PRAISE FOR *THE WISDOM*

"An intriguing exploration of philosophy as the ancients understood it: as a way of life, care for the soul, and the key means of understanding reality. I recommend this book to anyone who seeks to lead a more meaningful and thoughtful life."

—Crystal Addey, PhD, University of Wales, Trinity St. David and Cardiff University

"For most modern Pagans, the blessed lady that we know as Hypatia of the great Library of Alexandria is but a name that we repeat with honor as we chase it down the corridors of time. *The Wisdom of Hypatia* brings her era and her teachings into our time with beautiful clarity and coherence. After reading this book when you speak her name, you will know the power of living a well-examined Pagan life. I strongly recommend it as a guide to becoming closer to the Divine in all its forms."

—Ivo Dominguez, Jr., author of *Spirit Speak*

"Dr. MacLennan has reclaimed the secrets of living well from the old tradition and reframed them for today's seekers. *The Wisdom of Hypatia* is grounded in solid scholarship, lucidly written, and, above all, practical. This book reunites spirituality, philosophy, and psychology into a path for our time, and for all times. Read it. Practice it. You will never be the same."

—Leonard George, PhD, Capilano University

"A brilliant introduction to the wisdom traditions of Pagan antiquity, The *Wisdom of Hypatia* presents ancient philosophy as it was: not a corpus of sterile abstractions, but a living path of personal development toward that rarest of all human qualities, wisdom. This book belongs on the shelf of every modern Pagan, and indeed that of anyone interested in any of the spiritual traditions of the Western world."

—John Michael Greer, author of *The Celtic Golden Dawn*
and *The New Encyclopedia of the Occult*

"The end result of this book is a deepening of our own spiritual relationship to the ancients and to ourselves. All the chapters are wonderfully organized, offering a nine-month program designed to bring about in the careful and dedicated reader a more spiritually enlightened life according to the example of the philosophers of antiquity."

—Danielle A. Layne, PhD, Georgia Southern University

THE WISDOM OF
HYPATIA

ABOUT THE AUTHOR

Bruce J. MacLennan, PhD, has been a student of ancient Greek and Roman philosophy and religion for more than forty years, and for the past twenty-five he has studied the relationship between Neoplatonic spiritual practices, Jungian psychology, and neurotheology. He has published journal articles and book chapters on these topics, and has presented his work at meetings of the International Society for Neoplatonic Studies and the Society for the Scientific Study of Religion. MacLennan offers regular workshops on Neoplatonic spiritual practice, Pythagoreanism, theurgy, and related subjects. In his professional capacity as a professor of computer science, MacLennan researches artificial intelligence, autonomous robotics, artificial life, artificial morphogenesis, self-organizing systems, and the mind-body connection, including the relation of the brain to consciousness and the collective unconscious. He has published several books and more than sixty scholarly articles, and he is regularly invited to give international presentations on his work. He lives in Tennessee.

THE WISDOM OF
HYPATIA

ANCIENT SPIRITUAL PRACTICES FOR A MORE MEANINGFUL LIFE

BRUCE J. MACLENNAN, PHD

Llewellyn Publications
Woodbury, Minnesota

First Edition
First Printing, 2013

Book design by Donna Burch
Cover illustration: Eric Williams/The July Group
Cover images: iStockphoto.com/18268927/sbayram, 16908874/James Steidl, 9955928/Elena Garbar
Cover design by Kevin R. Brown
Interior art by the Llewellyn Art Department

Llewellyn Publications is a registered trademark of Llewellyn Worldwide Ltd.

The Cataloging-in-Publication data for *The Wisdom of Hypatia* is pending.
ISBN: 978-0-7387-3599-3

Llewellyn Publications
A Division of Llewellyn Worldwide Ltd.
2143 Wooddale Drive
Woodbury, MN 55125-2989
www.llewellyn.com

Printed in the United States of America

CONTENTS

PART III THE SECOND DEGREE OF WISDOM

PART IV THE THIRD DEGREE OF WISDOM

ACKNOWLEDGMENTS

In writing this book on practical Neoplatonic philosophy, I am standing on the shoulders of giants indeed. In particular, it would have been impossible without the enormous efforts of many philosophers and historians of philosophy, both living and deceased, who have investigated and explicated ancient philosophy, and in particular Neoplatonism. Many of their works are cited in the endnotes and bibliography, although neither is comprehensive. I have also benefited from discussions with scholars at conferences of the International Society of Neoplatonic Studies, where I have presented some of these ideas. In particular I am grateful to Drs. Crystal Addey, Marilynn Lawrence, and Danielle Layne for valuable discussions and advice. Nevertheless, I take full responsibility for my misunderstandings and for the inevitable simplifications required by a book such as this. In addition, I am grateful to Drs. Michael Betz, Gene Bocknek, Gordon M. Burghardt, Jo Lynn Cunningham, Neil Greenberg, Doris Ivie, Sandra J. McEntire, and other members of the "Spirituality and Critical Inquiry" colloquy at the University of Tennessee, Knoxville, who carefully read an earlier draft of this book. Our discussions and their comments and criticisms gave me valuable feedback, which has improved this book. Finally, I cannot adequately express my gratitude to Elysia Gallo, senior acquisitions editor at Llewellyn, whose suggestions have enormously improved the readability and accessibility of this book. While I took all of this valuable advice seriously, I did not always follow it, and so I must accept final responsibility for the result.

PART I
PRELIMINARIES

CHAPTER ONE

INTRODUCTION

AN ANCIENT PATH FOR MODERN TIMES

If you are like me, you have a range of spiritual aspirations. As a start, you would like to live a joyous, peaceful, and fulfilling life, regardless of circumstances (health, wealth, and so on). Beyond this, you would like to be able to be tranquil in the face of life's pain and disappointment, and to know how to respond wisely to these circumstances. But these are only a beginning. Most people discover sooner or later that to live a truly fulfilling life, they need to live with purpose. But how do you discover the purpose of your life, not in vague generalities, but specifically? As you will discover in this book, there is a little-known ancient spiritual path that can help you to live a meaningful life in joy, freedom, and tranquility. With it you can contact the deepest wellsprings of life's meaning, whether you think of this source as God, the gods, or psychological archetypes. It is not an Eastern practice, such as Buddhism, Yoga, or Daoism; nor is it one of the well-known Western religions: Judaism, Christianity, or Islam. It does have some interesting similarities to Eastern thought, however, and it flows like a subterranean river from ancient Paganism through the heart of Western religions, but it is a philosophy of life and a system of spiritual growth independent of them all. Its sources are deep in prehistory, but its practice has been documented for nearly 2,600 years. Though ancient, it is not primitive; indeed it is more compatible with contemporary understanding of nature and human nature than many younger systems of spiritual practice.

Enough suspense. I will follow custom and call this tradition "Platonism," but this familiar term is misleading—first, because it often suggests an intellectual system rather than a spiritual practice and, second, because the tradition predates Plato, stretching back to Pythagoras (sixth century BCE) and before him to the semi-mythical Orpheus and the Persian Magi. Furthermore, it has not been stagnant since Plato's time. Like any living tradition, it has evolved over the centuries, but its core practices are still valuable because they are based on an understanding of the essence of human and divine nature, and that essence has not changed for many thousands of years.

In this book you will learn the way of life and spiritual practices taught by the most famous female philosopher of antiquity: Hypatia, a Pagan spiritual teacher who died nearly 1,600 years ago. I've picked her because she taught in the ancient Egyptian city of Alexandria, where she had Pagan, Jewish, and Christian students (Islam did not yet exist), which shows that her philosophy is compatible with many religions (and indeed with agnostic views). Although she taught more than sixteen centuries ago, her ideas and practices are even more valuable in our world than in hers. She also stands out as a woman in an otherwise male-dominated history of philosophy and religion, and so she is a better model for our time.

Socrates said that the unexamined life is not worth living, and Epicurus said that a philosopher's words are empty if they don't cure any human ills. In my own life I have studied many systems of thought and spiritual practice, Eastern as well as Western, and I have found much of value in them. Over the years I have learned, however, that this tradition of spiritual practice and understanding that lives hidden in the heart of Western culture can help us to live meaningful lives with joy, tranquility, and spiritual well-being today. As I continue to study, learn, and practice, my appreciation only deepens.

As you work through the exercises in this book, you will learn this system of spiritual development through three stages of progressively deeper understanding and practice, which I call "three degrees of wisdom."

THREE DEGREES OF WISDOM

You are embarking on a new way of life, but it is neither wise nor practical to make sudden far-reaching changes in your life; in fact, most people will give up. You shouldn't enter the Ironman Triathlon without doing some training and before succeeding in less-demanding competitions! It is the same with spiritual development, which involves a change in attitude as well as behavior. Our goal is wisdom, and the wise path is to become proficient at one level of practice before attempting the next.

The ancient Greek word *therapeia*, from which we get "therapy," means both "cure" and "care." In this sense, ancient philosophy was *therapeia*—both cure and care—for the soul. Like many cures, philosophy must proceed in stages, starting with your current condition and proceeding through successive phases until the cure is successful. But philosophy is also care of the soul—a tending to its health, like regular exercise—which should be appropriate to maintain and to advance your level of spiritual progress. Indeed our goal is loftier than cure and care of the soul; it is the soul's *spiritual transformation*.

Fortunately, there is a natural progression of spiritual attainment in the three most important philosophical schools of the Hellenistic Age (the period following the breakup of Alexander the Great's empire after his death in 323 BCE). The first degree is represented by Epicureanism, which despite the modern connotation of the word, seeks tranquility through moderating the desires. The second degree is Stoicism, which seeks freedom and serenity through detachment from the things outside our control, and the third is Platonism, which is the foundation of Hypatia's philosophy. In ancient Athens, where these philosophies originated, Epicureanism was taught in the enclosed Garden of Epicurus outside the city walls; Stoicism was taught on the painted Porch (*Stoa* in Greek) in the Athenian *agora* (market and meeting place); and Platonism was taught in the Akademia, a sacred olive grove outside the city, which was a walled sanctuary dedicated to Athena, the goddess of wisdom. The Garden, the Porch, and the Grove thus symbolize three degrees of spiritual attainment, the *three degrees of wisdom*. Remember these nicknames for the three degrees of wisdom; you will see them frequently in this book.

In ancient times, when people wanted a deeper spiritual experience than the popular religions could provide, they were initiated into one or more of the mystery religions, such as the Eleusinian Mysteries, the Dionysian or Bacchic Mysteries, and Orphism. As you will learn later, initiation proceeded through three degrees—*purification, illumination,* and *revelation*—in which the initiate had direct experience of the gods. These stages correspond to the three degrees of wisdom through which you will pass as you practice the exercises in this book.

Much has been made of the secrets revealed only to the highest initiates, but the real secret is that for the unprepared—the unpurified and unilluminated—the hidden truths are meaningless and sometimes dangerous. The Mysteries guard themselves; human secrecy is not required. Practice is the key that unlocks the Mysteries.

A NINE-MONTH PROGRAM

To help you through this system of spiritual development, I have designed a nine-month program, which is reasonable for most people, but does not need to be followed rigidly. Depending on your prior spiritual practice and the time available, you may be able to do it more quickly or you may need more time. Keep in mind, first, that philosophy is a way of life, not an accomplishment, and so the goal is to integrate these spiritual practices into your life, not to try them once or twice and move on. Second, they are called spiritual *practices* because they must be *practiced*! This means, first of all, that it is not enough to read about them; you have to do them. You can't learn to swim by reading about it or by watching other people swim; you have to get in the water! Third, they must be practiced *regularly*; otherwise you won't acquire and retain your skill in the practice, and it won't have its transformative effect. Think again of health. It won't do you much good just to read about healthy eating, or to eat one or two healthy meals; it has to become part of your life. So also with these spiritual practices.

Everyone wants to get right to the good stuff, the advanced spiritual techniques that put us in contact with divinity, but all authentic spiritual traditions agree that it's best to do things in order. Ancient Platonists said:

> *According to the Rules of Order,*
> *little things must precede the greater,*
> *if we would make the ascent.*[1]

If you attempt the Ironman without proper training… well, the results might not be pretty. In our culture of instant gratification, this is a hard pill for many to swallow. True philosophers—spiritual adepts—have more discipline. (There is no harm, however, in reading this book through so that you see your destination. But don't fool yourself into thinking that you have learned the practices. Go back and do them diligently.)

As you will see, each of the degrees of wisdom provides a foundation on which the next degree rests. The effects, the transformations, build incrementally, but that doesn't mean that you can forget earlier practices after you have moved on to more advanced ones. Often you will find it is worthwhile to go back to the lower degrees, just as the piano student who has advanced from practicing scales to playing complex études finds it worthwhile, from time to time, to repeat the scales.

So let's begin. The next chapter will give you a brief overview of the spiritual practices common to all the ancient philosophies and will get you started on your spiritual transformation. The following chapter is a summary of the history of the Platonic tradition, from a thousand years before Hypatia up to the present day.

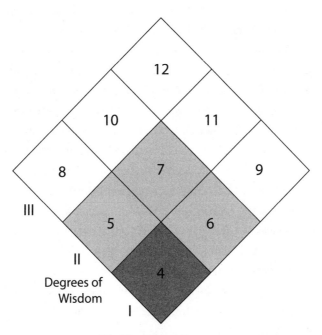

The Nine-Month Program

Next you will begin a nine-month program of spiritual growth (see the figure). Chapter 4 is devoted to the first degree of wisdom, which teaches Epicurean spiritual practices as a way of living with greater tranquility. The following three chapters (5, 6, 7) teach the second degree (Stoic philosophy), where you will learn three disciplines to help you face with equanimity the challenges and opportunities of a socially and politically engaged life. The final five chapters are devoted to the third degree of wisdom, the Platonism of Hypatia. The first two (8, "The Macrocosm" and 9, "The Microcosm and the Archetypes") help you to understand the Platonic view of reality. The remainder (10, 11, 12) teach three different ways of ascent to the divine.

But first, let's learn a little more about Hypatia, her world, and its similarity to our own.

HYPATIA, THE MOST HOLY
AND REVERED PHILOSOPHER[2]

You may wonder why I have chosen Hypatia as our guide on this path of spiritual development. She was the most important teacher of philosophy in Alexandria at the end of the fourth century of the Common Era. Students from all over the ancient world, from Rome and Constantinople, from Cyrene and Syria, journeyed to study with her. Many attended her public lectures, but a few were privileged to become her private students, to whom she taught a spiritual practice directed toward personal contact with divinity. She was a confidant and adviser to public officials, some of whom had been her students. The intellectual life of Alexandria, a very cosmopolitan city, revolved around Hypatia. Yet she came to a terrible end.

Ancient authors said that Hypatia was modest, just, considerate, and wise. Her students went further, calling her "the most holy and revered philosopher," "the blessed lady," and "divine guide"; they spoke also of her "divine spirit" and "oracular utterances." She never married. Her attitude seems to have been aristocratic, perhaps aloof, steeped in the excellences of Greek culture, but she wore the coarse, white, woolen cloak that was the traditional insignia of philosophers. Yet she was at home in the highest social circles of Alexandria.

Hypatia was a mathematician and scientist as well as a philosopher, and she assisted her father, Theon, in his projects editing and commenting on the work of famous astronomers and mathematicians. She probably learned her science and philosophy from her father, an important scientist and mathematician, for there is no mention of other teachers or of her traveling outside Alexandria to study.

Theon was a member of the Museion, perhaps its head. The Alexandrian Museion (often misleadingly translated "Museum") had been established about 300 BCE, and by the time of Theon and Hypatia it had been in operation for seven hundred years. The term "Museion" refers to a temple or sanctuary for the Muses, the divine patrons of creative activities, including the arts, but also astronomy and mathematics. The head of the Museion was a Pagan priest.

The Museion was more like a research university than a museum. It had facilities to support the resident scholars, such as Theon, who were paid by the emperor. These included a communal dining hall, a tree-lined walkway, and small meeting areas with seats arranged in an arc to facilitate collaboration, discussion, and presentation to small groups. There was also the famous Alexandrian Library, which may have been part of the Museion or nearby it. At its height, it was reported to house 700,000 volumes, including all the greatest works available to the Roman Empire (and no doubt lots of mediocre stuff, too!). This would have been the primary resource for the Museion scholars.

Theon is the last Museion scholar known to us, and the Museion may have ceased to exist in the early 390s, a victim perhaps of the religious and civil strife in Alexandria at that time. Hypatia's name is never connected with the Museion, and so we suppose that she taught elsewhere, in public lecture halls and her home.

Although she was a Pagan at a time when the empire was officially Christian, and Pagans were increasingly persecuted, her students included Christians who later became important religious and civil leaders. In spite of her religion, she was welcome in the highest circles of Alexandrian society and government. The reason seems to be that her true allegiance was to her philosophy, which was mostly compatible with the beliefs of the Pagans, Jews, and Christians who were her students. She does not seem to have involved herself in the escalating violence among these three groups.

Nevertheless, Hypatia was drawn into these civil conflicts, for she was an adviser to Orestes, the Prefect (Governor) of Alexandria. Although he was a Christian, he came into increasing conflict with Cyril (later, Saint Cyril), the Christian Patriarch of Alexandria, who was very ambitious. He was installed as bishop in 412 after three days of fighting between his supporters and those of a rival candidate (the one favored by Orestes). To some extent, the conflict of Orestes and Cyril was between civil and religious authority, but it also pitted the wealthy upper classes, allied with Orestes, against the poor lower classes, which followed Cyril. These conflicts came to a head in 415.

Although there is some doubt about Hypatia's birth date, we know that by 415 she was a mature woman, at least in her mid-forties, perhaps as old as sixty, a widely respected figure of dignity, moderation, and wisdom.

According to church historians, Cyril was passing through the streets of Alexandria, and came across a crowd at the door to a house. There were young men and wealthy citizens with their horses and chariots blocking the road. Cyril turned to a companion and asked, "Whose house is this?" and he was told, "It is the house of the philosopher Hypatia." According to this historian, Cyril became jealous of her popularity and influence, for "the whole city doted on her and worshiped her."

We do not know how much Cyril was directly responsible for the ensuing events, but at the very least he encouraged his followers to stir up popular resentment and fear against her. In the ancient world, astronomy was hardly distinguished from astrology, and they both were considered parts of mathematics, which the popular mind considered a kind of magic.

Hypatia was accused of being devoted to "magic, astrolabes, and instruments of music"![3] Thus, given Hypatia's known activities, and the fact she was Pagan (which many Christians considered devil worship), it was not hard to spread the rumor that she was a witch and had used black magic to cast a spell over Orestes, over Christians, and indeed over all of Alexandria. It was whispered that Orestes had stopped attending church and that Hypatia was converting him to Paganism. Thus, especially among the uneducated followers of Cyril, the suspicion and distrust of Hypatia grew.

The *parabolani* were strong young men who had been recruited by Cyril to help the clergy, in particular to do the "heavy lifting," such as moving sick or disabled people from their homes to the hospitals. But they also served as a kind of paramilitary force, loyal to Cyril, and it is hard not to see them as fifth-century "Brownshirts" (Hitler's storm troopers). They helped to spread the slander against Hypatia.

One day in March, during the season of Lent, a hotheaded minor church functionary called Peter the Reader gathered the parabolani, and they led a mob toward Hypatia's house. She was being driven home, but the mob blocked her chariot and pulled her out of it. They dragged her through the streets and ripped off her clothing; we can imagine her cries of fear and indignation.

They dragged her into a church and gouged away her flesh with sharp, broken ceramic roofing tiles. No doubt her shrieks of agony echoed off the church walls, and the floor ran with her blood. "While she was still feebly twitching, they beat her eyes out."[4] We can only hope that she had passed out or died before the next crime, for they dragged her bloody body through the streets until body parts were scattered all over Alexandria (as one church historian put it). Their savagery glutted, they gathered her remains and burned them. (This kind of barbarism was not unique; in 361 and 457 the Christians dragged two of their bishops through the streets until they were dead, and then burned their bodies.)

Obviously there was widespread indignation and revulsion at Hypatia's murder, even among the Christians, and it became a blot on Cyril's record as a church leader. Nevertheless, no one was punished in any significant way for the crime, although the parabolani were restrained to some degree and made to report to the Prefect. Orestes himself was withdrawn from Alexandria by the emperor, or perhaps he asked to be withdrawn, having seen the city and its people at their worst. Cyril had won.

Hypatia's murder is sometimes said to be the end of philosophy in Alexandria, and to mark the end of the classical world, but this is an exaggeration. Certainly philosophers kept a low profile, continuing to teach but staying out of civil affairs. Mercifully, Theon had died a few years before and didn't have to witness his daughter's gruesome end.

If you know anything at all about Hypatia, you probably know the story of her horrific death, although many versions of the story are embellished or distorted to fit the teller's inclinations. Nevertheless, this book is not a history of Hypatia and her times (which can be found in other books; see the "Additional Reading" section), but a guide to practicing her philosophy as a way of life that is valuable to us now.

WHY HYPATIA'S PHILOSOPHY IS IMPORTANT TODAY

You might ask why a 1,600-year-old philosophy would be of interest to anyone but historians of philosophy, but there are several reasons it is valuable to you and me, the most important being that it teaches a system of spiritual development especially suited to contemporary Western culture.

In Hypatia's time, which like ours has been characterized as an Age of Anxiety, people were seeking new spiritual insights and practices that would show them how to live rewarding and fulfilling lives, in spite of the stresses of their world. They were unsatisfied with the common dogmas, whether religious or secular, and sought direct spiritual experience as a source of meaning in their lives. Many people feel the same way today, for they are dissatisfied with organized religion on one hand and with scientific materialism on the other. Hypatia's philosophy, which is called Neoplatonism, has the advantage that it teaches spiritual practices to connect us with the deepest sources of meaning in our lives and to live them with divine purpose; in this, it is like Buddhism and the other great wisdom traditions of the East.

Although spirituality is a very important component of Neoplatonism, it is a philosophy, and so (like Buddhism, which has been called a religion without God) it is compatible with many religions and even with atheism, as I will explain later. Therefore, in addition to Pagan Neoplatonists, over the centuries there have been many Jewish, Christian, and Muslim Neoplatonists. Indeed, the techniques taught by Hypatia are the core of the spiritual practices of all these religions, and so they are a common point of agreement. This religious neutrality is why Hypatia had Jewish and Christian students (of course Islam did not yet exist), and why her Christian disciples, including one who became an important bishop, remained Neoplatonists as long as they lived.

There is no evidence of a falling out between Hypatia and her Christian students, and her murder must be seen as a particularly brutal political assassination, not as religious persecution. Although there were certainly religious overtones (Cyril's faction referred to her as "that Pagan woman"), she was caught between the political aspirations of two Christian factions who were not above torture and murder.

In our own time, when there is so much strife among mutually intolerant Christian, Jewish, and Muslim extremists, I think that we cannot ignore a system of Pagan philosophy and spiritual practice that all these faiths have found valuable, and which contributed to their contemplative and mystical traditions. Hypatia's philosophy offers itself as a common core of spiritual practice compatible with these and other religions, including contemporary Paganism and Wicca.

Remarkably, this ancient philosophy is quite consistent with the modern worldview, including modern depth psychology, and so it is very applicable now. This is because, as a spiritual discipline, it did not depend significantly on ancient scientific ideas, which have been superseded. Rather, it depended on spiritual practices that took students into their psychological depths and on to the divine sources of meaning common to all people. The structure of the human psyche has not changed in many thousands of years, and so Neoplatonic practices are as useful now as they were then. Nevertheless, we have learned a few things over the past 1,600 years, and in this book I will suggest some places where I think Hypatia's philosophy needs to be updated.

On the other hand, Hypatia's philosophy has been tested by time. When she was teaching, this spiritual tradition had already been practiced and refined for at least one thousand years (as you will see in chapter 3). Although her philosophy was a culmination of this development, Neoplatonism has continued to evolve—in various guises—and is still alive in our time.

Like most ancient philosophers, Hypatia taught a *way of life*, not an academic subject to be studied but not practiced. This does not mean that they did not investigate and debate abstruse topics, but these intellectual pursuits were a means to an end: living well. This is the approach to Hypatia's philosophy that I take in this book: *a way of life*. Therefore, its focus is on spiritual practices and exercises directed toward your spiritual transformation and well-being.

What's in it for you? A system of practical techniques for living a happier, more spiritually enlightened life. Whether you are Pagan, like Hypatia, or Jewish, Christian, Muslim, or Wiccan, or whether you are a skeptic or nonbeliever, you can use these spiritual practices. With them you can learn to live a more joyous life in spite of the inevitable disappointments and tragedies. And you can learn to access a source of insight and guidance—of divine wisdom—that will give your life deeper purpose and direction. Who doesn't want to live with joy and purpose?

This book is not intended to be an academic study; that is not its purpose. Many excellent scholars have studied Neoplatonism and continue to do so, and I have benefited from their work. If you want to learn more about Neoplatonism from an academic perspective, please look at the "Additional Reading" section at the back of this book. Also, although I avoid technical terminology so far as possible, I have included a glossary at the back to help with the terms that are unavoidable.

A few remarks on my conventions: I have adopted the modern convention of capitalizing *Pagan* like the other religions. I have also used the modern scholarly and culturally neutral notation for dates: CE (Common Era, instead of A.D.) and BCE (Before Common Era, instead of B.C.). I do not capitalize *god* and *goddess* when they are used generically (e.g., "the gods and goddesses of ancient Greece"), but I do capitalize them when they are used as names for monotheistic or duotheistic deities (e.g., "if you worship God or Goddess or both"). I also follow the common convention of capitalizing the names of Platonic Forms or Ideas (e.g., Truth, Beauty, Justice), which are closely connected with deities. Indeed, in ancient Greek Paganism, these words were sometimes the names of gods or goddesses (e.g., Gaia = Earth, Eros = Love, Nike = Victory, Dike = Justice, Hygiea = Health, Hestia = Hearth, Nemesis = Retribution). Occasionally, I capitalize words used as names with special meanings (e.g., "the ancient Mysteries" refers to religious rituals, not old detective thrillers!). Names of specific exercises and practices are also capitalized. Finally, English speakers usually pronounce "Hypatia" as *high-PAY-shah*, but in her time it would be more like *hü-pah-TEE-ah* (where *ü* is pronounced as in German). Her name means "highest" or "supreme."

CHAPTER TWO

SPIRITUAL PRACTICES

PHILOSOPHY AS A WAY OF LIFE

I have mentioned several times that in the ancient world, philosophy was not so much an academic discipline as a way of life. Therefore, as a way of learning the techniques and practices taught by Hypatia, I think it will be helpful if I tell you a little about the role of philosophy in the ancient world. Then, as now, people's spiritual interests and activities varied widely. Some were ardent believers and devoted practitioners, while others participated only because it was socially expected. Many were initiated into the Pagan Mysteries, such as the Eleusinian and Bacchic Mysteries, but many fewer experienced the illumination and spiritual transformation that the mysteries were intended to produce. This is what Plato meant when he quoted an ancient Orphic saying:

The wand-bearers are many but the Bacchi are few.[5]

In other words, many carry the wand of Bacchus in the religious processions, but those truly inspired by the god—the Bacchi—are very rare.

In every age and every part of the world, however, there have been spiritual masters offering systems of spiritual development intended to increase their students' spiritual depth and understanding, to improve their lives by revealing the secrets of reality, and to allow them to interact personally with the divine powers governing it. In the ancient Greek and Roman worlds, these teachers and seekers of a deeper spiritual life were called *philosophers* (lovers of wisdom).

The same is true now. Whether you are a Pagan like Pythagoras, Plato, Hypatia, and the rest, or Wiccan, or a follower of one of the "religions of the book" (Judaism, Christianity, Islam), you may find yourself seeking a deeper experience of the sacred and a spiritually more enlightened life. If so, you are of the same mind as the ancient people who sought out the philosophers. Welcome!

The ancient philosophical schools were very different from what we think of as philosophical instruction now. It wasn't primarily a matter of teaching the student complex systems of thought or techniques for analyzing intellectual ideas, but a method of improving the student's way of life. Since the philosophical teacher was supposed to guide the student into a new, philosophical way of living, the method depended a great deal on where the student was beginning, on their present psychological and spiritual state, so it was very individualized. Like a doctor treating a patient, the teacher first had to diagnose the student's condition and then to apply the appropriate treatments. Philosophy is both *cure* for the soul, which depends on its prior condition, and also ongoing *care* for it afterward, which depends on the character of each soul, for this affects its dispositions, strengths, and weaknesses. Philosophy is a process, not a one-time achievement.

Picture a teacher, the "master," meeting with a small group of students, the "disciples," in a home, garden, or similar location. ("Teacher" and "student" are the literal meanings of *magister* and *discipulus* in Latin.) They might begin by discussing a text from the sect's founder or another sage, with the teacher answering the disciples' questions. The purpose was to teach the students reasons and conclusions that would help them live in accordance with the philosophy; it was not doctrine for its own sake.

After the discussion, each student might report to the group, in an atmosphere of mutual affection and trust, about his or her success in living philosophically. They might bring up, for group discussion, particular problems they were having. Later the teacher would meet with the disciples individually to address issues that might be too personal to discuss openly in the group. The mentor, like a coach, would review, either individually or as a group, each disciple's progress in his or her spiritual practice, and perhaps recommend changes.

If this scenario sounds like modern psychotherapy, it should! It might also remind you of Eastern guru-centered spiritual traditions, if you are familiar with those. (*Guru* just means "teacher.") The reason is that these are age-old methods of spiritual guidance that have evolved independently in different cultural contexts; they are repeatedly rediscovered because they work. (In later chapters I will illustrate ancient philosophical instruction in a number of dramatic dialogues.)

Philosophy, in the ancient sense, is supposed to teach you a new way of life, but learning to live in a new way requires *practice*. Therefore, ancient philosophical instruction included a number of *spiritual practices* or *exercises* that are still useful in learning to live wisely. In this chapter I will describe them briefly; in later chapters you will learn to practice them systematically in order to advance your spiritual transformation.

Since philosophy is a continual striving after wisdom, rather than a one-time attainment, these exercises become part of a lifelong practice of philosophy, the "philosophical way of life." Therefore, if you want to live Hypatia's philosophy, you will want to establish a regular habit of practice.

The role of spiritual exercises in a philosophical way of life is analogous to the role of physical exercises in an athletic way of life. It is no coincidence that Plato located his school, the Academy, next to an exercise field. This reflected the idea that free, strong, independent citizens need exercises for the body, for the soul, and for the body and soul together. The body was exercised through athletics. Exercises for the soul were directed toward guiding one's attitude and behavior in accordance with the philosophy's moral norms, so one might live wisely. Finally, exercises for the body and soul together were directed toward tempering and fortifying the body and soul through ascetic habits and practices. *Spiritual exercises* are those that involve the soul, with or without the body.

For all the ancient philosophies, the ideal sage was godlike, a "divine man," and therefore the aim of the spiritual exercises was to make you more like a god, and the "imitation of god" was the basis of the philosophical life. There are two broad approaches to becoming godlike. One approach is to approximate external or transcendent divinity, which encompasses the universe. By these exercises you *expand* your awareness to become godlike. The other approach is to seek the god within, immanent divinity, by concentrating your soul into the innermost divine core of the psyche. By these exercises you *concentrate* to become godlike.

These are really two paths to the same place, for the outermost horizon is also the innermost horizon. A Hermetic text from the twelfth century (but expressing a Platonic idea) "described the nature of God as a circle whose center was everywhere and its circumference nowhere." [6] It was a popular saying among Neoplatonists and has been widely quoted. "As within, so without; as without, so within" expresses the same idea. Thus the greatest expansion and the most focused concentration reach the same place. Therefore the philosopher uses practices of both sorts to become godlike. In this chapter I will outline the most common spiritual practices. Don't worry if the descriptions seem a bit abstract; I will give more specific and practical instructions later; my goal here is a quick overview.

CONCENTRATING INWARD

The practice called *Concentrating Inward* is a kind of meditation that effects a separation of the psyche into two parts; by concentrating into itself, the "I" leaves the rest of the psyche behind. One important effect is a separation or detachment of what is fundamentally *you* from the various feelings, desires, fears, worries, regrets, as well as physical ailments, discomforts, and pleasures, connected with you as an individual embodied biological organism. The exercise is a turning toward the *inner self* or *true self* (however you understand it) and a turning away from your ordinary, egoistic everyday self. The result is assimilation to deity in the sense that you are focusing on the universal and eternal perspective of Nature or God (depending on the philosophy) and are setting aside all the particularities and partial perspectives of your ordinary, mortal life. By this practice, philosophers maintain tranquility and independence in the midst of life's circumstances. You will learn several versions of this practice.

In his dialogue *Phaedo*, Plato has Socrates ask rhetorically, "Is not philosophy the practice of death?"[7] The idea of philosophy as the *Practice of Death* is central to the Western philosophical tradition, but it is not so grim and morbid as it sounds to our ears, for meditation on death is simultaneously meditation on life. For example, the philosopher Epicurus, whom we'll meet in the Garden, wrote:

The exercise of living well
and the exercise of dying well
are one and the same thing.[8]

Just like many modern people, most of the ancients thought that upon death some sort of immortal soul separated from the body, perhaps to be reincarnated later into another body. Therefore, inward concentration can be an exercise in "dying before you die." In it, the parts of the psyche that have the character of eternity and immortality separate from the body and from those aspects of the psyche that are entangled and enmeshed in the particularities of an individual human life. Regardless of your thoughts about the afterlife, dying before you die will help you to live in the present and make the most of this life. It will help you to live in the Isle of the Blessed, the Summerland, Avalon, or Heaven while still on Earth.

Another variant of the practice of inward concentration is to *Focus on the Present* and to turn away from the past and future, with their burdens of regret and worry. Here again the philosopher adopts the eternal divine perspective, for the eternal is outside of time, atemporal, timeless, the ever-present, whereas mortality is limited existence-in-time, defined by a finite past and future. The present moment is perfectly complete and self-contained.

This practice helps you to live in the present, which is the only thing at all within your control, for the past and future do not exist and are not in your control; therefore the present is the home of self-awareness and hence of wise action and of wise experience. Like the practice of death, concentrating in the present helps you to live each moment as though it is your *last*, savoring every moment of life, but it also helps you to experience each moment as the *first*, imbuing it with freshness and delight, an opportunity to act in joyful wisdom.

The present moment is the crux of morality, for it is in the present that you make choices. Nevertheless, the present moment involves both the past—represented by present recollection—and the future—represented by present intent. In order to make these choices more wisely, philosophers practice the *Examination of Conscience*. In this your past actions and attitudes are submitted to an "inner judge," who compassionately evaluates them and decides how they can be improved so that you can live better in the future. This same inner judge may award praise for your progress. This objective assessment of your own moral state is one of the meanings of the maxim inscribed on the temple of Apollo at Delphi:

Know thyself.[9]

Therefore all ancient philosophies used the practice of *Morning and Evening Examination of Conscience*, as recorded in the *Pythagorean Golden Verses*:

> *Don't suffer sleep at night to close thine eyes,*
> *Till thrice thine acts that day thou hast o'er-run:*
> *How slipped? What deeds? What duty left undone?*
> *Thus thine account summed up from first to last,*
> *Grieve for the ill, joy for what good has passed.*[10]

Each of your acts is classified as (1) an error of commission, (2) a virtuous deed, or (3) an error of omission. This practice is a way of judging your progress: celebrating your successes and establishing your intent to do better in the future. It also develops your memory, so that you will be more able to recall your intent and past actions in your present choices. According to different philosophers, this review should be practiced at night, at both waking and retiring, or at three times each day (e.g., morning, noon, and night). You can begin this practice today. Don't wait!

Ancient philosophers also practiced *group confession* and *fraternal correction* as a means to more objective examination of conscience. Conversely, they supported and praised each other for progress made. In our time, too, it is easier to make spiritual progress in a like-minded community. Think about whether there are other people who could work through this book with you.

Examination of conscience is directed toward the past, but other exercises address the future. For example, Porphyry said that Pythagoras recommended careful contemplation of your intentions at the beginning of the day:

> *As soon as thou hast waked, in order lay*
> *The actions to be done that following day.*[11]

This is also a practice that you can begin right away.

Another exercise, *Premeditation of Misfortunes*, was also directed toward the future. In it you vividly imagine possible problems that you might face in the future, or have faced in the past and might face again, along with the proper philosophical response to them. This exercise increases the likelihood that you will respond wisely if the situation occurs. You will learn the technique in chapter 6.

The ideal sage has internalized the philosophical way of life; it has become part of his or her character, and so the sage instinctively acts wisely. For imperfect philosophers (seekers of wisdom), such as us, however, it is valuable to have rules readily at hand, ready to be applied in order to act wisely in the present. For this purpose, you need rules expressed in short, pithy formulas (*maxims* or *aphorisms*); you should be able to grasp their meaning in a single intuition. Similarly, you need short, persuasive *demonstrations*, or arguments, to establish your certainty in a rule. That is, you need to know both the conclusions and their reasons (called *theorems* and *proofs*).[12]

Maxims are valuable for another philosophical practice: governing your inner discourse. We often run negative and counterproductive mental "tapes"—dialogues or monologues—that reflect habitual ways of responding to situations. The philosophical maxims provide alternative inner narratives that can help you live the philosophical life.

Therefore, an important practice is to memorize these maxims and to spend some time contemplating them. Then they will be ready to apply when you need them. For this purpose I have included many maxims (mostly from ancient philosophers) in this book. They are displayed in a distinctive way (for examples, see "Don't suffer sleep …" and "As soon as thou hast waked …" earlier in this chapter). You should copy down the maxims you find useful, or that speak to you, and memorize them.

You can invent your own maxims too, to express philosophical rules and their explanations. It is especially useful to find new, striking, fresh expressions of philosophical doctrines, if the old ones have become stale. (Much of Marcus Aurelius's *Meditations*, which we'll explore in Part III, is devoted to reformulations of Stoic maxims.)

To be effective, the maxims must be potent, but they lose their potency with time and repetition. They are like magical spells, and they work because they work *on you*. Some define magic as "the art of changing consciousness at will,"[13] and in this sense philosophical maxims are magical, but in Neoplatonism we use them to change not only consciousness, but also the unconscious mind. They can transform circumstances and ourselves.

You may be familiar with the idea of *affirmations*, which you repeat to yourself to bring about some change in your life. Most contemporary theory and use of affirmations is a resurrection of ideas from the New Thought movement in American spirituality, which was very popular at the beginning of the twentieth century.[14] You can see that it has much older precedents. In any case, many of the rules for affirmations, such as that they should be in the present tense and positive, are also applicable to philosophical maxims. The reason is that affirmations and maxims operate by the same psychological principles.

Commonplace books (or, more briefly, *commonplaces*) have been used for hundreds of years to collect general ideas and rules for living, as well as other material that you want to remember. In pursuing the philosophical way of life, you too will find it useful to compile commonplaces. For example, as you read this book, you can use your commonplace to record quotations, summaries, ideas, and other things worth remembering. It's kind of like a school notebook. Alternately, if you think of the maxims like magical spells, then your commonplace is a "book of shadows."

The purpose of the commonplace is to record universal verities, which will be valuable throughout your life and may be useful to other people too. Therefore it is impersonal, except insofar as the formulations strike a chord in you. If you wanted, you could make it public on a webpage or blog (as many people already do with their favorite quotes). In this respect it is different from a journal, which I'll discuss shortly.

In any case, while in the past commonplaces were notebooks, you may find it more convenient to keep yours on a computer, so you can easily print, edit, and reorganize it. On the other hand, you might find it more psychologically effective to calligraph the maxims in an attractive notebook that you've made by hand. You can decide right now how you will keep your commonplace. If you are going to use a notebook, you can start shopping for it or making it.

Ancient philosophers practiced the *art of memory*, a collection of well-tested memory techniques, so that they could remember the maxims, the demonstrations justifying them, and other essentials of their philosophical systems. We don't attach much importance to memory these days, because we have notebooks, computers, smartphones, and the Internet as repositories for knowledge, but they are of little use for philosophical practice. To act in the moment, you need to have philosophical principles readily at hand; there is no time to look them up, even in a notebook or portable device. When you have practiced the Morning and Evening Examination of Conscience for a while, you will discover that your memory is improving.

Finally, many ancient philosophers, like modern psychotherapists, recommended *Examination of Dreams* as a spiritual practice. This was because recurrent images or events might reveal issues on which the student needed to work. For example, if someone dreamed they were being cruel or greedy, or if the person had frightening dreams, an ancient philosopher might interpret these as indicating unhealthy mental states. Conversely, the absence of these dream elements might indicate spiritual progress. Similarly, in modern times Jung taught that dreams can reveal forces mobilizing in the unconscious, both heralding and facilitating spiritual growth. I will have little to say about dream interpretation in this book, but if you are really interested in this spiritual practice, you should explore Jungian psychology.

EXPANDING OUTWARD

Having surveyed ancient spiritual practices that concentrate inward, I will next describe those that expand outward. In these practices we take some version of a "god's eye view" of the universe.

In the exercise that I will call the *Viewpoint from the Center*, you visualize yourself expanding to include the entire universe, attempting to comprehend it intuitively in its entirety in your mind. You look out on the planets, then the stars, then the galaxies, and see them moving in their billion-year-long dance. Like the concentrative exercises, this also effects a separation of the divine from the mortal, but instead of focusing on the divine kernel within, you identify with the divine All.

Therefore you have a deity's perspective on the universe, comprehending it in its universality and eternity. You experience the entire universe as ideas in the divine mind, which is your transcendent mind. You have separated from—by expanding beyond—your individual, mortal life, which now appears as an insignificant part of the whole. However, you realize that the essential you is the eternal part, and so you can look objectively on your role in the grand scheme. You will learn versions of this practice in chapters 8 and 11.

The *View from Above* is a similar exercise, but it is more an "angel's eye view," for it keeps the earth in view. You imagine yourself ascending into the sky so that you can see the entire earth; you lose sight of individual people, and then of cities, and finally of countries, until you see the earth as a blue orb in space. Simultaneously time speeds up, so that individual lives blur by and eventually you can see the ages quickly rolling by. This gives you an altered, angel's-eye view of all the things we normally consider so important, but from this perspective, they do not seem very important. The View from Above is a kind of Practice of Death, because you are seeing the world from a perspective outside of your human life; you are seeing it from the perspective of an immortal soul. I'll give you more specific directions in chapter 6.

A third expansive exercise is the *Viewpoint of Science*, in which you use whatever understanding of science you have in order to see yourself as a nexus of past causes and future effects, as part of the continuous fabric of causality in the universe. If you know a little about general relativity, quantum mechanics, or superstring theory, you can view the universe from any of those perspectives. If your knowledge is less technical, or those perspectives seem too abstract, you can simply visualize yourself in the complex web of nature: all the complex biochemical processes in your cells interacting with all the many living and nonliving things in your ecosystem—the plants, animals, air and water, the bacteria in your gut, the gravity and light from distant stars, etc. The goal is to have an intuitive comprehension of the whole shebang. This exercise can effect a simultaneous concentration into the present (that causal nexus) as well as an expansion into the entire universe. You'll learn a version in chapter 6.

ADDITIONAL PRACTICES

I will mention briefly a few other spiritual practices that are neither especially concentrative nor expansive, such as keeping a *spiritual journal*. In it you can record your difficulties and successes in your other practices, as well as the insights you gain from them. In contrast to your commonplace, which contains eternal verities, your journal is for your thoughts, feelings, and intuitions of the moment. Therefore, it is more ephemeral and personal, although of course you may show it to your teacher or to others whom you trust. In some respects, the difference between the commonplace and the journal corresponds to the difference between the perspectives of the universal, timeless god within and your individual self embedded in the infinite particularity of everyday existence. Both are important in a balanced philosophical life. Make plans now to start a spiritual journal if you don't already have one.

As we have seen, ancient philosophy was not in general a solitary activity, and it can benefit today from a support group. The key is to find a group of mutually supportive, trusting people with whom you can share your philosophical way of life. A reading group studying this book and related books, and putting the ideas into practice, could form the nucleus of a philosophical community. Think about who would be interested in practicing with you and contact them.

Likewise, most ancient students of philosophy learned it from a teacher, who acted as a spiritual guide and life coach. Nowadays we are uncomfortable with the connotations of a master-disciple relationship, and there are many examples of abuse and exploitation in the spirituality business. Nevertheless, a more advanced philosopher can help a student move forward when they are stuck, and view their situation more objectively, helping them avoid pride and other traps. In the best case the teacher shows by his or her example that living the philosophical life is possible and desirable.

Another common practice is *Contemplation of the Sage*.[15] All of the ancient philosophical traditions had images of the ideal sage, often the founder of the tradition, and this is the way we must understand ancient biographies of Pythagoras, Plotinus, and similar figures. They were not intended as fact, but as an inspirational goal. They were meant *not to inform, but to form*.[16] The sages became ideal figures that the disciples could strive to emulate, even though they set a standard of perfection that few could expect to meet.

Individuals might ponder, and groups might discuss, how a sage might act in various circumstances or how they might respond to difficulties, along the lines of "What would Jesus do?" The image of the sage permitted philosophers to think concretely about dilemmas and issues they might face. Thus this practice is related to Premeditation of Misfortunes.

As you will learn in later chapters, there are several characteristics common to ancient sages, each in some way godlike. First was a sort of cosmic vision—that is, a sort of "god's eye" perspective on the universe and everything in it. This does not mean that a sage was supposed to know every last detail about the world, but that they had a comprehensive understanding of reality sufficient to live with true wisdom. The expansive exercises facilitate this cosmic understanding. Second, ancient sages were like gods in their tranquility, independence of circumstances, self-sufficiency, and freedom. These mental states are facilitated by the inward practices. However, as you will see, true freedom and peace depends on understanding human nature and humanity's place in the universe, and therefore on cosmic understanding. Finally, sages are like the gods in their providential care for humankind. Thus sages are characterized by *philanthropy* (literally, love of humanity); they are dedicated to curing and caring for souls as spiritual guides, teachers, and the founders of philosophical traditions.

Summary of Spiritual Practices	
Concentrating Inward	Practice of Death
	Focus on the Present
	Examination of Conscience
	Premeditation of Misfortunes
	Governing Inner Discourse
	Memorization of Maxims
	Compilation of Commonplaces
	Examination of Dreams
Expanding Outward	Viewpoint from the Center
	View from Above
	Viewpoint of Science
Other Practices	Contemplation of the Sage
	Spiritual Journaling

LIVING PHILOSOPHICALLY

There is more to the philosophical way of life than these mental exercises. Spiritual practice involves the whole of your being, and so it affects your actions as well as your thoughts. Philosophy, in the ancient sense, is not a weekend activity, but a new way of living every moment.

As you will learn in the following chapters, self-mastery is an important part of living the philosophical life. This includes a kind of vigilance: becoming more aware of your mental state and acquiring some control over it. For example, many of our troubles arise from our desires, from our likes and dislikes, and from our fears. We are also troubled by pain and suffering, and by stress and striving for wealth and fame. Therefore philosophy teaches you to govern these mental attitudes and, where necessary, to alter them so you can live better. Self-mastery also includes the quieting of undesirable dispositions (e.g., anger, greed, harmful speech) and the encouragement of desirable ones (e.g., tranquility, compassion, generosity). In this book you will learn ancient, time-tested techniques for self-mastery.

All of the above deals with the manner in which we ought to *live*, but there is also the fundamental question of what we should *do*. What, if any, are our duties to ourselves, to our family and friends, to society, to deity? Ancient philosophy provides guidance in these issues and teaches you how to make it a way of life. Progressing through the degrees of wisdom, you will arrive in the sacred Grove, where you will learn Hypatia's techniques for receiving divine aid and guidance.

CHAPTER THREE

SOURCES FOR HYPATIA'S PHILOSOPHY

PYTHAGORAS AND PLATO

In this chapter I will present—very briefly—the history of Hypatia's philosophy, which is called *Neoplatonism* (see the timeline on page 29). This information is not essential to its practice as a living philosophy, but I think it is helpful to see the long ancestry of Hypatia's philosophy and its roots in common human spiritual experience. If you are not too interested in history, then I suggest you skim this chapter; you might be more inclined to come back to it later. If you are anxious to get on to the practices, then skip to the next chapter, which teaches the first degree of wisdom.

Pythagoras is a good place to begin, for he coined the word *philosophia* from *philo-* (love of) and *sophia* (wisdom). The idea was that only the gods are truly wise, and the best that mortals can hope for is to love wisdom and pursue it by living philosophically.

Pythagoras was born in about 570 BCE on the Greek island of Samos (just off the coast of modern Turkey; see the map on page 30).[17] Ancient biographies tell us that as a young man he studied with the sages of Egypt, Persia, Phoenicia, Judea, Chaldea, and perhaps India, but these biographies were written hundreds of years after his death and mix considerable legend with the facts. (Remember, they are meant more to *form* than to *inform*.) When he was about forty years old, Pythagoras settled in Croton (modern Crotona), a Greek colony in southern Italy. Shortly after his arrival he gave speeches in turn to the men, women, and youth of the city, encouraging them to live according to his spiritual principles. According to the biographies, the citizens were very impressed by his teaching and wanted to learn more. Pythagoras founded a society or philosophical order organized around his teachings. The character of applicants was examined, and if they were deemed worthy, they were admitted to the outer circle, where they were obliged to remain silent for five years. The apparent goal was that the neophytes learn humility and the basics of the philosophy before presuming to question or contribute to it. If a member proved to be unworthy, they were banished from the order, their property was returned to them, and they were henceforth considered dead by Pythagoreans and mourned as such. The inner circle of Pythagoreans learned the secrets of philosophy from the master himself, which they were banned from revealing to non-Pythagoreans. This sort of secrecy, analogous to modern trade secrets, was common in the ancient world. It shows that Pythagoreanism was like the ancient Mysteries, which also required vows of secrecy from initiates. The point is that without proper preparation, the esoteric doctrines are likely to be misunderstood and even perhaps to be harmful. This is why there are degrees of initiation.

The Pythagoreans were very influential in the government of Croton and nearby Greek colonies, reorganizing the systems of government in accordance with their philosophical principles. Pythagorean spiritual practices, which you'll learn in the third degree of wisdom, probably provided some of the insights that led to these principles. The Pythagoreans thus afford an example of how spiritual practices can make a positive contribution to society and practical affairs.

Unfortunately, this involvement in politics led to the destruction of the Pythagorean order. Obviously there was much resentment of Pythagorean influence in government, especially from the rich and powerful. The precipitating cause may have been when Cylon, scion of a wealthy and influential family, applied for membership, but was rejected for bad character. He forged documents, which he used as evidence of a secret Pythagorean conspiracy, and gathered a mob, which set fire to a Pythagorean meeting hall, burning the people inside. It is unclear whether Pythagoras died at this time, or whether he managed to escape to another city. In any case, the old guard organized uprisings in many Greek colonies and banished the Pythagoreans; it was the end of their political influence. The Pythagorean order survived and spread throughout the Greek-speaking world, but they were more focused on personal spiritual practice and scientific investigation than on political action. This is a subtler but slower means of effecting change.

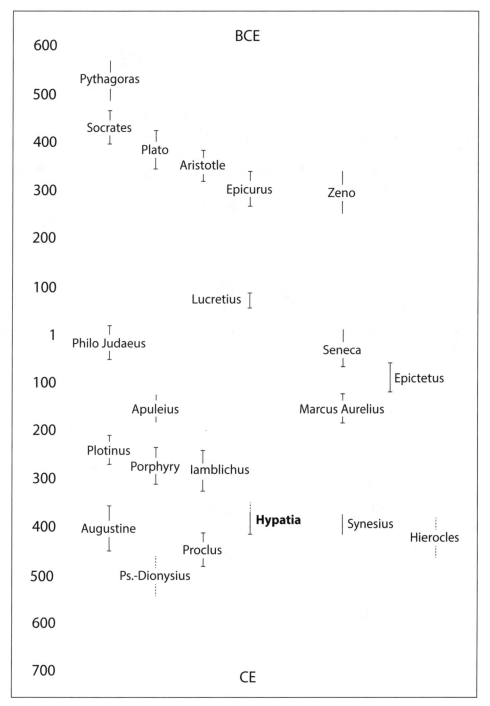

Timeline

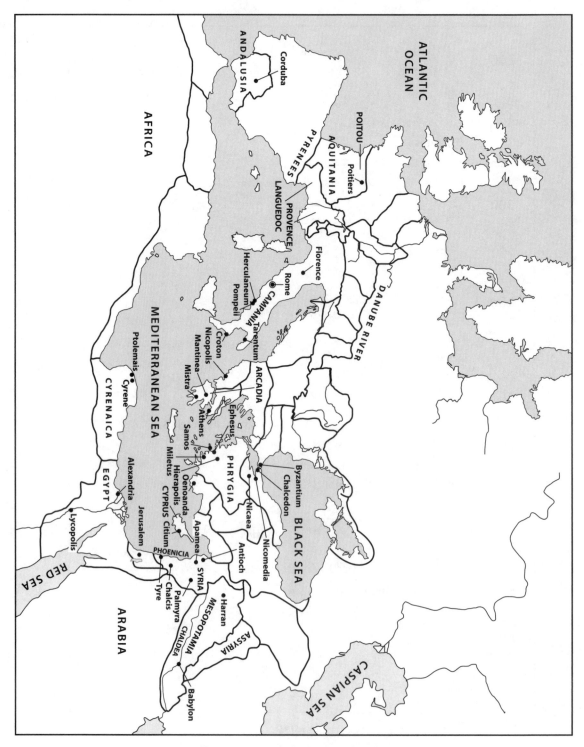

The Ancient World in the time of Hypatia

There is intriguing indirect evidence that Pythagoras learned some of his spiritual practices from shamans, whom the Greeks first encountered when they opened trade routes to the Black Sea region in the seventh century BCE, a century or so before Pythagoras was born. Essential to shamanism is the idea that the soul can be separated from the body, and this idea seems to have entered Greek thought about this time.

Many of the legends of Pythagoras have shamanic themes, and Pythagoras himself has many of the characteristics typical of shamans.[18] In particular, ancient biographies say that he was visited by Abaris, an emissary from Hyperborea, the "land beyond the North Wind," who was led to Pythagoras by his magical golden arrow or dart, which he gave to Pythagoras. Abaris's name seems to refer to the Avars of central Asia, and the story suggests that he was a shaman from Mongolia or Tibet, where a ritual dart or dagger (the *phurba*) is used as a magical tool and token of divine sanction. He was also called a "skywalker," which is an Asian way to refer to shamans and to the magical arrows by which they travel. This and much other evidence suggest that Abaris conferred a shamanic initiation on Pythagoras, thereby establishing a Western spiritual tradition with roots in Tibet.

Shamans are the psychotherapists of indigenous cultures, negotiating and coordinating the spiritual relations among people, the natural world, and higher powers. Since they are specialists in the structure and dynamics of the soul from a practical perspective, they use their techniques for care of the soul and cure of its ailments. A common operation is *soul retrieval*, a means of helping a patient suffering malaise due to a wandering or stolen soul. Nowadays we would probably diagnose depression. Shamans also identify and banish malignant spirits (perhaps neurosis, psychosis, or schizophrenia).

Shamans help to ensure that their communities live in accordance with nature and the divine order, which their spiritual practices allow them to understand. This ensures ecological balance, with the aim of ensuring good hunting and the health of livestock and crops. Thus the Pythagoreans' spiritually-based social programs were not inconsistent with the shamanic tradition.

Shamanic ideas also appear in Orphism, a Greek religious movement dating from at least the sixth century BCE, which has many interconnections with Pythagoreanism, Platonism, and Neoplatonism. Orphism taught the separability of the soul from the body, reincarnation (also a Pythagorean belief), and spiritual practices intended to ensure a blessed afterlife. (You may know the ancient Greek myth of Orpheus and Eurydice, which is an allegory for Orphic ideas.)

The Greeks might have learned shamanism from the Persian Magi, who were spiritual teachers, prophets, and magicians of ancient Iran. Indeed, our words *magic* and *magus* come from the Persian word for these spiritual specialists. Pythagoras and several of his followers were said to have been students of the Magi. Some of Plato's ideas have been traced to the Magi, and according to Plato's personal secretary, a delegation of Magi visited Plato when he was on his deathbed and made offerings to him as to a demigod.

There are no surviving authentic writings from Pythagoras, and in fact it is most likely that his teaching was entirely oral. To a certain extent scholars can reconstruct his philosophy from later philosophers, but it is always difficult to separate his ideas from those of his followers. Much of what we do have comes from the Neopythagoreans, who revived his philosophy in the first century of the Common Era, and whose philosophy is closely related to Neoplatonism. Pythagoras was an almost divine progenitor for all these philosophers, and their writings show us what they considered most important of his philosophy (at least as they understood it).

Number was of central importance in Pythagoreanism. If you know nothing else about Pythagoras, you probably remember learning the Pythagorean theorem in school. (Remember it? "In a right triangle, the square of the hypotenuse is the sum of the squares on the other two sides.") Attributed to Pythagoras is the discovery that concordant musical pitches could be expressed in simple numerical ratios (for example, a string half as long will sound an octave higher, strings in the ratio 2:3 sound at the interval of a fifth, and so forth). This was a key discovery in the history of science, for it showed how complex natural phenomena could be understood mathematically; it is the ancestor of modern mathematical physics.

Hypatia and her father, Theon, were interested in Pythagorean number theory because they both were mathematicians and astronomers. However, their interests were not purely technical, for in Pythagorean philosophy numbers have a spiritual dimension, which in our time has been explored by psychologists such as Carl Jung. Although it may seem unlikely, the numbers are potent symbols of deep psychological structures, as revealed in symmetric diagrams such as mandalas, and so they have a role in the more advanced topics of Neoplatonism, which are taken up in the later chapters of this book.

There were many famous Pythagoreans, but I will pass over them, since my purpose here is not to write a history of philosophy, but to present the sources of Hypatia's philosophy.

The direct ancestor of Hypatia's philosophy was Plato, and she would have called herself a Platonist. The term "Neoplatonism" was originally a derogatory term invented by certain nineteenth-century scholars to name what they considered to be a degeneration of

Platonism from its earlier "purer" form. But Hypatia and her contemporaries intended their Platonic philosophy to be a further refinement and development of Plato's work. Nowadays, "Neoplatonism" is a purely descriptive term that has lost its negative connotation among scholars; it refers to Platonism after 245 CE.

Plato (427–347 BCE) was probably born in Athens; he came from an aristocratic family, and Socrates (c.469–399 BCE) seems to have been his principal teacher in philosophy. However, many scholars have perceived an important Pythagorean influence on Plato's thought. He was friends with a number of Pythagoreans, and Pythagoreanism seems to have influenced his political philosophy and the spiritual importance that he attached to mathematics. According to a story written 750 years after Plato, over the door to his school was inscribed:

Let no non-geometer enter!

This was an allusion to a common inscription over the doors of temples: "Let no unjust person enter!" Regardless of whether the story is true, it embodies a truth: mathematics is the quickest entrée to Platonism. But don't worry; you don't need to be a mathematician to practice Platonism!

When Plato was about forty years old, he founded his school outside the city walls of Athens in an exercise field and olive grove sacred to Athena, the goddess of wisdom. It was called *Akademia*, and from it we get *academy*, *academic*, and related words, the original "groves of academe." The location was appropriate—for in the exercise field, young men practiced and exercised their physical bodies, developing their strength and coordination, while in the Academy they exercised their minds and learned to practice wisdom and virtue. "A sound mind in a sound body" was an ancient Greek proverb.

Starting with Plato, the Academy operated under a continuous succession of heads for four hundred years. It suffered a period of disorganization after the Roman invasion in 88 BCE by Sulla, who cut down the trees to make war machines, and many philosophers left Athens. The Athenian Academy was reestablished toward the end of the fourth century CE and continued in operation under a continuous succession of heads, until Justinian I in 529 CE closed all the Pagan schools. The Academy continued to exist after Justinian's edict, but no longer as an educational institution.

PLOTINUS

While many philosophers contributed to the development of Platonism, an especially important figure for our purposes was Plotinus (204–70 CE), for he inaugurated the phase of Platonic philosophy that scholars call Neoplatonism. He was probably born in Lycopolis (modern Asyût) in Upper Egypt, but as a young man he traveled to Alexandria to study philosophy. He tried each philosopher in turn, but was dissatisfied with them all until he came to Ammonius Saccas, who had founded a school at the beginning of the third century. We know little about Ammonius, except that ancient Neoplatonists said he was born a Christian but converted to Paganism. He was called "Saccas," supposedly, because he dressed in a sack! [19] In any case, Plotinus found in Ammonius what he was searching for, and exclaimed, "This is the man I was seeking!" [20] He studied with Ammonius in Alexandria for eleven years.

We know very little about the philosophy of Ammonius Saccas, for he wrote no philosophical treatises. What little we do know must be inferred from the philosophy of Plotinus, who said he owed everything to Ammonius, and from his fellow students Origen and Longinus.

In 243 Plotinus left Ammonius to join the campaign of Emperor Gordian III against the Persians. Most likely he did not go as a soldier but as a scientific adviser, and he seems to have been motivated by a hope to contact Persian Magi and Indian sages. In particular, Mani, the great Persian religious reformer and founder of Manichaeism, was supposed to be accompanying the opposing army. However, Gordian's adventure proved to be a failure and Plotinus's plans were unsuccessful.

Therefore Plotinus, who was about forty years old by this time, headed for Rome, where he set up his school (about 245). Like many of the ancient schools, it admitted women, and in fact a wealthy woman, Gemina, provided space for Plotinus and his school in her house.

For the first ten years (until about 253), Plotinus's instruction was completely oral, as befits the teaching of philosophy as a way of life. Rather than setting out a philosophical system in organized lectures, Plotinus's teaching method was to respond to his students' questions and problems, and to use this to illustrate more general principles, but eventually his students convinced him to write down his doctrines. His method was to first formulate his expositions completely in his mind. No doubt he used the ancient "art of memory," which arranges knowledge into organized images that can be vividly visualized and remembered. Once the ideas were organized in his mind, he would write them out in one go; he rarely revised his texts, for his eyesight was bad and it was difficult for him to read. These essays were later collected and edited by his student Porphyry.

Plotinus was highly respected in Rome, and many senators attended his classes. The emperor Gallienus and his wife, Salonina, were especially taken by his philosophy, and they agreed to his plan to establish a city, "Platonopolis," in Campania (southern Italy). This was to be a home for philosophers and governed by Platonic principles, but it seems that the project was scuttled by court intrigue.

Gallienus was assassinated in 268, and around this time Plotinus's sickness, perhaps leprosy, worsened. Most of his disciples stayed away, and eventually he left Rome and retired to an estate in Campania. Plotinus died in 270 at the age of 66; his last words were:

Try to bring back the god in you to the divine in the All.[21]

PORPHYRY AND IAMBLICHUS

Porphyry (c.232–c.305 CE) was a Phoenician from Tyre (in modern Lebanon), who studied under Longinus at Athens. Longinus and Plotinus differed on some philosophical matters, and so Porphyry, defending his teacher, engaged in a formal debate with one of Plotinus's students. Eventually Porphyry was won over to Plotinian philosophy and studied under this new teacher for six years (263–268). Toward the end of this period Plotinus perceived that Porphyry was contemplating suicide, and so the master sent him to Sicily with spiritual exercises to practice. These apparently worked, but Plotinus died in 270 while Porphyry was away. Porphyry returned to Rome and wrote his teacher's biography, which we have, and edited and collected his essays into a book called the *Enneads*, which has survived and is a rich source of Neoplatonic philosophy.

Porphyry wrote about sixty philosophical works of his own, but less than a dozen survive; they are very valuable for understanding his philosophy. From these it appears that he was more interested in the spiritual dimensions of philosophy than was his teacher. For example, he wrote about the philosophy in the *Chaldean Oracles*, about which I'll have more to say later. Porphyry lived about a century before Hypatia, and his philosophy is perhaps the most similar to hers.

Iamblichus was born about 240 CE in Chalcis (modern Qinnesrin) in Syria. He was from an aristocratic family, which is perhaps why he kept his Semitic name at a time when most wealthy families chose Greek names; for example, Porphyry changed his Phoenician name *Malchus*, meaning King, to Greek *Porphyrios*, which means "Purple" (referring to the royal purple). Iamblichus's decision may reflect his opinion that the Greeks had too little respect for the ancient wisdom of the "old nations" of the Middle East. As was typical, he traveled around studying philosophy, and eventually became a student of Porphyry, who was just four years older. We are unsure how directly the two interacted.

Around the year 305, Iamblichus returned to Syria, where he founded his own school in Apamea, near Antioch. Much is made of the disagreements between Iamblichus and Porphyry, but they are more a matter of emphasis than of fundamental difference. In particular, they disagreed about the importance of ritualistic (as opposed to contemplative) spiritual practices, which were intended to lead to mystical insights. Iamblichus designed the definitive Neoplatonic curriculum. It began with his *Collection of Pythagorean Doctrines* in ten "books" (scrolls), but only four of them survive, along with fragments of a fifth. His surviving book, commonly known as *On the Mysteries*, is a valuable explanation of the theoretical principles underlying his spiritual practices; I'll discuss it in a later chapter. Iamblichus died around 325, some seventy-five years before Hypatia's teaching activity.

Scholars think the Alexandrian Neoplatonists tended more to the Porphyrian than to the Iamblichan position on ritual, and so we might expect this of Hypatia too, but there is evidence that both Theon and Hypatia incorporated ritual into their spiritual practice, including ritual invocations. Therefore I will teach you these spiritual exercises in an appropriate place.

HYPATIA'S PHILOSOPHY

So far as we know, Hypatia wrote nothing about her philosophy; it was all taught in person, which had been the traditional approach for more than a millennium. She did write about mathematics and astronomy, and her works, long thought lost, have been partly reconstructed, but that is of no use to us here. How then can we learn how to live her philosophy?

In fact, we can infer a pretty accurate picture of her philosophy. One historian writing twenty years after her death reported that "she succeeded in the school of Plato and Plotinus,"[22] and we are fortunate to have Plotinus's *Enneads*, which sets out his philosophy in detail, if somewhat obscurely. Also, as explained in the previous section, we have a number of important philosophical texts from Porphyry and Iamblichus, who lived only a century before her. We are also aided in reconstructing her philosophy by the fact that she was apparently not much of a philosophical innovator; she seems to have been satisfied with the philosophy she had learned from her father and their Neoplatonic predecessors. In a culture such as ours, which values innovation for its own sake, this can be considered a failing, but her goal was to teach her students to live well, not to change doctrine for the sake of novelty.

We know some of the philosophy of Hypatia's most prominent disciple, Synesius of Cyrene (c.373–c.414), who later converted to Christianity and became Bishop of Ptolemais (in Libya). Despite their religious differences, they remained devoted friends until death. We have 159 letters that he wrote to many contemporaries, including a dozen to Hypatia and his fellow students, several essays, and ten metaphysical hymns. Synesius sent two philosophical essays, which we have, to Hypatia for her approval, and it is reasonable to assume that they are consistent with her philosophy. (Unfortunately, we do not have Hypatia's replies to Synesius.) The hymns, including those written after his conversion, are also consistent with what we would expect of her Neoplatonic philosophy. Mercifully, Synesius, who had already lost his three sons, died before learning of the murder of her whom he called his "divine guide," "the most holy and revered philosopher."

We also know a reasonable amount about the Neoplatonic philosophy that was being taught in Alexandria shortly after Hypatia's death. For example, we know something of the philosophy of Hierocles of Alexandria, who was teaching just twenty years after her assassination. He was Pagan, but seems to have been interested in reconciling his philosophy with Christianity. Nevertheless, his views offended the powers in control, and he was banished from Alexandria for a time. He traveled to Constantinople, where he also managed to offend the party in power there, who had him beaten by a group of thugs.

Covered with blood, he plunged the cup of his hand into his own blood and sprinkled the judge with it, saying: "Here, Cyclops, drink this wine now that you have eaten human flesh." [23] (The quotation is from the *Odyssey*.)

You will not be surprised to learn that he was exiled from Constantinople! Later he was allowed to return to Alexandria and resume studies with his students. We have Hierocles's complete *Commentary on the Pythagorean Golden Verses* and fragments of works on providence and fate.

The surviving works of Proclus (415–485 CE) are some of our best sources for Neoplatonic philosophy in the years immediately after Hypatia's death. He was born in Constantinople, educated in Alexandria, and eventually settled in Athens, where he became the head of the Platonic Academy. In a sense he brought Pagan Neoplatonism to its final form, but most of his refinements are not especially relevant to the practice of Neoplatonism in our time.

By combining these sources, interpolating between her predecessors, contemporaries, and successors, we can get a reasonably accurate picture of Hypatia's philosophy, certainly accurate enough to be a guide for living well, if not for every technical nuance.

LATER NEOPLATONISM

As I said, my purpose is not to write a history of Western philosophy or even of Neoplatonism. Rather, I have tried to show the sources from which Hypatia got her philosophy and the sources from which we can reconstruct it. Nevertheless it's worthwhile to say a few words about Neoplatonism after Hypatia's time.

Hierocles and other Pagan philosophers continued to teach Neoplatonism in Alexandria, but after Hypatia's murder they kept a low profile and stayed clear of politics. Eventually, an Alexandrian Neoplatonic succession was reestablished by Hermeias (c.410–c.450) and his son Ammonius (440–521/517), and it was quite active in the fifth and sixth centuries.

Pagan Neoplatonism was also pursued in other parts of the Greek-speaking world, but it was curtailed after Emperor Justinian closed the Pagan schools in 529 CE. When this occurred, seven philosophers from the Athenian Academy traveled to the Middle East seeking a more tolerant culture, and they were welcomed at the court of the Persian king Chosroes. However, the philosophers were not happy, and so they returned to the Byzantine Empire, but not before Chosroes negotiated a treaty with Justinian, ensuring that the Pagan philosophers would not be persecuted. Some scholars believe that they settled near the border with Persia in a city called Harrân, which was still famous for Neoplatonic philosophy five hundred years later.

Many Neoplatonic ideas were incorporated into Christianity, which used Neoplatonism as a philosophical foundation for Christian theology. For example, Hypatia's disciple Synesius used Neoplatonic ideas to explain the doctrine of the Trinity. Also, St. Augustine of Hippo (354–430), a contemporary of Hypatia, was a Manichaean until about age thirty, when he began to study Neoplatonism, especially Plotinus and Porphyry. After he converted to Christianity he used Neoplatonism (and Stoicism) as a framework for Christian theology.

Especially important to Christian mysticism are four works written under the name "Dionysius the Areopagite" (Acts 17:34), but attributed by scholars to some pseudo-Dionysius of the late fifth or early sixth century. These works (*Mystical Theology*, *Divine Names*, *Celestial Hierarchy*, *Ecclesiastical Hierarchy*) are almost pure Neoplatonism, so much so that some scholars suspect the author of being a closet Pagan. Later, St. Thomas Aquinas (1225–1274) blended Neoplatonic and Aristotelian philosophy into his theology, and Meister Eckhart's (c.1260–1327) mysticism and negative theology owe a large debt to Neoplatonism. The ascent to divine union taught by St. Bonaventura (1221–1274) is based on the Neoplatonic ascent that I will explain in chapter 11. Platonic and Neoplatonic ideas and practices have been especially influential in Greek Orthodox Christianity.

Alexandrian Neoplatonic (especially Plotinian) ideas are prominent in the thought of a number of Islamic philosophers, including the Persian Ibn Sina (Avicenna, 980–1037), al-Farabi (c.872–c.950), al-Ghazali (c.1055–1111), Suhrawardi (1155–91), and Ibn 'Arabi (1165–1240). Neoplatonism was also important in Sufi thought, perhaps as early as Dhu'l-Nûn (died 859).

Neoplatonic and Neopythagorean influence is apparent in the Jewish mystical tradition, the *Kabbalah*, both in the doctrine of emanation and in the importance attached to the first ten numbers. Neoplatonic quotations can be found in the writings of Moses de Leon (c.1250–1305), whom Gershom Scholem, the eminent historian of the Kabbalah, credits with writing the *Zohar*, the principal kabbalistic text. Neoplatonism also influenced the Jewish philosophers Solomon ibn Gabirol (c.1021–c.1058) and Moses Maimonides (1135–1204).

Although never really absent from the Western intellectual landscape, Neoplatonism made an important reappearance beginning in 1438. In that year, the Council of Florence was convened in order to reconcile the Western and Eastern branches of the Christian church. The Eastern branch was represented by George Gemistos (c.1360–c.1450), who called himself Plethon. What was suspected, but not known until after his death, was that he was a Pagan Neoplatonist, and secretly practiced his religion with a small group of followers at Mistra (in the Peloponnese). When he died, his papers were discovered and most of them were burned, preserving only enough to prove his "crime."

However, at the Council of Florence he was representing the Greek Orthodox Church, and presented lectures arguing the superiority of Plato over Aristotle, who was favored in the West. His descriptions of the Platonic Academy so fired the imagination of Cosimo de Medici (1389–1464) that he decided to establish a Platonic Academy in Florence. Eventually he chose the young scholar Marsilio Ficino (1433–99) to head the Florentine Academy, which was established in 1462 in a villa at Careggi. Ficino's first task was to translate the texts of Plato and the Neoplatonists from Greek to Latin, which made them widely accessible in the West. Ficino came under some suspicion for engaging in Pagan rituals and spiritual practices in the Academy, and eventually he was obliged to reaffirm his Christian faith. In any case, his written works present a Christian Neoplatonic philosophy.

The Florentine Academy became a fount of Neoplatonic ideas and inspiration in philosophy, the sciences, the arts, music, and literature, which helped to precipitate the Italian Renaissance and the rebirth of learning throughout Europe.

One of Ficino's students was Pico della Mirandola (1463–94), who in some ways went further than Ficino, combining Christian Neoplatonism with Kabbalah and Hermetic magic. The church condemned some of his claims, and he had to recant. We still read his *Oration on the Dignity of Man*, with its famous quotation from a Hermetic text:

What a great miracle is man! [24]

The Cambridge Platonists were an influential group of seventeenth-century Cambridge University graduates, including Henry More (1614–87), Ralph Cudworth (1617–88), and Anne Conway (1631–79), who advocated Christian Neoplatonism for its harmony with reason.

An important modern Pagan Neoplatonist was Thomas Taylor (1785–1835), who was known in his time as "the English Platonist." He made many of the first translations into English of Neoplatonic texts, some of which are still valuable today. His writings significantly influenced the English romantic poets William Blake (1757–1827), William Wordsworth (1770–1850), and Percy Bysshe Shelley (1792–1822), as well as the American Ralph Waldo Emerson (1803–82) and the other Transcendentalists of the nineteenth century.

As you can see, the Platonic philosophy—from Pythagoras to Neoplatonism—has been a fruitful spiritual tradition for two and one-half millennia. That is what you will learn, but let's begin by entering the Epicurean Garden to learn the first degree of wisdom.

PART II
THE FIRST DEGREE
OF WISDOM

CHAPTER FOUR

SEEKING TRANQUILITY
IN THE GARDEN

GOALS OF THE FIRST DEGREE

You are embarking on a path of spiritual growth so that you can live a more fulfilling life by direct interaction with divinity. But this will be difficult to achieve if you are stressed out, working long hours, perpetually dissatisfied with how you spend your time, striving to advance in your career, anxious and fearful about the future, worried about money, and so on. Where will you find the time and energy—let alone the mental focus and peace—for spiritual practices? Therefore, you need to begin living a more tranquil life as a foundation for advanced spiritual practices. Nevertheless, most of us cannot devote our lives to spiritual pursuits; we need to work for our food, shelter, clothes, and other necessities, and living happily is easier if we have more than the bare necessities. How can we establish a base of happiness and tranquility on which to build a spiritual practice?

In this chapter you will learn the Epicurean way of life, which provides a background for more advanced spiritual practices. You'll learn how to analyze your desires so that you can decide which are worth pursuing and which less so. You will get help deciding how much is enough (of anything you want). You will get aid eliminating fear of death and fear of the gods, in case they trouble you. Finally, you will learn the Epicurean ways of dealing with ambition, justice, and friendship. All of this will help you live your life more tranquilly to promote your spiritual progress.

According to the study plan, you should take about a month learning the Epicurean way of life and making it a habit. Of course it won't take you long to read the chapter, but that won't do much good unless you *practice* the philosophy. That may come quickly (you might be doing much of it already) or it might take more than a month, especially if it is a very different way of looking at the world for you. You're not in a race, so keep returning to the practices until they become habitual; practice them whenever tranquility and contentment seem out of reach.

THE GARDEN

Nowadays, *Epicurean* is nearly synonymous with "gourmet," and Epicurean philosophy would seem to be about indulging in pleasure above all else, but it is not. The ultimate goal is in fact pleasure, but this is achieved largely by avoiding pain and seeking tranquility. Something of what Epicurus had in mind can be learned from a letter in which he wrote,

> I am thrilled with pleasure in the body, when I live on bread and water, and I spit upon luxurious pleasures not for their own sake, but because of the inconveniences that follow them.[25]

His philosophy is not so ascetic as this quote suggests, but it shows just how far the meaning of "Epicurean" has drifted! Rather, Epicurus taught how to live happily without too much effort, but before we get to the techniques, let me tell you a little about him.

Epicurus was born in 341 BCE of Athenian parents on the island of Samos (just off the coast of modern Turkey), where Pythagoras too was born; this was when Alexander the Great was sixteen years old and seven years after Plato's death. He first became interested in philosophy in his early teens after he had become disenchanted with mythology. His grammar teacher was presenting Hesiod's *Theogony*, which describes the origin of the universe:

First, Chaos, next broad-breasted Earth was made ...

Epicurus asked if everything came from Chaos, then where did Chaos come from? His teacher said that if he wanted answers to this kind of question, he would have to go to the philosophers. "Then I must go to them," said the boy, "for they know the truth of being." [26] In other words, Epicurus wasn't satisfied with simply accepting the traditional stories about the gods; he wanted to know the *reasons* for things. He had a *desire* for *wisdom*, which made him a philosopher (lover of wisdom).

He studied with various philosophers in various cities but later claimed that he was largely self-taught. He started his own school at the age of thirty-two, and after about five years he moved it to Athens, where he established the Garden. It adjoined a temple of Aphrodite, the goddess of love, beauty, and joy, who had a famous statue there. The Garden was renowned for the friendship among its members, as were other Epicurean communities, so that "his friends were so numerous that they could hardly be reckoned by entire cities." [27] Women as well as men, slaves as well as free people, the rich and the poor were all admitted and treated as equals. They came from all over the Greek world, including the Middle East and Egypt. The master of the Garden, who had a weak constitution, died in his seventy-second year (270 BCE), as I'll discuss later. We have his will, which reveals his kindness and generosity.

Epicurus's school continued to exist, under an unbroken succession of "masters" or "presidents" for six hundred years, until the time of Hypatia. "In a word, so long as Learning flourished in Greece, and Rome was preserved from the Barbarians, the School and discipline of Epicurus continued eminent." [28]

Epicurus required his students to memorize his maxims, and he worked to make them very clear, which is important if they are to be psychologically potent. In ancient times he was considered an exceptionally prolific author; he wrote over three hundred "books" (scrolls), and we have the titles of more than forty works. Unfortunately, almost everything has been lost (or destroyed). We have only three letters, two collections of maxims, and several dozen fragments (most only a sentence or two in length)—a total of less than fifty pages.

Fortunately, some of his writings are among the 1,785 charred scrolls from the Villa of the Papyri in Herculaneum (the sister city of Pompeii, both of which were destroyed by the eruption of Vesuvius in 79 CE). These scrolls belonged to a philosophical library, probably originally assembled by Philodemus, an influential Epicurean philosopher of the first century BCE. With the volcano rumbling above the villa, the scrolls were being crated so they could be moved to safety, when the pyroclastic flow—1,800° gas and rocks moving at 450 miles per hour—engulfed the library, instantly burning the scrolls nearly to charcoal and thus preserving them from decay. The carbonized scrolls cannot be unrolled because they crumble so easily, and in the more than two hundred years since they were discovered, scholars have been trying to find a way to read them. Fortunately, the latest technology is proving successful, and we may hope some valuable lost works will be reclaimed soon. Herculaneum's loss may be our gain.

One of the most important Epicureans was Lucretius (c.94–55 BCE), a contemporary of Philodemus. His long poem "On the Nature of Things" popularized Epicurean ideas in the Roman world, and influenced many other poets, including Virgil, Ovid, and Horace. There is a story (dating from the beginning of the second century CE) that he wrote the poem between spells of insanity caused by a love potion his wife gave him, and that he eventually killed himself. Historians doubt the story, but it inspired Tennyson's poem "Lucretius," which imagines his erotic dreams, despair, and consequent suicide.

"On the Nature of Things" was lost for a thousand years, but after it was rediscovered in 1417 CE, it had a significant influence in European intellectual circles, and stimulated the development of scientific atomic theory in the seventeenth century. Thus it is a direct ancestor of the contemporary scientific worldview.

The Garden has remained an inspiration and source of wisdom for many people over the centuries. For example, Thomas Jefferson wrote in a letter:

> As you say of yourself, I too am an Epicurean. I consider the genuine (not the imputed) doctrines of Epicurus as containing everything rational in moral philosophy which Greece and Rome have left us.[29]

ATOMS AND THE VOID

Epicurus founded his ethical theory on the atomic theories of Leucippus (fl. 440 BCE) and Democritus (460–370 BCE). In this he was following the pattern, first established in Plato's Academy, of many ancient philosophies, which were divided into three disciplines: *logic*, *physics* (natural science), and *ethics*. Logic specified the criteria of truth and how it might be discovered; its goal was *right discourse* (saying what is true, the rules of discourse). Physics, which was based on logic, studied nature (*physis*) in all its aspects, including cosmology, theology, and psychology; its goal was *right thought* (knowing the laws of nature). Ethics used the knowledge obtained from logic and physics to understand how people should live; its goal was *right action* (the norms of conduct).

According to Epicurus's atomic philosophy, the universe is made of *atoms* and the *void* through which they move. The atoms are the smallest bits into which things can be divided, for in ancient Greek, *atomon* means an indivisible (*a-tomon*) thing. Since we have split the atom, a more accurate translation would be *elementary particle*. The way in which the microscopic atoms connect and interact determines the properties of ordinary things, such as their color, hardness, and chemical properties. Epicurus's system was not completely deterministic, for he said that the atoms occasionally swerved for no reason.

The details of Epicurus's physics are not especially relevant to our purpose here. What is important is that his worldview is qualitatively very similar to contemporary scientific materialism in that everything, including the human mind, is made of elementary particles. The atoms of the soul, said Epicurus, are finer and subtler than those of the body, but they are atoms nonetheless. This is similar to the contemporary scientific view that the mind is nothing but the electrochemical activity of the brain. Thus, Epicurus's ethics do not require any particular spiritual commitments, and it is quite applicable in our secular world. It's a good starting place for us. We can take up matters of the spirit later.

Epicurus insisted that his atomism did not exclude free will. Although, as we will see, he was no friend of the traditional Greek religion, he said, "It would be better, indeed, to accept the legends of the gods than to bow beneath destiny that the natural philosophers have imposed." [30] Exactly how free will fit into his atomic theory is not entirely clear from the surviving texts, but his position is similar to the modern philosophical theory of *compatibilism*, which argues that if you understand free will correctly, then you see that it is consistent with both (nondeterministic) modern physics and (deterministic) classical physics. The basic idea is that if *my* choices are a result of *my* beliefs, desires, purposes, values, etc., then my will is free, in the only meaningful sense of "free," regardless of what the particles constituting me are doing. [31]

CLASSIFYING DESIRES

We can imagine a meeting between Epicurus and a dozen of his favorite students in the Garden. [32] They recline on couches, talking and enjoying olives, figs, nuts, and a little wine mixed with chilled water. On several of the couches couples recline together, including Metrodorus, one of Epicurus's most distinguished friends, and his wife Leontion, a former courtesan.

"Epicurus," says Metrodorus, "surely what separates wisdom from folly is the way we make our free choices, and so this issue is central to philosophy, which is the love of wisdom. Now, you teach us that everything in the universe is atoms and void, but how does that help us decide what to *choose* and what to *avoid*?"

Epicurus replies, "All animals choose pleasure and avoid pain; that is the way we are made—the way our atoms are put together. In fact, we can say that pain is nature's signal to avoid something and pleasure is the signal to choose it. Pain and pleasure are not matters of opinion; they are facts of nature."

Timocrates, Metrodorus's older brother, waves his goblet and sighs, "It's all so simple, isn't it? Pleasure is the only good, and we should always pursue pleasure. Everything that Socrates and Plato said is just hot air."

"My brother, you know that's false. If that were all there were to it, our master's philosophy would be the crassest kind of hedonism—and I've heard that you sometimes spread that slander—but it is not. For example, he's taught us that it's often wise to avoid pleasures if they will lead to greater pain, and that it may be wise to endure pains in order to gain a greater pleasure."

"That is correct," Epicurus replies. "We must apply reason to the direct experience of pleasure and pain, which includes mental pleasure or pain as well as physical pleasure or pain. Both are a result of the way the soul atoms are bouncing around with the body atoms and interacting with the atoms of things outside the body. The jostling of the soul atoms is the source of the pleasure and pain. In this sense these pleasures and pains are *real* and *true*; you cannot be mistaken about the fact that you are feeling pleasure or feeling pain. Therefore pleasure and pain provide a secure basis for choice and avoidance, but it must be subjected to judgment in order to act wisely."

"Teacher, how can we make such choices?" asks Mys, a female slave and one of Epicurus's best students.

"As a basis for judgment, here is a useful way to classify your desires. First, some desires are *natural*—that is, a function of our biological natures, including normal human psychology, whereas other desires are *non-natural* in the sense that they do not follow from our biological nature. Of course, the term 'non-natural' does not imply that these desires are in some way deviant or perverted! Of the natural desires, some are *necessary*, others are not. Of the necessary natural desires, some are necessary for life, such as the desire for food; some are necessary to remove bodily stress, such as the desire for rest when we are tired; some are necessary for happiness, such as freedom from anxiety and fear. That is, these desires are necessary either for survival or to remove bodily pain and mental discomfort."

"Why is it important to make this distinction?" asks Mys.

"The crucial point is that necessary natural desires are self-limiting, for the pleasure is maximized when the corresponding pain or discomfort is eliminated. For example, if you are thirsty and desire drink, when you have had enough, you will not be thirsty anymore. The pleasure is maximal because you cannot have *less* thirst than *no* thirst. So also with hunger. In all these cases, if you desire more than is necessary to satisfy the need, then this excess desire is still natural, but it is not necessary."

"Yes," Timocrates interrupts, belching, "but as the old saying goes, 'The stomach is insatiable.'"

"And I bid you remember," Epicurus replies, pointing at Timocrates:

> The stomach is not insatiable, as most people say;
> instead the opinion that the stomach needs unlimited filling is false.[33]

"Nevertheless, my brother has a point," says Metrodorus, "for people go to great trouble and expense to stuff themselves with delicacies."

Epicurus nods. "The desire for gourmet food or drink is an example of a *unnecessary but natural* desire, since it is merely unnecessary variation of a natural desire. Unnecessary desires are not self-limiting because they are not removing a bodily pain or mental discomfort, and so you run the risk of overindulgence, for they can exceed what is *sufficient* and have the potential to cause pain. So if you eat too much or too rich food, you may get indigestion, and if you drink too much, a hangover. Less obviously, you have to work harder to earn the money to buy expensive food. Remember:

> Nothing is enough to one for whom enough is very little.[34]

"I am not saying that you should avoid all unnecessary pleasures, for all pleasures have an inherent goodness—that is the teaching of the Garden—but they should be enjoyed in moderation. The sage weighs the likely pleasures and pains and makes a prudent choice."

"In other words," Leontion remarks, "we should remember the sacred Delphic Maxim, which is inscribed on the temple of Apollo at Delphi:

> Nothing too much![35]

"Indeed," Epicurus nods. "Now the non-natural desires are those that are not essential to our human nature. For example, the desires for wealth, power, and fame. These are matters of opinion, not facts of our biological nature. Certainly, all pleasures are good, but some pleasures bring greater pain in their pursuit or in their wake—especially those pleasures born of non-natural desires or even of natural but unnecessary desires. Therefore remember the following slogan; when you are feeling desire, use it to help decide how to address the desire:

Among desires, some are natural and necessary,
some are natural and unnecessary,
and some are unnatural and unnecessary,
arising instead from groundless opinion.[36]

We all desire many things. What Epicurus has taught us is a technique for becoming more conscious of the sources of our desires and their consequences. Then we can make wise choices about which to pursue and which to forgo, so we can live happier lives. Here is an exercise to give you some practice in classifying your desires:

Classify Your Desires: List all your desires, or at least your strongest desires. These can range from the most basic, such as food, to more abstract desires, such as love, knowledge, enlightenment, power, or peace. Part of the practice, of course, is to be honest with yourself, so try to list your actual desires as opposed to those you think you ought to have. Try also to be specific, so if you have a special craving for chocolate or books, list it. Now classify each desire as (1) natural and necessary, (2) natural but unnecessary, or (3) non-natural. This will require some thought, and not everyone will agree. For example, the desire for sex is certainly natural, but is it necessary or not? On the one hand, many people think sex is necessary for a normal life, but on the other, you're unlikely to die of sex starvation! This exercise can be a good topic for group discussion. In any case, record your thoughts in your journal.

After reading this description of Epicurus's ethics you may be thinking, "Well, that all sounds very good, but does it mean I should get rid of my smartphone?" Not necessarily (although I doubt Epicurus would have one, were he alive today). Obviously, desire for a smartphone in itself is non-natural, but a smartphone can serve other desires that are natural, either necessary or not. For example, you can use your smartphone for personal safety, which is a natural desire, or for keeping in touch with your friends, which is also natural.

The point is to be clear about the costs and benefits. How much do you have to pay for the smartphone itself and for smartphone service? What are alternative means for satisfying your primary desires (e.g., keeping in touch with friends)? Of course, this calculation will depend on your wealth: paying for an expensive smartphone will cause less financial "pain" for a rich person, but then you must consider the effort of becoming and staying wealthy. Therefore the Garden does not provide ready-made answers to all the decisions of life, but it does provide ways to think about them. Epicurus suggests:

> *Evaluate each of your desires by this question:*
> *"What will happen to me if that which this desire seeks is attained,*
> *and what if it is not?"* [37]

In my own life, when I want something that is expensive or will take a lot of hard work to get, I think about it in terms of Epicurus's three-way classification and ask myself that question. This guides my action and helps me do what will actually make me happier in the long run and avoid the pain of "buyer's remorse."

> *Modern Conveniences:* Take the smartphone or some other modern convenience that "you can't live without" and apply the Epicurean calculation to it. First, decide whether it is natural and necessary, natural but unnecessary, or non-natural. Next, investigate what other desires it serves, and whether these are natural and necessary, natural but unnecessary, or non-natural. Weigh these benefits against the costs. For example, for a computer, as well as the obvious purchase cost you should include the time to keep it working, the frustration when it doesn't, and the time you regret wasting online. Record your conclusions in your journal. Even if your analysis does not incline you to give up some gadget, it should give you a clearer understanding of what you are getting from it and at what cost.

TRANQUILITY

Epicurus distinguished pleasures that require activity from those that don't. *Static pleasure* is when you are suffering from neither pain nor desire; body and soul are comfortable; it is a state that will continue until pain, desire, or some other disturbance arises. *Active pleasure* arises from the act of satisfying some desire—that is, in eliminating some pain, or in doing anything else that produces enjoyment in body or mind. For example, quenched thirst is a static pleasure, but the act of quenching it is an active pleasure. Another kind of active pleasure is when you vary the pleasure without increasing it—for example, drinking when you're not thirsty.

Other things being equal, Epicureans prefer static pleasures to active pleasures because the static ones are more enduring; the absence of pain continues without effort until something happens (either inside the body or outside of it) to cause pain. Active pleasures, in contrast, require some effort to continue, which is a kind of pain or can lead to pain. Furthermore, they continue only until the original pain or discomfort is eliminated, and so they are limited in duration, whereas static pleasures continue indefinitely.

Nevertheless, active pleasures are essential to living well, if for no other reason than as a side effect of eliminating pain. The Epicurean sage does not reject active pleasures, but prefers static pleasures. Furthermore, pursuing an active pleasure can divert your mind from an unavoidable pain and in this way eliminate it or diminish its strength, at least for a while; this is the valuable practice of *replacing a pain with a pleasure*. For example, if you are suffering from some unavoidable physical or mental pain, you can try to replace it by doing something pleasant (say, eating a good meal or enjoying a conversation with friends), by remembering some past happy time, or by imagining some pleasure to come. We can focus our attention on only one thing at a time, and so the idea is to focus on something pleasant. This might not be easy at first, but it comes with practice. As you will see, spiritual progress depends on developing better control of your thoughts.

> *Passive and Active Pleasures:* Take your list of desires and classify each as *passive* (requiring no effort) or *active* (requiring some effort). Think about each and notice how passive pleasures can continue indefinitely, but active pleasures are self-limiting.

According to the philosophers of the Garden, the greatest pleasure is the absence of pain, for its absence is filled with enjoyment and delight (essentially the organism's recognition that it is flourishing). Further, they teach that mental pleasures are greater than bodily pleasures. Therefore, the principal goal of the philosopher, the greatest static pleasure, is a state of *tranquility*, a state in which the mind is not disturbed, uncomfortable, troubled, or in need; it is content.

> *But pleasantest of all is to be master of those high*
> *and tranquil regions fortressed by the teaching of the wise.*[38]

These lines remind us to take the philosophical "view from above" of troubles so that we are not caught up in the storm, and so we can act and react more wisely.

What you are doing in these and other Epicurean spiritual practices is gradually reprogramming yourself so that you are happy most of the time, and especially so that you are usually tranquil, which is the happy state that is easiest to maintain and the best for spiritual progress. It's hard to focus on spiritual practices if your mind is in turmoil. Achieving a state of tranquility may seem an unlikely possibility, but you still have much to learn in the Garden.

SUFFICIENCY

Now that you know the different kinds of desires and their pros and cons, we come to the question, "How much is enough?" Epicurus explains that when we properly understand pleasure, pain, and desire, we make a happy discovery. For satisfying a desire that is natural and necessary achieves the maximum pleasure by eliminating the corresponding need, and whatever satisfies that need yields the maximum pleasure. For example, hunger and thirst can be satisfied by simple food and water. (But, you might ask, don't I get more pleasure by eating tasty food and drinking wine? Perhaps, but the desire for this more interesting taste is a different desire, which is natural but unnecessary.) Therefore desires that are natural and necessary—the basic requirements of survival and of physical and mental comfort—are relatively easy to satisfy (that is, not expensive or hard to obtain). In this sense, like other animals, humans are by nature well adapted to existence; we and our natural environment fit together well.

> *Thanks be to blessed Nature that she has made*
> *what is necessary easy to obtain,*
> *and what is not easy unnecessary.*[39]

The difficulties come when our desires go beyond the necessary and beyond the natural, for they involve pain. But Epicurus does not say we should restrict our desires to the strictly necessary; on the contrary, the Golden Mean is best:

> *There is also a limit in simple living. He who fails to heed this limit falls into an error as great as that of the man who gives way to extravagance.*[40]

Rather, as dwellers in the Garden we are contented with simple pleasures, and so if a more luxurious pleasure is available we are able to enjoy it all the more. Thus Epicurus wrote to a friend:

> *Send me a little vessel of cheese,*
> *so that I can feast whenever I please.*[41]

Someone who continually expects gourmet foods will be less likely to be satisfied with Epicurus's jar of cheese, and so Epicurus has more opportunities for pleasure than the gourmand. The poet Euripides (c.480–406 BCE) wrote,

> *For the wise man the sufficient is enough.*[42]

Therefore you must apply your judgment to deciding what is sufficient. Because your happiness depends on it, it is important that you can obtain what is sufficient and be satisfied by it.

> *We regard self-sufficiency as a great virtue*
> *not so that we may only enjoy a few things,*
> *but so that we may be satisfied with a few things*
> *if those are all we have.*[43]

In other words, Epicureans are content even if they do not have much, but can enjoy themselves even better when they have more. For example, I try to pay attention to how good a slice of bread and butter tastes. It really does! Or how satisfying a bowl of oatmeal or beans and rice is on a cold day. Or how refreshing a glass of water is when I'm thirsty. If you appreciate simple things (not just food), then you can be delighted and grateful if you have the money and opportunity for fancier things. They are like surprise gifts. These maxims put it more succinctly:

Self-sufficiency is the greatest wealth of all.[44]

Freedom is the greatest fruit of self-sufficiency.[45]

Freedom is certainly important for happiness, and it's difficult to be happy if you are trapped, for example, in a miserable job so you can satisfy your unnecessary or non-natural desires.

The goal of self-sufficiency does not imply, however, that the philosophers of the Garden are egoistic isolationists, striving to be independent of everyone else, for mutually dependent friendship is an essential part of Epicurean blessedness, as we will see.

Satisfying Your Desires: Given the result of the exercise "Classify Your Desires," you are now going to determine how difficult it will be to satisfy them. Begin with your *necessary natural* desires, and for each one write down what you need to do to satisfy it. Then determine what is needed for *moderate* satisfaction of your *unnecessary natural* desires, and finally do the same for your *non-natural* desires. For a desire like food, this could be a monthly cost, but other desires, such as love, companionship, or time for meditation, will not depend on money. If you have done your classification well, this exercise should give you a good idea what you need in order to satisfy your most important desires—that is, to become self-sufficient in this important sense. Record your conclusions in your journal along with a tentative plan for achieving your desires.

Simple Pleasures: Make a list of your simple pleasures—that is, natural desires that are easy or inexpensive to satisfy. Make sure to indulge in them regularly and pay attention to the pleasure you feel. Everything else is icing on the cake.

PAIN

If you want to choose pleasure, then you want to avoid pain, which may be physical or psychological (mental or emotional). Let's begin with physical pain. Epicurus said that physical pain is always endurable, because if it is long-lasting, then it is relatively mild, whereas if it is intense, then it does not last long (in some cases because the sufferer dies, which stops the pain!).[46] While there is a nice symmetry to this idea, something seems to be wrong with it: we know that some people suffer from intense chronic pain. I will mention later how Epicurus dealt with his own extremely painful terminal illness, but it may be that the Garden does not have much to offer to the chronic pain sufferer, who might be better advised to continue on to the Stoics' Porch. This is, after all, only the first degree of wisdom.

> *Dealing with Pain:* Consider the various sorts of physical pain you have experienced. To what extent can you agree with Epicurus that "either the duration or the intensity is slight" and therefore that the pain is endurable? Does this apply also to mental or emotional pain? What, if any, actions have you taken to mitigate the pain in each case? Summarize your own strategies for dealing with pain.

> *Replacing Pain with Pleasure:* Pain is unavoidable, but it can be replaced often by an active pleasure. In preparation for future pains, make a list in your journal of some active pleasures you might employ. They could be purely mental, such as remembering a past pleasure or daydreaming about one to come. They could be more physical, such as enjoying a conversation with friends, having a good meal, playing with a pet, reading, playing some music, exercising, or sex. Everyone's list will be different, but you should pick activities that are pleasant for you and that will hold your attention. The next time you are suffering physical pain or mental discomfort, try replacing it by one of the active pleasures on your list. Afterward, record its effectiveness in your journal. In this way you will develop a toolbox of techniques for dealing with pain.

FEAR OF THE GODS

Mental pain or anxiety is, according to those of the Garden, a result of incorrect ideas, and these mental dis-eases can be cured by a proper regimen of Epicurean philosophy. Here we will look at the cure for a mental ailment that Epicurus thought was epidemic: fear of the gods.

The Garden was commonly condemned for being atheistic, but technically it is not, for Epicurus said that the gods exist, but that they are made of atoms like everything else. Since the gods are immortal, they have no needs, and so they have no desires, and therefore they are suffering no pain from unmet needs and desires. As a consequence, they are in a perfect state of tranquility, which is the utmost pleasure according to those of the Garden.

We do not have to accept Epicurus's claim that the gods are made of atoms in order to agree with his conclusion. If we accept the Epicurean ideal that the height of wisdom, goodness, and blessedness is tranquility, then it follows that the gods (or God) will not be subject to the weaknesses of anger and jealousy, nor be swayed by flattery, nor, for example, be offended, all of which are traits of imperfect mortals. Therefore we have nothing to fear from the gods. This argument is summarized in the following slogan:

> *That which is blissful and immortal has no troubles itself,*
> *nor does it cause trouble for others,*
> *so that it is not affected by anger or gratitude*
> *for all such things come about through weakness.*[47]

Both Epicurus and Lucretius considered this a very important conclusion, for it cured a significant cause of mental anguish and eliminated an impediment to human tranquility— namely, fear of the gods. But isn't it the fear of divine retribution that keeps people moral? More on that question later.

The Garden also seems atheistic because the gods don't interfere in our lives, for good or for ill, so they are irrelevant, except as models of the perfect Epicurean sage. This role is significant, however, since "imitation of the gods" (in their tranquility) is a goal of the Epicurean life. In effect, a god is just an immortal sage, and a true sage is a mortal god.

Because the gods are perfectly tranquil, Lucretius said that the wise do not worship them (for they are not swayed by flattery), but that philosophers might participate in worship services, for a tranquil human mind is capable of receiving the images of the gods that the gods send into it. By thus witnessing divinity, and contemplating the gods, the sage is able to become more godlike.

Obviously the Epicurean view of the gods differed from the beliefs of ordinary people, who thought the gods were touchy, vindictive, dishonest, greedy, jealous, egotistical, and—in general—displayed some of the worst qualities of mortals. This is how they act in traditional mythology. As Xenophanes (c.570–c.475 BCE) said, "Homer and Hesiod have ascribed to the gods all things that among men are a shame and a reproach—theft and adultery and deceiving one another." [48] But Epicureanism, like other ancient wisdom traditions, said that this picture of the gods is incorrect and that the gods are good.

Nevertheless, if you are reading this book, then your spiritual aspirations are probably rooted in belief of the existence of God or Goddess or both, or of the gods of ancient Greece or some other pantheon. Furthermore, you may be thinking, "I know the gods intervene in human affairs, because they intervene in mine all the time!" What's more, I have said that the goal of the more advanced spiritual practices of this book is contact and conversation with divinity. What's the point if they are uninvolved except as objects of contemplation?

Remember, therefore, that ancient philosophy is a cure for the soul that progresses in stages. As with many cures, the first stage is a sort of purging or detoxification—in this case, an elimination of toxic beliefs about the gods that may impede spiritual progress. The purpose is not to convince you that the gods don't exist, but to encourage you to examine your beliefs more carefully. By first loosening up the congestion in your beliefs, you will be better able to breathe in the fresh insights that will come in the higher degrees of wisdom.

Fear of God(s): Are you afraid of the gods (or God)? For this exercise spend some time thinking about your concept of divinity and your feelings about it. Do you think a god can feel angry or jealous? Do you think he or she would act on those feelings? Do you think that making fun of a god or using his or her name in vain could provoke divine retribution? Or do you think gods have only positive emotions? Record your musings in your journal. (If you are an atheist, you can skip this exercise!)

FEAR OF DEATH

The Garden also promises to cure us of another cause of mental discomfort: the fear of death. The reason is simple: at death our atoms dissociate, and therefore we are incapable of feeling anything, whether pain or pleasure:

> *Death is nothing to us;*
> *for what has disintegrated lacks awareness,*
> *and what lacks awareness is nothing to us.*[49]

Therefore it is foolish to disturb our peace *now* in anticipation of a *future* state in which we will feel no pain (or anything else); that would be suffering a present evil in anticipation of a future evil that will not occur.

You can see why the philosophy of the Garden has not been popular with religions that depend on notions of heaven and hell. Instead, Lucretius said,

> *And, verily, those tortures said to be*
> *In Acheron, the deep, they all are ours*
> *Here in this life.*[50]

He goes on to show how each myth of a sinner being punished in hell (Acheron) symbolizes the pains we experience in this life when we don't live wisely. He concludes,

> *In truth, the life of fools is hell on Earth.*[51]

My purpose is not to convince you that there is no afterlife; people much smarter and wiser than me have believed and continue to believe in an afterlife or in reincarnation. However, I do think our growing understanding of neuropsychology must inform our views, for our mental lives are highly dependent on the brain. Evidence comes from developmental psychology, for the child's mind changes as his or her brain changes; from mind-altering substances, which alter the chemical balance of the brain; and from brain injuries and degenerative diseases, which affect the mind. Also, diseases like Alzheimer's show that memory degenerates along with the brain, and it would be astonishing if memory were suddenly restored after death, when the brain is completely gone. Therefore, at least during life, the mind is highly dependent on the brain, and so it seems that if anything of the mind survives the dissolution of the brain, it would have to be rather ephemeral and loosely connected to the living personality. Contemporary embodied psychology has also concluded that human intelligence cannot exist or be understood independently from a body purposefully acting in the physical world. Nevertheless, some have argued that the brain acts more as a *receiver* of the mind than as its *generator*, and so the mind could exist without the brain. In any case you have to use your own judgment and reach your own conclusions. Even if your beliefs about death do not agree with the Epicureans', thinking about their view may help alleviate any anxiety you have about it.

We may return to our imaginary discussion between Epicurus and his students. Reclining together are Idomeneus, a dignitary of Lampsacus who came with Epicurus from that city, and his wife Batis, who is the sister of Metrodorus; recently they lost their only child. Epicurus has just explained that our state after death will be the same as our state before our birth: non-existence.

"Explain to me then," says Idomeneus, "why we should not choose the oblivion of death, and therefore absence of pain? This seems to me the best: eternal tranquility."

"We should not despise life," says Epicurus, "for life is fundamentally pleasurable. Remember:

> *The wise neither renounce life nor fear not living.*
> *Life does not offend them,*
> *nor do they suppose that death is any kind of suffering.*[52]

"This is because a wise person knows how to choose pleasure and avoid pain, and so to live a blessed life."

"It seems you have contradicted yourself," says Leontion. "Shouldn't we fear death because it puts a limit on pleasure?"

"A long life is not necessarily better than a shorter one," Epicurus explains. "For just as the sage chooses the pleasantest food, not simply the greater quantity, so too he enjoys the pleasantest time, not the longest.[53] That is, the *quality* of his life is more important than its *quantity*:

> *Unlimited time and limited time afford an equal amount of pleasure,*
> *if we measure the limits of that pleasure by reason.*[54]

"This is perhaps a difficult idea, but think of it this way. Pleasure and pain are experienced in the present moment. Even if we remember past pleasures or pains, or antic-
ipate future ones, that recollection or anticipation is experienced *now*, in the present.
The present is the only time that exists. Therefore present experience is eternal in the
sense of being timeless—that is, outside of time altogether. Hence the present experience of pain or pleasure is a *quality* of the moment, not a temporal *quantity*. The perfection of pleasure that the sage experiences in any given moment is like the perfect
roundness of a circle. This perfection is not altered by the size of a circle; a small circle
may be just as perfectly round as a large one. Likewise the perfection of a sage's life is
a quality that is not dependent on its length (its quantity). All sizes of circles offer the
same degrees of roundness. Think about it." [55]

In summary, the proper cure for the fear of death is to begin living the true Epicurean
life immediately so that in every moment you are tranquil and content, so far as possible.
During your evening Examination of Conscience, you can assess how well you have done
and how you can do better.

> *Fear of Death:* Meditate on your own feelings about death. If you fear it, what is it
> about it that you fear? Do you fear death itself or the process of dying? What do
> you think happens to you when you die, and what is the reason for your beliefs?
> Record your thoughts in your journal.

THE FOURFOLD CURE

The preceding observations on sufficiency, pain, gods, and death are summarized in one of
Epicurus's most famous slogans, the *Tetrapharmakos*, or *Fourfold Cure*:

God presents no fear,
death no worry.
The good is easy to obtain,
but evil easy to endure. [56]

LIVE HIDDEN

We have seen how the philosophers of the Garden make choices in their individual lives in order to be tranquil and happy, but how will they live in the larger world? The image of an enclosed garden suggests that they will withdraw from wider world of business and politics, and to an extent that was true of ancient Epicureans. Indeed, the master teaches that we do not have to be very ambitious in order to live happily:

> *One who perceives the limits of life*
> *knows how easy it is to expel the pain produced by want*
> *and to make one's entire life complete;*
> *so that there is no need for the things*
> *that are achieved through competition.*[57]

If we satisfy our natural and necessary desires, and the unnecessary ones in moderation, and pay little attention to the non-natural ones, then we will not have to work so hard. On the contrary, we should enjoy our limited lives, for we never know how long we have left, and should make sure to include leisure time:

> *We have been born once and cannot be born a second time;*
> *for all eternity we shall no longer exist.*
> *But you, although you are not in control of tomorrow,*
> *are postponing your happiness.*
> *Life is wasted by delaying,*
> *and each one of us dies without enjoying leisure.*[58]

Those in the Garden tell us that the stress, anxiety, and lost leisure of business and politics do not compensate for the empty desires they may satisfy.

> *We must free ourselves from the prison*
> *of public affairs and ordinary concerns.*[59]

Does this imply you should not be the CEO with multiple mansions? If you are not enjoying your life, and if you are experiencing stress and anxiety, or wonder if your work is meaningful, you might reassess costs and benefits (pains and pleasures). Of course each person must make the Epicurean calculation for himself or herself, but the master of the Garden reminds us that the highest pleasure is tranquility.

The crown of tranquility is incomparably superior
to the crown of the greatest political power.[60]

Therefore, one of the most famous Epicurean maxims suggests that is better to live happily in obscurity rather than unhappily in prominence.

Live hidden![61]

We will see in the next chapter that the Porch is more open to involvement in the wider world, and that it teaches techniques for living philosophically while doing so. But it's worth returning to the Garden whenever ambition becomes an end in itself.

The Epicurean idea of tranquility is summarized well by Synesius in his first hymn, which he probably wrote while he was studying under Hypatia:

But I would choose to lead a life serene,
Humble, by all, except my God, unseen—
A life most fit for youth, most fit for age,
In which wise poverty can calmly smile,
Untouch'd by all the bitter cares that rage
Round those who with the world their hearts engage.
Let me have but enough to keep me free
From suing beggary at my neighbor's door,
Lest hungry want should bend my soul to see
Nought but the loathsome cares that grind the poor.[62]

> *Ambition Assessment:* Spend some time thinking about your career and your ambitions. What are your goals? What desires are you attempting to fulfill? You are probably choosing present "pains" (work, stress, lack of leisure, competition, etc.) for the sake of future pleasures (wealth, recognition, power, influence, leisure, etc.), but what exactly are those hoped-for pleasures? Classify them and do the Epicurean trade-off. Record your conclusions in your journal.

JUSTICE

Although the ultimate ground of Epicurean ethics is individual experience of pleasure and pain, the philosophers of the Garden were well aware that it is difficult to be happy in isolation, first because we benefit from mutual aid, and second because companionship is itself a natural pleasure. Therefore, while the master pointed out the disadvantages of political and social ambition, he was also aware of the importance of society to human happiness. In fact, Epicurus taught a kind of evolutionary anthropology, tracing the development of human culture from a primitive and brutal "every man for himself" state to a social system recognizing justice as a central principle.[63] The Garden's justice is built on human nature refined by rational norms. The basis is "nature's justice," which is neither to harm another nor to be harmed:

> *Natural justice is a covenant for mutual benefit,*
> *to not harm one another or be harmed.*[64]

This justice, which is grounded in mutual aid, extends even to domesticated animals; they help us and in turn we care for them. Although animals cannot make contracts, among humans there should be an implicit social contract to neither hurt nor be hurt, as the master said:

> *Absolute justice does not exist. There are only mutual agreements among people,*
> *made at various times and places, not to inflict nor allow harm.*[65]

Evildoers are prevented from harming people by the threat of punishment. Epicurus is not concerned about punishment in an afterlife, for he says that the criminal cannot escape pain, either punishment now, or present anxiety in anticipation of future punishment. Even up to the moment of death, he says, criminals can never be sure they have escaped, and so they will be afraid. On the other hand, the life of the just person is free of such worry, as the following maxim reminds us:

> *The just man is the freest of anyone from anxiety;*
> *but the unjust man is perpetually haunted by it.*[66]

Therefore you can see that the philosophers of the Garden are not "noble savage" primitivists urging that everything would be well if we went back to living like our Paleolithic ancestors. Instead, they saw that human happiness depends on rational laws and constitutional government grounded in human nature.

> *Laws are made for the wise:*
> *not to keep them from doing wrong,*
> *but to keep them from being wronged.*[67]

The Greek word *dikê*, which I have been translating as "justice," means to give everyone what they are due.[68] All people are equal in that (1) they aspire to tranquility, (2) they have a right to it, and (3) they can achieve it. The means to achieving it is (4) the philosophy of the Garden. (These four truths are analogous to the "Four Noble Truths" of the Buddha.) Thus the Garden is democratic and egalitarian, and you can see why it welcomed everyone who wanted to pursue the Epicurean way of life. When everyone is Epicurean, they predicted, the whole world will be a Garden, a home for everyone, all living in justice and mutual friendship, with no need for laws. Thus Diogenes of Oenoanda, an ardent Epicurean of the second century CE, commissioned a public colonnade and engraved on 260 square meters of its walls his philosophy in 25,000 words (about a quarter of the length of this book). He looked forward to an Epicurean age:

> *Then truly the life of the gods will pass to men. For everything will be full of*
> *justice and mutual friendship, and there will come to be no need of city walls or laws*
> *and all the things we manufacture on account of one another.*[69]

In this ideal (if unlikely) worldwide Garden of Eden or Paradise, this return to the Golden Age, there would be no need for separate states, for Diogenes says:

> *The entire earth is a single native land for everyone,*
> *and the world is a single home.*[70]

Until this happy day, Epicurus reminds us that

> *The greatest gift of justice is tranquility.*[71]

This is perhaps the most important lesson for us, since we are not living in a worldwide Epicurean Garden. Although the wise have little to fear from each other, they can strive to create a society in which everyone is protected from harm and free to seek contentment by Epicurean practices.

I like to think of Epicurean justice in the following way. Everyone has a right to live in peace and contentment, and the Epicurean prescription will help them to do so. In addition, we should refrain from inflicting pain on others, whether physical or mental, so far as possible. Some pain is unavoidable, but we should try to avoid causing additional pain or anguish for our fellow humans. (Coping with unavoidable pain is addressed by the second degree of wisdom.)

> *Epicurean Justice:* Think about how the Epicurean sage will treat other people, non-Epicurean as well as Epicurean. Think about how you can treat other people with Epicurean wisdom. Record your intentions and regularly assess your success.

FRIENDSHIP

The Garden teaches a fundamentally individualist philosophy, grounded in personal happiness and self-sufficiency, which is why it is a relatively accessible place to embark on our search for wisdom, but social relations are also essential to the good life in the Garden. Lucretius claims that the social contract between neighbors for their mutual benefit naturally led to friendship between them. This may seem to contradict the old proverb "Good fences make good neighbors," but the ancient concept of friendship was somewhat broader than ours. It was not limited to emotional attachment, but included the social networks of mutual aid and support that were necessary for thriving in the ancient world. These were established through kinship, marriage, adoption, fostering, voluntary alliance, and common interests. Epicurus's utilitarian theory is supplemented by modern evolutionary psychology, which has shown that cooperation and social bonding are part of human nature. (This scientific support would have pleased the master, but not surprised him.) Those of the Garden acknowledged "the existence of a certain natural affinity among people, deriving from their likeness in body and soul." [72]

The master taught that friends should not be too demanding of each other, nor too reluctant to help. Indeed, he said, it is not so much actual acts of kindness that matter, as the alleviation of anxiety and the pleasure in the confidence that a friend will help: knowing they will be there when you need them. Epicureans said,

It is both more noble and delightful to do than to receive a kindness.[73]

Those of the Garden told the story that when Epicurus was forty-four years old, Demetrius besieged Athens, which caused a great famine in the city. The master saved his friends by sharing his beans equally with them. It may seem to be a tawdry sort of friendship that is grounded in mutual benefit, but Epicurus argued that the accompanying affection could develop into genuine love for one another, which then supersedes any possible benefit. Therefore true Epicurean friends feel each other's pleasure and pain, a friend may suffer pains for the sake of a friend's pleasure, and the Epicurean sage may even give his life for the sake of a friend.[74] The depth of Epicurean friendship was famous in the ancient world. The master said:

Friendship dances around the world,
bidding us all to awaken to give joy to one another.[75]

Of all things that wisdom acquires for living one's entire life in happiness,
the greatest by far is the possession of friendship.[76]

The noble soul is chiefly concerned with wisdom and friendship;
of these, the former is a mortal good, the latter an immortal one.[77]

When a friend dies, we should not feel sorry for them, since they cannot feel any pain. As for ourselves, we should avoid grief and choose instead to remember the joy we received from them, thus replacing present grief by remembered pleasure. The master says:

We sympathize with our friends not through mourning
but through thoughtful attention.[78]

Sweet is the memory of a dead friend.[79]

Philosophical Friends: Your spiritual progress will be accelerated if you form a community of "philosophical friends" with similar spiritual aspirations. Consider whom you can associate with who will aid your progress and not impede it.

THE DEATH OF EPICURUS

Many people who aren't afraid of death, are afraid of dying; that is, they fear the pain, incapacity, indignity, and other suffering associated with a terminal illness. This is an important issue, which I won't address in this chapter. Instead I will take as an example Epicurus himself, who died three days after his seventy-first birthday, having endured for two weeks the agony of a bladder stone. Yet he wrote to his friend Idomeneus:

> On this last, yet blessed, day of my life, I write to you. Pains and tortures of
> body I have to the full, but there is set over against these, the joy of my heart
> at the memory of our happy conversations in the past.[80]

Thus he applied the active pleasure of his memory against his present pain. To ease his passing he took a hot bath in a large bronze tub and drank a cup of unmixed wine (ancient Greeks usually mixed their wine with water). Then Epicurus died, conversing with his friends; his last words were:

> *Farewell, and bear my doctrines in your minds.*[81]

MISCELLANEOUS MAXIMS

Here are a few more of Epicurus's sayings that are worth thinking about and perhaps memorizing. Be sure to record the ones you like in your commonplace book and memorize them if you are so inclined.

> *One must laugh and seek wisdom*
> *and tend to one's home life and use one's other goods,*
> *and always recount the pronouncements of true philosophy.*[82]

Do not pretend to practice wisdom, but practice wisdom in reality;
for we need not the appearance of health but true health.[83]

It is foolish to ask of the gods that which we can supply for ourselves.[84]

Whoever has peace of mind disturbs neither self nor other.[85]

Insofar as you forget nature,
you will find yourself in trouble
and create for yourself endless fears and desires.[86]

A philosopher's words are empty
if they do not heal the suffering of mankind.
For just as medicine is useless
if it does not remove sickness from the body,
so philosophy is useless
if it does not remove suffering from the soul.[87]

Love for true philosophy
destroys every disturbing and troublesome desire.[88]

Unhappiness is caused by fears,
or by endless and empty desires;
but he who is able to rein these in
creates for himself a blissful understanding.[89]

Meditate on these and kindred precepts day and night,
by yourself and with a like-minded friend,
and you will never be disturbed whether waking or sleeping,
but will live as a god among people.
For people lose all appearance of mortality
by living in the midst of immortal blessings.[90]

There are many other Epicurean maxims that we can use to help us follow the Garden path; see the "Additional Reading" section at the end of the book for some suggestions. Of course, you can formulate your own maxims or learn Epicurean principles from other practitioners. Practice applying the principles of the Garden. When you have made them a part of your life, you may choose to advance to the second degree of wisdom, which can be found at the Porch. But you could choose to remain in the Garden and live quite well.

PART III
THE SECOND DEGREE
OF WISDOM

CHAPTER FIVE

THE DISCIPLINE OF ASSENT

GOALS OF THE SECOND DEGREE

We advance now to the second degree of wisdom, which is Stoicism, the philosophy of the Porch. Symbolically, we are proceeding from the secluded peace of the Garden into the more engaged and active life of the Athenian forum, where the Stoics' porch was located. You will find that while this philosophy has much in common with the Garden, it also differs in some of its doctrines. This might suggest that at least one of the philosophies must be incorrect, but that misses the point. Keep in mind that the goal of ancient philosophy is cure and care for the soul. As different medicines are required for different diseases, so different philosophical doctrines are required for souls in different conditions. For another analogy, a piano teacher will recommend different exercises for a beginning player or for a more advanced one. So also practicing the philosophy of the Garden has prepared you for the practices of the Porch, and those, in turn, are a foundation for Hypatia's philosophy.

As you will see, the Stoic way of life is based on three disciplines, and so I will devote three chapters to the philosophy of the Porch. This may seem like a lot, but Stoic practices provide a firm foundation for the Neoplatonic practices of Hypatia. Although we will ultimately abandon some of the Stoic doctrines as scaffolding, the practices are essential, which is why Stoic ethics were taken for granted in Neoplatonism. The chapters are divided into manageable parts, so take them one at a time; the goal, remember, is to make the practices of the Porch a way of life, and this takes some time and practice. If you follow my study plan, you should devote about one month to each chapter, but everyone will progress at a different rate.

In this chapter you will learn, first, a little of the historical background of Stoicism, including its origin and a few of its masters. Next, I will explain the goals of the Stoic way of life, which can be achieved only by living in accordance with nature. Therefore I will present the essence of the Stoic views of Nature and human nature, and you'll learn how these determine the three fundamental disciplines of the Porch. With these preliminaries out of the way, we'll turn to the first of the three disciplines, the Discipline of Assent, and you will learn how to apply it in your life.

HISTORICAL BACKGROUND

Stoicism was one of the most popular philosophies from the Hellenistic period (third century BCE) through the end of the Roman Empire, so there have been many Stoic philosophers. I will mention just four who were important or whose works survive.

The founder of Stoicism was Zeno of Citium (c.334–c.262 BCE), who was a contemporary of Epicurus (and not, incidentally, the Zeno who propounded Zeno's Paradoxes). He was born in the harbor city of Citium (modern Larnaca) in Cyprus, a city with a large Phoenician population, and he was probably of Phoenician descent.

When Zeno was a boy, he asked an oracle what sort of life he should lead, and the oracle replied that he should converse with the dead. Zeno interpreted the oracle to mean that he should read the books of ancient authors. Therefore his father, who was a merchant, regularly brought his son philosophical books from Athens.

When Zeno was about twenty-two, his father set him up in business with a ship, goods to sell, and money to lend. Thus Zeno went to Athens, where he was successful as an entrepreneur until his ship was wrecked. He accepted the accident with equanimity and said, "You do well, Fortune, to drive me to philosophy," and so he sought a teacher. This is an example of how Stoics turn the accidents of fate to their advantage.

According to an ancient biographer,[91] Zeno was standing in a bookseller's stall, reading about Socrates, and asked, "Where can I find people like this?" The Cynic philosopher Crates happened to be walking by, and so the bookseller pointed and said, "Follow him!" Thus Zeno began to study with Crates (c.368–c.288 BCE).

The Cynics were ascetic followers of Socrates (c.469–399 BCE), who sought happiness through freedom—in particular, freedom from desires, from emotions such as fear, grief, and anger, freedom from religious and societal customs, and freedom from family and other social obligations. They argued that the simplest life is the best and the only secure way to happiness.

Crates was born into wealth, but he gave it all away and adopted the Cynic way of life. He wandered around the city, entering the homes of friends to settle their disputes and to give other advice. Hipparchia, the wealthy sister of one of his students, fell in love with him, gave away her money, and married him. Crates treated her as an equal, which was remarkable at that time, and they lived the ascetic life together. They lived happily, not in spite of their poverty, but because of it. He is supposed to have written:

> *If this way of practicing philosophy is unpleasant,*
> *it is a shortcut.*
> *It leads to happiness*
> *even though we have to walk through fire.*[92]

It was considered a shortcut because it required only practicing the Cynic way of life but not studying and discussing philosophical doctrines. He also wrote:

> *Do not shun practicing,*
> *but avoid discussing,*
> *for the long road to happiness is through words,*
> *but the short way is through the daily practice of deeds.*[93]

Zeno was an excellent philosophy student, but Crates thought he was too modest and self-respecting to be a good Cynic philosopher, so to teach him a lesson, he had Zeno accompany him through downtown Athens carrying a pot of lentil soup. Zeno, who had a proud disposition, was ashamed to be seen carrying the pot, so he hid it under his cloak. When he saw this, Crates smashed the pot with his staff and the soup ran down Zeno's legs. Mortified, Zeno ran away, and Crates called after him, "Why are you running away, my little Phoenician? Nothing terrible has happened to you!" Here you have an example of ancient Cynic philosophical instruction: awakening Zeno to the difference between what is important and what is not.

Eventually Zeno became dissatisfied with Crates and turned to other philosophers, with whom he studied for twenty years. During this time he developed his own philosophy, and about 300 BCE he decided to begin teaching his philosophical practice. He might have been inspired by disagreements with Epicurus, whose Garden has been established just a few years earlier. Since Zeno was not an Athenian citizen, he could not buy property in the city, and so he took to teaching in the *Stoa Poikile*, the "Painted Porch," which was not so much a porch as a colonnade on the front of a building on the Athenian *agora* (market and meeting place). This colonnade was decorated with famous paintings and made a kind of arcade in which Zeno walked conversing with his disciples. Therefore his disciples became known as Stoics (those of the Stoa).

Zeno wrote at least twenty philosophical works, of which we have the titles, but none have survived, except in the form of isolated quotations by other authors. When the master died, his pupil Cleanthes (331–232 BCE) became the first of a long succession of leaders of the Stoic school. Due to its practicality as a way of life, Stoicism became the most popular philosophy in the Hellenistic and Roman periods.

The second Stoic I will discuss is Seneca the Younger (c.4 BCE–65 CE), who was born to an aristocratic family in Córdoba in Spain. He was brought to Rome as a young child, where he first became acquainted with Stoic philosophy.

Beginning after 31 CE Seneca held various government positions, during which he was sometimes in favor and sometimes out. About 49 CE he was appointed tutor to Nero, who was then twelve years old. When Nero became emperor in the year 54, Seneca became his adviser. For the next eight years Seneca was able convince Nero to behave, and the empire was relatively well governed. Unfortunately, Seneca's influence waned after the year 62, and so he retired from public life and devoted himself to philosophy. He also gave away most of his wealth. Seneca was accused of involvement in a conspiracy against Nero and was forced to commit suicide in 65 CE.

Although at least a dozen of Seneca's philosophical works have been lost, fourteen have survived, including a collection of 124 letters (in twenty "books") on philosophical topics to his friend Lucilius. They are not actual letters, but philosophical essays in the form of letters. They are filled with Stoic philosophical gems.

One of the most important Stoic philosophers was Epictetus (60–117 CE), who was born in Hierapolis in Phrygia (modern Pamukkale, Turkey) shortly before Seneca's suicide. His name means "Acquired," and so he was probably born a slave. In any case he was brought to Rome by his owner, a wealthy freedman of Nero, who permitted Epictetus to study with the famous Stoic G. Musonius Rufus.

Epictetus was eventually freed and began to teach Stoicism in Rome. His house was so poor it didn't have a lock, because it contained only the mattress and mat on which he slept. He taught there until 93 CE, when the emperor Domitian banished all philosophers from Rome and later from the rest of Italy. Epictetus moved his school to Nicopolis (on the

Gulf of Arta in northwest Greece). There he had many powerful and influential Romans as students, including perhaps the emperor Hadrian.

Epictetus's oral teachings were published by his disciple Arrian of Nicomedia as the *Discourses of Epictetus*, of which four of the eight books survive. In fact, all existing manuscripts of these four books appear to be more or less accurate copies of a single eleventh- or twelfth-century manuscript currently in the Bodleian Library at Oxford; but for this manuscript we might not have any of the *Discourses* at all! Arrian said that he tried to record the actual words of Epictetus, so as to reproduce the effects they had on listeners, so the *Discourses* give an idea of ancient philosophical instruction. We also have Arrian's summary of Epictetus's philosophy, called the *Handbook* (also called the *Manual* or *Encheiridion*, its Greek name). It is especially valuable as a source of Stoic maxims. Arrian was a student of Epictetus for a year or two and afterward applied Stoic principles in a successful political career.

Marcus Aurelius is perhaps the best-known Stoic. He was born in 121 CE, shortly after Epictetus's death, to an aristocratic family near Córdoba in Spain. He was educated by many well-known teachers and had already shown an interest in philosophy by age twelve. He began wearing the philosopher's simple robe and sleeping on the ground, but his mother objected and convinced him to go back to using a bed. Throughout the ages Stoics have adopted this practice from time to time as a way of returning to basics. (Camping is a good modern version of this practice.)

When he was about fifteen, Marcus met Apollonius of Chalcedon, a Stoic philosopher from whom he learned much, but he was influenced even more by the most distinguished Stoic philosopher of the time, Quintus Iunius Rusticus (c.100 – c.170), who might have studied with Epictetus. Marcus was influenced especially by Epictetus's *Discourses*, and perhaps by notes that Rusticus had recorded when he studied with Epictetus. Rusticus continued a Stoic tradition of "speaking truth to power" by criticizing bad emperors; his grandfather Arulenus Rusticus (c.35–93 CE) had been condemned to death by the emperor Domitian for his writings, and was considered a Stoic martyr. Iunius Rusticus was a successful statesman, as were Musonius, Seneca, and Marcus, for there is nothing contradictory about being a Stoic philosopher and leading an active life. When Antoninus Pius died in 161 CE, Marcus became emperor at the age of thirty-nine. He was an effective leader and is considered a good emperor, who had to deal with natural disasters including plagues, floods, and earthquakes. Furthermore, there had been trouble on all the borders of the empire following Antoninus's death, and Marcus died in 180 while defending the northern borders near the Danube.

Many people are familiar with the *Meditations* of Marcus Aurelius. It is actually titled simply "To Himself," and is his philosophical notebook, probably recorded in his later years each night before he went to bed. Thus it is a good example of how a practicing philosopher used his notebook to keep the maxims and demonstrations of the philosophy before his eyes in order to live by its principles. The *Meditations* is more like a commonplace book, recording general maxims in striking form, than a journal or diary recording the particularities of a life. It is especially valuable because Marcus was not living in a garden, out of the stream of affairs; he faced greater challenges and stresses than most of us.

Marcus's notebook seems to have been intended for his own eyes, and none of his contemporaries appear to be aware of its existence. We are probably fortunate that it survived. It seems to have escaped notice until the fourth century, but by the tenth century it was well enough known that complete manuscripts were circulating. However, the text that we have now comes from only two manuscripts, one of which has been lost, but not before it was published in 1559, and the other of which is still in the Vatican libraries, but missing forty-two lines here and there. We are lucky that the *Meditations*—a cultural treasure—has survived.

Marcus Aurelius's *Meditations* (except Book I) are filled with maxims expressing Stoic doctrines, and all the maxims in the Stoic chapters are from it, unless I note otherwise. The emperor's book is a treasure chest for you; find the maxims that speak most clearly to you and learn them.

Marcus's commonplace displays a philosophy that was not purely Stoic, but mixed with Epicurean and Platonic practices, and so it is especially relevant to practicing Hypatia's philosophy. In ancient times, the Garden and the Porch often regarded each other as opposed philosophies, but we will see that in their practices they are more alike than different. One difference is that, while the Garden teaches that happiness is relatively easy to obtain if we change our thinking, and disengage from the world, the Porch teaches that a deeper, more endurable serenity is obtainable by engaging in life and the world appropriately.

GOALS OF WISDOM

One of the goals of Stoics is to live with serenity and happiness, which they contrast with (Epicurean) pleasure. A second goal is autonomy—that is, the impregnability of the mind to outer circumstances, so that it becomes an "inner acropolis." A third goal is a sort of "cosmic consciousness," by which the philosopher's reason becomes identical with Universal Reason, the law of Nature, and in this sense identifies with the divine will. This goal is one way of becoming more godlike, a goal of all the ancient Greek philosophies.

These goals can be achieved only by understanding Nature (our own nature and universal nature) and by living in accordance with it, but this requires us to understand what is in our control and what it not. According to Stoics, only the present moment is in our control, since we cannot change the past, and we can affect the future only by what we do in the present. Furthermore, our control in the present moment is limited to (1) our judgment of what is true or not, (2) our evaluation of what is good or not, and (3) our intention to pursue the good. These mental actions are governed by the three Stoic disciplines (discussed later).

Further, control of the moment requires mastery of reason over the feelings, which are distracting. Therefore the perfect sage is serene in the face of circumstances. The result of controlling what you can control, and not trying to control what you cannot, aligns your life with Universal Nature, so you live in accordance with divine Providence, and experience a profound feeling of participation in Nature. This is the perfection of the moment, which, as those of the Garden also said, depends on its quality, not its quantity. A moment of joy is the supreme happiness, and is equivalent to an eternity of joy. As Seneca said, "Whether you draw a larger or a smaller circle, its size affects its area, not its shape." [94] All circles are perfectly round, no matter what their sizes.

NATURE

Like other ancient philosophies, Stoicism was divided into *physics* (the study of nature), *logic*, and *ethics*, which deal with *being*, *knowing*, and *acting*, respectively. Thus, some Stoics said philosophy is like an enclosed field. [95] Logic is the bordering wall, which with its carefully fitted stones delimits the discipline and controls what is allowed inside. Physics—the study of Nature—is the fertile ground and the trees growing in it. Ethics are the fruit, which we hope to harvest if we have maintained the wall and tended the soil and trees.

Although the Stoics developed a very sophisticated logic, in the end it is not very relevant to the other two, which were developed more intuitively. We will look briefly at Stoic physics since it provided the foundation for ethics. Of course natural science has made enormous progress since the ancient Stoics, but we will see that Stoic physics is more a way of looking at the world than a scientific theory, and hence its usefulness is largely independent of scientific progress.

Like Epicurean physics, Stoic physics was an account of Nature (*physis* in Greek), but this word was understood to mean everything that exists, not just the natural world as we think of it. It thus included things that we usually think of as nonphysical, such as the soul and the gods. In this chapter I'll use "Nature" in this broad sense, and for convenience "physics" will refer to the study of this Nature.

In many respects Stoic physics was opposed to Epicurean physics. Thus the Epicureans had an essentially mechanical view of the universe, with atoms bouncing off each other and interacting through inanimate forces, like billiard balls. The Stoics, in contrast, viewed Nature (everything that exists) as an organism, a living whole constituted of mutually interdependent parts (organs). Likewise, contemporary Pagans, but many other people as well, find it enlightening to see ecosystems, the earth as a whole (Gaia), and even the entire universe as super-organisms.

The Stoics analyzed Nature into two inseparable aspects: the active principle, which they sometimes called the *Cause*, and the passive principle, which they called *Matter*. Here "matter" does not have the same meaning it does in modern physics, but refers to the hypothetical formless and quality-less substrate of all things. The Cause gives form to Matter; it gives it its qualities. We may say that the Cause *informs* Matter (gives it form). In modern terms we might think of the Cause and Matter as the laws of physics and the "stuff" (matter and energy) that those laws govern, but the modern view is more mechanical than the Stoic view, which is organic.

For the philosophers of the Porch, the Cause is the origin of all change in the universe, and because the universe follows orderly laws, the Cause is considered rational, and in fact a sort of rational mind. For this reason Stoics call the Cause by many names, including God, Zeus, Jupiter, Force, Soul, Spirit, Destiny, Providence, Fate, Necessity, Reason, and Logos.

The word *logos* is essential to all ancient Greek philosophy, including Hypatia's. Its primary sense is "word" (e.g., "In the beginning was the Word," John 1:1), but its meaning is much richer. In broad terms it refers to the orderly principle of anything, whether an explanation in speech or thought, or an active organizational principle. In modern terms we may think of the Logos as the laws of the universe, not just as descriptions, but also as living, active, dynamical causes, rather like gods. This is the Stoic sense of the Cause.

Logos is central to the three parts of philosophy. It is the source of truth in logic, which investigates the laws of thought and rational discourse; here the role of Logos is *descriptive*. In physics Logos has a *constructive* role, for it is the governing principle of the universe. In ethics its role is *normative*, since the goal of philosophy is to live in accordance with Nature—that is, in accordance with the Logos.

Since, according to Stoic physics, Nature is one, a unified whole, so also the Logos is one and Matter is one. Furthermore, since there can be no unformed (quality-less) Matter, and no immaterial form, Logos and Matter are co-extensive; neither exists without the other. Therefore Deity informs all Matter, and thus pervades the universe, but there is also no Deity apart from Matter. The philosophy of the Porch is *pantheistic*, which means that Deity is immanent in nature, as opposed to being a transcendent being existing in some supernatural realm (heaven, for example). Therefore, Nature itself is divine and sacred. This is the common view in contemporary earth-oriented religions, such as Neopaganism and Wicca, but it is often controversial in those religions that emphasize the transcendence of God.

In summary, Stoics view the cosmos—Nature in the broad sense—as a living being imbued with an intelligence, the Logos, which governs it. All of the other intelligences in the cosmos, including gods, celestial beings, and terrestrial life, including humans, are split-off bits of this Cosmic Intelligence. This is important for understanding our role in the cosmos.

> *Divine Nature:* Reflect on your own views on the intelligible order of the universe and the role of divinity in it. How are your beliefs similar to and different from the Stoics'? Is Nature governed from within or from outside? Record your thoughts in your journal.

HUMAN NATURE

The philosophers of the Porch advise us to live in harmony with universal Nature, but to do so we need to explore Stoic ideas of *human* nature. Humans, as parts or emanations of Nature, have similar aspects to it. This is expressed by the ancient idea of the *macrocosm* and the *microcosm*. The macrocosm is the cosmos in its entirety, the universe, including the principles by which it is organized. The microcosm is the "little cosmos"—that is, the universe that is the individual human being, both body and soul. Many ancient philosophies taught that the microcosm is an image of the macrocosm—that is, a universe in miniature, and therefore that human nature is a reduced image of universal Nature. There is some truth to this notion, in part because human nature must be adapted to universal Nature in order to survive, and in part because human nature (specifically our sense organs and brains) is the lens through which we understand universal Nature.

Stoic physics analyzed the human being into three principal parts. First, we have a *body*, which is formed matter. Second, we have a *lower soul*: a vital energy, which maintains our life processes, including metabolism, healing, perception, movement, cognition, reproduction, and so forth. It is animating and gives life to living things, making them organisms as opposed to nonliving things.

Third, we have a *higher soul*, which is variously described as an intellect, a power of reflection, and a *guiding principle*. It is, as we will see, the power of conscious judgment and free choice. Since the Universal Reason is a unified whole, Stoics understand the higher soul as a portion of Universal Reason, and thus of God.

> *You must now at last realize of what cosmos you are a part,*
> *and that you subsist as an emanation of the governor of the cosmos.*[96]

According to those of the Porch, the higher soul, this split-off bit of the divine, which is enthroned in the body (in the wide sense, incorporating the body proper and the lower soul), is a *daimon*. The ancient Greek word *daimôn* (pronounced DYE-moan) has a completely different connotation from the English word *demon*. Originally it meant any divine being; later it became restricted to lesser divinities as opposed to the high gods (Zeus, Athena, etc.). In fact, *daimon* is closer in meaning to "angel," and in Platonic philosophy angels (*angeloi* in Greek) were considered one kind of daimon. Hence, the higher soul is the god within.

> *Every person's mind is god,*
> *and is an emanation thence.*[97]

The philosophers of the Porch say that your guiding principle or inner divinity is what is truly you; the rest (body and lower soul) is "exterior" (outside of the true you). This is important for understanding the Stoic way of life.

Notice that since everything is formed matter (that is, an inseparable composite of an active cause and passive matter), the soul is considered material, not immaterial or incorporeal. At death these two substances (body and soul) separate, but the Stoics did not think that the soul outlives the body for long. That is, they both disperse, and our lives as independent beings come to an end; we merge back into universal Nature.

Since the distinguishing characteristic of humans is our power of conscious reason and reflection—that is, our higher soul—for humans to live according to (human) nature means to live in accordance with this guiding principle. Your body and lower soul (which you share with other living things) is part of your nature, but not peculiar to humans. According to ancient philosophy, the aim of every being, human and otherwise, is to bring its own nature to completion and perfection. Since reason is the good that is peculiar to humans, we reach the end intended by Nature when we bring our reason to perfection. Therefore to live a *human* life, and also the most godlike life, your guiding principle should follow reason. Now let's turn to the method.

THREE FUNDAMENTAL DISCIPLINES

The Stoa teaches three fundamental *disciplines*, which are practices by which the guiding principle regulates its judgment, impulse, and desire. These three faculties govern the corresponding parts into which Plato divided the soul: the mind or rational part, the will or spirited part, and the appetites or desiring part; in other words—metaphorically—the head, heart, and belly. *Judgment* is the faculty by which we decide what is true and what is false. Our goal in judgment is to assent to the true, reject the false, and suspend judgment on the uncertain. As judgment is the realm of true and false, so *impulse* is the realm of choice and refusal, for our goal is to choose what we should do and refuse to do what we shouldn't. Finally, *desire* is the realm of the good and the bad, for we desire what's good, try to avoid what's bad, and should be indifferent to that which is neither. In order to behave in harmony with human nature, we should use reason to decide between true and false, between choice and refusal, and between desire and aversion. (At first blush, it may seem that desire and aversion are out of our control, but the next chapter teaches spiritual practices to gain that control.)

These three mental faculties correspond to the three divisions of philosophy: logic, ethics, and physics (natural science). It is pretty obvious that logic relates to truth and falsity, and ethics to choice and refusal, but the connection between physics and desire or aversion is probably more mysterious (we'll get to it). Therefore wisdom consists in three *disciplines*, of *assent*, *impulse*, and *desire*, which I'll explain in three chapters, along with the spiritual exercises that support them. (Remember them by the abbreviation AID.) Marcus summarizes where we will be going:

Every nature is contented with itself when it goes on its way well;

and a rational nature goes on its way well:

[1] when in its thoughts it assents to nothing false or uncertain;

[2] when it directs its impulses to social acts only;

[3] when it confines its desires and aversions to the things that are in its power;

and when it is satisfied with everything that is assigned to it by universal Nature.[98]

I have added the numbers to show that these are the disciplines of assent [1], impulse [2], and desire [3].

The Discipline of Assent

In our imagination we can look into a small room in the palace where the Stoic philosopher Iunius Rusticus, a man in his forties, is teaching Marcus Aurelius, still in his twenties. They sit facing each other, a scroll of Epictetus's *Discourses* lying unrolled on a side table. Rusticus leans forward with intensity:

"The goal of the Discipline of Assent is to exclude everything from your higher soul—the real you—that is not true. That is, to assent to the true, to dissent from the false, and to suspend judgment on the uncertain."

"Is such perfect judgment possible?" asks Marcus.

"It is possible because cognition is a two-step process. The first is the passive formation of an *impression*, such as an image, sensation, or feeling, in your mind as a consequence of the physical interaction of your lower soul and body with the rest of the world. That is, this impression is received passively from what is exterior to your higher soul. For example, this impression might be a very loud sound or a painful sensation. This process is involuntary, and may involve some reaction, as when you jump at the sound or say, 'Ouch!' from the pain.

"Next is an active process of inner discourse, by which your guiding principle— your higher soul—attaches a value judgment or interpretation to the impression, such as 'This is scary,' 'I am in agony,' or 'I am unhappy.' This is a voluntary process; this is where you may exercise your freedom, if you are wise! And this is the crucial step for those of the Porch, for as Epictetus says,

What troubles people is not things,

but their judgments about things.[99]

"The Stoic sage does not immediately attach the *habitual* judgment to an impression, but withholds judgment until a *reasoned* judgment can be attached. Therefore remember:

Suppress your judgment.[100]

"The goal is to make an *objective* judgment, which is a simple description of the event, without the additional *subjective* value judgment.

Do not draw inferences in excess of what first impressions report." [101]

"Wait," says Marcus as he fumbles to pull a tablet from the folds of his toga. He scratches the maxims on its wax surface.

"By all means, write them down," says Rusticus, "but they will do you no good impressed in wax; you must impress them on your soul and practice them daily.

"By the way," Rusticus continues, "another part of the Discipline of Assent is that just as we are obliged to govern our inner dialogue (our internal judgments), so also in our outer dialogue we should assent only to the true. That is, we should tell the truth and refrain from unjustified spoken judgments.

"Now, an objective judgment is a description of an event in its bare reality—that is, a value-neutral description, and one of our Stoic spiritual exercises is to practice doing this.

Make for yourself a definition or description of every object presented to you,
so as to see distinctly what it is in its own naked reality, complete and entire,
and tell yourself its proper name, and the names of the things of which
it is compounded and into which it will be dissolved.[102]

"Consider eating a good steak.[103] What is this in its naked reality? It is a piece of a muscle, cut from a dead cow, which (if it is well aged) has been allowed to begin to rot, which means that germs have begun to grow in the muscle fibers and decompose them. This piece of semi-rotten dead muscle has been burned, more or less, which kills many of the germs, and also thickens or clots the blood and other body fluids, trapping them in the dead muscle. When you chew a bite, your teeth crush the charred, dead muscle, releasing some of those body fluids, which are further decomposed by the spit in your mouth, and which chemically stimulate your tongue to produce certain impressions (called taste). Appealing?"

"You make me lose my appetite," Marcus laughed.

"Listen," Rusticus continues, "and I will give you a 'naked' description of sex, which men desire above everything else. It is merely a rubbing together of bellies, accompanied by the spasmodic ejaculation of a sticky liquid. That is all."[104]

"Master," Marcus replies, "you go too far! These so-called naked descriptions seem to be flesh-denying, ascetic, anti-life exercises in rejection of the physical world and its pleasures. It sounds like the ravings of those naked ascetics that hate the world and their own bodies. You would suck all the joy out of life!"

"Not at all!" says Rusticus. "Ideally, a naked description should be akin to objective scientific or clinical descriptions that are value-neutral, and therefore neither positive nor negative, simply factual. While I have used pleasurable activities to illustrate neutral description, the same technique applies to unpleasant things, and tends to eliminate the judgment of unpleasantness in the same way that the preceding examples eliminate the judgment of pleasantness. The goal is to eliminate the subjective value judgment, not to switch it to its opposite. We want to separate the bare impression, which we cannot control, from the subjective judgment, which we can. When we describe an impression to ourselves in its bare reality, we should think:

This you are in reality,
whatever else common opinion would have you be.[105]

"Neutral description is one example of how the Discipline of Assent sets aside subjective value judgments and governs your inner dialogue, your judgments about things. Since you are judging things from an objective, physical perspective, rather than from a personal one, you are judging them from the perspective of universal Nature or God—that is, from the divine perspective. This is one way in which the Stoic sage becomes more godlike."

Neutral Description: Write out neutral descriptions of a variety of things, events, conditions, or circumstances that seem either good or bad to you. Contemplate your descriptions and see if they modify your subjective reactions. Do the good things seem less compelling, and the bad ones less repulsive? Try to describe some things that occur on a regular basis in your life (e.g., eating food you like, getting stuck in traffic, an annoying person). Next time the situation arises, recall your neutral description and see if you are able to replace your habitual subjective judgment with an objective one. This will give you some conscious control over your judgments, some control over your inner chatter.

Rusticus continues. "Whereas the passive formation of an impression is involuntary, the subsequent value judgment is voluntary, and under your control. Therefore you do not have to allow any judgments that you do not want to allow. Your higher soul is thus like a *spiritual acropolis*, an invulnerable inner fortress to which you can retire in peace, admitting only what you choose. Think of the Acropolis in Athens, that walled high rocky cliff, to which the Athenians retire when under siege, which protects the temples, the sanctuaries of the gods, at its summit. And whose temple stands in the center of the acropolis in many Greek cities?"

"Why, Athena's, of course."

"And why hers?" Rusticus presses.

"Because she is the Protector of Cities."

"Good," Rusticus smiles. "She is Goddess of Wisdom and Goddess of War, for she brings cleverness, insight, and judgment to the protection of what is most sacred. Let Wisdom ward your citadel as well. Write this down:

> *The mind that is free from disturbances is an acropolis,*
> *for people have nothing more secure to which they can fly for refuge*
> *and be impregnable.*"[106]

After Marcus finishes scratching on his wax tablet, the teacher continues. "Judgment is an active and voluntary process. Therefore your guiding principle can choose whether to go out and meet exterior events by choosing whether to attach a value judgment to them, by choosing whether to judge or evaluate them. From your mental acropolis you can choose what to go out and meet and what to bring inside the walls. Remember:

> *Things stand outside the door, just as they are,*
> *with neither knowledge of themselves, nor report of themselves.*
> *What is it then that reports about them?*
> *The guiding principle.*[107]

"Moreover,

> *The things whose pursuit or avoidance disturbs your peace*
> *do not come to you,*
> *but you, rather, go to them.*
> *Let then your judgment about them be untroubled,*
> *and they will be quiet too,*
> *and you will be seen neither pursuing nor avoiding them.*[108]

"Your guiding principle is free to attach any value judgments it wills to the impressions it receives. Remember:

> *The guiding principle rouses and turns itself,*
> *and while it makes itself what it is and what it wills to be,*
> *it also makes everything that happens*
> *appear to be what it wills it shall be.*[109]

"But what should it *will* things to be? When should it judge something good and worth pursuing, or evil and worth avoiding? What is the best criterion for judgment? This is the topic we will take up when we meet tomorrow."

PRACTICING THE DISCIPLINE OF ASSENT

What do these ancient teachings mean for us nowadays? The basis of Stoic wisdom is a correct understanding of what is in your control and what is not. The Discipline of Assent helps us to understand that many of our reactions are habitual, and that habits can be changed. The raw impression is physical fact, but the judgment can be changed. Detaching the judgment from the impression allows you to begin reprogramming your reactions. It doesn't mean that you don't care about things. The ultimate goal is to get control over what you care about so that you can live a purposeful, socially engaged, but tranquil life. How about some examples?

Suppose your boss is in your face, screaming at you. A neutral description might be that someone is speaking to you loudly and wagging a finger in your face. That's the objective fact. You may have an immediate, involuntary reaction of fear or anger; that's also part of the initial impression. But any further judgment should be suspended. Is his or her anger justified? Have you done something wrong? Will you be fired? All that is uncertain; leave it outside the door.

Suppose the bank has foreclosed on your house. The bare fact is that you have received a piece of paper with some words on it. That is certain and you should assent to it. Is it a mistake? Can you fight it? Will you have to move in with friends? Live on the street? All this is uncertain, and so you should suspend judgment on it. You may have immediate, involuntary reactions—disbelief, anger, fear—when you read the words; these feelings are objective impressions. After acknowledging them, you set them aside and return to the primary fact: you have received a foreclosure notice. What should you do about it? That is the subject of the next two chapters.

Somebody cuts me off in heavy traffic. My immediate impression is surprise and I swerve or brake; fear, anger, or relief follows quickly. These are my immediate, involuntary reactions, to which I must assent. Beyond that, I should suspend judgment. That the other driver is an idiot, that he or she intended to scare me, that I have narrowly escaped death, and so on: all this is uncertain, and I should set it aside. The objective fact is that the other car pulled too close in front of me. Why allow the rest inside the walls, where it will only disturb my tranquility?

You read or hear in the news that some people are being tortured, that they are being imprisoned unjustly, or that they are starving and homeless. The bare fact is that you have been told these things; set aside your habitual judgments so that from a state of tranquility you can act more wisely (as taught in the next two disciplines).

Suspending judgment is not the same, of course, as apathy. You suspend judgment in order to break free of habitual reactions so that you can evaluate circumstances correctly and respond to them appropriately. The Stoic prescriptions for correct evaluation and action are the disciplines of desire and impulse, respectively, the subjects of the next two chapters.

Suspending Judgment: As you go about your daily affairs, pay attention as situations stir up your emotions, positive or negative. In your mind, separate what is certain—the naked description—from what is uncertain—your habitual judgment—and set aside the latter. Record your observations in your journal. Note your successes and failures in suspending judgment. (Remember the Evening Examination of Conscience?) Do you find that practicing the Discipline of Assent is giving you the ability maintain neutrality in the face of life's experiences?

CHAPTER SIX

THE DISCIPLINE OF DESIRE

INTRODUCTION

We come now to the second discipline of the second degree of wisdom. In many ways it is the most difficult of the three disciplines, since it requires the greatest reorientation of your thinking, and so you should plan on spending some time practicing it. The first discipline taught you how to suspend habitual judgments, in particular about whether something is good or bad, or to be desired or avoided. What then should you seek or shun? The second discipline will teach you how to reprogram your desires and aversions so that you can always obtain what you desire and avoid what you want to avoid, and so live in peace and happiness. To this end you will learn the complementary relation of desire and action, what it is you are truly free to choose, and how to detach yourself from what is out of your control. You will learn about your inner daimon, which makes these choices, and your guardian daimon, which guides them, and how to detach your feelings from things outside of your control in both your personal life and the world. Finally, I will explain the importance of understanding events, whether positive or negative, in terms of your personal destiny.

Desire, Impulse, and Nature

We can imagine a discussion between Rusticus and Marcus as they stroll through one of the palace gardens. Rusticus is speaking. "I explained yesterday that the Porch recognizes three mental faculties—judgment, desire, and impulse—with their corresponding disciplines. The first governs the higher soul—the head, we might say—but the last two, impulse and desire, regulate two complementary aspects of the lower soul; call them the heart and belly. Desire relates to *passion* in the sense of what we feel and also what we passively suffer, whereas impulse relates to *action*, to what we want to do, our active intention. Thus passion is a consequence of universal Nature, and hence of external causes, in contrast to action, which is a consequence of our human nature, and hence of internal causes. Therefore these two disciplines are based, respectively, on physics (the study of Nature) and ethics. So that you remember the cause of your destiny, say to yourself:

I have what universal Nature wills me to have;
and I do what now my nature wills me to do.[110]

"Together the Disciplines of Desire and Impulse are intended to coordinate universal Nature and human nature so that you fulfill your nature as perfectly as possible. Now from the Stoic perspective, universal Nature is God and human nature is the inner daimon, so these disciplines harmonize the god within and the god above all—that is, the individual logos with the universal Logos. Since the inner logos is a fragment of the universal Logos, this harmony is our natural state. Tell yourself:

First, nothing will happen to me that is not in harmony with universal Nature;
second, it is in my power never to act contrary to my god and daimon.[111]

"As you've seen, the Discipline of Assent gives us control over our judgments, so we assent to the true, dissent from the false, and withhold judgment from the uncertain. Given this control, how can we use it to decide truly what to seek and what to avoid?"

GOOD, BAD, AND INDIFFERENT

What an organism perceives as *good* is whatever it seeks to obtain and keep, and what it perceives as *bad* is whatever it seeks to avoid or get rid of. A philosophy, then, teaches a way of life by defining the good, which should be chosen, and the bad, which should be avoided.

We have seen that for those in the Garden, pleasure is good and pain is bad, as Epicureans understand pleasure and pain. Thus the Garden's philosophy is classified as *hedonism* because the ultimate standard of good and the goal of life is pleasure (*hêdonê* in Greek). Of course you have seen that life in the Garden is far from the sort of sensual self-indulgence that "hedonism" usually connotes. In contrast, the Porch's philosophy is a kind of *eudemonism* because its goal is happiness or spiritual well-being (Greek *eudaimonia*, literally, having an inner *daimon*—higher soul—that is doing well). How is this goal achieved?

The philosophers of the Porch say that we can live happily if we understand good and bad correctly, in accordance with our nature, for then we will see that the good is always obtainable and the bad always avoidable. This is the case if we understand good and bad in terms of what is in our power: namely, our *moral purpose*, which is our commitment to act in accordance with Stoic ethical principles (discussed in the next chapter). Therefore the only truly good things are what is morally good, right, noble, virtuous, and so forth, and the only truly bad things are what is shameful, disgraceful, base, vicious, and so forth. Since nothing can prevent us from choosing to act morally, the good is always obtainable and the bad avoidable. The Emperor affirms the Stoic definition of good and bad this maxim:

> *I have seen the nature of the good that it is virtuous,*
> *and the nature of the bad that is vicious.*[112]

The other side of the Stoic prescription is to eliminate value judgments from things that don't depend on us, to be "indifferent to the indifferent," and to accept what Nature or Destiny brings. That is, what is in our control, and what we should choose, is to act virtuously. But the results of our actions are not in our control, and so we should consider them neither good nor bad in this fundamental sense. Thus the Discipline of Desire brings about a transformation of consciousness, in which the higher self is experienced as a safe haven from the onslaught of Fate.

> *Be like the cliff against which the waves continually break;*
> *but it stands firm and tames the fury of the water around it.*[113]

The effect of the Discipline of Desire is not apathy, as you might suppose, but a more solid foundation and stronger fortress from which to act effectively and courageously in the world. Recognizing this intellectually and feeling it in your gut are, of course, two different things. How can we be indifferent when our plans come to naught or lead to disaster? How can we be indifferent to the trouble and pain in the world? We cannot, but dealing with them effectively requires a base of serenity and strength. This requires mental training and vigilance in your judgments until they become habitual. In modern terms, you are practicing *cognitive behavioral therapy*, in which new ideas and thinking are used to reprogram your

emotions and behavior. (In fact, cognitive behavioral therapy is based on ancient Stoicism.[114])
Let's see how it's done.

CIRCUMSCRIBING THE SELF

The Stoics teach a number of practices that are intended to transform the consciousness
of the philosopher. Here I will outline a concentrative practice described by Marcus, which
philosopher Pierre Hadot calls "delimiting or circumscribing the self" and describes as "the
fundamental exercise of Stoicism."[115] It elevates consciousness to the first level above that
of the non-philosopher.

The exercise is to progressively detach yourself from exterior circumstances by judging
them as "indifferent"—that is, neither good nor evil. It is like stripping away the layers of
an onion to get to the inner daimon (the essential you). First, you must withhold judgment
about what others say or do. Second, you must detach yourself from memory of past suffering or fear of future suffering; this involves focusing on the present moment. Third, you
withhold value judgments from involuntary emotions. As mentioned in the last chapter,
the early stages of sensation are beyond voluntary control, but it is in our power to withhold judgment. The Stoic sage certainly feels pain, grief, sickness, and so forth; he or she is
not insensitive. But the sage withholds judgment on them. Fourth and finally, you detach
yourself from the flux of exterior things and events, including those in the body and lower
soul. This is a detachment from the flow of Fate. Naturally you must do what is necessary
to preserve your body and lower soul (this is required by Nature), and you also have to act
appropriately toward other people, as discussed in the next chapter.

The overall effect of circumscribing the self is a detachment from things that are not
essentially yours—that is, from things not pertaining to your higher soul, which is to say
from things that are not your business, but the business of God (Destiny, Fate, Nature,
Goddess, whatever the name). What is in your power is to act virtuously, which should
be the object of your desire. What happens "lies in the laps of the gods," as the ancients
said, and so getting disturbed by it will only interfere with your ability to seek the good in
future choices. In this way you come to a state of spiritual serenity in all circumstances.
This exercise prepares the way for the second level of philosophical consciousness, which
aligns your reason with the Universal Reason of Nature (discussed later), for by suspending
judgment on what is not in your control, you accept your role in the unfolding drama of
Destiny.

Has someone said something very nasty to you? Or very nice? That was outside of your direct control (your moral purpose), so be indifferent to it. Of course, it's natural to feel a little annoyed or pleased, but indifference means you don't attach any great importance or moral significance to it. Did you lose some money? Unless it was a consequence of your own moral mistake, be content that your inner daimon is unscathed. Stewing in sadness or seething with anger will confuse your future choices, which are made best in a state of serenity. The practice of circumscribing the self will help you to concentrate your awareness into your guiding principle, the quiet source of your autonomy and freedom.

At the end of his description of circumscribing the self, Marcus says, "You make yourself like the Sphere of Empedocles, a pure orb, proud of its joyful uniqueness." [116] This is an important image. Empedocles (490–430 BCE) was a Pythagorean sage who argued that the universe alternated between phases governed by Love, a force of attraction, and by Strife, a force of separation. In the phase when Love had reached her maximum strength, the entire universe was a well-rounded sphere, united by Love. The poet Horace (65–8 BCE) reveals why the Sphere of Empedocles is a good symbol of the higher self:

Who then is free? The sage, who keeps in check
His baser self, who lives at his own beck,
Whom neither poverty nor dungeon drear
Nor death itself can ever put in fear,
Who can reject life's goods, resist desire,
Strongly, firmly braced, and in himself entire,
A hard smooth ball that gives you ne'er a grip,
'Gainst whom when Fortune runs, she's sure to trip. [117]

The polished sphere is an image of the imperturbable guiding principle of the sage.

Circumscribing the Self (Sitting): There are two ways to perform this practice: either as a sitting meditation or in ordinary life circumstances. For a sitting meditation, find a place where you can sit without serious disturbance from other people or hard-to-ignore distractions (radio, TV, phone, etc.). However, you do not have to be in a special place that is isolated, nor do you need to sit in any special posture. Your eyes can be open or closed. The basic practice is to go through the steps outlined on page 94. (1) Put aside and judge as indifferent anything that is not in your control. This could be things other people are saying or doing, or other things that are happening in your world (pleasant as well as unpleasant). If anything comes to mind, say to yourself, "I am indifferent to X," and let it go. If nothing comes immediately to mind, then probe your day a little, and you will probably find something. Gently banish it with a judgment of indifference. *You are now in yourself.* (2) Next turn to the past and future. Are you worried about something, or happily anticipating something, that is not in your control? Then affirm your indifference to it. Do the same with the past: regrets, resentments, anger, happy memories; let them go. *You are now in the present moment.* (3) Turn your attention to your current feelings. This includes discomfort or pain in your body, but also pleasant or unpleasant emotions and moods. You cannot change these, but you can affirm your indifference to them. It may help to inspect them from the perspective of bare reality. For example, "My empty stomach is sending nerve impulses to a part of my brain, signaling its emptiness." "A bird is making sounds—vibrations in the air—that my brain interprets as melodious." *You are now in a state of indifference to indifferent things.* (4) Rest serene and tranquil in the present moment, experiencing your higher self as the imperturbable Empedoclean sphere: smooth, simple, shining, perfectly reflective, suffused with tranquil well-being and loving-kindness. Pleasant or unpleasant thoughts may arise in your mind, but banish them gently with an affirmation, "I am indifferent to that." You can rest in this state as long as you like, but when you rise for your other activities, try to keep the serene state of mind.

Circumscribing the Self (Active): After you have practiced circumscribing the self as a sitting meditation, you can practice applying it in the circumstances of everyday life, especially when you are stressed, angry, worried, or suffering in some other way. Wherever you are, go through the steps in your mind, briefly acknowledging the impressions that are disturbing you and affirming your indifference to them. Finally, visualize your higher soul as the Empedoclean sphere, tranquil because the exterior turmoil is reflected from it or slides off of it. If you practice circumscribing the self, you will be able to use it when you feel under assault from exterior circumstances.

INDIFFERENCE TO MISFORTUNE

How can we be indifferent to disease, injury, death, and the like? We have to think differently about them, and one way to do this is to see them from the perspective of universal Nature. For the same Nature that has enabled humans to evolve and thrive also enables the viruses and bacteria that cause disease and death to survive. Indeed, without competition and death there would be no evolution at all, and we humans would not exist. If there were life on Earth at all, it would be at the level of bacteria.

Our tendency is to judge disease, aging, and death negatively when they happen to *us*, but the expanded perspective of universal Nature shows us that they are necessary to the processes of Nature, which helps us to be indifferent to them, to consent to them, and even to welcome them. (This is a version of the Viewpoint of Science discussed in chapter 2.)

Neutral Description of Disease: Give a neutral description of disease in general, or of a specific disease, as a purely natural process, which allows you to view it indifferently, from the perspective of universal Nature as opposed to your own perspective. After you have some experience describing conditions with no direct relevance to you, try it on something that matters to you (e.g., a disease that you have or someone close to you has).

When we understand physics and evolution, we see that—in spite of indeterminate and random aspects—they are rational: that is, orderly, intelligible, and in a sense even purposeful, by which I mean that there is an intelligible progression from simpler to more complex organisms. We can also see that the aspiring philosopher should study Nature in order to be familiar with the necessity and interrelationship of all things, and to be able to apply the Viewpoint of Science.

Nevertheless, being indifferent to calamities is not easy, and so philosophers of the Porch also practice Premeditation of Misfortunes (described in chapter 2). This lessens the impact of misfortunes, because we have anticipated them, understood them as the workings of Nature, and can be indifferent to them. Epictetus gives a shocking example: he says that when you kiss your child you should think, "Tomorrow you will die." [118] The point of this apparently morbid thought is to acknowledge a real possibility, and so to better appreciate the present moment. So also for anything that you love or value, consider that Fate may snatch it away at any time. Clearly such a practice can be overdone, which would in fact undermine the Stoic objective of concentration on the present. Seneca reminds us:

> A soul obsessed with the future is miserable indeed;
> it is unhappy even before any misfortunes. [119]

Therefore the goal of the Premeditation of Misfortunes is not to worry about everything bad that could happen, but rather to see that these things are not really misfortunes, because they are independent of your moral purpose, and so you should be indifferent to them. You do not need to dwell on every possible future calamity, but whenever one occurs, consider the question:

> What is there in this that is intolerable and past bearing? [120]

Let's try an example. Think about what you will do the next time you get stuck in traffic. Naturally, you will be frustrated at first, but what in it is intolerable and past bearing? Nothing. It's happened before; it will happen again. Will the situation prevent you from acting morally? Certainly not, which should please you. You can be compassionate toward the other drivers, cooperate with them, and make sensible decisions. Will you be late for your meeting? Perhaps, but that is out of your control; treat it with indifference. This does not mean you take no action. Rather, with your tranquil mental state you will be better able to decide what to do, such as phoning to say you may be late, or seeing if you can get off the road and take a detour. This is much more effective than banging on your steering wheel, yelling at the other drivers, or crying. By premeditating the situation and your Stoic response to it, you will be better able to face it when it occurs (and you know it will!).

Think about something we all dread: being diagnosed with a serious medical condition. Should you commit suicide? Probably not, in which case, by definition, it is not unbearable. Of course, the condition and its treatment may be very unpleasant, but that is largely out of your control: treat it with indifference; accept it. Certainly, you should try to get well (if that's possible) and to minimize the pain and discomfort, since that will help you to act effectively. But so long as your condition does not impair your ability to make moral choices, you remain free in the only sense of freedom consistent with human nature.[121] If you desire the good in the Stoic sense, then you cannot be prevented from satisfying your desire. Though your body may be disabled and wracked with pain, you can remain serene and untroubled in your Empedoclean sphere.

Well, that's the theory; I'm not claiming it's easy. This is why you need to premeditate possible misfortunes, beginning with the lesser ones. That's why you need to practice Stoic indifference in the lesser trials of life, so that you are better prepared for the greater ones, which will come. Like learning and practicing self-defense, or learning first aid, Premeditation of Misfortunes is a way to prepare yourself to deal with situations that you hope will never arise (but, in some form, surely will).

Premeditation of Misfortunes: Think about various misfortunes that could occur in your life, visualize them vividly, and visualize your own Stoic response to them. Start with minor mishaps, not with the big ones like loss of loved ones. Like all exercises, it is best to begin just a little beyond your capabilities, and then to practice until you can do better.

> *Detachment*: Epictetus[122] suggests a daily exercise that begins with little things, such as breaking a cup, proceeding to the loss of some clothing or a pet, then to loss of land, then to injuries to your body or loss of limbs, finally to loss of loved ones. (You can make up your own list.) This is an exercise in gradual detachment. In each case ask yourself, "What in this is past bearing?" Recalling people who have borne these or worse misfortunes will help you realize that they are not past bearing. At the same time, by acknowledging that you could lose these things at any time, you become more appreciative of having them now. All these things are exterior to your higher self, and not truly your own; in effect they are on loan from the universe. Remember the following two maxims from Epictetus.
>
> *Purify your judgments,*
> *and see that nothing that is not your own is attached to you.*[123]
>
> *Don't set your heart on them, and they won't be necessary.*
> *Don't tell yourself they're necessary, and they're not.*[124]
>
> Your possessions, your loved ones, your body, and even your life: none of these are fundamentally yours. They are on loan from Nature or Fate, who may take them back at any time. Be prepared!

PERSONAL AND TRANSPERSONAL GUIDES

Regular practice of the preceding exercises will lead to your inner daimon—that is, your higher self—becoming more serene and benevolent. (Recall that the self, intellect, power of reflection, guiding principle, and inner daimon are all names for the higher self.) The goal of philosophy then is to preserve your inner daimon from disturbance and compulsion, so that it is secure and free in its spiritual acropolis. Marcus offers these maxims:

It is sufficient to attend to the inner daimon and to reverence it sincerely.
And to revere it means keeping it pure from feelings and frivolity
and discontent with what comes from gods or humans.[125]

What then can be our guide?
One thing and one thing only: philosophy.
And this consists in keeping the inner daimon unwronged and unscathed,
master of pains and pleasures,
doing nothing at random, nothing falsely or with pretense.[126]

Chrysippus (c.280–c.207 BCE), who headed the Stoic school after Zeno and Cleanthes, said happiness is living "in accordance with the harmony between the daimon within each one of us and the will of the governor of the universe."[127]

Your guiding principle is your personal conscious ability to determine your judgments, desires, and impulses (the three disciplines). But we find hints in Epictetus of a *transpersonal guide*, a transcendent source of norms deriving from the Universal Reason of Nature. He says God has placed this "guardian daimon," a small portion of Zeus, in each of us. In scientific terms it is an unconscious regulatory system common to all humans (a collective unconsciousness, rooted in innate neural structures, discussed in chapter 9). Your higher self may enter into dialogue with this guardian daimon so that you can live more in accordance with Nature. The practices for doing so, however, are more the business of the Grove than the Porch, and I'll defer them for now. Epictetus says we have a faculty equal to that of Zeus, for:

He has set by each person a daimon to guard him,
and committed him to its care,
indeed to one who never sleeps and cannot be beguiled.[128]

The Emperor advises:

Live with the gods!
And he lives with the gods who constantly shows them that his soul is satisfied with its lot
and obeying the daimon that Zeus has given each person
as guide and guardian.
This is each person's mind and reason.[129]

THE VIEW FROM ABOVE

In chapter 2 I briefly described the *View from Above*, an expansive spiritual practice used by all the ancient philosophies; we can listen in as Rusticus explains it to Marcus.

"I want you to practice the View from Above, which is an exercise in which you rise in your imagination above the earth, so that all the ordinary affairs of life, which usually seem so important to us, shrink to insignificance. Humans, scurrying about in their busyness, in their intrigues and treacheries, in their loves and desires, seem like so many ants swarming in the dirt. National borders, too, which otherwise seem so important, vanish; all you can see are oceans and land masses. But just as the View from Above shrinks the human distances to insignificance, it also shrinks human lives to insignificance. And so we see humans being born, rushing about in their brief lives, and dying, to be replaced by yet more humans. Empires rise and fall—even the Roman Empire—and fame and fortune disappear into the void of endless time."

"What's the purpose of such imaginary visions?" asks Marcus.

"The View from Above has several goals. The first is the Discipline of Desire, for it helps us to appreciate the fundamental valuelessness of most of what we ordinarily consider valuable, for on the global scale, and over the long term most of it makes no difference. The Roman Empire will fade. No one will care that the revolt of the Brigantes was put down."

Marcus is shocked. "Surely the heroism of Lollius Urbicus will live on!"

"He too will be forgotten. Use this exercise to refocus your attention from passing events to the core Stoic values: the only good is moral good, and the only evil, moral evil. All the rest is just means to this end."

"But this view seems so depressing," Marcus replies. "It cries 'Everything is vanity!' like some dismal philosophers."

"On the contrary, my son—rightly viewed—this vision is liberating. First, by revealing the unimportance of so many issues and by focusing on the few that are important, it frees us to concentrate our effort on the few things that really matter, and to let the rest go. Second, it reveals the pageant of the earth's history, and indeed of cosmic history, and how we are a part of it. Though each of us is a small part, the universe is the totality of such small parts. Finally, through this exercise you experience the exhilaration of a mind that can expand outward to encompass first the earth and then the universe."

View from Above: Sit comfortably and close your eyes. Begin by imagining yourself exactly where you are. Then imagine yourself rising in the air, on your own or in a vehicle, whatever seems most vivid and natural to you. As you rise vertically into the air, the buildings, the streets, and eventually the city shrink smaller and smaller. The people, cars, and so forth shrink, just as they do when you take off from an airport. Soon the city is lost in the topography of the land. You can barely perceive myriads of dots moving around in chaotic patterns: humans, going about their business, getting and spending, loving and fighting, but the details are too remote now to see. Next, by a shift in your consciousness, or by engaging a time machine in your vehicle, you see time on Earth begin to accelerate. The dots move faster and faster. Soon human lives go by in the blink of an eye. Buildings are erected and crumble in moments. Countries are founded, flourish, and decline to extinction while you watch. Populations grow and shrink, and shift around the globe, their national borders visible only to them. People become rich and famous, but are soon forgotten. Soon the languages in which they were praised are forgotten. Eventually the sun expands into a red giant, and the earth and everything on it are vaporized. The sun shrinks back, leaving empty space, but myriads of other stars shine in the cosmos. Now return to ordinary time and space. Meditate on your experiences for a while, and then reflect on them in your journal.

PROVIDENCE OR CHAOS?

Marcus often contrasts the providential world of the Stoics with the Epicurean world, which he characterizes as chaotic and ruled by chance. He reminds himself of the difference by the dichotomy:

Either Providence or atoms.[130]

Marcus obviously prefers the Stoic view, but his point seems to be that even if the Epicureans are correct, and the world is ruled by chance, that does not imply that human beings should not use reason.

> *If God, all is well,*
> *and if random, don't you be random.*[131]

For even if Stoic natural science is false (and certainly some of it is, from the perspective of contemporary science), the philosophers of the Porch argued that people should still live in accordance with human nature, of which reason is the characteristic property. This implies that we should be indifferent to indifferent things, that the only authentic good and evil is moral good and evil, and that this is the only realm of true human freedom.

Furthermore, reason and experience teach us that the world is not completely random; there is order in it, and in this sense it is governed by Universal Reason (Logos). Therefore, details aside, there is obviously some truth in the Stoic worldview.

Such terms, however, as *Providence, Destiny, Reason,* and *God* suggest more than simple orderliness; they suggest an orientation toward the future, some purpose, some care for what happens. If you are a believer in God or Goddess, or in a whole pantheon of gods and goddesses, then you are probably comfortable with the notion of a purposeful Providence. On the other hand, you may see the universe as more chaotic, subject to chance and accident, with little evidence of divine purpose. Furthermore, as you know, randomness plays an important role in contemporary science, from the Heisenberg Uncertainty Principle to the random mutation and genetic recombination that fuels evolution. Indeed, randomness, and in particular the random motion that we call heat, is the principal driver of the creation of order in the physical universe.[132]

On one hand, we have a dilemma. Reason or randomness? Providence or chance? In any particular case it is difficult to know, which is why Marcus's recommendation is valuable: "don't you be random." In other words, no matter what happens, for whatever divine purpose or lack of purpose, you are free to respond in accordance with *your* moral purpose. This brings us to the next lesson of Rusticus.

CONSENT TO DESTINY

Rusticus is sitting on a garden bench besides Marcus, who is speaking.

"I've been practicing the View from Above. It has shown me that in the infinite span of history the events of an individual life—even being declared Caesar—have little ultimate significance. But it is difficult to be indifferent to the calamities that Fate brings us."

"By being indifferent to indifferent things," Rusticus replies, "the Discipline of Desire teaches us to accept what Nature or Destiny brings. Indeed, you should welcome what Destiny brings, because this is the destiny tailored especially for you. Write this down in your tablet:

> *The characteristic of the good person*
> *is to delight in and welcome what happens*
> *and is spun for him by Destiny;*
> *and not to defile the daimon enthroned in his breast,*
> *or disturb it by a crowd of impressions,*
> *but to preserve it in serenity,*
> *following it obediently as a god,*
> *neither saying anything contrary to truth,*
> *nor doing anything contrary to justice.*[133]

"The first part is the Discipline of Desire; the last two lines refer to the Discipline of Assent and the Discipline of Impulse: the good person says nothing false and does nothing unjust."

"I understand," Marcus says, "that we should be indifferent to difficulties and unpleasant circumstances, but it seems unnatural to welcome these things."

"Think of this, my son. Many people go to the temples of the healing god Asclepius in order to be cured of physical and mental ailments. What happens there?"[134]

"Typically," Marcus replies, "after prayer, fasting, and other practices, they have a healing dream in which the god prescribes a cure, if he does not heal them outright. Thousands of dedicatory plaques testify to the success of the god's ministrations."

"Yes," says Rusticus, "and just as doctors do, the god may prescribe unpleasant cures or difficult practices for the patient, as appropriate to their condition, and the patient accepts them in order to be cured. So also, Providence prescribes circumstances to each of us, appropriate to our personal destiny, and we should consent to them, difficult or unpleasant though they may seem to everyday, philosophically uninformed opinion. If all this seems difficult, it's helpful to remember Seneca's remark:

> *Life is not made for delicate souls.*[135]

"Like the members of your own body, we are all members of the Universal Organism, Nature, and so we should welcome the part we are destined to play. What would you think of your foot if it complained about getting muddy, or your teeth if they didn't want to grind against each other?"

"I would think," Marcus replies, "that they do not know their own nature or their purpose as part of the whole."

"Likewise you have a destined place in the cosmos. Think of masons building a pyramid. They put squared stones into places perfectly fitting them, and thereby assemble a harmonious structure. So also the Architect of the universe shapes our individual lives and arranges them in circumstances fitting to them.

For there is one harmony in all things.
And as the cosmos is made up out of all bodies to be the body it is,
so out of all causes Destiny is made up to be the cause it is.[136]

"Like the ancient Orphics and Platonists, we Stoics talk of the Fates, three crone goddesses who spin, measure, and cut the thread of each person's life. They weave the fabric of Destiny, the Tapestry of Fate. Remind yourself:

Whatever may happen to you,
it was prepared for you from all eternity;
and the plaiting of causes
was from eternity weaving into one fabric
your existence and the coincidence of this event.[137]

"Everything is woven together in mutual causality. Therefore, when something bad happens, or even something especially good, you should say to yourself:

This comes from God.
This is from the decree and spinning of the thread of Destiny
and some such coincidence and chance.[138]

"Hence, you can see that true piety corresponds to the Discipline of Desire, for it leads us to consent to the divine will or Logos. Through the interweaving of Destiny everything is implicated in everything, in mutual interdependence, sacred interconnection, and sympathy, and the cosmos is a single living organism with consciousness and will."

Always think of the cosmos as one living being,
having one substance and one soul,
and how all things trace back to a single sentience,
and how it does all things with a single intention,
and how all things are the causes of all that exists,
and how intertwined is the fabric
and how closely woven the web.[139]

There is one cosmos made up of everything,
and one god immanent in everything,
and one substance and one law,
and one Logos common to all intelligent beings,
and one truth.[140]

It may be difficult to accept that the circumstances of your life—the blown head gasket, the layoff, the broken leg, the robbery, the rape—were prepared by the gods just for you, but that's often the best way to think about them. They happened, nothing can be done about that. But you are free to choose how to interpret them. Often a good way to make the best of a bad situation is to ask yourself what Providence is trying to teach you, or in what direction the Destiny is leading you. Get a new car? Get a new job? Advocate for universal health care? Learn self-defense? Start a support group? Regardless of whether the cause was chance or the hand of Providence, it is more helpful to make it part of your destiny. This attitude will also bring you greater peace in all circumstances. This may seem like fooling yourself or self-delusion, but remember: magic is the art of changing consciousness at will. Practice this magic! (The practices of the Grove will help you to discern your destiny better.)

The Web of Fate: This exercise is intended to help you accept and even welcome your destiny. Look back over your life and pick out some major event, one that you have been accustomed to consider either positive or negative. First apply the Discipline of Assent, withdrawing subjective evaluation from what was not in your control. Then consider all of the preceding circumstances and events—many of them apparently accidental or coincidental—that converged to create this event. Meditate on the uniqueness of your destiny. This event is just one scene in the world drama, in which you have a role that you want to perform well! Next turn your attention to what has happened since this event, the many unanticipated consequences that have followed on it. Eliminate value judgments from them insofar as they were not results of your intention. The goal is to achieve a better appreciation of the focal event as an essential knot in the fabric of your individual destiny.

Accepting Your Destiny: As a mental exercise, pick some calamity from your past and suppose some benevolent deity has caused this to happen. Based on the assumption that some greater good should come out of it, think about how you can turn it to the betterment of yourself or the world. Record your conclusions and your intentions for the future in your journal.

UNIVERSAL LOVE

We learn in the Porch that our attitude should be a joyous and enthusiastic participation in this universal life. Marcus says, "The cosmos loves to produce that which must occur."[141] That is, Cosmos/Logos/God/Goddess/Nature produces and sustains all its parts, for this is what Nature—*physis*—means in Greek: that which produces and nourishes. Therefore the cosmos loves its parts, including us, which is called *Providential Love*. Furthermore, since the desire, inclination, and disposition of the cosmos is to do exactly what it must do, this should also be the desire, inclination, and disposition of each of its parts, including us. That is, each part of the cosmos loves to fulfill its function in the whole, and in this sense loves the whole, which is called *Returning Love*. So also it is natural that the parts love each other, for they are all parts of one organic, mutually sustaining whole (*Mutual Love*).

Marcus recommends a view of Nature that will resonate with many adherents of earth-oriented religions, Nature spirituality, and deep ecology:

> *Meditate often upon the intimate union and mutual interdependence*
> *of all things in the cosmos.*
> *For things are somehow mutually intertwined,*
> *and thus all things are friends to one another.*
> *For one thing follows in order after another*
> *by reason of their tight resonance,*
> *the sympathy that breathes through them,*
> *and the unity of substance.*[142]

The myriad lines of mutual interdependence and causality are bonds of natural behavior (what each thing "loves" to do) and therefore friendship. They are also bonds of tension, pulling each thing in many directions, conveying a "vibration" or "spirit" that unites the whole by "sympathy" (joint response). (Recall our discussion in the last chapter of the Cause/Logos/Spirit that unites and coordinates the Stoic cosmos.)

We have here again the image of the Sphere of Empedocles united by Love. Each higher soul is an image of the universal Empedoclean Sphere—a sphere with its center everywhere (in each person), but its boundary nowhere (for it encompasses everything). Therefore, if we practice the Discipline of Desire, then each of us becomes a vehicle through which the cosmos loves itself. The cosmos loves each of its parts, including us, who love it in turn, and therefore should love its other parts (Providential, Returning, and Mutual Love, respectively).

THE STOIC GOD

The Stoic God, who is equivalent to Providence, Universal Reason, Logos, Nature, Goddess, Destiny, Fate, etc., may seem rather impersonal. For many people this is just fine, but others will consider this an impoverished substitute for a personal god. It seems unlikely anyone would pray fervently to Providence or Destiny (even though Stoics give them mental qualities). Nevertheless, philosophers of the Porch are comfortable switching between more or less personal conceptions of Universal Reason. For example, the ancient maxim "Follow the gods"[143] is interpreted by Stoics to mean "Consent to Destiny."

Marcus sometimes thanks the gods for their aid, but he withholds judgment about whether they are capable of pity, for pity is a human emotion, which even humans should try to avoid. This requires some explanation, for as we will see, Stoic morality emphasizes altruism, but the Stoics argued that the *feeling* of pity clouds judgment. Those of the Porch are altruistic because it is right, not because they feel pity. Therefore, if the Stoic sage renounces pity, we should certainly expect the same of the gods. In any case, Marcus recommends that we not expect divine pity, but strive to deserve it:

> *Is Providence susceptible to pity?*
> *Then make yourself worthy of divine assistance.*[144]

Prayer also raises problems from a Stoic perspective, for if we think that by prayer we can cause Providence to change its direction, then that implies that the Universal Reason is not perfect. Either it was incorrect and was righted by the prayer, or it was correct and the prayer has diverted it from the right course. Thus Seneca remarks, "If divine majesty had done something that it later had to modify, it would be an affront and the admission of an error."[145] Nevertheless, communication is part of human nature and the most natural way we have of relating to other humans and to animals; therefore it is natural to personalize divinity and relate to it in this human way. When we look more closely at Hypatia's philosophy, we will see that it has a better account of prayer and other spiritual aspects of philosophy.

The Discipline of Desire helps us to see that whatever I am experiencing was destined for me and that the entire cosmos is implicit in it. It also shows us that while we desire moral good and reject moral evil, and are indifferent to the rest, we should nevertheless love what occurs, for it is our destiny and the result of divine will. Epictetus gives a short prescription for tranquility:

> *Ask not that events happen as you will,*
> *but will that they happen as they do,*
> *and you shall have peace.*[146]

Of course you cannot will a specific event in advance, because you don't know what will happen. But you can desire that Nature be in control and guide the universe in the best way. The specifics might not always be what you want from your more limited perspective, but you will have greater peace—and therefore be able to act more effectively—if you assume that whatever happened is the work of Providence. Follow the gods.

In each event in your life, whether big or small, you have the choice to interpret it as chance or destiny. If you decide it's just chance, then try to be indifferent to it; it "just happened." If you choose to interpret it as destiny, then you will want to understand what Providence or the gods have in store for you. As you will learn, the third degree of wisdom is especially useful for engaging actively with Providence, but in the meantime you can notice *synchronicities* (meaningful coincidences) in your life, which are evidence of an overarching order in the cosmos and of the hand of Destiny in your life. You shouldn't become superstitious, searching for meaning in every trivial, chance event, but if you are sensitive to the synchronicities, you will begin to discern your destiny.

A kind of cosmic consciousness results from circumscribing the self, concentrating on the present moment, consenting to the will of Nature in each moment, and recognizing that each event implicates the entire cosmos. As a result you may experience yourself as an integral part of the cosmos, a self-transcending experience, and more godlike. As the Discipline of Assent taught you the independence of your higher self from Fate, which is the first level of Stoic consciousness, the Discipline of Desire, with its consent to Destiny and reintegration into the cosmos, is the second level. These disciplines teach you how to apprehend reality and make your choices, but in the next chapter you will learn to use the Discipline of Impulse to act in harmony with Nature and Universal Reason.

Remember that these disciplines must be *practiced* in order to be effective. Reading about how to swim will not keep you from drowning unless you have practiced in the water.

Assessing Your Progress: Make a regular practice of assessing your progress toward the perfection of the sage. In which indifferent things are you confident of your indifference? Which are you still inclined to judge good or bad? Remember, the goal is progress, and some backsliding is inevitable. The Evening Examination of Conscience discussed in chapter 2 is a good mechanism for assessing progress.

CHAPTER SEVEN

THE DISCIPLINE OF IMPULSE

INTRODUCTION

We come now to the third of the three disciplines of the Porch. The Discipline of Assent teaches you to see things in their naked reality without attaching habitual value judgments. The Discipline of Desire shows you that your only desire should be to act virtuously, for this desire can always be satisfied, and that you will be more serene if you accept circumstances as the will of the gods. Practice of these disciplines reprograms your attitudes toward life, but they don't teach you much specific about how to act virtuously. This is the purpose of the Discipline of Impulse. We begin with the Stoic conception of human nature, for like the Epicureans the Stoics have a theory of human nature, but it is more refined than that taught in the Garden. This will lead us to three criteria for being a good human being. The first criterion is social and addresses our duties to other people, including friends and foes. The second teaches us how to accommodate the imperfections of the real world to treat people with justice. The third shows us how to act wisely by accommodating ourselves to Fate and recruiting all circumstances to our moral purpose. We wrap up the second degree of wisdom with a summary of its disciplines and how they embody respect for Nature. So let's get going!

ACTION AND NATURE

The Porch can be considered a sort of golden mean or middle way between the asceticism of the Cynics and the disengaged serenity of the Garden. Whereas the basic Epicurean attitude is relaxation, the basic Stoic attitude is tension or vigilance: constant monitoring of your inner discourse, your desires, and your intentions to act so that they accord with Nature. With practice this vigilance becomes habitual and creates the foundation on which Hypatia's spiritual practices are built.

Marcus and Rusticus are leaning on a palace balcony, watching the busy crowds in the Roman forum.

"This constant vigilance sounds like a great burden," Marcus sighs.

"It's not so onerous as it sounds," Rusticus replies. "While living the authentically human life requires assessing each moment in its totality and acting with your whole soul, this is a source of joy. Remember:

> *Salvation in life depends on examining everything*
> *in its entirety and its reality,*
> *what is its Matter and its Cause;*
> *and with all your soul to do justice and to speak the truth.*
> *What remains except to enjoy life*
> *by joining one good thing to another*
> *so as not to leave even the smallest gap between?* [147]

"We should minimize frivolous or pointless activities and treat each moment as though it is our last, as indeed it might be, since we can suffer a heart attack, a stroke, or something similar at any time.

> *This is the mark of perfect character:*
> *to pass through each day as though it were the last,*
> *without agitation, without torpor, without pretense.* [148]

"This is accomplished by constant attention to your actions:

> *In every action ask yourself:*
> *How does this affect me? Shall I regret it?*
> *A little time, and I am dead, and all is gone.*
> *What more do I seek,*
> *if my present work is that of an intelligent and social being,*
> *one under the same law as God?*" [149]

Marcus asks, "What is this law, which such intelligent and social beings should use to guide their behavior?

"Our goal is to act in accordance with Nature, but we have four natures: universal, vegetative, animal, and human.

"Our *universal* or *common nature* is what we share with all other things in the universe, for we are bound by common laws. Acting in accordance with universal Nature means accepting Destiny or Fate, about which I'll have more to say later. We must act in accordance with this common nature, but not if it worsens our higher nature, our more characteristic or specific natures.

"Our *vegetative nature* is what we share with all other living things, which includes metabolism and the capacity to reproduce. Therefore we have to nourish ourselves, avoid getting too hot or cold, and do other things to preserve life, but not if it worsens our nature as a rational animal.

"We share our *animal nature* with all other animals, and it includes our faculties for perception, mobility in the world, and our ability to remember, learn about, and adapt to our environment. It includes our abilities to seek food and to protect ourselves, and to cooperate and compete with others of our kind. We must live in accordance with our animal nature, but not in such a way that it prevents our ability to act as humans.

"Finally, we should live in accordance with our *human nature*—that is, with the capacities most characteristic of human beings. This includes our consciousness, ability to reason, self-reflective capacity, and human culture. Remember:

For a rational being,
the same act is according to nature
and according to reason."[150]

In modern terms, all living things must take appropriate actions in order to survive as individuals and as species. However, what other living things do naturally—that is, largely automatically and involuntarily—we do by decision and choice, but this is in fact our nature. This ability makes our behavior flexible and adaptable, but it also gives us the unique ability to choose inappropriate actions, to act against our nature. Thus ethics is an issue for humans much more so than for other animals (some of which also have to learn appropriate behavior, but to a lesser degree than humans).

"How can we act in accordance with human nature?" Marcus asks.

"We Stoics say that you should choose actions that are socially motivated, take account of worth and justice, and make exceptions for Fate. These are the three criteria of the Discipline of Impulse, and I will explain each in turn.

CRITERION I, FIRST STANDARD: ALTRUISM

Rusticus continues. "We can begin with the social criterion and those natural tendencies common to all humans beyond the behaviors necessary for survival as living
beings. These include our inclinations to form enduring pair bonds; to mate and have
children; to love our children, parents, siblings, and other kin; to associate with other
people in a community; to cooperate in group activities; to compete for authority; and
so forth. I am not trying to give you a complete list, but only an indication of the sorts
of inclinations common to all people. To the extent these things are out of our control,
they are indifferent, neither good nor evil. Nevertheless, they are part of human nature,
and so our moral purpose—which is in our control—should take them into account."

The notion of human nature is slippery and somewhat treacherous, since it can be used
as an excuse for undesirable and unphilosophical behavior: "It's just human nature to be
greedy, cruel, egotistical, deceitful, whatever." The discipline of evolutionary psychology is
beginning to offer a scientific understanding of human nature, but here it is sufficient to take
a commonsense view, and subject our intentions and actions to the Discipline of Impulse.

Fundamental to the philosophy of the Porch is the observation that human beings are social creatures, and therefore that the domain of appropriate action is social. Marcus regularly
reminds himself that rational beings (humans) are made for each other's sake, as expressed
in these maxims:

The rational being is also a social being.[151]

The prime principle in human constitution is social obligation.[152]

There is a deep basis for this community of humankind, for just as there is a "soul" (the
Logos) common to everything, there is a more particular soul common to all humans. Here
we see an application of the Stoic doctrine of the interconnectedness of everything, of which
the interconnectedness of all people is an aspect. Marcus says that just as the light of the sun,
although interrupted by walls, mountains, and many other things, and apparently broken
up into parts, is nevertheless one, so also in the cosmos there is one substance, one soul, and
one rational principle binding everything together.[153] We all share a common human nature.

Like an organism's body, humankind as a whole can be considered an organized, mutually interdependent system of organs or members. Each part contributes to the proper functioning of the whole, and thereby benefits itself. This is an important Stoic metaphor.

I am a member of the organism of rational beings.[154]

It is part of the function of a foot, for example, to be walked upon, and as part of that activity to get muddy and to step on thorns. Epictetus quotes Chrysippus, who said that if a foot had the power of thought, it would want to get muddy, for it is thus fulfilling its proper function, and so also should we welcome the circumstances of our lives, even illness and hardship, if it is our individual destiny (the Discipline of Desire).[155] In some cases the foot might even have to be amputated for the good of the body.

Both Epictetus and Marcus remark how grotesque it is to see a detached body part, such as an amputated foot.[156] Separated from the body, it is unable to perform its natural function for the body, or to survive isolated from the body's lifeblood. However, unlike body parts, we have freedom, and so we may choose to separate ourselves from the body of humanity, neither benefiting from its support nor fulfilling our natural function; that is, we have the freedom to act unsociably. However, the miraculous thing is that we, unlike detached body parts, can choose to reunite ourselves with the greater whole and resume our proper role.

For the Stoic sage altruism is its own reward, for the sage is acting in accordance with authentic human nature.

Are you not content
when you have done something in harmony with nature?
Does the eye demand a reward for seeing,
or the feet for walking?[157]

Therefore the Emperor reminds himself (and us) to think:

Have I done something for the general interest?
Well then I have my reward.
Let this be always present to your mind,
and never grow weary.[158]

Indeed, ideal sages will help others spontaneously and unselfconsciously, since that is their natural function, which they fulfill as naturally as the foot does its function, as naturally as bees produce honey, and vines produce grapes.

> *A person who has done a good act*
> *does not call out for others to come and see,*
> *but goes on to another act,*
> *as a vine goes on to produce again the grapes in season.*[159]

Philosophers who are not perfect sages, however, will have to devote some conscious attention to acting philosophically until it becomes a habit. This is in fact the Discipline of Impulse.

What does this mean for you? You probably know that in a healthy ecosystem many species—animals, plants, and microorganisms—exist together in a thriving community, co-operating and competing with each other. While no individual is essential, they all contribute to the health and vitality of the ecosystem, and in turn benefit from it. You can apply the philosophy of the Porch by thinking of humankind and yourself in the same way. Imagine the whole of Nature and see the contribution you are making, but also the myriad ways that you benefit from others, nonhuman as well as human. This does not imply that you should passively accept your current place in life. Your destiny may lie elsewhere. Keep your eyes open for the signs and seize the opportunities. (More systematic techniques for discerning your destiny are taught in the Grove; we'll be there soon!)

The Body Politic: Sit in a comfortable position with your eyes closed. Imagine society as a huge person or other animal. Watch it going about its business, looking for food and shelter, defending itself, getting sick or wounded and then healing, and so forth. When you have a clear image of this living *body politic*, then become aware of its myriad parts, its members and organs. Next imagine yourself as one small part of the body politic (e.g., a finger, a muscle, the tongue, a tooth, the stomach, a gland, an eye, a bit of cortex); if you like, pick a part that has a similar function to your occupation. Some parts are more important than others, but all have their functions, and many are indispensable. Now imagine that your part is cut from the body politic and placed beside it. Picture your part on the left and the injured body on the right. First notice how the body is disabled by your part's absence: it might be partially blind, sick, weak, or disabled in some other way. Now turn your attention to your part, lying separate from the body. Notice its uselessness on its own; it is just a piece of flesh or bone. And soon, separated from the lifeblood of the body, it will die and begin to rot. It is no better than garbage, medical waste. Feel the urgency of the situation, and like a surgeon reattaching a severed limb, imagine your part being put back into its place in the body. Feel the rejuvenating lifeblood flowing back through your part as it is reattached to the neighboring tissues. As life returns, feel the growing urge to resume your function in the body, to make it complete and fully abled. Finally, allow yourself to rest content as a fully reintegrated part, both benefiting and benefiting from the body politic. Record in your journal any insights that you receive.

CRITERION I, SECOND STANDARD: DIFFICULT PEOPLE

You must deal especially with the imperfection of others, for that too is part of human nature, a consequence of our freedom and limited knowledge and capacities. For example, Marcus advises that when you are offended by someone's obnoxious behavior, you should say to yourself,

Is it possible that there should be no shameless people in the world?
It is not possible.
Do not, therefore, require what is impossible.[160]

This affirmation (which does not excuse their behavior) helps you to deal with ignorant, dishonest, and uncooperative people. As emperor, Marcus had to deal every day with many of them, probably more than most of us do. Therefore he practices the following exercise, which is worth quoting in full:

> Begin the morning by saying to yourself: I shall meet with the busybody, the ungrateful, arrogant, deceitful, envious, unsocial. All these things happen to them by reason of their ignorance of what is good and bad. But I who have seen the nature of the good that it is virtuous, and the nature of the bad that it is vicious, and the nature of him who does wrong, that it is akin to mine, not only of the same blood or seed, but that it participates in the same intelligence and the same portion of divinity, I can neither be harmed by any of them, for no one can make me vicious, nor can I be angry with my brother, nor hate him. For we are made for cooperation, like feet, like hands, like eyelids, like the rows of upper and lower teeth. To act against one another then is contrary to nature; and it is acting against one another to be vexed and to turn away.[161]

Stoics, Epicureans, and Platonists all traced their philosophical descent from Socrates, the preeminent Greek sage, who taught that people are bad only through ignorance; if they truly understood themselves and the world, they could not avoid being good. Referring to Plato, the philosophers of the Porch asserted:

"No soul is willingly deprived of truth."
And it is the same with justice, moderation, loving-kindness, and all the like.
It is essential to keep this ever in mind,
for it will make you gentler toward all.[162]

When we think of willfully ignorant people—of liars, cheats, and criminals; of abusers, exploiters, and exes; of rapists, murderers, and terrorists—we may smile at the apparently naïve optimism of Socrates, but there is much of value in this view. Fundamentally, everyone (I will admit a very few exceptions) wants similar things: peace, freedom, material comfort, security, love, a better future for their children, and the like. If you ask political opponents, religious fanatics, or even terrorists, they will agree with everyone else on basic wishes such as these. Where we disagree is on the exact form these desires take and on the means to satisfy them. There are very few irremediably evil persons, but there are very many confused, thoughtless, irrational, ignorant, emotionally disturbed, and opinionated people, who may be swayed easily by others. Moreover, intelligent, educated, and thoughtful people can dig themselves into their own cognitive holes, which may be very deep and difficult to escape. What can we do?

Think about the people you most love to hate (for example, a political party, occupation, or religious group). Of course they think they know the truth. Just ask them! Usually they also have specific ideas about justice and injustice. Some of them might not seem interested in moderation, but the Greek word I have translated as "moderation" in the preceding maxim means "knowledge of the good to be chosen and the evil to be avoided." [163] That's exactly the knowledge that the folks in the "other" political party or "other" religion say they have. Often they also claim loving kindness and the like, but we might not think they show much of it.

By acknowledging that all people are fundamentally alike in their basic needs and desires, we open the way to resolving our difficulties without the use of explosives. If we can grant this common human nature, then we can begin to address the different ways we interpret such words as freedom and justice, and to resolve our disagreements about how to achieve them. Our common goal should be the best understanding of truth, goodness, freedom, and justice, which was precisely the goal of ancient philosophy. Therefore, the sage's first obligation to bad people is to try to teach them. You may say to yourself or to them:

> *Not so, my friend.*
> *We are constituted by Nature for something else.*
> *I shall certainly not be injured,*
> *but you are injuring yourself, my friend.* [164]

You will not be injured because you have learned to suspend the judgment of injury, to which you should be indifferent. As one of my favorite maxims from the emperor says:

> *Set aside the judgment, and you set aside "I've been harmed."*
> *Set aside "I've been harmed," and you set aside the harm.* [165]

On the other hand, the bad person has injured himself or herself in the only way possible, by incorrect moral choice. Therefore, Marcus reminds himself to explain specifically but compassionately how such action goes against human nature and the person's own good.

> *If someone is mistaken,*
> *instruct him kindly and show him his error.*
> *If you are not able to do this, blame yourself,*
> *or blame not even yourself.*[166]

That is, assume the person is wrong through ignorance and try to correct him or her. If you are unsuccessful, then give the person the benefit of the doubt and assume the fault lies with your instruction. Or, if you have done your best, consent to a failure that was destined. Accepting failings includes accepting your own; forgiveness begins at home.

In any case, you should undertake any such correction with tact and gentleness, and without anger, for their fault is due to ignorance.

> *I will be mild and benevolent toward everyone,*
> *ready to show his mistake to this very person, not reproachfully,*
> *nor yet as making a display of my forbearance,*
> *but nobly and honestly.*[167]

The emperor reminds us that there is nothing admirable about anger:

> *And let this truth be present to you in the excitement of anger,*
> *that to be moved by passion is not manly,*
> *but that mildness and gentleness are more manly,*
> *just as they are more in conformity with human nature.*[168]

Therefore, if in our anger we find we are priding ourselves in being tough, then we should remember this maxim, and take the more courageous (and more human) path of mildness and gentleness. Any beast can be angry, but humans can restrain their anger.

> *Teach them and show them without anger.*[169]

In teaching others we are genuinely trying to help them, but if we cannot do it without reproach, criticism, or an air of superiority, which likely will make them resentful and resistant to change, then it is better perhaps to let them be. After all, philosophers are only *seekers* of wisdom, and don't know everything.

If they have not had their habits of thought corrected in the past, or if they cannot be corrected now, then this incorrect thinking prevents them from acting correctly. Epictetus suggests that we think of them like blind or crippled people who are physically disabled through no fault of their own. We should not be harsh with them, but treat them with gentleness and compassion, and try to help them. Indeed, by being kind to them, we emulate the gods, who are kind to less-than-perfect mortals:

> *If you are able, correct by teaching those who do wrong;*
> *but if you cannot,*
> *remember that charity is given you for this purpose.*
> *And the gods too extend charity to such persons,*
> *helping them attain health, wealth, reputation—*
> *so kind they are.*
> *And it is in your power too.*
> *Who hinders you?* [170]

Patience, benevolence, and forgiveness are appropriate, for these people are our kin, sharing a common human nature.

> *People exist for the sake of one another.*
> *Teach them or bear with them.* [171]

Marcus suggests the following meditation for when you think someone has injured you:

> *It is peculiar to humans to love even those who do them wrong.*
> *This happens, if when they do wrong you remember they are kin,*
> *and wrong you through ignorance and unintentionally,*
> *and soon both of you will die;*
> *above all, that the wrongdoer has done you no harm,*
> *for he has not made your mind worse than it was before.* [172]

Thus you exercise the Discipline of Desire, and treat their wrong indifferently, even welcoming it as willed by Destiny.

> *Benevolence is invincible if it be genuine,*
> *and not merely an affected smile and playing a part.*[173]

Indeed, it is reasonable to love those with whom we are connected through Destiny as well as through family:

> *Harmonize yourself with the things to which you are linked by Destiny.*
> *As for the people to whom you are linked;*
> *love them, but genuinely.*[174]

You may be thinking, "Yeah, I can really see myself teaching my boss that his actions are inappropriate, that he's only harming himself, or patiently showing this irate customer her error." True enough. You have to pick your battles wisely. Sometimes you can find common ground, even if you disagree on many specific issues. If not, remind yourself that these people are our greatest teachers for, like sparring partners, they teach us how to take the blows without going down. Focus on the benefits you gain from them. In a few pages I'll explain how to treat people justly even if they see things very differently from you.

Premeditation on Difficult People: An exercise similar to the Premeditation of Misfortunes can help you to respond philosophically to difficult people. It is similar to Marcus's exercise, but in it you think of specific people or specific classes of people (e.g., grumpy customers) whom you are likely to encounter. Think of the things they do that are most annoying, or that you find most difficult to bear in other ways. Practice each of the disciplines. The Discipline of Assent, especially the practice of Neutral Description, will help you to withdraw extraneous judgment of the situation and to see it objectively. Exercising the Discipline of Desire will help you to realize that their behavior cannot injure you, because it cannot affect your freedom of moral choice. The Discipline of Impulse guides your actions toward compassion, forbearance, gentleness, and justice (as explained later in this chapter). Imagine the situation and your response as vividly as you can, since this will help you to apply the same techniques when the situation, or one like it, actually occurs.

CRITERION I, THIRD STANDARD: FRIENDS

Like the Epicureans and other ancient philosophers, the Stoics valued true friendship, which is based on a common commitment that the good resides in virtue, not in the accidents of fate. Under these conditions friendship is deeply rooted and secure. The Neoplatonist Hierocles, a younger contemporary of Hypatia, wrote:

> *Friendship is the most excellent virtue*
> *and outshines all the rest in perfection.*
> *For the end of all the virtues is friendship,*
> *and their principle is piety.*[175]

He was commenting on these *Pythagorean Golden Verses*, which explain how we should choose our friends and treat them:

> *Him that is first in virtue make thy friend,*
> *And with observance his kind speech attend;*
> *Nor (to thy power) for slight faults cast him by;*
> *For power is neighbor to necessity.*[176]

The first verse means that we should choose friends of outstanding moral character. The second says that friends should listen to the advice of their true friends (which comes in the form of "kind speech"), for they agree in their moral purpose. Furthermore, friends should be tolerant of their friends' minor failings, for they are confident of each other's fundamental character, which is all that really matters. According to Hierocles, "power is neighbor to necessity" means that necessity proves that we are able to do more than we think we can do, and so we should bear as much as possible from our true friends and try to help them. He adds that even unjust people should be treated justly, lest we become unjust ourselves, and that human kinship dictates that we show kindness and a degree of affection even to bad people:

> *The Wise hate no person,*
> *but love only the virtuous.*[177]

Review of Friends: Think about your friends. What is the basis of your friendship? There are many possibilities besides a shared philosophy of life and moral purpose, including common interests, regular association, shared work, kinship, mutual aid, and living nearby. How stable is the basis? Could it change, and what would that mean for your friendship? How would you react if they did something you consider wrong? The purpose of this exercise is not to get you to "write off" casual friendships, but to achieve a greater conscious understanding of their basis and to help you appreciate better your true friendships. Record your analysis in your journal.

CRITERION II: WORTH AND JUSTICE

Marcus and Rusticus have turned around and are leaning on their elbows, back against the balcony.

"I think I understand the criterion of altruism," Marcus remarks, "but you said there are three."

"Correct," Rusticus replies. "The second criterion of the Discipline of Impulse is to take account of worth and justice. We philosophers of the Porch may be perfectionists in regard to our own behavior, but we are realists in our expectations of others. We are well aware that non-Stoics might not reject the false and uncertain, that they are generally not indifferent to the indifferent, and that their impulses are undisciplined. Nevertheless, they are part of Nature, and so we must accept them and choose actions according to their relative worth or value. Say to this yourself:

> *Now it is in my power to allow no evil in my soul,*
> *nor desire, nor perturbation,*
> *but looking at things, I see what is their proper nature,*
> *and I use each according to its worth."* [178]

"How do we evaluate the worth of things?" Marcus asks.

"There is a hierarchy of values: intrinsic value, value to other people, and value for a purpose. First, actions should be evaluated according to an intrinsic scale of worth. Highest is their absolute worth—that is, their moral goodness or badness, or their conformity to human nature. Second is their support for the practice of virtue; for example reputation and wealth, while not worthy in themselves, make it easier for the sage to act virtuously. Things may be more or less worthy in this regard. Last are those things that are properly indifferent, but may promote more worthy things under appropriate circumstance."

For an example of absolute worth, consider health. Stoic sages will be *indifferent* to illness but *prefer* health, because it is their natural state. For an example of aiding virtuous action, consider wealth. Stoic philosophers are technically *indifferent* to wealth, since poverty or wealth does not affect their ability to make moral choices, but they *prefer* wealth over poverty, as it gives them greater means to contribute to the public good. An online social network might be an example of something that is worthy under appropriate circumstances, such as organizing a just demonstration or a democratic revolution.

"Second," Rusticus continues, "actions and things may be chosen according to their *perceived worth* by others. That is, the sage may help people to achieve ends that they consider worthwhile, but that the sage knows are indifferent. This might seem to contradict Stoic values, but it is an act of benevolence, and accepts people as they are. It is also a way of becoming more godlike, for it is what gods do. Remember:

You must be well disposed toward them.
And the gods too aid them in all ways, by dreams, by signs,
toward the attainment of their aims." [179]

For example, the ideal Stoic sage is indifferent to imprisonment and torture, because they cannot breach the walls of the inner acropolis (although they prefer the opposites of freedom and no torture for their intrinsic worth). However, most people are not Stoics (that is a fact), and so the sage will prefer to work for other people's freedom from torture and unjust imprisonment. To take a more pleasant example, many people value the Internet for watching movies, playing games, and social networking. Although sages are indifferent to these values, they might work to broaden Internet access because it makes people happier. This is a way of becoming more godlike because most people think the gods will help torture victims and the unjustly imprisoned (unless they have a higher purpose in mind). Will they grant you greater bandwidth? I can't say ...

Back to Rusticus. "Third, you should choose actions according to the worth of the people involved. This is not simply moral worth; for example, you can treat people according to their legal guilt or innocence. Further, you may employ people according to their abilities, characteristics, or fitness to certain purposes. This is another sense of worth: worthiness for a task.

> *It is impossible to create such people as you wish to have,*
> *but it is proper to employ those in existence*
> *for tasks for which they are fitted.*[180]

"In this way too the philosopher imitates Providence or Deity, who allots roles according to worthiness for the sake of the Whole.

"To sum up, action according to reason and the worth of things constitutes the Stoic concept of justice—that is, giving each person what they are due. Therefore:

> *Reason that is right doesn't differ from reason that is just.*"[181]

At first blush it might seem that the Stoics are recommending that we "use" people in a cold and calculating fashion, ignoring their character, but their intent is not so sinister. They are simply saying that we must consent to Destiny and accept that most people are not Stoics, but we must live and work with them anyway for the good of the whole. If you have plumbing problems, you should employ a reliable plumber. If you have legal matters to take care of, you should hire an honest lawyer (please! no jokes!). A Stoic sage who knows nothing of plumbing or the law will do you no good in these circumstances.

On a more public level, there may be followers of religions or advocates of political positions with which we have profound—even moral—disagreements. Nevertheless, it is sometimes *worthwhile* to make common cause with them for the greater good. Often below our differences we can find a core of common concerns, goals toward which we can work together.

Evaluating Worth: Acting according to worth (just action) is a criterion for every action, and so philosophers of the Porch have to get used to evaluating possible actions quickly. The best way to acquire this skill is to apply it when there is time for a more conscious evaluation of your choices; then it will become habitual. It is especially valuable to apply this criterion to your long-term or regular choices, such as your career, leisure activities, and the like. Evaluate each according to their *intrinsic value, value to other people,* and *value for a purpose*. Does this evaluation incline you to act differently in the future? Record your conclusions in your journal.

CRITERION III: RESERVATION

Marcus and Rusticus have strolled through the palace to a balcony on the other side, which overlooks a terrace with a magnificent temple of Apollo and its adjoining library. After admiring it silently for a few minutes, Marcus asks, "What is the third criterion of the Discipline of Impulse? You said something about making exceptions for Fate."

"That is correct," Rusticus replies. "We call it *reservation*. Never forget that only the ideal sage has infallible judgment and can act with certainty; as for the rest of us, who are fallible seekers of wisdom, remember what Seneca said:

We go where reason—and not the absolute truth—leads us.[182]

"Therefore we imperfect philosophers must act reasonably, according to probability, taking advice as appropriate. That is, we must think carefully about the situation. If it is clear what to do, then do it; but if it is not clear, then seek help from someone else, keeping justice in mind and acting for the common welfare, which are the first two criteria. This is the way to be contented. Remember:

Whoever follows reason in all things
is both tranquil and active at the same time,
and also cheerful and collected."[183]

"But what of reservation, the exception for Fate?" asks Marcus.

"Although the sage has a firm intention to act for the good, circumstances may prevent the intended outcome. The sage may will it, but Providence must will it as well, and a wise person yields to Providence. Therefore the sage's intention is always *with reservation*, accompanied by an (often implicit) added 'exception,' which says, 'I intend to do X, *if nothing prevents me.*' In effect, it is equivalent to adding 'God (or Providence) being willing.' As a consequence, the sage's action is complete and perfect in each moment, because the intention is to act in a certain way—with a moral purpose—not to achieve an outcome.

> *You must set your life in order by accomplishing your actions one by one;*
> *and if each of them achieves its completion, insofar as is possible,*
> *then that is enough for you.*
> *What is more, no one can prevent you from achieving its completion."*[184]

This may seem like an odd sort of fatalism or self-delusion, like tripping or fumbling something and then saying, "I meant to do that!" But it is just the Discipline of Desire, which is fundamentally the recognition of what is in your power and what is not. What is in your power is to act in the present moment to achieve your moral purpose in the best way, as determined by your own thinking and the advice of trusted others. If you do this, then you have done all that you can do, and you should be content in that knowledge, remembering that the final outcome is out of your control. Your action is complete and successful in this moment, even if the later results were not what you hoped.

Rusticus continues. "Thus the sage concentrates on each moment as it comes and takes satisfaction in it:

> *Take pleasure and comfort in one thing,*
> *in passing from one social act to another social act,*
> *thinking of God.*[185]

"That is, the sage acts with the best intention, but desires that the divine will be done, which is the Discipline of Desire. Remember:

> *The sage desires what Destiny dictates."*

"That is a very neat idea," Marcus remarks, "but I don't think it makes sense. You can't mean that I should desire what has already happened, because desire is directed to the future. And how can I desire beforehand what is destined to happen when I don't know the future?" He gestures toward the temple below. "Even the oracles of Apollo are obscure and subject to interpretation. This is a peculiar sort of desire!"

"You are correct," Rusticus answers. "We cannot desire *specifically* what will happen, because we don't know the future. What we can do is to desire *in general* that the divine will be done, that the gods have us in their care. It's really a matter of attitude. You can torment yourself with grief over the accidents of Fate and what might have been, or you can serenely and optimistically assume that Providence has arranged things for the best for the world, and perhaps for you. Then you can work to make it so, assisting the gods to achieve the best future as you understand it."

"And how can I do that?" Marcus asks. "Consult the soothsayers?"

"Certainly, you can pray to the gods for guidance, and divination can help discern the currents of universal Nature, but we Stoics rely most heavily on reason. Think it through, consult with advisers you trust, then act with reservation."

"And if the action fails?"

"It cannot fail. If you have willed what is appropriate and acted on it, then you have been successful, in spite of the outcome. In effect, if an action does not turn out as hoped, then you switch from the Discipline of Impulse to the Discipline of Desire, adjusting your desire to what is willed by Nature—that is, by consenting to Destiny."

Marcus shakes his head. "I cannot accept this attitude of surrender, of resignation and acquiescence in whatever occurs. This is not the courage of a Caesar!"

"It is not surrender, but rather an attitude of continual adaptation to circumstances with skill and whole-hearted devotion to right action. Consent to Destiny is not easy, but the practices of the Porch will give you the strength. As you know, Premeditating Misfortune may help you to prepare for what may go wrong, and so to meet it with greater peace and preparation."

For example, you may be working for the election of a political leader in support of the moral purpose of greater social justice (a *worthy* cause, in the sense of Criterion II). If in each moment you make the best choices that you can, following reason, then you have done all that you can do. What happens if your candidate loses? The cause might have been chance, cheating on the other side, inadequate organization on your own, the will of the gods, or all of the above. Regardless, you have no choice but to accept what Destiny dictates and move on to your next action. (Challenge the results? Work for election reform? Begin organizing for the next election?) In the third degree of wisdom you will learn techniques that will help you to discern the direction of Providence.

As the sun sets, Marcus and Rusticus watch priests, attendants, and worshippers gathering at the altar that stands before the temple of Apollo. "I think I see your point," Marcus muses, "but what should we do when we're defeated or some disaster happens?"

"The sage accepts what Fate decrees," Rusticus replies, "and acts appropriately in the next moment. An obstacle may arise, but:

> *By cheerful acceptance of the hindrance*
> *and by being content to adopt that alternative,*
> *another opportunity of action is immediately put before you*
> *in place of what was prevented,*
> *and one that will fit in the whole of which we are speaking.*[186]

In other words, the Stoic goes to "Plan B." Things might not have worked out as we hoped, but we must play the hand we are dealt. Through ignorance, chance, or Nature, this is what has happened. What's the best way forward? We've all heard stories of people who have suffered terrible illness, injuries, or other disasters, but have turned these misfortunes to the benefit of themselves and other people. It's difficult, which is why we have to practice on the lesser misfortunes so that we're prepared for the greater ones. Let's listen in again to Rusticus.

"The sage turns every such occurrence to advantage:

> *The mind converts and changes every obstacle to its activity*
> *into an aid,*
> *so that obstacles in our path only make it easier.*[187]

"It's a matter of attitude. When disaster strikes, you can think of it as punishment, and so it will be. Or you can think of it as a mysterious gift, an opportunity to learn and grow, and a challenge, uniquely part of your personal destiny. Think: What good can I make of this?"

"That takes courage," Marcus remarks.

Rusticus points toward the raging altar fire. "The sage's intention is like an all-consuming fire. You know what happened when Rome burned: for six days the fire consumed everything in its path; obstacles became its fuel and made it stronger. Don't forget:

> *That which rules within us*
> *makes material for itself out of what opposes it,*
> *as fire lays hold of what falls into it.*
> *A little flame might have been extinguished,*
> *but the blazing flame instantly assimilates what is cast on it,*
> *and rises higher by means of this very material.*[188]

"You too, be a blazing flame, not a little one. Think of Nature, who converts everything to her own will; the sage does the same, in this way becoming more godlike, for we have received this power from the gods.

> *As universal Nature molds to her purpose*
> *whatever interference or opposition she meets,*
> *and gives it its predestined place and makes it a part of herself,*
> *so also can the rational animal convert every hindrance*
> *into its own instrument and use it to further its purpose."*[189]

"Do you mean," Marcus asks, "that I should doggedly pursue my goal until I succeed?"

"Of course not," Rusticus replies. "Your failure may be the gods' way of telling you that you have the wrong goal. You must try to perceive the good at which Providence is aimed, think your actions through, and consult those whom you trust, for you should be willing to be convinced by others and to change your intention. You are not giving in, but exercising your freedom of choice. A trap for us philosophers is to imagine we're wiser than we are, and arrogantly cling to our cherished ideas. Be willing to change.

> *Remember that to change your mind*
> *and to follow whoever corrects your error*
> *is not a surrender of freedom.*
> *Your action follows your own judgment and understanding*
> *and keeps the course your mind has set.*[190]

"Epictetus says it is like playing a dice game well.[191] You cannot control the roll of the dice that Fate has allotted you, but you can use your reason to make the best of it, while awaiting the next roll."

This is perhaps a good place to mention Epictetus's most famous maxim:

Bear and forbear.[192]

This is the usual English translation; a more literal translation might be "hold up and hold back." That is, you should endure what is inevitable and abstain from that which is not prescribed by Stoic ethics. Epictetus said that remembering these two words is a good way of avoiding wrongdoing and living a peaceful life. It is a good way of governing your actions and reactions.

> *Examination of Conscience*: This exercise was described briefly in chapter 2 and can be applied to any system of philosophical practice. Here you apply it to assessing your progress in putting Stoic principles into practice in your life. Do the exercise at least in the evening before you go to sleep, but if possible also during other breaks in the day, such as when you first awake or at lunchtime. Go over your actions and reactions, and classify each as (1) an error you made, (2) some virtuous action you missed, or (3) some success in applying the disciplines. Congratulate yourself on your progress and, without being too hard on yourself, think about how you can do better in the future.

Nature's Sympathy

We find Marcus and Rusticus in the temple garden below the palace, strolling among the trees under a clear and starry sky.

"Listen to the chorus of cicadas!" Marcus exclaims. "They will awaken the sleepers!"

"Indeed they will," Rusticus muses. "Their song celebrates their rebirth after a long time underground. Now they are united in love. They hymn Apollo and the Muses and fly in ecstasy to heaven. They show us the way."

"These pious thoughts seem far removed from the Discipline of Impulse," Marcus remarks.

"Not at all. By living in accordance with their own nature, they are obeying Mother Nature; their very life is a hymn and prayer. So too the true philosopher's."

"What do you mean?"

"The Discipline of Impulse teaches us that injustice is impiety, for universal Nature has made humans for one another and to help each other according to worth. To do otherwise is impiety to Mother Nature, the most venerable of deities. Likewise, lying is impiety to this goddess, for Nature is everything that is and their cause, and so she is named Truth. Even ignorance is impiety, for the ignorant act against Truth and neglect the power of distinguishing truth from falsehood, a gift from Dame Nature. Further, one who seeks pleasure and avoids pain is impious, for they will find fault with the goddess, accusing her of distributing these things unfairly, although pleasure and pain are indifferent. And so on, for whoever disobeys Nature and human nature is impious." [193]

Marcus looks up into the trees. "The cicadas have returned after many years. Has Apollo called these singers up from the underworld?"

"Learn this law of Nature," Rusticus replies. "All things that share in a common element have an affinity for their own kind.[194] This is the case even for inanimate nature, for earth clings to earth and water to water. It extends to non-rational animals, such as swarms of bees, herds of cattle, and flocks of birds, which hang together, behave like one super-organism, to their mutual benefit. So also we rational beings associate in families, friendships, and communities, although we also have the freedom to separate from each other. What is more, higher beings have an even greater affinity for one another, though apparently separated.

All that shares in universal intelligent Nature
has a strong affinity for what is akin.
For the measure of its superiority to all other things
is the measure of its readiness to blend
and coalesce with that which is akin to it.[195]

"This is the case even among the celestial deities, such as the stars, whose affinity and coordinated movement we should emulate:

But in the things that are still superior,
a sort of unity in separation even exists,
as in the stars.
Thus the ascent to the higher degree

is able to effect a sympathetic connection
even among separated things.[196]

"Thus in our ascent toward divinity we should strive for this hidden unity in separation, this magical sympathy connecting all things in Nature."

Marcus shakes his head. "You have given me much to think about today."

"So that you don't miss the forest for the trees, remember Epictetus's summary of our philosophy:

You must discover [1] the art of assent,
[2] and with respect to impulses pay good heed that they are
subject to reservation, to social interests, and to worth.
[3] And you must abstain from inordinate desire,
and show no aversion to things not in your control.[197]

"Here you have [1] the Discipline of Assent, which governs judgment; [2] the Discipline of Impulse, with its three criteria regarding the reservation for Fate, altruism, and worth (for justice); and finally [3] the Discipline of Desire, with its indifference to indifferent things and its acceptance of Destiny."

The four "cardinal virtues" or "excellences" of classical Greek philosophy are truth (practical wisdom), moderation, justice, and fortitude.[198] The first three correspond, respectively, to the Disciplines of Assent, Desire, and Impulse. The fourth excellence, fortitude, represents the vigilance required to apply the disciplines throughout our lives.

Rusticus claps Marcus around his shoulders. "You are tired, my son; I think that is enough for today. Be strong and practice these disciplines; ask yourself:

Does the light of the lamp shine without losing its radiance
until it is extinguished?
Shall the truth and justice and moderation that is in me be extinguished?"[199]

If you have practiced the philosophy of the Porch diligently, then you are prepared for "the ascent to the higher degree," which you will learn in the Grove. Press on!

PART IV

THE THIRD DEGREE
OF WISDOM

CHAPTER EIGHT

THE MACROCOSM

GOALS OF THE THIRD DEGREE

You have come now to the third degree of wisdom, that taught by Hypatia and other Neo-platonic philosophers. Having become more moderate and sensible in your desires in the secluded Garden, and more tranquil and benevolent in the busier Porch, you are prepared to enter the Grove, where you will learn a higher order of spiritual practice. As you will see, each of these degrees focuses on one of the three parts into which Plato divided the soul (although, of course, each philosophy addresses all three parts). The Garden focuses on the appetites or desiring part of the soul (the "belly"); the Porch focuses on the will, impulse, and feeling (the "heart"); and we will see that the Grove focuses on the mind (the "head"). Each degree of wisdom is directed also toward its own characteristic form of joyous tranquility: the Epicurean's lack of disturbance (Greek, *ataraxia*), the Stoic's freedom from suffering (Greek, *apatheia*), and the Neoplatonist's mental stillness (Greek, *hêsychia*) leading to spiritual enlightenment.

As the practices of the Porch build on those of the Garden, so also the Grove builds on the Porch, and Stoic ethics are taken for granted by Neoplatonists. This does not mean that you can forget the first two degrees. If you are like me, you cannot devote all your time to spiritual pursuits; you have a day job and other obligations. The practices of the Garden and the Porch will help you to live your everyday, active life in peace and happiness, so that you have a firm emotional and spiritual foundation for the more advanced practices of the Third Degree.

If you have not succeeded yet in making the Garden and the Porch your way of life, then come into the Grove anyway so you can see where you are headed. Remember, philosophy—the love and desire for wisdom—is a process, not an achievement, and the image of the ideal Sage leads us and draws us onward. I know that you are anxious to learn the advanced spiritual practices of Hypatia, and you probably haven't spent the time to make the first two degrees habitual, to reprogram your mind. That is natural, but don't forget that to succeed in the more advanced practices you will need to acquire the necessary skills (remember, magic is the art of changing consciousness at will).

The philosophers of the Garden and the Porch talk of God, the gods, Providence, Destiny, Universal Reason, and so forth, but their focus is on living well in *this* world. The philosophers of the Grove also teach a way of living on Earth, but they do this by paying much greater attention to the spiritual dimensions of reality. Sometimes this is called the "second voyage" of Socrates in search of wisdom after he failed to find it in the naturalistic philosophies of his "first voyage." [200] This will be our quest too. While it is often the voyage of the second half of life, it need not be so.

Before embarking, it will be helpful to recall the philosophers of the Grove from whom we'll be learning; we already met them in chapter 3, where you'll also find a timeline. Plato (fourth century BCE) is of course central, but he was working in the tradition of Pythagoras (sixth century BCE) and was a student of Socrates (fifth century BCE). For comparison, Epicurus was born a few years after Plato's death and was a contemporary of Zeno the Stoic. Plotinus (third century CE) took Platonic philosophy in a new direction, which modern scholars call Neoplatonism. Plotinus is a key source for us, because contemporaries of Hypatia, who was murdered in 415 CE, tell us she "taught the philosophy of Plato and Plotinus." Other sources are the surviving works of her disciple Synesius (c.373–c.414) and the Neoplatonist Hierocles of Alexandria (fl. 400–450 CE), a younger contemporary of Hypatia.

Neoplatonic spiritual practices are based on a systematic understanding of the cosmos, including psychological and spiritual phenomena as well as physical phenomena. Therefore, an overview of this system is a prerequisite to understanding the practices. In fact, we are proceeding through the stages of the ancient mysteries (such as the Eleusinian and Bacchic Mysteries). As I will explain in more detail later, the first stage is *purification*, which is accomplished by progress through the first two degrees of wisdom, which teach virtue through *philosophy*. The second stage is *instruction*, which explains the psychospiritual world through *theology*; it is the topic of this chapter and the next. The third stage is *revelation* through the practices of *theurgy* ("god work"), the advanced spiritual practices of

Neoplatonism; it is the topic of the last three chapters. However, as in the Mysteries, these practices depend on the spiritual transformations of the first two stages.

In this chapter you will learn about the four planes of reality charted by ancient Platonists, but I will explain them out of order, because that is the easiest way to understand them. First, we'll look briefly at the World Body, which is the familiar physical universe, before turning to the World Mind, which is central to Platonic theology. As Plato did, we will approach it first from the perspective of mathematical forms, such as triangles and circles, and then look at the Platonic Forms or Ideas more generally. This will help you understand the difference between Becoming in the World Body and Being in the World Mind. After considering the reality of such Platonic ideas as Truth, Beauty, and Justice, we will turn to the World Soul, which connects the Mind and Body. It is crucial for theurgical practice, for it is the bridge connecting the everyday world to the realm of the gods. Therefore, you'll also learn a little about Nature, Wisdom, and mediating spirits as helpers on the path. Finally we come to The Inexpressible One, the first principle of the Platonic system, and discuss the ways in which it is similar and dissimilar to "God." Having completed this tour through the Platonic cosmos, I will teach you several visualization exercises that will help you to imprint this map of reality on your mind, which will be valuable as you learn to navigate the higher spiritual realms.

I will present the Platonic system first from the perspective of Pagan polytheism, which is the historical and cultural context in which it developed. This will be familiar if you are Pagan or Wiccan, but may seem a little unusual if you are not. Nevertheless, it's not hard to understand, and in the next chapter I will explain how the Neoplatonic worldview is compatible with monotheistic beliefs (as in Judaism, Christianity, and Islam) and indeed with nontheistic beliefs. With appropriate translations between terminologies, all these systems are describing fundamentally similar psychospiritual structures. But we'll come to that later.

The World Body

We can imagine Hypatia in one of her public lectures.[201] On benches sit several dozens of eager listeners, including her private students, who have the best seats. Hypatia arrives, dressed in the simple but dignified white woolen robe of a philosopher. She ascends the dais, sits in a chair, and, with little ado, begins her exposition of the Neoplatonic worldview. "The cosmos can be understood in terms of four *levels* or *planes of reality*.[202] The lowest level is the one we are ordinarily involved with: the material plane of physical objects and processes, the sort of things that we can experience with our senses. This is our everyday world of matter and energy. In a sense this material world is hard to understand, because everything is in a state of change, as Heraclitus pointed out when he said, 'You cannot step in the same river twice.' Nothing stays the same; everything is coming to be and passing away. Nevertheless, the change is not totally chaotic, because it is obvious there are patterns. Heraclitus also said, 'All things come into being in accordance with the Logos.' Things of the same or of related kinds change in similar ways, and Nature exhibits orderly processes."

Pythagoras is supposed to have coined the word *cosmos* to refer to the well-ordered universe. It refers to orderliness and harmony, and is also the root of the word *cosmetics*! It is often translated "world," but we must understand that it includes everything, not just the physical world. That is, it includes not only the physical universe charted by cosmologists and other astronomers, but also the worlds of the human body and mind, and of whatever other things we think exist in the universe. (I use *cosmos*, *world*, and *universe* interchangeably.)

As we will see, ancient philosophers drew an analogy between the *macrocosm* ("big cosmos") of the universe and the *microcosm* ("little cosmos") of the individual person, taken as a whole (that is, including mind, soul, spirit, etc., as well as body). This view is expressed in the well-known Hermetic saying, "As above, so below; as within, so without." Since we have some intimate acquaintance and understanding of ourselves (the microcosm), we can transfer this knowledge and use it as a basis for understanding the macrocosm.

According to this analogy, the physical world corresponds to the human body; both are organized physical objects with systematic physical processes. As a consequence, in Neoplatonic philosophy physical reality may be termed the "Cosmic Body," "World Body," or "Universal Body"—that is, the physical body of the universe. The World Body is the lowest level in the Neoplatonic map of reality. Our next stop is the realm of the gods.

THE WORLD MIND

Some of the students scratch notes on their wax tablets, while Hypatia continues: "A higher level of the cosmos is the Cosmic Mind, which is a realm of Ideas or Forms. The easiest way to understand them is by thinking about geometrical objects, such as triangles, squares, and pentagons. This is why Plato posted 'Let no non-geometer enter' over the entry of the Academy: an understanding of geometry is a prerequisite to spiritual progress. Let me explain.

"We have a clear and simple idea of a perfect equilateral triangle, but no physical triangle can be perfect. A perfect equilateral triangle has all its sides of exactly the same length, but no triangle that we draw, carve, or construct can be so exact; there will always be errors.

"Nevertheless, in a very important sense, a geometrically perfect equilateral triangle is real. We can prove things about the equilateral triangle, such as that all its angles are equal, and, less obviously, that all triangles' angles add to two right angles (180 degrees). We can prove things about other triangles as well. An example is the famous Pythagorean theorem, which says that in a right triangle the square on the hypotenuse (the diagonal side) is equal to the sum of the squares on the other two sides."

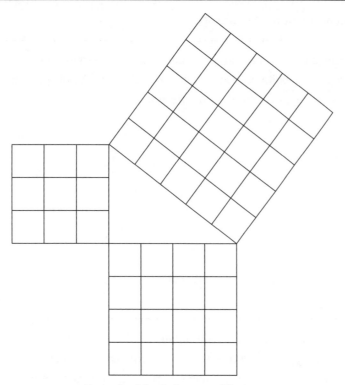

Example of the Pythagorean Theorem

In our times Platonism is still the working philosophy of mathematics, because mathematicians are continually confronted with the fact that mathematical objects have a reality independent of human wishes or desires; the existence of objects and the relationships among them are possible or impossible, true or false, independent of people's subjective beliefs and desires. Thus all mathematicians, no matter what their cultural background or beliefs, come to the same mathematical truths. For example, the Pythagorean theorem was discovered by many cultures before Pythagoras lived (but he might have been the first to prove it). All mathematicians are investigating the same nonmaterial but objective reality, the same world of abstract *forms*.

Some readers may object that there are disagreements about the philosophy of mathematics, and that is true. You may know that there are non-Euclidean geometries (essentially geometries of curved space) in which a triangle's angles might not sum to 180 degrees. In the Platonic realm of modern mathematics, any non-contradictory mathematical object exists, and that object has objective relations to other mathematical objects.[203] Later, when we have explored further the realm of Ideas and Forms, I will say a little more about the psychospiritual reality of mathematical objects.

We can imagine Hypatia pausing in her presentation to introduce a simple exercise. She props up a white board with a black equilateral triangle painted onto it (see the figure below) and explains the exercise as follows.

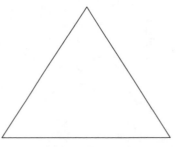

Equilateral Triangle

Triangle Contemplation: Look at the image of the equilateral triangle for a few moments. As you will discover soon, it is only an imperfect sensible image or representation of the ideal Equilateral Triangle. Now close your eyes, but keep the image of the triangle before your mind's eye. If it is not too clear—that is okay, because we are not interested in the sensory image; we are interested in the idea behind it. So visualize the perfect Equilateral Triangle, with its three sides perfectly straight and of exactly the same length.

Triangle Contemplation (continued): Notice this astonishing fact: although the three sides are exactly the same length, they have no specific length. Your mental image has no size! Nevertheless, if you wish, you can make it smaller or larger, but still with no specific size. Isn't that peculiar when you think about it? You can discover facts about the Equilateral Triangle. For example, in your mind rotate the triangle one-third turn, so that one of the other points is upmost. Since all three lines are the same length, you know this rotated triangle must coincide with the original one. And you can see that its three angles must be identical, since they can be superimposed. Move the top point up a little, and you will see that the two sides must get longer than the base, but stay the same length as each other. Move the point down, and the opposite happens. What happens to the lengths of the sides if you move the top point horizontally to the left or right?

Make another equilateral triangle with a side exactly half as long as the original. You can see that you can fit exactly four such smaller triangles in the original one. This is enough of this exercise for now; we will draw some conclusions. Notice that your mental triangle is not in space, because it has no size. Indeed, it has no place. Where is it? Hovering two inches in front of your nose? Between your ears? So this triangle is not a physical object. Nevertheless it does exist in time, since you can change it. Therefore, you are not directly experiencing the ideal Equilateral Triangle in the world of Forms. Rather, you are experiencing a mutable projection of it into your own time-bound soul. Nevertheless, this exercise demonstrates how you can begin to ascend above the level of sensible forms and can begin to contemplate and investigate the realm of ideal Forms. If you had some trouble with visualizing the triangles and manipulating them, don't worry; you will get better with practice. Of course you can use any geometric forms; there's nothing special about equilateral triangles.

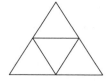

Bisected Equilateral Triangle

THE PLATONIC FORMS

Platonists look at all "universals" (general terms) and concepts the same way as mathematical ideas. That is, just as there is an ideal-form Equilateral Triangle, of which all physical equilateral triangles are more or less accurate copies, so also there is an ideal substance Gold, and chemists and physicists can tell you many of its properties, such as atomic weight, density, hardness, and electrical conductivity; but any actual sample of gold will contain impurities. So also for the ideal-form Horse, of which all physical horses are more or less accurate copies. Thus biological species can be understood as ideal Forms (but this notion must be modified in the light of modern biology, as I'll explain later).

There is much that can be said about this theory, and philosophers (including Plato) have been debating it since Plato's time. It has a certain commonsense appeal, and that is really all that matters here. For example, if you have never seen a wombat, but I show you a picture of one, there is a good chance you will recognize other wombats. If I show you liquid mercury, you will probably recognize it again. You will have acquaintance and a little knowledge of the forms Wombat and Mercury.

In a sense, just as mathematicians study ideal triangles, but may use physical diagrams of triangles to help them understand ideal triangles, so other scientists study ideal species, substances, processes, etc., by means of specimens, samples, and observations in the field and in the laboratory.

Since ancient philosophy was a way of life, Socrates, Plato, and their successors were especially interested in applying their analysis of ideal Forms to ethical ideas. Is there an ideal Form of Justice, to which all just acts are only approximations? Are there ideal Forms of Courage, Truth, Beauty, Piety, and Wisdom? Is there an ideal Form of the Good? These are the sorts of questions addressed in Plato's dialogues.

If there are such ideal Forms, then can a philosopher explore the nature and relation of ethical concepts the same way a mathematician investigates mathematical concepts? Might one discover ethical universals, independent of historical time and culture, in this way? This has been the goal of Platonists and other idealist philosophers through the ages.

Before proceeding it will be worthwhile to take a brief excursion through etymology, which will help you to understand the Neoplatonic understanding of these "forms" or "ideas." The Greek word *idea*, from which get our word, is related to a verb meaning "to see." Thus *idea* originally meant the visual appearance of something, especially its *shape* or *form*, that by which it might be recognized. Already before Plato, the meaning of *idea* had been extended to include any property or characteristic of something, even a symptom. It was further extended to refer to the class, kind, or species of things, and to the power that gives anything its potential, its potency. All of these meanings are implicit in the word *idea* (and its Latin translation, *forma*) when used by Plato and his successors.[204]

Often, as is customary, I will capitalize *Idea* and *Form* when I mean them in the Platonic sense, or somewhat redundantly I will write "ideal Form" to emphasize that I do not mean "form" in the ordinary sense. Nevertheless, as you have seen, the ordinary meaning is part of the Platonic meaning. I will also capitalize the names of particular ideal Forms, such as Equilateral Triangle, Horse, Gold, and Justice.

BEING AND BECOMING

Hypatia continues her explanation of the Forms. "An important difference between the ideal realm and the material (or sensible) world, according to Platonism, is that the Ideas are eternal and unchanging, while things in the physical world are always changing, and nothing lasts forever. The Equilateral Triangle is a good example. First, the mathematical object is unchanging, whereas any particular physical triangle that we make will come into being at some point in time (when we make it) and eventually decay (for it is made out of matter). In the meantime, it will be changing, perhaps slowly and imperceptibly, perhaps more rapidly. Second, and more importantly, the ideal Equilateral Triangle is eternal, not so much in the sense that it will last forever, but in the sense that it is out of time altogether; that is, the concept of time does not apply to it, since it is not a thing in the physical world, where time exists. It is, we say, *atemporal*—that is, timeless.

"The ideal realm is called the realm of Being (where things either are or are not) in contrast to the material world, which is called the realm of Becoming (where everything is in the process of becoming something that it was not). Therefore the individual Ideas may be called *Beings*.

"Since the Ideas exist independently of us, we can think of them existing in some place separate from individual human minds. Plotinus says they are *there* or *beyond*, not *here*, but where is *there*? Where can we find the ideal Equilateral Triangle? In a sense this universe of independently existing Ideas constitutes a 'Cosmic Mind.' Mind here is taken to be equivalent to its contents: its ideas and the relations among them. There is no thinking Mind separate from the Ideas it thinks, but we cannot assume that the Cosmic Mind is conscious in the sense that our minds are conscious.

"Essential to Platonic philosophy is the primacy of the ideal Forms. For example, the ideal Equilateral Triangle is the *real* equilateral triangle; individual physical equilateral triangles are imperfect images or reflections of that ideal reality. Therefore, generalizing, the Ideas are considered the ultimate causes of physical things and processes, which are their effects. Furthermore, to explain something, we Platonists look to the Form in which it participates (that is, of which it is an image). If you want to understand why a particular triangle has the (approximate) properties it does, then study the mathematical Triangle that it approximates. If you want to understand why a horse is eating hay, then study the ideal Horse. To understand a just act, study Justice."

This is still very much the perspective of science, at least in its more mathematical forms. Scientists have discovered various mathematical laws that describe how objects behave. If they want to explain why something happens in the physical world, they appeal to these laws by way of explanation. For example, Newton's laws explain why a cannon ball travels in an (approximately) parabolic arc. Although our knowledge and understanding of the laws of physics change as science progresses, the laws themselves (even if we do not understand them perfectly) are eternal. These unchanging laws describe the Form of the processes of change in the material world. Contemporary science is very Platonic—indeed, Pythagorean.

"Since the Ideas are causes," Hypatia continues, "we cannot think of them as purely passive; there is an active aspect to them too. Plotinus describes the Ideas as *Thoughts*, which means both timeless acts of thinking and the things thought about."

Aedesia, who is one of Hypatia's Pagan students and wears the simple white woolen robe of a philosopher, raises her hand and asks, "What are 'timeless acts of thinking'?" [205]

"They are eternal connections and relations among the Ideas (the Thoughts), such as the timeless relations between the Equilateral Triangle and the Lines that make up its sides. The Cosmic Mind, as the totality of Thoughts, in both senses, is both the object of thought and the subject doing the (timeless) thinking, so at this level, subject and object are two sides of the same reality. Nevertheless it is important to keep in mind that this is not thinking in the everyday sense of that word, but eternal relationships among ideal Forms.

"If you think of the Ideas not only as static Forms, but also as causes and as acts of thought, then you can see that they also have the character of mind. That is, they are individual Minds in the Cosmic Mind. Thus each Thought is a coincidence of subject and object, of Mind and Idea. Plotinus says that each of these Minds is a special form or aspect of the Cosmic Mind. We might describe them as different projections of the totality called the Cosmic Mind, like different shadows of a three-dimensional object. Or, to change similes, as different facets of a multifaceted gem. Since the Ideas are characterized by both causation and cognition, they are in a certain sense alive, and we Platonists attribute power, life, and mind to the Beings populating the Cosmic Mind and to the Cosmic Mind as a whole."

Therefore Pagan Neoplatonists also viewed the traditional gods as archetypal Beings (Minds in the World Mind), for they were considered the causes and explanations of many phenomena in the world. This is reinforced by the belief that the Ideas are, in a timeless sense, alive and thinking. At a somewhat superficial level, ancient Pagans took the gods to be the causes of natural phenomena; for example, Zeus (Jupiter to the Romans) causes thunder and lightning, Poseidon (Neptune) causes earthquakes. But many philosophers (including the Epicureans and Stoics) sought to explain natural phenomena without recourse to the gods. Now we understand them as the result of atmospheric electricity, plate tectonics, and the like. Ancient Pagans also attributed psychological phenomena to the gods. For example, a sudden feeling of sexual attraction might be understood as an effect of Aphrodite (Venus) or Eros (Amor); everyone is familiar with the idea of being shot by Cupid's arrow (Latin *cupido* = desire).

If the gods are Beings in Cosmic Mind, then they are eternal (timeless), which we would expect, but they are also impassive because they are unchanging; that is, they cannot be affected, they are eternally tranquil. We have seen this view of the gods before, with the Epicureans and Stoics. It implies that the gods cannot be swayed by prayer (although, as I will explain later, that does not imply that prayer is useless). The gods are like other cosmic laws (such as the law of gravity), with which we can cooperate, but which must obeyed and cannot be altered. This may contradict your experience; you might say, "I pray to God or Goddess and they hear me; they intervene directly in my life." I don't disagree, but please have patience for a few more pages, and you will learn the Neoplatonic explanation.

Since the Cosmic Mind contains all the Forms that cause and govern the physical processes that create everything in the universe, Neoplatonists often identified the Cosmic Mind with the *Demiurge* (Craftsman), the mythical creator god described in Plato's *Timaeus*. There is a sense in which the Cosmic Mind is a creator, but anthropomorphizing it can be misleading. First, according to Neoplatonic philosophy, the creation of the world does not take place at a particular point in time, for creation is a continual process of emanation from the eternal Cosmic Mind. Second, this creation is not chosen or willed by the Demiurge, but is a necessary and natural consequence of the Cosmic Mind.

TRUTH, BEAUTY, AND JUSTICE

Seated upon her dais, Hypatia was perhaps herself an embodiment of austere and timeless beauty, for in her life she exemplified the perennial Platonic ideals of Truth, Beauty, and Justice. "Among the Ideas in the Cosmic Mind," our imaginary lecture continues, "is ideal Beauty, but the Cosmic Mind as a whole is also called 'Beauty.' This is because philosophers identify beauty with harmonious form, which is supremely exemplified by the Cosmic Mind. For, firstly, the Cosmic Mind is the totality of the ideal Forms, and secondly because each such Form includes all of the rest in itself. Therefore, because each is an 'all-in-all,' the Forms are united into a whole in the most harmonious way possible. This is why Plotinus calls the Cosmic Mind 'Beauty,' and as you know, the Greek word *cosmos* refers to order, harmony, and beauty."

A student named Hierocles raises his hand and asks, "For what sorts of things are there Ideas? It is hard to imagine that there are Platonic Forms of mud and excrement."

Hypatia nods in agreement. "This is one of the questions addressed by Plato that he never resolved. We may accept that there is ideal Truth, Beauty, and Justice, that there are immortal gods in the ideal realm, but what about ideal Evil, ideal Disease, and ideal Decay? This is an important question, but I must leave it for another time."

It is worth mentioning that over the centuries there have been many objections to Plato's theory of Forms and its successors. The "problem of universals," the nature of universal terms, such as "horse," and their relation to the world and our minds, is a perennial problem in philosophy. Fortunately, for the purposes of spiritual practice, we do not need a definitive solution.

Are the Ideas defensible? In the *Sophist*, Plato has the Stranger say that the contest between materialist and idealist explanations of reality is like the mythological battle between the giants and the gods. The giants

> are dragging down all things from heaven and from the unseen to Earth, and
> they literally grasp in their hands rocks and oaks; of these they lay hold, and
> obstinately maintain that only the things that can be touched or handled have
> being or essence, because they define being and body as one, and if anyone

else says something incorporeal is real, they are utterly contemptuous and will not listen to another word.[206]

On the other side, the gods

are cautiously defending themselves from above, out of an unseen world, mightily contending that true essence consists of certain intelligible and incorporeal Forms. The bodies of the materialists, which by them are maintained to be the very truth, they break up into little bits by their arguments, and affirm them to be, not real Being, but generation and becoming.[207]

That is, materialists always mock the notion that there is anything of significance in the world that they can't—metaphorically speaking—lay their hands on. Against them the idealists contend that the impermanent physical objects out of which the materialists build their reality cannot stand up against the timeless, immutable Ideas or Beings that govern the Platonic cosmos. The empirical universe of the materialists is built on a foundation of forms, ideas, and consciousness.

THE WORLD SOUL

If the World Mind and the Ideas it contains are eternal—outside of time—organized in an immutable structure, a timeless connection of Idea to Idea, then there cannot be much *thinking* taking place, for thinking, as we ordinarily understand it, is a process taking place within time. Or to use the scientific analogy, the World Mind is like a static system of equations. Although these equations, like Newton's laws of motion, may describe how objects move, the equations themselves are not changing at all. How does a static description of motion get translated into actual motion? Furthermore, how can a single law of motion govern many moving objects?

We can listen in, as Hypatia continues her explanation. "Our world is manifestly not a world of static, eternal Ideas. It is in flux and ever changing, but in an orderly way; it is a living organism, growing, developing, and evolving. What connects the timeless Being of the Cosmic Mind to the flux of Becoming we see around us in the Cosmic Body?" She pauses and scans her audience. "It is the Cosmic Soul. For just as any living thing has a soul, which is the principle of orderly motion that governs its body in accordance with its proper Form, so the cosmos in its entirely has a Soul that includes the souls of everything inside it. The timeless form Horse is an abstraction, an Idea, but each living horse has a soul, which is an orderly and organized system of processes that govern, in accordance with the timeless Form of its species, the matter and energy that constitute the individual horse's body. Thus the Cosmic Soul connects the unity of the ideal Horse to the plurality of individual horses."

"But wait," you might object, "modern biology has shown that biological species, such as the horse, are not timeless ideal Forms; they are populations of interbreeding individuals, which evolve slowly through time." That is correct. Nevertheless, it makes scientific sense to talk about horse physiology, horse anatomy, horse diet, horse behavior, the horse genome, and so forth. That is, the horse species (say, *Equus ferus*, to be precise) is a well-defined, stable scientific concept and subject of scientific investigation. Certainly, species evolve, but biological evolution itself is a natural process, subject to mathematical laws, and thus a manifestation in time and space of an ideal Form.

To return to the Cosmic Soul, consider a more contemporary example: you may have a DVD with the latest video game on it, but it is a coded, static description of the program, which includes descriptions of how the people, species of animals, and kinds of objects behave; this is analogous to the Cosmic Mind. You need a computer to read the disk, interpret the program code, and enact the static description into dynamic behavior in time, which is analogous to the Cosmic Soul. In particular, the executing computer creates in its memory instances of the people, animals, and other objects that behave in accordance with the descriptions of their kinds. With the aid of the computer, the images of individual things appear on the screen and interact with you; you see them with your eyes, hear them with your ears, and interact with them using your hands and input devices.

Hypatia continues. "The Cosmic Soul is the enactment of the Ideas in time and space. This enactment takes place on the stage of the Cosmic Body—that is, the plane of material reality. Thus, the Cosmic Soul creates Becoming from the Being of the Cosmic Mind. It is the plane between the planes of the Cosmic Mind and the Cosmic Body, a mediator or middle principle joining the other two together. It therefore has intermediate properties, for while the Cosmic Mind is eternal (timeless) and unchanging, and everything in the Cosmic Body is mortal (of finite duration) and changing, the Cosmic Soul combines one characteristic of each, for it is eternal (that is, unending) but changing. Likewise, the Cosmic Soul mediates between the non-spatiality (or spacelessness) of the Ideas and spatiality (or existence in space) of physical things by multiplying each Form into a multitude of individual souls, which are instances of the Form governing physical processes in time and space. The Cosmic Soul joins The One and the Many."

Hypatia moves on to a deeper level of inquiry. "If we think carefully, we see that each level of reality has three aspects, which we call *Abiding, Proceeding*, and *Returning* (turning backward). This is the *Triadic Principle*, and many of the threes in Platonic philosophy are a consequence of it. (This might seem to be an inessential technical detail, but I mention it for the sake of my more advanced students, for it helps us understand Platonic spiritual practices. Those who intend to navigate the nonmaterial realms need to know their way around.) According to this principle, the Cosmic Mind *abides* in itself as an eternal system of Ideas. However, it also *proceeds* out from itself and, just as *we* utter *our* ideas, it creates a temporal expression of itself, thus generating the Cosmic Soul, which enacts the Ideas in time. However, the Cosmic Soul also *turns back*, looking toward the Cosmic Mind, 'contemplating' the Ideas, which means that the Cosmic Soul acts in accordance with these ideal Forms. Thus the Cosmic Mind simultaneously abides in itself, while proceeding outward to produce the Cosmic Soul, which simultaneously turns back toward the Cosmic Mind."

In more modern terms, the procession of the World Mind creates the possibility of change (the unprogrammed computer, as we might say), and the looking back of the World Soul to the Forms in the World Mind (the program) makes change orderly and lawlike.

Nature, Wisdom, and Daimons

"The Triadic Principle applies at each level," Hypatia continues, "and so the Cosmic Soul in its turn abides in itself, but also produces the material world, the Cosmic Body, which in its turn looks back toward the Cosmic Soul to get its guidance.

"According to Plotinus, the Cosmic Soul 'orders, administers, and governs' processes in the material world.[208] Since these processes are self-organizing, living, and evolving, the Cosmic Soul is the generative and vivifying principle of the universe. In particular, the Universal Soul is the origin of all orderly motion in the universe, and hence of all life.

"Plotinus calls the Cosmic Soul 'the final goddess' because everything below her is material reality, which she produces.[209] She stands at the gateway between the realm of the gods (the Cosmic Mind or Empyrean) and our world. And she has a name, for according to Plotinus, Nature (*Physis* in Greek, *Natura* in Latin) is the part of the Cosmic Soul that is nearest to material reality, lowest on the plane of the Cosmic Soul. But highest on this plane—that is, the highest part of the Cosmic Soul, in direct contact with the Cosmic Mind—is Wisdom (*Sophia, Sapientia*).[210] Thus the goddess of Nature and the goddess of Wisdom stand as guardians at the extremities of the Cosmic Soul.

"The Cosmic Soul as a whole is a temporal unfolding of the Cosmic Mind, and thus an image of it. Therefore Plato defined time as 'the ensouled image of eternity.'[211] Furthermore, each individual Idea or Being (which, you will recall, is a sort of life and mind) has images in the Cosmic Soul, which are individual souls."

This remark will be easier to understand if you know that the word *soul* (*psyche* in Greek, *anima* in Latin) is used in ancient philosophy to refer to the animating force of anything that is self-moving. And so, in this sense, plants have souls.

Our teacher continues. "The Ideas in the Cosmic Mind emanate, form, and inform souls in the Cosmic Soul, which in turn animate and govern individual bodies in the Cosmic Body. Thus each living thing is in a lineage, descending through the Cosmic Soul from a Being in the Cosmic Mind.

"There are souls other than those governing plants and animals (including humans). As a class they are called *daimons*, by which I mean living beings lower than the gods and in some way less corporeal than ordinary plants and animals. Some of them have subtle or airy bodies, and some philosophers believe they dwell in the air. Others have no body at all, and are in that sense disembodied souls.

"Of especial importance for Platonic spiritual practices are those daimons in the lineage of specific gods—that is, the daimons descended from the gods. (Less anthropomorphically, these daimons are the images in space and time of particular divine Beings.) Since the gods are impassive and eternal (outside of time), they have little direct interaction with individual people. However, each god's attendant daimons, which are images and emanations of that god, are in time and in the Cosmic Soul, which governs processes in the material world. Therefore the daimons are not impassive, and since they act in time and space, they can be more involved with individual humans. They are the ones that hear prayers and communicate with people. Therefore, the daimons act in effect as ministers and messengers of the gods." (If daimons sound like angels, they should, for *angelos*—Greek for "messenger"—was one of ranks of daimons, according to some Platonists.)

Gods, angels, and daimons! How primitive! How superstitious! You may wonder how the philosophers who laid the foundations of Western philosophy, logic, mathematics, and science, and who posed questions and proffered solutions that still engage us, could have entertained seriously such apparently primitive ideas. Eurocentric scholars of the past talked about "Orientalism" and "Eastern irrationality" infecting a supposedly purely rational Greek philosophical tradition. We now know that these scholarly opinions were prejudiced oversimplifications. On the contrary, contemporary analytical psychology has found that the ancient concept of daimons is an effective way of understanding and dealing with complexes and other psychological phenomena, as I will explain in more detail in later chapters. As Epicurus said, "Empty are the words of the philosopher who has cured no one's soul," [212] and Neoplatonic philosophers were interested in practical psychospiritual results, for which these concepts are important.

The Inexpressible One

Before commencing the culmination of her lecture, Hypatia pauses a moment in silent contemplation. "I turn now to the highest level of the macrocosm, *The Inexpressible One*. Unity is necessary for anything to be what it is, and therefore unity is prior to all Being. I mean prior in a logical sense, not prior in time. Unity is obviously essential for organisms, but also for nonliving things, insofar as they are *things*. However, unity is even essential for groups of things—for a colony, army, team, or flock, for example, would not be what it is without being unified in some way. *The One* refers to this principle of unity, the ultimate and absolute ground of Being.

"My dear student Synesius braved an earthquake to return to us from his stay in Constantinople, and we are happy to have him back in Alexandria; he is sitting here in the first row." Hypatia gestures in his direction, and he bows his head modestly. "Synesius has written words praising The One in a hymn that he composed here last year. Please recite it for us."

Synesius rises, turns to face the audience, and chants:

Fount of all founts, of all beginnings first,
O Root, whence every living root hath burst;

Unit of Unities, of Numbers all
The Source, the Mind that hast all ever known,
Both what has been, and what is yet to be;
One before all; of all the Sum alone;
Seed of all things; the Root and highest Branch.[213]

"Thank you," Hypatia says as he returns to his seat. "Despite Synesius's eloquent words, we must be careful to distinguish The One from the Cosmic Mind. For the Cosmic Mind, in contrast to The One, is characterized by multiplicity, for there are many Ideas, all different from each other. *To be* is to be *something*, so Unity is above the realm of Being, the Cosmic Mind, which is, in contrast, the realm of Duality, of differences between one Idea and another. The Cosmic Mind is also characterized by duality in another way, for it looks toward itself, in the sense that its constituent Thoughts are related in various ways to each other, but it also looks upward toward The One, from which the individual Ideas and the Cosmic Mind as a whole get their unity. So in the Cosmic Mind there is a differentiation between subject and object, which is not present in The One. Let's look at this in a little more detail. It's subtle and difficult, so pay attention!

"In accordance with the Triadic Principle, Plotinus considered there to be two aspects of the emanation of the Cosmic Mind from The One: *procession* and *return*. The One produces an Indefinite Duality, which is like itself (unified), but no longer simple, for it permits differentiation within itself. It is sort of the raw material for the realm of Ideas, and is therefore an *indeterminate Mind*, an indefinite mental continuum, and the highest level of the Cosmic Mind. This indeterminate Mind looks back toward The One, from which it proceeded, and, trying to impose unity on its indefiniteness, can do so only by breaking up the indeterminate continuum into determinate Ideas or Forms. Thus, by contemplating The One, the Cosmic Mind *informs* itself. That is, it copies the unity and simplicity of The One into the many Ideas that are images of The One, but determined or defined in different ways. Therefore, each Idea is a different Thought about The One. In effect, the *object* of all the Thoughts is the same, but from different *subjective* perspectives. Since each of the Beings, as Minds, are images or projections of the same Whole, each Mind is its own cosmos, but they all are perspectives on one common cosmos."

Permit me to interrupt Hypatia to explain these ideas in different terms. The One is an abstract notion of unity and stability, but it raises the question of how there can be multiplicity in the World Mind, which is an image of The One. Think of The One as a perfectly sharp mathematical point; it is absolutely definite and unified in itself. Now imagine defocusing the point so it spreads into an ever-widening field of blackness. It is still unified (because it's all the same), but it provides a continuous field of different possibilities (i.e., different locations), but they are undifferentiated and indeterminate, as in pitch darkness. This is the Indefinite Duality (because it *permits* differences but doesn't *define* them). However, in this infinite field of possibility there is space to make definite images of The One, like stars appearing in the night sky; these are the Ideas or Beings. Thus the unlimited potential of Indefinite Duality creates definite Beings by copying The One. For this reason, some Platonists understood The One to have two complementary aspects, the *Monad* (another word for "one")—a principle of unity—and the *Indefinite Dyad* (i.e., duality)—a principle of separation. Since together they create the Beings, which include the gods, they can be identified with the father and the mother of the other gods—that is, with God and Goddess. The father gives them their form; the mother gives them individual existence. However, we must beware of thinking of abstract principles anthropomorphically.

If these ideas seem a little abstract, let's try extending our DVD analogy. Remember that the videogame DVD is analogous to the World Mind with its timeless structures of interrelated Forms and Ideas: the videogame's reality. The blank DVD, before the game has been burned onto it, corresponds to the unlimited potential of the Indeterminate Mind, which can hold different systems of Ideas, different realities. Each reality, however, is represented on the DVD by a pattern of ones and zeroes, and as you may know, each "one" is a small hole in the metal layer of the DVD blasted by the intense laser light of the DVD writer. Thus, the ones that, through their arrangement, constitute the videogame's reality are all images of The One of the laser light.

Like all analogies, this one is imperfect, since it suggests that The One creates the World Mind sequentially in time, like writing a DVD, whereas the emanation of the World Mind from The One is timeless. Nevertheless, I hope it makes these esoteric ideas a little clearer. Let's get back to Hypatia.

"Since The One is above Being, above what *is* or *is not*, it cannot have any definite being or have any specific properties ascribed to it. It cannot even be said to exist or not to exist, for Existence is an Idea at the level of Being."

"How then can we think or talk about It?" Hierocles asks.

"Ultimately, we cannot, at least not in any precise way. Therefore it is called Inexpressible or Ineffable. Synesius puts it well in another hymn, which he sent to me:

Father unknown, transcending thought,
Unspeakable, no tongue can sing
Thee, Mind of minds, Thee, Soul of souls,
Thee, Source whence natures all must spring.[214]

"Of course, to call The One 'Father' or any of these other things is misleading."

"Then how can we learn anything about it?" Hierocles asks.

"Ultimately The Inexpressible One can be grasped only through a process of union, which is a practice for my more advanced students." Some of her private students nudge each other and exchange smiles, swelling a little with pride. Their teacher continues, "Nevertheless, we attach attributes and names to The One (including 'The One') as a way of helping the mind to grasp it. Plotinus often adds 'so to speak' to his descriptions of The One as a reminder that they are just crutches to help us comprehend it. With this caution in mind, I will mention a few attributes that help lead us to The One.

"The One is *infinite*—so to speak—because the setting of bounds or limits is characteristic of duality, and The One is prior to duality. That is, a bound separates one thing from another, even if the other thing is nothing, and so if there is a limit there must be at least two things. The One is also *infinite in power*, in the sense that it is the cause of everything, of all the eternal Ideas or Forms, and through them of all the natural process in the Cosmic Soul, and by means of them, of all the coming to be and passing away in the material world. It is the productive power behind the universe.

"The One is called The Good for the following reason. A good may be defined as anything something else seeks in order to preserve its existence and its being—that is to say, its unity. This applies even to inanimate things, such as fires and hurricanes, for which fuel and warmth are 'good.' Without it, the fire or hurricane ceases to exist; it *is* no more. But The One, which is the ultimate cause of existence and being, cannot be in need of anything. Further, to need something implies duality—that which needs and that which is needed—but duality is posterior to The One.

"Since The One is what everything needs, ultimately, to exist and be what it is, The One can be considered the Ultimate Good. In some sense, unity is what everything seeks in order to exist, to *be* something. It is The Good to which everything at every level looks for its being. You should not confuse The One as Ultimate Good with the

Idea of the Good, which resides in the Cosmic Mind and is opposed to the Idea of the Not-Good, or Evil, and so is in the realm of duality."

Petrus, a Christian student, raises his hand and asks, "Is this why we know that God is good?"

Hypatia quickly replies, "The Good is not necessarily good in the sense of *doing good* in some human terms, which is what someone usually means when they say, 'God is good.' The most we can say is that this thing we call The Good is what everything needs in order to be. This is part of the trap of using loaded words, such as *good*, which are properly applied to human actions, to the utmost ineffable metaphysical abstractions, but let us continue down this treacherous road a little further.

"For instance, as the Ultimate Good, which all things seek and pursue, The One can be called the Supremely Lovable—that is, that which everything loves. Since it is its own Good, it can be said to love itself, and thus—so to speak—to *be* Love; it is simultaneously Love and The Beloved. Again, The One is above the *Idea* of Love, and so it is metaphorical and ultimately inaccurate to call The One 'Love.' But we philosophers do it.

"The Inexpressible One is also characterized—so to speak—by Beauty. It is not Beauty Itself, for Beauty is a matter of Form, and so, as I've explained, the Cosmic Mind in its totality is Beauty. Nevertheless, since the Cosmic Mind is a direct emanation of The One, Plotinus calls The One 'the Beauty that transcends all Beauty.'[215] These metaphorical descriptions of The One might seem to be dangerously misleading, but Plato showed how beauty is the basis of a spiritual practice that can lead us upward from bodily beauty, through the beauty of the soul, to ideal Beauty, and from it toward The One, the Beauty that transcends all Beauty.[216] I will conclude by reciting again from a hymn of my devoted disciple, Synesius:

O Unity of Unities,
Thee, Thought of Thoughts, I ever sing—
Father of fathers, only Spring
Of all beginnings, Thou bidst flow
All founts, and mak'st all roots to grow;
Thee only good—who world on world
And star on star through space hast hurl'd.
Fathomless Beauty, seed unknown,
Source whence the wings of Time have flown,

Father of spirits pure, that dwell
In spheres whose place no tongue can tell."[217]

"Thank you for your attention. Farewell." As Hypatia leaves the dais, her students lead the rest of the audience in applause.

THE GOD OF THE PHILOSOPHERS

Inevitably, The One, the cause of everything that *is*, was treated as a kind of deity (indeed, a supreme deity) and simply called "God." Furthermore, in conformity with the conceptions of the age, this deity was envisioned as an anthropomorphic male god, the Father.

This terminology is treacherous, however, since it inclines us to think of God as some being behaving in time, observing human behavior, hearing prayers, making decisions, allotting punishments and rewards, and otherwise behaving like a bigger-than-life person (typically a father figure). We must remember that the Cosmic Mind is already outside the realm of time, and that Neoplatonists regard the gods, who exist at this level, to be impassive. How much more remote and abstract must The One be! This is not a god to cozy up to, or with whom you can have heart-to-heart colloquies! Arguably, much of the appeal of Christianity, Judaism, and the popular Pagan religions as well lay in their more approachable and anthropomorphic ideas of deity.

Therefore Neoplatonist philosophers with a more religious or spiritual orientation find a more approachable concept of divinity at the level of the daimons. As I've explained, these beings are in the lineages of gods, but exist in time and space, and so are able to interact with people. This does not mean that the gods themselves, as Beings in the World Mind, are irrelevant, but they are impersonal dynamic forces, which engender and govern the personal daimons in the World Soul. So if you pray to Diana and she answers, in actuality it is probably one of her daimons who takes the call. (If you are a monotheist and getting impatient with this talk of gods and daimons, think of them as angels for now. I will have more to say later.)

When considered as a religious orientation, Pagan Neoplatonism is often characterized as *henotheism* rather than *monotheism*, because it has a multiplicity of gods, but one is supreme. This is one reason, as a philosophy, it was able to accommodate the monotheistic religions (more on this in the next chapter). For example, Maximus Tyrius, a Platonist of the second century CE, expresses the henotheistic view:

In such a mighty contest, sedition and discord, you will see one according law and assertion in all the earth, that there is one god, the king and father of all things, and many gods, sons of god, ruling together with him.[218]

The One, the Ultimate Good, is sometimes known as "the God of the philosophers" to distinguish it from more popular notions of deity. Recall that *philosopher* means "lover and seeker of wisdom," so "the God of the philosophers" does not refer to some academic theological concept, but to the understanding of divinity achieved by these seekers of wisdom.

The Inexpressible One, with its incomplete descriptions as the Good, Love, Beauty, and God, is a concept in spiritual philosophy and theology, and we may seem to have come a long way from Forms exemplified by the objects of mathematics and the equations of physics, and from the World Soul as Nature and its processes. Can The One cohabit with a scientific worldview?

I believe that it can. If we ascend upward (or descend inward: pick your image) from the equations of physics (that is, the laws of gravity, electromagnetism, etc.—whatever the correct equations might be), conceived as the Forms governing different aspects of material reality (gravity, electromagnetism, etc.) and psychical reality (perception, motivation, behavior, the unconscious, etc.), we must encounter a Form (abstract law) governing reality as a whole (that is, not separated into different phenomena). We may not be able to express this law in discrete mathematical equations (as when the Forms are separated), but this principle of universal orderliness, of cosmos and not chaos, approaches the limit that is The One, the cause of everything. So I think that The One can be identified with the ultimate causal principle of the universe, even if it is inexpressible in mathematical equations, but it is essential that this principle be the cause of *all* phenomena in the universe, not just physical phenomena; in particular, it must account for consciousness, the unconscious, and other psychical phenomena. This conception of The One could be called "the God of the scientists."

IMAGES OF THE COSMOS

There are several ways to visualize the Neoplatonic cosmos, and different ones work better in different circumstances. You may find one or more of them useful as the basis of visualization exercises. I suggest that you practice the visualizations that work best for you, since they will help to imprint the Neoplatonic cosmic map on your mind.

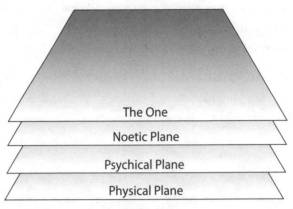

The Planes of Reality

One way to understand the cosmos is as levels or planes of reality. The lowest is the earthly plane, on which we live. Above it is the World Soul, the realm of divine Nature and the daimons, which is the boundary or connecting link between our world and the World Mind. It is also called the *psychical plane*, because it is the level of the soul (*psyche* in ancient Greek). The next level, the World Mind, is the eternal realm of ideal Forms, including the archetypal gods; we might think of it as heaven. It is also called the *noetic plane* because, as will be explained in the next chapter, it is the realm of the thoughts (*noeta*) of the World Mind (*nous*). The highest plane, then, is The One, identified with God, which is absolutely simple.

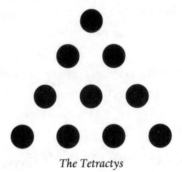

The Tetractys

The ancient Pythagorean symbol called the *Tetractys* is a way of remembering this structure (see figure). At the top is one dot, which represents The One. Below it are two dots, which represent duality, and thus being/non-being, true/false, is/is-not, subject/object, thinker/thought, and thus the plane of Being, the realm of the Ideas in the World Mind. The three dots represent the World Soul in two ways. First, because the three dots represent mediation (one dot between the other two), and the World Soul is the media-tor joining the Ideal World to the Material World. Second, because the World Soul is the realm where time first appears and, according to Pythagoreans, the three dots represent the beginning, middle, and end of any process. They also represent the three dimensions of physical space. The four dots on the bottom represent the Material World by means of several symbols. For example, it can be the four elements (earth, water, air, fire), which also symbolize our world: land, sea, atmosphere, and fiery phenomena (lightning, sunlight, etc.). The four dots can also represent the four quarters of the earth (North, South, East, West), or the four seasons of the year—the cycle of Nature—and so forth. Remember this simple symbol, and you can easily recall the four planes of the Neoplatonic cosmos.

At the point where the *Pythagorean Golden Verses* turn from the practices of the second degree of wisdom to those of the third, we read:

> *These study, practice these, and these affect;*
> *To sacred virtue these thy steps direct.*
> *Eternal Nature's fountain I attest,*
> *Who the Tetractys on our soul impressed.*[219]

The last two lines are the sacred oath of the Pythagoreans, which is quoted frequently (with slight variations). The philosopher swears by the sage Pythagoras, who first taught the Tetractys, which (in a slightly longer version) is described as "the fount and root of everflow-ing Nature." It represents the entire outflowing of The One into material reality, the flux of coming-to-be and passing away. The Neoplatonist Hierocles, who might have attended Hypatia's lectures, wrote this in his *Commentary on the Pythagorean Golden Verses*:

> *For "the fount of everflowing nature,"*
> *the Tetractys,*
> *is the First Cause,*
> *not only of the Being of all things,*
> *but likewise of their Well-being,*
> *sowing and diffusing through the universe the Good,*
> *innate and natural to it,*
> *as a pure and intellectual Light.*[220]

THE GEOCENTRIC IMAGE

As you know, ancient people believed in a geocentric cosmos—that is, that the earth is at the center of the universe. Although we now know that the earth orbits the sun, and that the entire solar system is moving in the Milky Way galaxy, the geocentric perspective is useful for visualizing the Neoplatonic cosmos. I'll call it the *Geocentric Image* (see figure). In the center is the earth, our material world. Surrounding it is the air (especially the luminous upper air, above the clouds), which symbolizes the World Soul that enwraps us and fills us with vital spirit (air, breath). According to ancient ideas, the daimons live primarily in the air. Above the air is the celestial realm, the heavens, where the gods dwell. Because the stars do not appear to change or move with respect to each other, they are good symbols of the impassive gods and the eternal Ideas. Indeed the forms of the constellations might have inspired geometric thinking about the Forms. Much ancient mathematics was devoted to astronomy and astrology. As I've mentioned, Hypatia was a highly regarded mathematician and astronomer, and her few surviving works are on these topics. The highest heaven, the black void behind the visible stars, symbolizes The Inexpressible One, with its ineffability, infinity, and impenetrability. Therefore you can go outside on a starry night and experience the Neoplatonic cosmos, as Hypatia might have done with her own students.

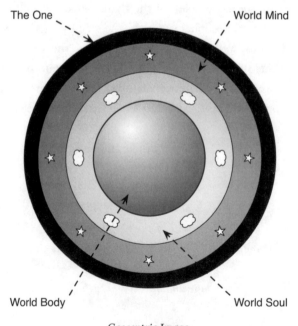

Geocentric Image

The Geocentric Ascent: Go outside on a warm, cloudless, moonless night and sit comfortably, preferably in a reclining position. First you will visualize a simple ascent to The One. Begin by looking around you at the plants, trees, houses, or whatever else is in sight. Imagine their solidity and materiality but also the myriad physical processes taking place in them, which will cause all of these things, even the rocks, to decay eventually. Now shift your gaze upward into the air, above the tops of the trees, and above the clouds if any are visible, but not so high as the stars. Be aware that you are looking at the air, which surrounds the entire earth with a continuous fluid, a breath-spirit, that enters into the depths of every plant and animal. For the oxygen goes into your lungs and through them into your blood and thence into every cell of your body. This all-permeating air not only envelops but also connects all living things. Now shift your attention upward to the stars. Set aside any astronomical knowledge you might have and admire the beauty of these fiery points of light. They have been there forever, and your ancestors gazed on them in wonder as you do now. They are perfect points separated by vast impassible voids, giving each a perfect identity. Yet they are not independent, for they are related to each other, creating eternal forms that are as evocative for us as they were for our ancestors. Contemplate them, trace out their patterns. Finally, project your attention into the black void beyond the stars, the perfect silence and invisibility out of which have emanated the stars and all else. This will take some mental effort, but focus on the black sky *behind* the stars. Rest for a while in the Abyss, the perfect simplicity and infinity of The One.

The Geocentric Descent: This exercise continues the preceding one by descending back to our world. After you have meditated on the Void and achieved a state of peace, calm, and tranquility, begin to notice the faintest stars (but don't strain to see them). You are witnessing the emergence of the Ideas and the Forms from The One. Continue to broaden your attention to take in more of the starry firmament, and try to hold the whole sky in your awareness. Know that these Beings of light are the causes of everything. Though motionless in their heaven, they are the governors of the cosmos. Next let your attention descend into the atmosphere, the all-pervasive spirit, moving in currents large and small to connect the earth into one living organism. Think about the air moving through all living things, keeping them alive, but also creating the weather that drives natural processes. Finally, return your attention to the physical things around you, but experience them as emanations and effects produced by all the levels above you. When you finish the practice and get up, try to take with you the feeling of the interconnectedness of all things, both horizontally to other things on the same level, and vertically as emanations of The One.

THE CENTRAL LIGHT

Another way of visualizing the Neoplatonic cosmos, and the one most commonly used by Plotinus, turns the geocentric perspective inside out. In the center is a perfect point of light, representing The One, the source from which everything emanates, so I will call it the *Central Light Image* (see figure). The immediately surrounding sphere, irradiated by The One, represents the World Mind. We can see how the infinitesimal point of The One expands into an indefinite continuum of differentiation (the Indefinite Dyad). We see this continuum divide into rays corresponding to the discrete Ideas in the World Mind, as a prism divides the continuum of white light into individual colors. Surrounding this sphere is that of the World Soul, which is further differentiated and darker, because it is farther from the source of light and unity. In it the rays further ramify, like light through a crystal, into the many rays emanating from each Being. The outermost regions where the light reaches is the realm of organized matter, the World Body. In the outer darkness, where no light reaches, is the realm of absolute chaos and indeterminacy. It is utter negation, non-being, and non-existence. This chaotic, indeterminate matter is furthest removed from the Good, but that does not mean that it is positively evil, only that it lacks the light of the Good and is beyond the reach of the organizing principle.

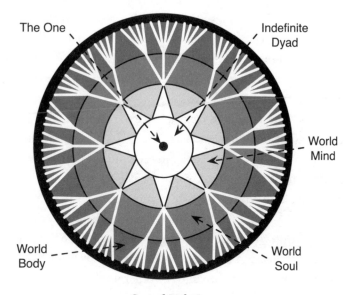

Central Light Image

Journey to the Central Fire: This exercise will help you to internalize the Central Light Image. Most everyone is familiar with the mythological image of the "fires of hell" in the center of the earth, but the ancients were more likely to imagine the fire in the heart of Mother Earth as a hearth fire bringing the warmth of life to all things on Earth. The Pythagoreans especially teach the mystery of the Central Fire, the Hidden Sun. This exercise builds on this imagery. Hypatia might have guided her students' visualization as follows. Sit quietly and close your eyes to prepare for an imaginary trip to the center of existence. There are many ways to begin your descent. For example, you can visualize the mouth of a cave in a verdant sacred grove. It is obviously a holy place; there are altars and statues adorned with colorful fresh flowers and fruit as offerings. You enter this sacred grotto. Alternatively, following Jung's example, you may prefer to imagine a door in your basement that, astonishingly, you have never noticed before.

Journey to the Central Fire (continued): You open the door and step through. Or you may imagine entering a door in a pyramid. It is your choice, but imagine yourself entering a sacred portal into the earth. You descend down long, dimly lit stone steps. Finally you come to a large chamber; the walls are so far away you cannot see them in the dark. Just inside the door is an altar, and upon it there is a golden oak branch or wand. Instinctively you pick it up, and it begins to shine, giving some illumination. You are shocked to see some very old bones lying about, and you have an inexplicable feeling they are your ancestors, but you cannot imagine how they got here. You go forward slowly and come to a shallow, slow-moving stream or canal. In the distance to your left you can see ghostlike apparitions of the dead, waiting to be ferried to the other side, the land of the dead. In the distance on the right you see a vast swarm of glowing butterflies, crossing from the other side to yours, where they disappear in the distance; they are newborn souls entering incarnation. The light of your wand shows you that there are some stepstones immediately in front of you, and you use them to cross the stream into the other world, where you come to a Y in the path. The branch to the left leads to a white cypress, where the souls of the dead who have crossed are drinking from a spring; it flows from Lêthê, the River of Forgetfulness, where Sleep and Death dwell. This is not your path, so you take the branch to the right, which leads to a black cypress; you drink from the spring by it, which flows from the Lake of Memory.

The cool, refreshing water wakes you up, and you notice that behind the black cypress is a passage into the hillside. This short passage through the hill takes you into a completely different world, the Elysian Field or Isle of the Blessed. It is sunny and a gentle breeze is blowing. It is an idyllic setting, with many flowers, soft grass, and trees for shade. All around are men and women, or perhaps ghosts—it's hard to tell—dressed in the clothing of many times and places. Some of them are talking together; others are engrossed in engaging activities. This is the land of blessed spirits and daimons—the saints, the wise and holy people of all cultures. As you pass through you recognize a few—perhaps Pythagoras and Plato, or Moses and Jesus, or Mohammed and Rumi; perhaps Buddha, Kuan Yin, or Lao Tzu—many others are unknown to you. Some of them notice your glowing wand and smile benevolently at you.

Journey to the Central Fire (continued): On the opposite side of the valley is a magnificent temple built into the side of a mountain; four rivers flow quietly from
the mountain in the four directions. You cross to the temple, leave your golden
bough or wand as an offering on the altar in front of the temple, and go inside.
It is so bright inside that at first you are blinded, but as your eyes adjust, you
discover that you are within a huge circular chamber filled with many shining
figures. They are immobile like statues, but they seem full of life and power.
You may recognize them as gods, such as Zeus, Athena, and Apollo, and all
the rest, in their typical poses. Or they might be choirs of angels, including
perhaps the archangels, such as Michael, in recognizable forms. Or they might
not be easily identifiable; in any case they shimmer, and the glare is so bright it
is hard to see them clearly. Ethereal music fills the interior.

You proceed slowly down a labyrinthine walkway that winds ever toward the
center, and as you do so the forms become less distinct, more like abstract forms
and indistinct lights. At the walkway's end, in the center of the hall, you come to
a golden dome embedded in the floor; it is the inner sanctum, and you know that
within it is the Holy of Holies. You pull open its door, but the light is so blinding
that you close your eyes. Nevertheless you can "see" that you are peering into a
huge spherical chamber. At its very center is a point of light infinitely brighter
than the sun. It fills the cavity with such brilliance that nothing else is visible. But
amazingly, the intense light is not harsh; rather it is comforting and filled with
life, which permeates your body and soul. Nevertheless the light is so intense
that you are forced to withdraw and close the door.

Having journeyed to the Central Fire, you now retrace your steps past the
divine beings, back to the temple entrance. Retrieve your wand and let it guide
you back through the peaceful realm of the blessed and wise, past the dead and
unborn, and finally again to the river that separates the divine realms from ours.
Cross the river and return to the stairs. Leave the golden bough or wand on the
altar, ready for your next journey. Climb the steps and return to your everyday
world. When you are ready, open your eyes and record any impressions you may
have.

THE GOLDEN CHAIN

Here is another way to look at the central light. Think of the rays emanating from the central One to all things in our world. Each of these rays may be traced back to its source, The One. Neoplatonists talk about rays, but also cords or chains, suspended from The One. The image of the Golden Chain has its origin in Homer's *Iliad*, where Zeus (Jove) says of himself:

And know, the Almighty is the god of gods.
League all your forces, then, ye powers above,
Join all, and try the omnipotence of Jove.
Let down our golden everlasting chain
Whose strong embrace holds heaven, and earth, and main:
Strive all, of mortal and immortal birth,
To drag, by this, the Thunderer down to earth:
Ye strive in vain! If I but stretch this hand,
I heave the gods, the ocean, and the land;
I fix the chain to great Olympus' height,
And the vast world hangs trembling in my sight!
For such I reign, unbounded and above;
And such are men, and gods, compared to Jove.[221]

Here Zeus the supreme god may be identified with The One (with all the caveats about anthropomorphic images of The One that I made earlier). With his unbreakable chains of causation God binds the cosmos, which *depends*—literally hangs—on him.

Besides chains or chords, Pagan Neoplatonists also spoke of lineages (it's actually the same word in Greek). Thus all the gods and goddesses (in the realm of Beings) are born of The One, who is then called the Father (and Zeus had the title "Father of Gods and Humans"). The daimons, angels, and other souls in the Cosmic Soul are likewise descended from one or another god or goddess. Finally, everything in the material world, including non-living things, is in the lineage of angels, gods, and The One. Thus we are all children of God.

All these images may be helpful and inspiring, but keep in mind they are just models or metaphors to help the understanding; they can also mislead. The higher levels are not literally higher than the lower ones (in the geocentric image) or deeper than the others (in the Central Light Image); this is just a spatial mapping or representation of their logical relationships, to make them easier to think about. Furthermore, you should avoid thinking of these relationships temporally; for example, that The One creates the World Mind, which *then* creates the World Soul, which *then* creates the World Body. First of all, this makes no sense, for The One and the World Mind are timeless—that is, outside of time altogether. Second, when we say that The One is *prior* to everything else, we do not mean earlier in time, but logically and ontologically prior, which means that The One implies and causes the rest. Higher/ lower, prior/posterior, and so forth are not spatial or temporal relationships, but logical and ontological relationships.

CHAPTER NINE

THE MICROCOSM
AND THE ARCHETYPES

MICROCOSM: THE TRIPARTITE SOUL

In the previous chapter you learned how Hypatia and the Neoplatonists of her time under-stood the structure of the world at large, and I explained some ways to understand it in more contemporary terms. Now we must turn inward, for the structure of the psyche is especially important for understanding Neoplatonic spiritual practices. First you will learn how the embodied mind—the microcosm—mirrors the macrocosm, which you learned about in the preceding chapter. Next I will explain how the Neoplatonic map of inner and outer real-ity can illuminate the beliefs of both polytheistic Pagans and monotheists. It is also valuable, however, for agnostics and nonbelievers, for it is an accurate map of the psyche irrespective of the transcendent existence of deities. Therefore the remainder of the chapter explains the connection between Neoplatonism and contemporary evolutionary Jungian psychology. You will learn about the archetypes and how they evolve, about complexes and their relation to daimons, about your Shadow and why you should befriend it, and about your highest or true self—the deity within—and how you can discover it. So let's begin by imagining how Hypatia might have explained the microcosm in one of her public lectures, which is already in progress.

"Democritus, the founder of atomic theory, said, 'A person is a small cosmos.' That is, since humans are emanations of The Inexpressible One through the levels of the

Cosmic Mind and the Cosmic Soul into the Cosmic Body, we too have all the same levels, and so we are microcosms, images of the macrocosm. I will go through the levels in order and describe their connections to the macrocosm on one hand, and to the individual person on the other. It is clearest to use the Central Light Image, since that places the body on the outside, which is how we normally see each other."

Hypatia sets up a drawing of the Central Light Image, such as you saw in the previous chapter. She explains that corresponding to the World Body, each of us has an individual body, located in space and existing for a finite period of time. Our bodies consist of formed or organized matter and energy. Hypatia would have described it in terms of the four elements, but we describe it in terms of proteins and other organic chemical compounds, as well as in terms of electricity and other physical forces.

Pointing to the diagram, Hypatia says, "Within your body is your own soul, which is an image of the World Soul adapted to an individual body. It permeates your entire body, like a second, subtle body, since it must regulate the processes in every part of your body. The soul governs the movement and transformation of matter and energy in your body; that is, it includes all the processes that make a *body* from a mass of disorganized matter and energy. In this sense all living things have souls, for it is their souls that make them *organisms*."

From a contemporary standpoint, we might add to the list of things with souls those self-organizing *nonliving* processes, such as hurricanes and ecosystems, that gather free energy from the environment and create order by dissipating this energy in a degraded form.

As a concession to the general audience, Hypatia provides some background: "The soul can be divided into various faculties or parts; for our purposes, two will do. The *lower soul*, which humans share with other animals, has two subparts. First, the *vegetative soul*, which all living things have, organizes the basic processes of nutrition, respiration, growth, reproduction, and metabolism. Second, the *animate soul*, which all animals possess, organizes the processes of perception, memory, emotion, intention (or will), and movement. The lower soul is distributed throughout the body, but takes on specialized forms and purposes in the various organs.

"The *upper soul* may be visualized as localized in the head, or even in the brain, which is approximately true. The upper soul is the *rational soul*, which is the faculty of discursive reason—that is, our capacity to talk internally to ourselves in order to analyze situations, reason to conclusions, and express thoughts in verbal form. The rational soul seems to be unique to humans, because it depends on a level of linguistic capacity that other animals apparently do not have. Notice that the rational soul deals with abstract ideas, but the process of thinking is sequential, taking place in time, which is why it is part of the soul."

Pointing to the diagram, Hypatia continues. "You may think that the true you is your soul, but deep within the soul is another faculty, which corresponds to a kind of mind that is an image of the World Mind: the *nous*. For the divine Plotinus says,

Each of us is a noetic cosmos."[222]

Here, for the sake of clarity and accuracy, it is necessary to use the ancient Greek word *nous* (pronounced "noose"). It is often translated "mind" or "intellect," but these translations are vague and may be misleading. *Nous* is in fact the word I translated previously as "Mind" in "World Mind." Here, however, we have to be more careful. In a Neoplatonic context, the nous is not the reasoning mind, which thinks sequentially in time. Rather, the nous is the *intuiting mind*, which grasps the Ideas and their eternal (timeless) connections. Sometimes we can translate *nous* as "intuition," but intuition itself is not well defined. Likewise, "Thoughts" here and elsewhere translates as *Noêta*—that is, the "Intuitions" in the Nous.

These concepts will be clearer if you remember that the individual nous is an aspect of the World Mind (that is, the World Nous), and therefore that each individual nous comprehends, from its own perspective, *all* the Ideas. To extend my analogy from the previous chapter: if the World Nous is like the DVD with the video game on it, then your individual nous is like the copy of that game installed on your computer. It is still static and inactive, until the computer executes it. Likewise, your individual nous is a static structure of Ideas until they come to life in your soul.

Hypatia continues. "In the innermost depths of the individual psyche is an image of The Inexpressible One, which we may call the individual One, the individual Good, the God image, or the like. We Platonists sometimes call it the *Inmost Flower of the Nous*; some other philosophers call it the *highest self* or *true self*. This is the divinity within us all. It is the source of light at our center. As in the macrocosm, The One is the source of eternal Being in the Cosmic Mind and is the providential governor of Becoming in the material world, so in the microcosm the highest self is the unified individual expression of all the unconscious archetypal Ideas common to humankind and is therefore the regulator of our individual destinies as humans. Thus, in this third degree of wisdom, your spiritual progress depends on coming to know, so far as possible, this God image, your individual source of psychological unity." Hypatia is describing the process Jung later called *individuation* (becoming *individuus*—undivided), which I'll discuss later in this chapter.

"Thus," Hypatia continues, "beginning at the exterior of the body, we may penetrate into the inmost depths of the soul to reach the inner divinity. This is the basis for some spiritual exercises, which I teach to my advanced students."

POLYTHEISTIC PAGAN INTERPRETATION

It is not my purpose in this book to explain the theology of any religion, past or present. But it is my purpose to offer Hypatia's philosophy as a contemporary spiritual practice and way of life. Since it arose in a time and culture very different from ours, it's necessary to say a little about how it fits with contemporary worldviews.

Neoplatonism developed in regions where the dominant and official religions were polytheistic and Pagan: ancient Greece, Rome, Egypt, and the Middle East. Therefore the religious connections of Neoplatonism are most apparent in Pagan polytheism. This will be familiar ground if you are Pagan, Neopagan, or Wiccan, but Neoplatonic philosophy will give you additional insights into the nature of the gods that will be useful in the more advanced practices taught in the remaining chapters. Let's hear what Hypatia has to say.

"The eternal Beings in the World Nous are themselves Minds of a sort and Beings with a kind of life. (I will explain the qualifiers in a moment.) Therefore it is natural to identify these Beings with the gods that we Pagans worship. Although Platonists make this identification, the Platonic understanding of the gods diverges from the popular notion in several ways.

"First, the Beings in the World Nous are eternal, not in the sense of living forever, but in the sense of being *atemporal*, entirely out of time. (Recall the analogy of the ideal Equilateral Triangle.) Therefore Platonists agree with Epicureans and Stoics in saying that the gods are *impassive*; that is, they are unaffected by occurrences in the material world, including our prayers and our behavior."

In the audience a distinguished man raises his hand and asks, "Is that why Epicurus says the gods are essentially irrelevant to human life? They might do us no good, but they also do us no harm, and so we have a nothing to fear from them."

"That is correct," the teacher answers, "but for Platonists the gods are not irrele-vant, for they are real Beings in the World Nous, conveying an image of The One into the lower orders, into the World Soul, and even into the material world, where they have real effects in space and time. Therefore, the Platonic gods are like laws of Nature, which are timeless, yet regulate processes in space and time.

"Furthermore, since they are eternal Minds, and Thoughts in timeless relation to other Thoughts, the gods especially regulate psychological phenomena in the lower orders. Thus, for example, Aphrodite (or Venus) is that goddess—that aspect of the World Nous—who especially regulates human love and sexual desire. Ares (or Mars) is the god who governs human courage and aggression, especially their psychologi-cal aspects. Thus the gods are very much involved with our lives, but in ways that are common to the human species as a whole, rather than peculiar to individual persons."

A woman in the audience raises her hand.

"Yes, Alexandra?"

"What about the daimons?" she asks.

"The gods are in the Cosmic Nous," Hypatia replies, "but each god engenders in the Cosmic Soul innumerable daimons that are images of that god. These are incorporeal souls that nevertheless exist and behave in space and time, and are thus capable of interacting with us. On the one hand, looking 'upward,' they are in contact with the gods from which they have descended; on the other, looking 'downward,' they can interact with the material world. Therefore daimons serve as mediators between our world and the divine world. Like all souls, they can govern material processes, and thus have physical effects in the material world, but primarily in our minds."

Various Neoplatonists divided the levels of the World Nous and the World Soul into mul-tiple sublevels. Corresponding to the sublevels are ranks of gods in the World Nous and ranks of daimons in the World Soul. In some cases these subdivisions are based on dialec-tical analyses of these higher realms; in others they are based on direct experiences of the higher realms arising from spiritual exercises. Nevertheless, these "maps" of the immateri-al world are not completely consistent with each other. Fortunately, the detailed structure is not very important for spiritual practice, and so we do not need to be concerned with it. Plato and Plotinus did not seem to bother about it, and perhaps Hypatia didn't either.

Just as we each have an individual soul, residing in the World Soul and descended from a Mind in the World Mind, so we have personal daimons accompanying our souls and descended from higher-ranked daimons and gods. We have already encountered this concept with the inner daimon and the guardian daimon of Stoicism. Neoplatonists recognized an inner daimon (the flower of the nous) and a personal guardian daimon. Some also recognized a personal "bad daimon," which tends to lead each person astray according to each soul's dispositions. Socrates was known for the "little daimon" (*daimonion*) that he consulted on a regular basis. He would stand silently in meditation—sometimes for hours—in communion with his guardian daimon.

Hypatia continues her discourse down the great chain of being:"Since everything in the universe is ultimately connected back to The One, all things exist in lineages. As we have seen, daimons are in lineages descending from particular gods. So also our humans souls, and even our bodies, which are formed by these souls, are in lineages descending from Beings in the Cosmic Mind. Therefore each of us has a progenitor Being in this realm where the gods reside, and in this sense each of us is descended from a divine Being who gives us our specific nature."

Alexandra raises her hand again and asks, "What do you say of the stories that some people are the son or daughter of a god or goddess? They say that Helen of Troy was sired by Zeus, that Aeneas was born of Aphrodite, and that Pythagoras was the son of Apollo."

"Some people's souls are descended from a god, and so completely informed by that god—that is to say, such a faithful image of that god—that they are like a son or daughter of the god. As you say, Pythagoras was rumored to be a son of Apollo. Likewise some people say that the divine Plato is also a son of Apollo, which makes him half-brother to Asclepius, the healing god. They say that just as Asclepius heals people's bodies, so Plato heals their souls. In any case, such people are spiritual leaders because they exemplify more than most people their divine origin. In Greek we call such people 'heroes' and consider them semidivine demigods. Conversely, an ordinary person, through spiritual practices, can make their soul more like their divine forebear, and thus make themselves more godlike."

This assimilation to the divine was a common aspiration of ancient spiritual practices (we have already seen it in the Garden and the Porch), and was the genuine meaning of *deification* in ancient philosophy. I will explain spiritual deification in the next chapter.

As we have seen, in Pagan Neoplatonism The One stands above the World Nous and is the cause of all the gods and of everything else in the universe. This Supreme Absolute was often called Zeus or Jupiter after the chief god of the Greek or Roman pantheon. However, this name is a mere convenience, and connected Neoplatonism to the traditional Pagan religions, but it was inaccurate (like "the Good" or "God"). The Inexpressible One is not an anthropomorphic god and cannot be well characterized positively; it is often more informative to say what it is *not*.

MONOTHEISTIC INTERPRETATION

Although most ancient Neoplatonists were Pagan, and the philosophy developed in a poly-theistic culture, there were monotheists involved too, especially in Alexandria. For example, monotheistic Jews were prominent in the Mediterranean intellectual world, and some of them, such as Philo Judaeus of Alexandria (20 BCE – 50 CE), made important contributions to Platonism. Further, Christianity had been spreading in the centuries before Hypatia, and some Christian philosophers saw in Neoplatonism a basis for Christian theology. These in-cluded St. Augustine (354–430) and Hypatia's disciple Synesius (c.373–c.414), who became Bishop of Ptolemais (in Cyrene, modern Cyrenaica, in Libya). Later, in the fifth or sixth cen-tury, St. Dionysius (or St. Denys), the pseudo-Areopagite, made important contributions to Christian mysticism based on the philosophy of the Pagan Neoplatonist Proclus (412–485), who was born shortly before Hypatia's murder. Dionysius might even have been a student of Proclus. Much later, during the Renaissance, Marsilio Ficino (1433–1499) was a key figure in defining a Christian Neoplatonism. Also, after Islam arose in the seventh century of the Common Era, Muslim philosophers, such as Ibn Sina (980–1037), Suhrawardi (1155–91), and Ibn 'Arabi (1165–1240), sought to reconcile Neoplatonism with their religion. Neoplatonism has remained an important, if not obvious, element in all three of these monotheistic reli-gions. In this section I will explain briefly how Neoplatonism fits into a monotheistic reli-gious context; if you are not a monotheist, feel free to skim it.

There is a disturbance at the back of the auditorium where Hypatia is speaking. A man known as Peter the Reader shouts, "You are spreading Pagan lies!" and storms out.

Amidst murmurs in the audience, Hypatia sits quietly for a moment, but then she continues. "I know that many of you listening to me today are Christians and Jews, and that you do not believe in the Hellenic gods. Even my dear Synesius has turned to the religion of the Galilean from his ancestral religion, although he traces his ancestry back 1,700 years to that hero who first led the Dorians to Sparta. I respect his courage in actively choosing a spiritual path rather than passively accepting one, and he has been kind enough to explain many points of Christian dogma to me. So now I want to address those of you who do not believe in the Hellenic gods and explain where Platonic philosophy agrees with your religion and where it does not.

"Monotheist philosophers naturally identify The One with their God, and we who honor many gods also sometimes call The One 'God' and 'Father' and treat it as a supreme deity. When I first learned about the Christian Trinity, I thought, 'Oh, this is just the three levels of reality,' for there is a natural correspondence between the three immaterial levels of the Platonic macrocosm and the three persons of the Trinity. The One, of course, is the Father. The Cosmic Mind, as an emanation of The One, corresponds naturally with the Son, especially because as *Logos*, or articulated thought, it corresponds to the Demiurge or Craftsman—the creator god in Plato's myth—and to the Creator-Logos of Christian theology. Finally, the Holy Spirit corresponds to the Cosmic Soul (also called Spirit), which brings the timeless Forms into life in time and space. But Synesius has explained to me that many Christian theologians do not agree, for this view makes Christ and the Holy Spirit subordinate to God the Father."

The theological position that Hypatia described is called *subordinationism* and was common doctrine in the first centuries of Christianity, including in Alexandria in Hypatia's time, but some Christian sects consider it unorthodox or even heretical.[223]

"As I've mentioned, Platonists sometimes analyze the levels of reality into sublevels, and even sub-sublevels. Often we divide a level, according the Triadic Principle, into three aspects—Abiding, Proceeding, and Returning—operating within that level. Some Platonists, such as Porphyry, have described a three-in-one structure at the highest level. The One remains in itself, but simultaneously proceeds outward through indeterminate 'spiritual matter,' but then, by turning back toward The One, creates and consolidates the structure of the Nous or Logos. The elements of this triad within the level of The One are sometimes named, first, Existence or Being; second, Power or Life; and third, Nous. These are complex matters and beyond the scope of this lecture, so let me just remark that Synesius and other Christian Platonists understand the Trinity in these terms. The One exists as the Father and, by his power or creative will, which is the Holy Spirit, he engenders the Nous, which is the Logos or Son. The three persons of the Trinity are therefore at the same level, and none is subordinated to any other. Synesius praises this Trinity in one of his hymns:

Thee Trinity, Thee Unity, I praise,

One and yet Three alike in all Thy ways;

The severance our minds admit is still

The one and only Person of God's will.[224]

"From the standpoint of orthodoxy there are several issues with the identification of God and The One, but monotheistic Platonists have resolved them to their satisfaction. The first issue is the impersonality of The One. As I have explained, The One is an ineffable abstraction, existing outside of time, impassive, and so it is quite different from the anthropomorphic Father of popular monotheism. The One does not easily inspire a devotional attitude.

"Second, according to Platonism the entire cosmos, everything that exists, is an emanation of The One, which causes and sustains the levels of reality, including the material world. Therefore Platonism is a kind of *pantheism*, because divinity permeates everything; as it is expressed, God is *immanent* in the world."

Technically, Neoplatonism is classified as *panentheism* (note the *-en-*), because divinity is immanent in the material world, but also transcends it, in the levels above the Cosmic Body.

"On the other hand, most monotheistic religions emphasize the transcendence of God—that is, that there is a crucial separation between God and the material world. Therefore, while the beauty of nature may lead us to God, Nature is not in itself divine.

"Third, most Platonists believe that your soul is an emanation of The One and that it remains connected to The One through the multiple levels of reality. Therefore there is a genuine spark of divinity in each person. They say that the individual soul is 'undescended.' As a consequence, individuals, by free choice and spiritual practice, are able to turn back toward their origin and to ascend to union with The One, and thus achieve a kind of deification.

"On the other hand, some Platonists, such as Iamblichus, who lived a century ago, taught that the individual soul descends completely, which means it is cut off from The One. Therefore it is unable to ascend by its own power, but requires divine assistance, an act of grace. These Platonists use spiritual practices, which I teach to my private students, to make themselves receptive to this grace, should it come. Similarly, monotheistic Platonists, who accept the transcendence of God, stress the role of grace in the ascent toward divinity.

"Another point of disagreement between the monotheistic religions and Platonism concerns the creation and eternity of the world. Most philosophers think the world is eternal, with no beginning and no end, although some say it goes through cycles of destruction and recreation. As I've explained, Platonists do not explain the emanation of the world from The One as a creation taking place in time. Indeed, that idea would be incoherent, since time is, in effect, created by the Cosmic Soul, and so it does not make any sense to speak of something happening *at some time* except at the lower level of the Cosmic Body. Individual bodies (including the earth as a whole) might come into being or pass away, but the cosmic structure as a whole, including the rays of emanation from The One, is eternal.

"At least at a superficial level, the Platonic eternity of the world contradicts the accounts in Genesis of God creating heaven and earth 'in the beginning.' More importantly perhaps, the eternity of the cosmos seemed incompatible with the notion of 'end times,' a specific event in which the world as we know it would come to an end to be replaced by the Kingdom of God. I think that, for the most part, Christian Platonists solve this problem by abandoning the eternity of the world in favor of the biblical idea.

"Most Platonists also differ from the monotheist religions on the issue of reincarnation. Since according to Platonists the emanation of The One into the World Mind and from there into the World Soul is atemporal—that is, outside of time, these relations are timeless, in the same sense that $2 + 2 = 4$ is timeless. This implies that all the individual souls in the World Soul exist eternally. Since our bodies are mortal, our souls must exist before we are born and continue to exist after our bodies die. Thus most of us interpret the eternal existence of souls to imply some form of reincarnation, which has been a common belief of philosophers at least from the time of Pythagoras, a thousand years ago."

Although some early Christians accepted reincarnation, the position that became orthodox is that people live once and will not be resurrected until the arrival of the Kingdom of God. Likewise, a minority of Jews and Muslims has believed in reincarnation in some form.

"Also," Hypatia continues, "it is probably worth mentioning another difference between the Christian concept of resurrection and Platonic reincarnation. Christian orthodoxy emphasizes a bodily resurrection, whereas Platonists understand the soul to exist independently of the body (in fact, it is the cause of the body). Because the soul exists outside of time, it is impassive like the gods, and therefore insensitive to events—whether external or psychological—that take place in time. As a consequence, nothing of our memories or concrete personality is preserved from one incarnation to the next, which is why we do not remember past lives. Thus from the Platonic perspective, the immortal soul is a sort of impersonal life force, and there is no reason to suppose the survival of much that we would call our personality or conscious identity." We may leave Hypatia's lecture at this point.

A major problem for a monotheistic interpretation of Neoplatonism would seem to be the multiplicity of gods in the Cosmic Nous. However, these were simply reinterpreted as angels, and the World Mind was renamed the "Angelic Mind." In Christianity this reinterpretation was pioneered by St. Dionysius, who translated Proclus's levels of reality into ranks of angels. According to the Triadic Principle, there are three "choirs" of angels, and each choir is divided into three ranks, also according to the Triadic Principle. Corresponding to the *Abiding* aspect are the Seraphim, Cherubim, and Thrones; *Proceeding* are the Dominations, Virtues, and Powers; *Returning* are the Principalities, Archangels, and Angels.

From a monotheistic perspective, the highest ranks of angels are differing aspects of God. Like the Pagan gods, they have various offices or spheres of activity that they govern. And like God, they are impassive, somewhat like laws of Nature. The lower ranks of angels, which correspond to the Pagan daimons and are involved in time and space, are the angels that interact directly with individuals. Since they are not impassive, they can know the particularities of a person's life and intervene in specific events. These are the beings that can respond to prayers, bring messages from God, execute his will, and enforce his laws. Some of these angels are devoted, in effect, to individuals, and so the monotheist idea of a guardian angel corresponds to the Pagan guardian daimon.

Although saints and heroes are different in many respects and come from different cultural contexts, the Pagan idea of a hero corresponds to the monotheist's saint. Both have become more godlike than ordinary people and manifested to a remarkable degree in their lives the attributes of divinity. Furthermore, in both the Pagan and non-Pagan traditions extraordinary, godlike accomplishments ("miracles") are attributed to these people.

One characteristic of the contemporary monotheistic religions that separates them from the popular polytheism of the ancient world is that God is considered omnipotent and good, whereas the polytheistic gods are not omnipotent and, at least according to the ancient myths, did things that we would not consider good. But even in ancient times the philosophers protested against the myths that depicted the gods as deceitful, adulterous, rapacious, and violent; they said that if the gods were not good, they didn't deserve to be called "gods."

We have also seen that even though the nature of The One is inexpressible, Neoplatonists were inclined to call it both "God" and "The Good." We must recall, however, that this does not mean that The One *does* good, like a good person, but rather that The One is the Principle that everything seeks. Monotheistic religions are more inclined to interpret the goodness of God in anthropomorphic terms—that is, referring to a God who *does good*, treating humans and all of Nature benevolently.

In any case, the notion of a God who is both good and omnipotent raises the "problem of evil." It was put concisely and dramatically in the so-called "Epicurean Paradox":

Either God wants to abolish evil, and cannot; or he can, but does not want to. If he wants to, but cannot, he is impotent. If he can, but does not want to, he is wicked. If God can abolish evil, and God really wants to do it, why is there evil in the world? [225]

Over the centuries many theologians posed solutions to the problem of evil, but many people find them hollow when confronted with human suffering as a consequence of natural calamities and human wrongdoing.

One explanation of the problem of evil, which appears in one form or another in the Western monotheistic religions, is Satan. Originally a relatively minor figure in the Bible, his role has increased into the "arch-enemy" of God. Thus Satan constitutes an all-evil polar opposite to the all-good God. There is no comparable being in the Pagan religions, since calamities and bad behavior can be explained by the limited power of the gods and by conflicts among them. Even Pagan Neoplatonism, with its identification of The One as The Good, explains evil purely negatively. That is, like light spreading from a central star, it gets weaker with distance, ultimately fading into the dark void. Evil, according to Neoplatonists, is not a positive force, but a result of the limited reach of the organizing and harmonizing power of The One. Evil and ugliness are merely the absence of The Good and Beauty.

Another consequence of a monotheistic God who only does good is that his emanations, the angels, are also dedicated to good. To complement them, the monotheist religions have often included evil spirits allied with Satan who assist him in causing evil. (Of course malignant spirits are common in the traditional beliefs in many cultures.) In English these evil spirits are called "demons," perhaps because the Pagan daimons dwell in the World Soul, and hence in space and time, and thus they can be swayed and therefore corrupted. "Who cares?" you ask? These medieval ideas may seem to be irrelevant to living Hypatia's philosophy today, to be a relic of the Dark Ages, but they have psychological implications that I'll explain in the next section.

As you can see, there are a number of places where Neoplatonism and the monotheistic religions do not fit together smoothly. Nevertheless, many Jews, Christians, and Muslims through the centuries have managed to negotiate an accommodation between their religion and the philosophy of the Grove. Neoplatonism has proved to be a spiritually rewarding way of life irrespective of religion.

> *The Problem of Evil*: Set aside some time to think about the problem of evil. Especially if you believe in a good God or a beneficent Providence, how do you account for the fact that "bad things happen to good people"? You have learned the Epicurean and Stoic answers to this question, but you should think it through yourself. Think about people close to you who have suffered from accidents, disease, or natural disasters. Record your thoughts in your journal.

EVOLUTIONARY JUNGIAN PSYCHOLOGY

One of the strengths, I believe, of Neoplatonism as a contemporary way of life is that it does not depend inherently on any particular religion, whether polytheist or monotheist. This is why over the centuries there have been Pagan, Jewish, Christian, and Muslim Neoplatonists. Indeed, although Neoplatonism is definitely spiritual, it does not require any religious commitment at all.

I think that the best way to understand Neoplatonism from a nontheistic perspective is by means of the psychological discoveries of Carl Gustav Jung (1875–1961).[226] Indeed, Jung was deeply influenced by Neoplatonic philosophy, as well as by related spiritual traditions such as Gnosticism, which has Platonic roots. Jungian psychology is nontheistic but not atheistic; that is, it is compatible with the existence of God, or gods. Jung himself was deeply religious, and his psychology has a strong spiritual orientation. He said that most psychological problems are at root spiritual problems.

Therefore, in the remainder of this chapter I aim to show how Neoplatonism and its spiritual practices can be understood from the perspective of evolutionary Jungian psychology.[227] I hope to convince you, even if you are skeptical about gods, daimons, and other spooky ideas, that Neoplatonic spiritual practices are valuable for us in the twenty-first century. On the other hand, if you are a believer, whether monotheist or polytheist, you may suspect that my goal is a materialist reduction of spiritual phenomena, in effect saying that the divine is all in your head, and thus an illusion. However this suspicion is based on a false premise, that if something is in your mind then it's not real. On the contrary, if we set aside the dualist assumption that the mental and the material are mutually exclusive, then we can begin to understand both spiritual and physical phenomena as equally real manifestations of one underlying reality (which is the way Jung understood them). Ultimately, we seek an understanding of Nature that is both spiritual and scientific.

THE ARCHETYPES

You have seen how in Neoplatonism the microcosm and the macrocosm are reflections of each other. We might suspect that they are in some way the same thing from different viewpoints. This is in fact one of the implications of evolutionary Jungian psychology, for it shows how the microcosm of a person is an image of the universal macrocosm, but that conversely the macrocosm is a creation of all the individual microcosms. Thus there is a sort of circular causality between macrocosm and microcosm, which reveals a self-creative cosmos.

Jung discovered that images and circumstances occurred in his patients' dreams that had detailed similarities with motifs in mythology and art from around the world, even though his patients had no acquaintance with these sources. He called these recurrent psychological patterns the *archetypes of the collective unconscious*. Over the years Jung and his successors have investigated the archetypes, and refer to them by names such as the Mother, the Father, the Maiden, the Wise Old Man, the Trickster, and so forth.

Jung stressed that the archetypes are not simply images, but that they are dynamic structures, akin to instincts, governing perception, motivation, and behavior in order to serve biological purposes. They are more like characters in a video game than pictures in a gallery. The archetypes therefore have a sort of life of their own.

The archetypes are unconscious structures, and so they cannot be experienced directly. We know they exist only indirectly, because when they are activated they manifest in consciousness through their effect on conscious experience (including dreams), altering motivation, perception, and behavior. By triangulating between these conscious experiences we can infer something of the hidden structure of an archetype, but we can never know it completely (at least not with contemporary scientific methods).

Since the archetypes are patterns of human behavior, and govern our thinking and how we live, they have the characteristics of life and mind. In this they are similar to archetypal Ideas in the Neoplatonic sense, for they are Beings, eternal patterns of life and mind. Indeed, Jung borrowed the term "archetype" from Neoplatonism. Therefore it is reasonable to identify the collective unconscious with the Universal Mind.

It is apparent that the archetypes correspond to the gods of the polytheistic pantheons, although the latter incorporate, of course, many peculiarities that are not universal but particular to each culture. This is why we find gods with similar characteristics and functions in all the pantheons, and the appearance of these figures in dreams is part of what led Jung to discover the archetypes. This correspondence agrees with Neoplatonic philosophy, which identifies the gods with certain Beings (Forms of motivation, perception, and behavior) in the World Nous.

For example, most pantheons have a goddess of love and sex, such as Aphrodite among the Greeks and Venus among the Romans. This is the archetype that is activated when we see or think of someone who is sexually attractive. As we all know, this can transform conscious experience, restructuring perception, motivation, and perhaps behavior in order to serve biological ends. The ancients said that you had been pierced by the arrow of her son Cupid or Eros, to which not even the gods were immune. In the next chapter you will learn how this potent force can be used to achieve divine union.

Like most archetypes, the Venus archetype is morally neutral. Her effects are positive when they lead to loving union and responsible reproduction, but they are negative when they lead to cheating, dishonesty, or sexual exploitation and abuse.

Have you ever been seized by sudden anger? Maybe you heard of an injustice, or perhaps you felt "dissed" by someone. Most likely you were under the influence of another familiar archetype, who is represented by Ares in the Greek pantheon and by Mars in the Roman. In broad terms this archetype governs our response to threatening and challenging situations. As we know, this archetype can be triggered by all sorts of challenges beyond physical threat, such as a perceived insult or competition at work or in romance. It certainly has served a valuable biological purpose, for it helps us to defend our families, our homes, our communities, and ourselves, so that we can survive and thrive. It gives us the courage to defend and pursue our values. When you are fired up to fight the good fight, Ares is awake in you. It encourages us to compete in order to excel and to identify leaders so we can cooperate more effectively. But the problems resulting from letting Ares seize control of consciousness are all too familiar. War, violence, anger, ruthless competition, and bullying are just a few.

Zeus (Roman Jupiter or Jove) displays many of the characteristics of the Father arche-type. Indeed he was called "Father of Gods and Mortals." In addition to being (in mytholo-gy) the literal father of many gods and mortals, he was the head of the family of gods, and a source of masculine moral authority and familial responsibility. What about The One? I will discuss it later.

Are the archetypes real, or are they "all in the mind"? This question arises with many spiritual experiences, and so it will be worth considering briefly. Certainly, if you are gripped by sexual passion or by rage—that is a real enough experience!

Generally speaking, we consider phenomena to be *objective* if they are not *subjective*—that is, dependent on particularities of an individual subject or observer. Objective phe-nomena are those on which (qualified) observers can agree, and objective knowledge is useful because it is potentially applicable to all people at all times. Science, of course, strives to confine its attention to the objective, even if it is not always successful. I have stated these criteria as absolutes, which is an oversimplification, but in broad outline it is easy to distinguish the objective from the subjective.

By these standards the archetypes are objective phenomena. When suitably disentan-gled from cultural and personal details, we find that all people have the same archetypes. Of course, we cannot observe them directly and must infer their properties from what can be observed in experience and behavior, but this does not make them unreal. Indeed, science often infers the existence of unobservable entities (they are usually called "theoretical enti-ties"). For example, although we can now image them by means of complex instruments, atoms were unobservable for a century after their existence was accepted, and the elemen-tary particles that are the foundation of contemporary physics are still unobservable (in any simple meaning of "observation").

In summary, a century of exploring the archetypes has established them as objective phe-nomena; they are independent of the observer and they are universal, in the sense that they are common to all people. This is why Jung said they reside in the *collective* unconscious, which he also called the *objective psyche*; it is collective because it is a common to all people (biologists call it *phylogenetic*—that is, common to our species). The collective unconscious is not some supernatural realm beyond science, as sometimes supposed. Nevertheless, the objectivity of the archetypes as phenomena does not explain how they arise, what is their cause, what defines their structure, or how they regulate consciousness. We do not need to know these things to live in the Grove, but a little knowledge will help to convince you of the archetypes' reality and to refine your spiritual practice.

Archetypal Events: The purpose of this exercise is to help you to identify archetypal events in your life, both recent and older. Identify events in which each of the following archetypes had a significant effect on your motivation, perception, or behavior: Aphrodite/Venus (or another god or goddess of love and sex); Ares/Mars (or another god or goddess of defense, aggression, strength, or competition); Zeus/Jupiter (or another god of masculine parental authority, leadership, and responsibility); Hera/Juno (or another goddess of feminine parental authority, leadership, and responsibility). These are just examples; you can choose your own from familiar legends, sacred scriptures, and mythology. The common characteristic of these archetypal events is that either at the time or in retrospect you felt like you were living a myth or legend, acting out a sacred drama, or being carried along by universal forces beyond your control. Try to see the universal pattern behind the particulars of your life and give it a name, either one from literature (e.g., Aphrodite, Odysseus, Moses) or a more generic archetype (e.g., Hero, Seductress, Wounded Healer).

EVOLUTIONARY NEUROPSYCHOLOGY AND THE ARCHETYPES

Jung explicitly related the archetypes to human instincts—that is, to the innate patterns of behavior common to all people. Normally scientists study the instincts of various species from the *outside*—that is, by observing behavior. We can study human instincts the same way, but we have an additional perspective, for we can investigate them from the *inside*, from how they affect our own mental state and activity. That is, by personal experience and by asking other people we can learn how particular instincts, when they are triggered, affect our perceptual experience, motivational state, and inclination to act. This is the manifestation of an archetype in conscious experience, for an archetype is the psychical (mental) aspect of an instinct, including its effects in consciousness.

So far as we know, the instincts are implicit in the structure of the brain, in the complex interconnections among brain regions, and in the neurotransmitters that allow one neuron to influence another. This neurophysiological structure is common to all human beings. Like the instincts, the archetypes are determined by the brain's neurophysiology, but the relationship is not simple. Furthermore, some instincts, and therefore some archetypes, may depend on processes that are not confined to the brain, for example hormone release and the population of gut bacteria, and therefore these archetype-instincts are at least partially physiological, as opposed to neurological.

Jung said that as we probed deeper into the causes of the archetypes, we would come to neurological processes, then to physiological processes, and ultimately to physical processes. That is, the archetypes are psychical correlates of natural, physical processes common to all humans. Inside and outside, they are coordinated aspects of an integrated human nature.

What gives the archetypes their specific forms? The archetypes are the psychical aspects of the instincts characteristics of *Homo sapiens*—that is, of the motivational-perceptual-behavioral patterns innate to humans. These dynamical processes are implemented by neural structures in the human brain as well as by other physiological structures. These structures are formed during embryological development by cells acting under genetic control.

Everything that is characteristic of the human species—including the human instincts and therefore the archetypes—is encoded in the human genome. It is worth recalling that the human genome is a mathematical Form. It is usually written as a string of the letters A, C, G, and T (abbreviating the amino acids adenine, cytosine, guanine, and thymine) approximately 3.2 billion characters in length, one for each amino acid base pair.[228] Since one of these letters is equivalent to two bits of information, an 8-bit byte can hold a sequence of four characters, each A, C, T, or G. Therefore the human genome is about 800 megabytes in size.

I am making these facts concrete because this mathematical Form contains all the information necessary to define *Homo sapiens* as a species. In principle, we or other beings with an appropriate technology could create humans by means of this code. Synthetic biologists have already assembled several simple organisms from scratch by using their genetic codes. The point is that our contemporary understanding of the genetic control of the development of an organism has many similarities to the Neoplatonic view. The human genome—a mathematical Form—indirectly defines the structure of the human instincts, and therefore also the structure of the archetypes. Therefore the archetypal realm—the collective unconscious—is an "emanation," an elaboration, of a mathematical Form, and a Form in itself.

The Form of the archetypes is invariable (because implicit in the genome), but it governs processes evolving in time, and so it has an image in each person's soul. First, the Form of the genome governs the development of the brain and the rest of the body, both prenatally and after birth at least through adolescence. Second, and most importantly, the

Forms of the instinct-archetypes govern our instinctual reactions, which unfold in time and space. This translation of timeless Form into embodied action is, according to Neoplatonists, a function of the soul.

I think it will be helpful to explore in a little more detail the accounts given by Jung and the philosophers of the Grove of the archetypal Ideas. According to Neoplatonism, each of us has a nous, which resides in the World Nous and is an image, perspective, and aspect of the entire World Nous. Similarly, each of us has an image of the collective unconscious embodied in our brains and physiologies. As each individual's nous is a perspective on the World Nous, so each individual's embodiment of the archetypes is a variant of the human collective unconscious. In biological terms, each of us has our individual *genotype* (our individual genetic code), which belongs to the general pattern called the *human genome*.

Your individual nous (your personal copy, so to speak, of the collective unconscious), as encoded in your genotype, is a timeless Form, but as embodied in your brain and physiology it is capable of modulating your experiences in time and space. The neurophysiological processes in your body correspond to your individual soul in the World Soul, which projects your nous into time and space.

COMPLEXES AND DAIMONS

The *complex* is an important concept in Jungian psychology, but it is frequently misunderstood. Complexes result from associations that are stored in our brains when archetypes are activated repeatedly or in highly charged situations. That is, complexes form by association around an archetypal core. Since complexes form as a result of the circumstances and events of an individual's life, they are peculiar to that person. That is, complexes necessarily involve personal content, whereas archetypes are universal or common to all people.

In common discourse complexes are supposed to be abnormal, undesirable, and perhaps pathological, but this is not correct. The formation of complexes is a natural consequence of the associative powers of the brain and of the normal activation of archetypal patterns of behavior. In effect, complexes personalize the archetypes to our individual life circumstances and biographies. Although in broad terms complexes allow us to adapt these species-wide instinctual patterns to our individual circumstances, which is part of what makes human behavior flexible, these largely mechanical associative processes can sometimes result in the formation of maladaptive complexes. Thus complexes are usually healthy and indeed necessary to normal mental function, but they are sometimes pathological.

Like the archetypes, complexes reside in the unconscious mind, in the sense that they are not present in consciousness, unless they are activated and begin to modulate conscious experience, and so they can be known only indirectly. Thus, Jung distinguished the *personal unconscious*, in which the complexes reside, from the collective unconscious, the realm of the archetypes. This is because complexes involve personal content but archetypes do not; complexes are individual, while archetypes are universal.

For example, the Eros archetype regulates the psychology of love and sex characteristic of *Homo sapiens*, but your complexes around this archetype influence your individual patterns of perception, motivation, and behavior in the domain of love and sex. Therefore, what "turns you on" is a result partly of biology, partly of culture, and partly of your individual life history.

So also with all the archetypes. The complexes that have grown around your Mars archetype will affect what pushes your buttons and how you respond to the button pushers. Your complexes around the parental archetypes will affect how you respond to people who trigger those complexes (to those who are, perhaps, unconsciously perceived as parents), and how you will act in parental situations (either as an actual parent or fulfilling a parent-like role).

Jung showed that complexes can behave like autonomous personalities residing in the personal unconscious, and he compared them to daimons. Since they are engendered by an archetype, they are like the daimons in the lineage of a god.

An activated complex can in effect seize control of consciousness, "possessing" a person, and influencing them to behave in accordance with the pattern encoded in the complex. This sounds like an extraordinary and perhaps pathological occurrence, but it is much more common than most people think. For example, many "knee-jerk reactions" are results of complexes. Also, a complex is generally involved when we react out of proportion to circumstances. Have you ever got unreasonably angry at a casual remark, or overly afraid in a non-threatening situation, or inappropriately sexually aroused in a non-sexual encounter? When such a reaction is peculiar to you, and not a common human reaction, it betrays the activity of a complex in your personal unconscious.

In the ancient world, such reactions might be interpreted as possession by a daimon, which might be desirable or not. If a poet were inspired by a Muse, it would be productive and a blessing; but if a person reacted to a situation with unwarranted anger and violence, it would be a curse. On the one hand, someone might pray to be filled with the strength, courage, attractiveness, eloquence, inspiration, or wisdom of a god. On the other hand they might beg to be protected or released from the sort of madness that each deity can bring (rage, power lust, racism, compulsive sex or lying, etc.).

The complexes serve a similar function to the daimons as mediators between people and gods. The archetypes are *transpersonal* and largely unchanging through adult life, for they are implicit in the brain's structure. The complexes adapt the archetypes to your individual life. Like the daimons, they act as messengers and ministers of the gods.

Complexes develop as a consequence of the activity of an archetype in your life, and continue to adapt as you live your life. In a significant sense they "know" you and your biography because they have incorporated into their structure material from your life, internal as well as external. While the archetypes, like the gods, are impassive and unchanging, the complexes, like daimons, are not, but respond to you as an individual and personalize the archetypes' relation to you.

It is also worth remarking that there are *group complexes*—that is, complexes that a group of people have in common. They develop through the common experiences of the group, which causes a similar complex of associations to develop in each group member. A shared culture of beliefs, practices, and so forth can reinforce the shared complex and cause it to persist from one generation to the next. Thus there are complexes shared by families, religious groups, ideologies, ethnic groups, nations, people of a certain historical period, and so forth. From a Neoplatonic spiritual perspective, these group complexes correspond to daimons associated with the groups, either for good or for ill (generally, both).

Your Complexes: Think about the archetypes you considered in the previous exercise (*Archetypal Events*). Based on your familiarity with your own psychology and your observations of others' behavior, can you identify circumstances in your life that have engendered your personal complexes? What are some of the cultural, familial, and individual factors? For example, if certain things set you off, but don't seem to have the same effect on most other people, can you find a reason in your life history? Do your standards of beauty differ from those of the culture at large? Why? What about parental complexes (in both roles: as child and as parent)?

THE SHADOW

Jung identified one very important complex, which he called the *Shadow*. As we grow up we learn the norms of our culture, community, and family, and eventually we develop our own values. These (often subconscious) norms constitute what we consider right, good, and just. The opposites of these—what we consider wrong, evil, and unjust—along with our own tendencies in these directions, are repressed and form a complex around the archetype of Evil. This is your Shadow. (It corresponds to a person's "bad daimon," as discussed by some Neoplatonists.) We all have one, and denying its existence often leads to acting out its inclinations, truly a kind of demonic possession!

For example, personally I find self-promotion distasteful; it is part of my personal Shadow, and as a consequence, I am put off by someone who seems to be bragging. More importantly, when such a person activates my Shadow complex, I risk projecting my entire Shadow onto them, perceiving them not only as boastful, but as having all the bad attributes of my Shadow. I risk perceiving them as "evil" and treating them accordingly. This is unfair to the other person, distorts my perception of them, and may lead me to behave inappropriately. I am blaming them for parts of me that I have projected onto them.

This is one danger of ignoring your Shadow; another stems from the fact that your Shadow is constituted from natural inclinations that you have repressed. Of course, it is good for ourselves and for society that we don't act out many of these inclinations; the problem is when we deny their existence. ("Doing such and such is bad, and of course *I* would never do anything so despicable.") The insidious fact is that when these Shadow characteristics are activated in you, you will not recognize that you are "possessed" and will even deny it in the face of evidence. For example, if I ignore or deny my personal Shadow characteristic of self-promotion, then I run the risk of bragging without the self-awareness I'm doing so, or of deceiving myself. ("I'm not bragging, I'm just being honest.")

You have seen that two problems with ignoring your Shadow are that you will inevitably project it onto others and that you may unintentionally act out its inclinations. Therefore it is important to recognize your Shadow, so you notice when it is intervening in your life. "Know your enemy" could be the moral, but I want to go further and encourage you to *befriend* your Shadow. This is because, as Jung stressed, your Shadow possesses many traits and characteristics that you have unconsciously rejected, but may have something positive to contribute to your life.

For example, thinking is my preferred way of dealing with the world; no doubt that fact has contributed to my choice of an academic career and to my interest in philosophy. But according to Jung, thinking and feeling are complementary orientations toward the world, and therefore an emotional orientation has been relegated to my personal Shadow. Other people's approach to life is more feeling-oriented, with thinking relegated to their Shadows. Neither is better, but both are incomplete.

For example, my thinking faculty has been developed and refined over many years, but my emotional intelligence is relatively undeveloped and unrefined. Therefore my emotional responses tend to be more raw or primitive than those of someone with a feeling orientation, who responds with more emotional finesse. I can become a more balanced person by acknowledging, practicing, and developing my emotional skills, which are owned by my Shadow. Who knows what talents hide in a human's psyche? The Shadow knows!

The same applies to all of us; we have all unconsciously buried traits and personality characteristics that for some reason we have deemed unacceptable. They have much to offer us, if we learn to embrace them consciously and not to act them out unconsciously. The method is to become better acquainted with your Shadow, to discover the gifts it can give you, and to recruit its aid in becoming a more complete and integrated human being. You will learn the techniques for doing so in the following chapters.

Know your Shadow; befriend your Shadow.

Seeing Your Shadow: It is important to recognize your Shadow, and this exercise will teach you to do it. Like all complexes, your Shadow resides in the unconscious mind, and so you cannot experience it directly, but you can probe it indirectly by investigating what sorts of people can wake it up. Do not make the assumption that your Shadow corresponds to behaviors you *consciously* consider bad (murder, rape, cruelty, lying, etc.); we are after something deeper. Sit quietly and think of the people—both specific people and kinds of people—who really rub you the wrong way. They may not be evil in any significant way; they might be merely, for example, lazy, pushy, casually dishonest, greedy, selfish, whiny, aggressive, cowardly, ignorant, pretentious, hyperrational, cold, or irritating to you in some other way. Spend some time going through all the people in your life who really bug you. In each case, try to identify the characteristics that annoy you. When you have finished you will have a (probably incomplete) list of the personal characteristics you have unconsciously rejected. If you try to picture a person with all these characteristics, you will have a good picture of your personal Shadow. Yuck! But keep in mind that these are rejected attributes and that some of them may be useful to you in some circumstances and worth reclaiming.

THE EVOLUTION OF THE ARCHETYPES

I have skimmed over a few details in order to present the parallels between the Neoplatonic and Jungian perspectives as clearly as possible. Now it is time to return to them, for I think they are actually quite important. On the other hand, they relate to a scientific understanding of the archetypes, so if your main interest is spiritual practice, feel free to skip to the next section.

I hope I have convinced you that the collective unconscious with its archetypes corresponds to the World Mind with its Ideas. There is, however, an important difference in the way they are usually understood, for according to Neoplatonists the World Mind is the changeless realm of Being, whereas the collective unconscious, as a function of the human genome, evolves in time as the human species evolves. This is a critical difference from the perspective of Platonic metaphysics, but not so important to practical spiritual practice, for in human terms the genome evolves very slowly. In fact it probably takes a thousand years or more for evolution to produce a noticeable change in human nature, and then it would be noticeable only to a careful observer. Furthermore, the change would be statistical—that is, in the relative frequency of genes leading to a difference in the instinct-archetypes. For the human genome is a mathematical abstraction, a sort of average, reflecting the population of genotypes of humans living at any given time. As people, with their individual genotypes, are born and die, the human genome slowly changes, and this change is human evolution. Therefore the archetypes are not perfectly changeless, though they may be practically so, unless we are looking over thousands of years of human history. (Behind the archetypes are the physical laws of the universe, to which the human mind is subject; these laws do not change and are literally Forms, but I will leave them aside for now.)

Individuals have their own genotypes, which contribute to the pattern of the human genome. Therefore, just as we all have somewhat different faces, but we all have *human* faces, and just as we all have slightly different brains, but we all have *human* brains, so we all have slightly different versions of the collective unconscious, but they are all images of the *human* collective unconscious. Hence, we each have slightly different perspectives on the archetypes, but they are fundamentally the same archetypes, innate to all humans.

Unlike the genome, which is a sort of slowly moving average, your individual genotype is a timeless mathematical Form. Since you have two complete genetic sequences (from your mother and father), it is 1.6 gigabytes of data, and in fact it corresponds to a nearly four-billion-digit-long number.[229] Each person has his or her own number (except that identical twins share the same number). Nowadays, for a modest price, you can find out your personal number (i.e., have your genotype sequenced).

So in this sense the Form in the World Mind corresponding to *you* is more real and more literally eternal than the human genome, which is a changing abstraction. Of course, the physical body generated from your genotype will last for only a relatively short time, but the genotype itself is as eternal as the number 2 or the Equilateral Triangle.

Furthermore, as you know, through cloning it is in principle possible to create another body genetically identical to yours. Such a person would have an identical perspective on the archetypes as you do, but be a different embodied person with their own complexes (or personal daimons) acquired through their own life.

The preceding observations lead to an interesting and, I think, important conclusion: the incarnation of humans is necessary for the evolution of the gods. Or, to put it anthropomorphically, gods create living humans in order that the gods themselves can evolve. This is because our individual genotypes define our individual images of the archetypes. The combined images of these individual perspectives determine the transpersonal archetypes—that is, the archetypes (gods) common to humankind as it exists at any given time. As we individuals prove ourselves to be better or worse adapted to our environments, we are more or less likely to contribute our genes to the gene pool that constitutes the human genome. To anthropomorphize again, it is the nature of the gods, who are otherwise unchanging, to manifest as archetypes slightly differently to each of us, and in this way they determine their own future manifestation.

As I said at the beginning of this section, this is a very unconventional perspective on the gods, who in Neoplatonic philosophy are unchanging and indeed timeless. Fortunately, whether you take this evolutionary view of the gods or the traditional view, it will not affect your practice of the Neoplatonic way of life.

This picture may seem to be an odd mixture of evolutionary biology, Jungian psychology, and Neoplatonic spirituality, but it provides an answer to why the souls should descend into bodies at all: it is the way that the gods ensure their own evolution and development. It is also a source of dignity and meaning for us as individuals, for through our individual lives, and our individual efforts to live well, we each contribute in our small way to divine evolution, to the evolution of the cosmos.

There is another interesting conclusion that we can draw from an evolutionary understanding of the archetypes. There is a mechanism that evolutionary biologists have known and understood for over a century by which learned behaviors can become encoded in the genome.[230] Roughly, the process is as follows. Suppose there is some learned behavior that helps a population adapt to its environment. For example, it could be a tendency to cooperate or a means of communication. As new individuals are born into this population, some will be able to learn this skill more easily, some less; this is a result of genetic diversity. Other things being equal, those who can learn it more easily will have an advantage, and the genes that contribute to learning the skill will spread in the population. Over the generations natural selection will favor those traits that accelerate learning the skill, and therefore the skill itself, or at least its precursors, will become encoded to some extent in the genome. Thus there is a tendency for advantageous *learned* traits to become *innate* traits; for, if you like, nurture to become nature.

Now let us see what this process implies about complexes and archetypes. Complexes of associations nucleate around archetypes, and some of these complexes will be advantageous; they will facilitate adapting the archetypes to a population's environment. Some people's genotypes may facilitate the formation of a particular adaptive complex, while others' will not. Therefore, we will expect the genes that facilitate this advantageous complex to spread in the population. In effect, some of the complex, or at least a predisposition toward the complex, is becoming part of the archetype (the innate structure). In the more anthropomorphic terms of Neoplatonic spirituality, an advantageous personal or group daimon will tend to be incorporated into its progenitor god. Thus a god ensures its own evolution by engendering daimons that are active in the material world, and in effect trying variations on the god's own nature, with a result that the god acquires traits from the successful daimons in its lineage: divine parents learning from their mortal children. But this is a process that takes millennia.

THE SELF AND THE INEXPRESSIBLE ONE

What of The One, the highest point of the Neoplatonic macrocosm and the inmost light of the Neoplatonic microcosm? The key is that it is the unity that causes all the archetypal Ideas. In terms of neuropsychology, the archetypes are only different aspects of the unified mind-brain. Although the archetypes are identifiable motivational-perceptual-behavioral *syndromes* (literally, things that run together), they are ultimately ideas that we use to organize and to comprehend the totality of the human psyche. Therefore there is a unity behind the pantheon of archetypes, embodied in the integrated brain, which is an integral component of an organism, which functions by means of the universal laws of nature. As Jung said, the roots of the collective unconscious reach through our physiology and terminate in pure physicality.

Jung called the totality of the archetypes the "Self" (with a capital "S"); others call it the "highest self," "true self," and "inner guide," but it is also the central core of the unconscious mind. It is the image of The One in the individual psyche, and therefore it is also called "the God image" by Jung and his followers.

Jung stressed that the Self is paradoxical and even contradictory, because it is a totality and must embrace all the opposites. Therefore, like the Neoplatonic One, it is inexpressible (incapable of being described in words, or captured in concepts), it is beyond Being (what *is* and *is not*). The Self can never be known completely, as a totality, because a totality is necessarily contradictory. Therefore we can only know it from one aspect at a time—that is, from the perspective of one archetype or another. In this and many other respects the Jungian Self is like the Neoplatonic One. In the following chapters you will learn the spiritual practices that will bring you into contact with the divine archetypes and lead to direct understanding of The One in the only way possible: divine union.

INDIVIDUATION

The Jungian understanding of the psyche, and the correlative Neoplatonic philosophy, has important implications for how we live our lives. Our instincts are part of our human nature, and (short of germ-line genetic engineering) can be changed only over many generations. Therefore the archetypes are also effectively invariable, which means that, in their essence (though not their cultural trappings) the ancient gods are still with us. These archetype-gods, which served us well through two hundred thousand years or so of *Homo sapiens'* hunter-gatherer past, before we discovered agriculture ten thousand years ago, are still active forces in our lives, although they are sometimes at odds with contemporary civilization and social conditions (such as population density). Further, they are *good* only in a biological sense: they have promoted the survival of our species up to the present day.

We may try to repress the archetypes and the complexes they generate, but the attempt is futile and creates greater problems. As Jung said, a repressed archetype tends to return, but in an even more primitive form. Therefore psychological health in contemporary culture requires some accommodation with these ancient gods, something between acting out and repression, for repression eventually leads to even cruder acting out. For example, it is no surprise that religious and political figures with puritanical ideas about sex are regularly discovered to be doing exactly what they condemn.

Fundamental to accomplishing this is humility in the face of the archetypes. We are inclined toward the arrogant assumption that our conscious ego is in control of our mental life, and in particular of the unconscious mind, both collective and personal. But Jung has been credited with a "Copernican revolution" in psychology, for he showed that the conscious ego orbits around the unconscious Self, rather than the opposite, which in our egotism we would like to believe. The ego is just one complex among many, orbiting the Self as the planets orbit the Sun. Nevertheless, the conscious ego is not irrelevant; it should not simply submit to the Self. For the ego is the uniquely human faculty of conscious introspection, evaluation, and judgment, and so it plays an essential role in living a *human* life.

Therefore the goal is neither to repress the unconscious Self nor to abandon the conscious ego, but to use our conscious faculties to reach a rapprochement between the conscious ego and the unconscious Self—the inner God image—thus using our conscious minds to draw strength, vitality, intuition, and inspiration from the Self, and to devote it to the Self in order to serve humankind.

Jung used the term *individuation* to refer to the lifelong process of integrating the ego and the Self, the process of becoming psychosomatically undivided (Latin, *individuus*), of becoming integrated in body and soul. Many analytic techniques in depth psychology are directed toward this integration, and we will see that they are similar to Neoplatonic spiritual practices directed toward the same end. This is the topic of the remaining chapters, which will teach you the path into the sacred Grove where the gods dwell.

CHAPTER TEN

THE PATH OF LOVE

THREE PATHS OF ASCENT

You are crossing the threshold into the Neoplatonic mysteries, which will bring you into contact with the gods and divine union. These advanced spiritual practices are the subject of the remaining three chapters and of the last third of your nine-month program of study. In this chapter you will learn the first of three paths of ascent to the divine, the Path of Love. Each of these paths has four initiatory stages corresponding to the four levels of the Tetractys, and you should devote at least a week to practicing each of them. You should be flexible, however, since some of these stages will be easier to learn than others. Also, you will probably want to study the other paths before you have mastered the Path of Love. What is the source of these practices?

Many of the Neoplatonists were inspired by the *Chaldean Oracles*, which they treated as inspired or revealed texts. They date from the late second century CE and were supposed to have been written by Julian the Chaldean and his son Julian the Theurgist; most likely the father used the son as a "medium" for receiving the texts, allegedly from the spirit of Plato. Many Neoplatonists attached great importance to the *Oracles*, including Porphyry, Iamblichus, and Proclus. In fact, Proclus said he would be content if all philosophical texts were lost except Plato's *Timaeus* and the *Oracles*.

In the century before Hypatia, Porphyry, whose philosophy was very close to hers, wrote a book *Philosophy from Oracles*, which was based on the *Chaldean Oracles*. Unfortunately, only fragments of it survive, as is also the case with the commentary on the *Oracles* by Iamblichus.

Of the *Oracles* themselves, a complete text may have existed as recently as the eleventh century, but now we have only about two hundred fragments, none longer than seventeen lines, some as short as one word! Nevertheless, scholars have been able to reconstruct an outline of the Chaldean system from these fragments and from the fragments of Neoplatonic texts that discuss them.

Many readers will doubt the value of such "channeled" texts, and it is certainly wise not to accept them blindly. However, the ancient Neoplatonists believed they were the result of advanced spiritual exercises, and that they were consistent with the results of the Neoplatonists' own spiritual investigations. In modern terms they are phenomenological investigations of spiritual experiences and the structure of the psyche. The *Oracles* retained their revered status for at least a thousand years, well into the Christian era in Europe, and Plethon (George Gemistos) and Marsilio Ficino wrote commentaries on the fragments in the fifteenth century.

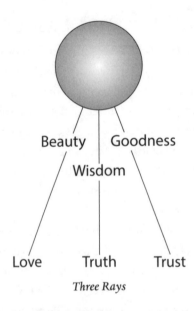

Three Rays

Hypatia is about to teach a lesson in her home to her private students. A dozen of them are seated in a semicircular arc around her chair. She enters from an adjoining room and, standing by her chair, surprises her students by quoting the words that are spoken by the Hierophant in the Eleusinian Mysteries:

I speak to those who lawfully may hear;
depart all ye profane and close the doors.[231]

Sitting, she pauses in contemplation before beginning. "According to the *Chaldean Oracles*, The One has three attributes or aspects: it is *beautiful*, *good*, and *wise*; these are the three *Chaldean Virtues* or *Excellences*. Therefore, three primary names of The One are Beauty, Goodness, and Wisdom, but please don't forget that The One is ineffable and inexpressible, and so all its names, including 'The One,' are limited attempts to capture some aspect of it in language. Corresponding to the Chaldean Virtues are three primary relationships: Love, Truth, and Trust (or Faith); we love beauty, we seek wisdom through truth, and we trust (or have faith in) goodness."

Usually, I will translate Greek *pistis* as "trust" rather than as "faith," since *faith* sometimes suggests belief in the absence of evidence or even in contradiction to it. This is different from the *trust* we have in a close friend or parent, or the *trust* we have in our senses, even if they sometimes fail us. Such trust is not the result of rational analysis, but neither is it groundless. Trust is earned, not granted blindly. In the context of Neoplatonism, "trust" expresses the meaning of *pistis* better than "faith."

Hypatia continues. "Beauty, Wisdom, and Goodness *abide* with The One as its primary aspects, but they also *proceed* through the levels of reality, like rays from the sun, imparting their virtue on everything that exists. We are all illuminated by their light, and consequently, by means of the third term of the Triadic Principle, we can use them to *return* to The One. They serve to connect the here below to the there above, and are like three powerful hands that reach down to draw us up. As a consequence, there are three ways of ascent to The One—the Ascents by Love, Truth, and Trust—and I will explain each in turn.[232] They emphasize the three parts of the soul that Plato described: the faculties of *desire*, *reason*, and *will*. Each ascent involves all three parts, of course, but they differ in the part that is used most in the process. Platonists differ about whether certain ascents are more or less powerful in their ability to reach The One. You should learn them all, but each has its strengths and different ascents may work better for different people."

Gaius asks, "How do we know which path is best for us?"

"If you worship a goddess or god of love, such as Aphrodite or Eros, then the Path of Love may be for you. Also, if you are filled often with the spirit of love, which comes from these deities, then you may find this path to be the best. Likewise, if you are filled with love and adoration for any gods. Remember also that in this ascent you are drawn upward by divine Beauty, and so if you are especially sensitive to beauty, it may aid your progress. Do you understand?"

Gaius blushes and nods eagerly.

"As for the other paths," Hypatia continues, "I will give you some advice when we come to them.

"Just as each of us is an emanation from The One, through the World Mind and World Soul, so these ascents reverse the process, descending into the depths of the soul, to reach The One within. Remember that The One within mirrors The One above, for these spatial locations are just metaphors, so the ascent is also a journey inward.

> For every thing
> when it enters into the unspeakable depths of its own nature
> will find there the symbol of the Universal Father.[233]

"The principle of all these ascents is 'like knows like,' and so to know The One, we must become like it—that is, unified, utterly simple, and tranquil. Platonic philosophy teaches that this unification is 'salvation,' the restoration and preservation of the integrity of the soul. Each thing, nonliving as well as living, is 'saved' through its principle of unity. Union with The One—that is, union with God, is also called 'deification'—that is, becoming godlike insofar as it is possible for humans; recall that the common goal of all philosophy, as taught by the ancient sages, is to become godlike.

"Each of the ascents proceeds through the same three stages, traditionally called *Purification*, *Illumination*, and *Perfection* (or *Union*). The meaning of these terms will be clearer after I describe the practices. They correspond approximately to the three degrees of initiation in our ancient mystery religions, such as the Eleusinian Mysteries."

Now you know the goal of this chapter, and of the next month of your practice: to use the power of love to become godlike and to achieve divine union.

HISTORY OF THE ASCENT BY LOVE

Before teaching the Ascent by Love, I will present the highlights of its history, for it has existed for at least two and one-half millennia and stretches through the Pagan, Jewish, Christian, and Muslim traditions. You do not need to know this history to practice this path, but it will help you to see more possibilities in its practice. The Ascent by Love has its origin, at least in the West, in Plato's *Symposium*, where it is explained to Socrates by a wise woman, Diotima, from Mantinea (a district in Arcadia, Greece). She may have been a real person, since most of Plato's characters were, but she is unknown to history except from the *Symposium*. Her ascent is the foundation of the one you will learn in this chapter.

The Ascent by Love was adapted to a Christian framework by St. Augustine (354–430), a contemporary of Hypatia, in his *Dimensions of the Soul*, and by St. Bonaventura (1221–1274), in *The Mind's Road to God*. More generally, the "mysteries of love," especially in their Neoplatonic form, had a profound influence on the mystical branches of Judaism (e.g., Kabbalah), Christianity, and Islam (e.g., Sufism).

The mysteries of love were at the core of the medieval doctrine of courtly love and of the art of the troubadours, which gave us the legends of the age of chivalry, with King Arthur, Parsifal, Lancelot, Guinevere, the Grail Quest, and the rest.[234] They are the basis of some of practices you will learn. One source of the troubadours' art was a tradition of Arab mystical poetry, which expressed longing and love for God, who is addressed as "the Beloved." This tradition began in the ninth century, but is most familiar to us in the poetry of Jalal ad-Din Muhammad Rumi (1207–1273). The following poem plays on the Persian word *shams*, which means the sun, a symbol of God the Beloved, but is also the name of Rumi's mortal beloved, the dervish Shams-i Tabrizi:

> Love is longing and longing, the pain of being parted;
> No illness is rich enough for the distress of the heart,
> A lover's lament surpasses all other cries of pain.
> Love is the royal threshold to God's mystery.
>
> ...
>
> Love is dangerous offering no consolation,
> Only those who are ravaged by Love know Love,
> The sun alone unveils the sun to those who have
> The sense to receive the senseless and not turn away.
> Cavernous shadows need the light to play but light
> And light alone can lead you to the light alone.
> Material shadows weigh down your vision with dross,
> But the rising sun splits the ashen moon in empty half.
> (*Raficq Abdulla, trans.*[235])

Arab mystical poetry drew from many sources, including Neoplatonism and Manichaeism, a dualistic Gnostic religion that was very popular from Rome to China, especially in the third to seventh centuries CE. From these sources came its ideas of love and desire for union with the divine, ideas which were considered heretical because, according to orthodox Islam, a finite being (such as a person) cannot love an infinite being (such as God). Indeed, several Sufi poets were tortured and executed for heresy, including al-Hallaj (857–922), known as "the martyr of mystical love." The charges against him said, "To adore God from love alone is the crime of the Manicheans…" Therefore it was necessary to be somewhat vague about the identity of "the Beloved." Al-Hallaj wrote of union with the divine Beloved, the inner God image:

> I am He whom I love, and He whom I love is I.
> We are two spirits dwelling in one body,
> If thou seest me, thou seest Him;
> And if thou seest Him, thou seest us both.[236]

There were many routes by which the Arab poetic traditions came to Europe, and especially to Provence and Poitou in France, the birthplace of courtly love and the troubadour tradition.[237] In addition to coming back with the Crusaders, these poetic traditions came across the Pyrenees from Spain, which had learned them from the Arabs in Andalusia. Thus it is not too surprising that half of the surviving songs of the first known troubadour, William of Poitiers (1071–1127), agree with a certain form of Arab mystical poetry (the *zajel*) in their detailed metrical structure and conventional expressions.

William, sixth Count of Poitiers and ninth Duke of Aquitaine, was a descendant of Agnes of Burgundy, who established connections with the Neoplatonic academy at Chartres in the early eleventh century. Among other Platonic ideas, this school viewed the Cosmic Soul as a force pervading the universe, a source of inspiration and wisdom, whom they personified as divine Wisdom (Sophia, Sapientia). They also identified the Cosmic Soul with the Holy Spirit (as explained in chapter 9), an idea that was considered heretical.

Also influential was Catharism, the "Church of Love," which had Manichaean roots. Beginning in the third century these ideas spread across Europe and as Far East as China, but they were especially welcomed in the Languedoc region. The Cathars had a good God of Love, but also an evil Creator (or "Great Arrogant"), who had created the material world, which they considered evil. They said their Church of Love was the opposite of the Church of Rome: AMOR vs. ROMA. (Indeed, according to legend, when Aeneas, the son of Venus, founded Rome, he gave it three names, as was customary: a common name *Roma*, a sacral name *Flora*, and a secret name *Amor*.)

According to the Cathars, salvation could be won from a female divinity, existing from the beginning of time, known by various names: Maria, Wisdom, Faith (*Pistis*), and others. She had borne Jesus to show souls the way to escape from matter and to reunite with their angelic spirits, who had remained in heaven. This divine feminine figure, who was also called the Form of Light, resided in the believer's spirit as well as in heaven (consistent with the Neoplatonic Nous). She met the believers' souls after they died, and greeted them with a kiss and salute.

Catharism was apparently quite popular among the nobility of southern France, and Cathar themes pervade the troubadours' songs. No doubt some of the troubadours were practicing Cathars, while others were simply reflecting the values of their patrons. The Cathar belief system was poetic rather than rational, and so music played an essential role in maintaining the faith of the believers.

In addition to an increasing appreciation for the feminine principle, both mortal and divine, the eleventh century saw a revaluation of physical love. Some poets had discovered that being in passionate love could change their consciousness, and so they began to see love and sex as means of spiritual illumination. Ancient texts such as Ovid's *Art of Love* and *Cure of Love*, which dealt with love's transformative power, were read with new appreciation, but the empire was officially Christian, and so these ideas had to be fit into a more or less orthodox Christian framework.

The Cathars considered themselves Christian, but the Roman Church considered many of their beliefs heretical. Furthermore, there were competing, but more orthodox, movements within the Church, which attempted to accommodate the improved social status of women and growing recognition of the divine feminine. For example, Joachim of Fiore (c.1132–1202) prophesied the dawning of an "Age of the Spirit" in which the Holy Spirit would incarnate as a woman. Also, St. Bernard of Clairvaux (c.1090–1153) taught the mystical ascent of the soul through Love in his sermons on the *Song of Solomon* and transformed the Cistercian order, emphasizing mysticism devoted to the Virgin Mary and divine Love.

In 1170, Eleanor of Aquitaine (c.1122–1204) established her Court of Love in Poitiers (where William, the first known troubadour, had lived thirty years before); it became a hotbed of courtly love. She was patroness of Chrétien de Troyes, who wrote the earliest versions of the Arthurian stories, including the Grail quest; he claimed to have heard the story from Countess Marie of Champagne, Eleanor's daughter.

The Cathars presented a doctrinal threat to the medieval Church, which declared the Albigensian Crusade against the Church of Love in 1208. Lasting until 1229, it was a systematic massacre culminating in the destruction of the Cathars' mountaintop castle Montségur, in the south of France. Montségur is traditionally identified with Monsalvat, the Grail Castle, and with the Venusberg (Venus Mountain) and its legendary subterranean temple of Venus. After Montségur fell, 211 Cathar men and women were executed by burning. This catastrophe forced the Cathars underground, but it scattered the troubadours and their heretical ideas throughout Europe. Although the Cathar leaders had been exterminated and many of their congregations destroyed, their ideas did not vanish, but reappeared in many sects and movements. These had in common an ambitious spirituality incorporating a doctrine of "radiant joy," praise of poverty, anti-clericalism, vegetarianism, and an egalitarian attitude that sometimes verged on communism. Heretical beliefs, especially denial of the Trinity, were also common.

These influences converged on Dante Alighieri (1265–1321), the author of the *Divine Comedy*, which presents an Ascent by Love. He belonged to the *Fedeli d'Amore* (The Faithful of Love), a group of poets practicing a spirituality based on love, which can be seen as an application of chivalric ideas (including courtly love) to the regeneration of society. The Fedeli were expected to write only about their own mystical experiences, so actual practice was mandatory, and they apparently had a system of degrees representing the levels of spiritual progress.

Their system was based on psychological and spiritual doctrines, probably including an Ascent by Love based on the six stages of St. Bonaventura, who divided each of Plato's three stages in two. They correspond to Dante's six guides in the *Comedy* (Virgil, Cato, Statius, Matilda, Beatrice, St. Bernard). The Fedeli's practice also included training the imagination to hold the image of the divine Beloved in the form of one's lady, since the pure light of The One would be too much to bear. Some of the group's doctrine was set forth by their leader, Guido Cavalcanti (1250–1300), in his long and elaborately structured poem *Donna me prega* ("A lady bids me ..."). Ficino and other members of the Platonic Academy considered it to be "a supreme Neoplatonic statement of love."[238] Some scholars regard *Donna me prega* as the manifesto of a secret group devoted to divine Sapientia (Wisdom).[239]

Dante attempted to contact the Fedeli in 1283 by writing a poem to them, as was common practice. In it he described a dream in which Amor (Love) appeared with his beloved Beatrice, and he invited the Fedeli to interpret the vision. Several people responded, including Guido Cavalcanti, who replied in identical meter and rhyme to Dante's poem. (Such exchanges of poetry were also common among the troubadours.) Subsequently Dante was invited to join the Fedeli d'Amore, and he accepted. This is one of Cavalcanti's poems, in which the Beloved, accompanied by Love, is addressed as a deity:

Who is she coming, whom all gaze upon,
Who makes the air all tremulous with light,
And at whose side is Love himself? that none
Dare speak, but each man's sighs are infinite.
Ah me! how she looks round from left to right,
Let Love discourse: I may not speak thereon.
Lady she seems of such high benison
As makes all others graceless in men's sight.
The honor which is hers cannot be said;
To whom are subject all things virtuous,
While all things beauteous own her deity.
Ne'er was the mind of man so nobly led,
Nor yet was such redemption granted us
That we should ever know her perfectly.[240]

The Ascent by Love was also popular in the Renaissance, and we have versions by, among others, Marsilio Ficino (1433–1499), founder of the Platonic Academy in Florence; his friend Cardinal Pietro Bembo (1470–1547); and the diplomat Baldassarre Castiglione (1478–1529), the author of *The Courtier*. Ficino coined the term "Platonic love" (*amor platonicus*), which originally referred to the ascent described in Plato's *Symposium*. In his *Dialogues of Love*, Judah Leon Abrabanel (c.1465–after 1521, also known as Leone Ebreo) presented a comprehensive philosophy of love, which includes an Ascent by Love, incorporating Platonic, Jewish, and Islamic elements.[241] The two characters of the dialogue are Philo (Love) and Sophia (Wisdom); their union would be Philo-Sophia. Courtly love was revived in the court of Henrietta Maria of France (1609–1669), Queen consort of Charles I of England. It inspired the plays of Sir William Davenant (1606–1668), whose *Platonic Lovers* introduced that term into English (with a certain amount of irony). So you see the Path of Love has a long pedigree; let's see what it's about and where it can lead you.

PURPOSE OF THE ASCENT BY LOVE

Before explaining the purpose of the Ascent by Love, I need to mention a grammatical convention. For convenience I will use the pronoun *she* for the lover, who is the philosopher, and *he* for the Beloved, but it will become apparent that the genders are irrelevant. In the *Symposium*, for example, they were both *hes*. It doesn't really matter, of course, but traditionally the soul is grammatically feminine and God masculine, and it is the philosopher's soul that ascends to God. Listen now, as Hypatia explains the powers and energies that you use in the Ascent by Love.[242]

"What is the Triadic Principle?" Hypatia asks.

Athanasius eagerly raises his hand and answers, "Each level of reality *abides* in itself, *proceeds* outward to lower levels, and *returns* as these levels look to their source."

"Good. Notice how this applies to the Love of The One. Of course it abides in The One as one of its aspects, but it also proceeds outward as *Providential Love*, which the Cause has for its effects. Providential Love is the natural perfecting and maintaining power of The One, not a desire or choice to do good. It generates a reciprocal *Returning Love*, the intense desire of everything to love its source and return to it. In the Ascent by Love, you withdraw into your soul and follow the ray of Returning Love up toward The One, drawn upward by divine Beauty. In each case—Providential and Returning—Love is the intermediary between the lover and the Beloved. It is one of connecting 'rays' between the human and the divine. This eternal ring of love binds the cosmos into one, like the Sphere of Love of Empedocles."

Hypatia might have explained that each of the ascents is under the guidance of a goddess and a god. For the Ascent by Love, they are Aphrodite (Venus) and Eros (Amor, Cupido), goddess and god of love. We are familiar with cute images depicting Cupid as a cherub, but the ancient world treated him much more seriously, understanding him as a potent deity, to whom even the gods are vulnerable. His swift and silent shafts were able to instantly turn a life inside out, opening and exposing the soul, for good or ill. Indeed, in the *Symposium* Plato has Phaedrus say, "Eros is a great god, a marvel to both people and gods"; he is "the oldest of the gods."[243] He quotes both poets and philosophers in support. For example, in Hesiod's *Theogony* (eighth century BCE), beginning with the line that convinced Epicurus to study philosophy, we read:

First Chaos, next broad-breasted Earth was made,
the ever-sure foundation seat of all
immortals on Olympus' snowy peaks,
dim Tartaros in depths of wide-pathed Earth,
and Eros, fairest of the deathless gods,
who loosens limbs of every god and man,
their minds and clever counsels conquering.[244]

Diotima has a different opinion, for she says Eros is a "great daimon," intermediate between humans and gods and attendant on Aphrodite:

> He acts as an interpreter and means of communication between gods and
> people. He takes requests and offerings to the gods, and brings back instruc-
> tions and benefits in return. Occupying the middle position he plays a vital
> role in holding the world together. He is the medium of all prophecy and
> religion…[245]

This daimon possesses the lover, imparting a divine madness—that is, an intense, all-
consuming desire for the beloved. The two views are not inconsistent, for in psychological
terms, Hesiod's god Eros is the archetype and Diotima's daimon is the complex generated by
it. Gods and their descendant daimons are often known by the same name.

In a well-known story from the *Metamorphoses* or *Golden Ass*, by the Platonist Apuleius
(c.125–c.180), Eros saves Psyche (Soul) and carries her away from the ordinary world. It is
an allegory for the salvation of the soul by love. After various trials she is elevated to divinity and united with Eros. Here again we see the ability of Eros to capture the soul and
transport her to the divine realms; this is the goal of the Ascent by Love.

The lover does not see her beloved in the same way as other people do. We all know this.
Certainly, other people may think he is attractive, charming, and so forth, but to the lover,
her beloved is *numinous*, radiant with allure, imbued with supernatural charm, charisma, and
beauty. The beloved possesses *glamour* in the original senses of that word: magic, enchant-
ment, spell, magical or fictitious beauty, delusive or alluring charm.[246] This transformation of
perception and mental state is evidence of possession by Eros, or in psychological terms, of
activation of the Eros archetype.

The beloved's beauty is *supernatural* in the literal sense that it is not purely natural—a
consequence of physical characteristics—but it comes from above. According to Neoplatonic metaphysics, the body is created and moved by the soul, and the soul is an emanation
of the Forms, and so it is illuminated by ideal Beauty; and in particular, the human soul is
illuminated by the ideal Human Beauty.

This idea is captured by the concept of *grace*. The English word, like its ancient Greek
and Latin translations (*charis, gratia*) means both a beautiful naturalness of movement and
a gift, especially from the gods. Grace is the ideal movement of the soul, and to the extent
that the soul is able to govern the material of the body, the body's movements are also
graceful. Furthermore, the soul governs the movement of cells during the development of

the embryo, and this graceful process creates beauty in the physical body. Thus Leonardo da Vinci said, "Beauty is nothing but fixated grace." [247]

The ultimate source of this grace is the Good, which defines the ideal movement of each species, its natural grace. Therefore beauty and grace are indeed gifts of God, manifesting in the physical body. Because Beauty and Grace are emanations of the Good, which everything desires, they ignite desire in the lover's soul, warming it, exciting passion. Love gives the soul wings by which she may ascend toward the Good.

Greek *charis* (Latin *gratia*) refers to a gift or other act of kindness, but also to the mutual feelings of joyous goodwill in the donor and recipient. The giver is happily caring, gracious, and benevolent; the receiver is grateful and delighted. This shared joy is the state of grace.

Does this mean that people who are beautiful (by contemporary standards) are better than other people? Of course not. Perhaps you don't think of yourself as beautiful or graceful. (Certainly, they are not words I apply to myself!) Rather, the more important, more enduring beauty resides in the soul, for that is the beauty that is created by the gods and refined by the way you live your life. The Path of Love will help you to sculpt a beautiful soul.

In Plato's *Symposium* each of the guests at the drinking party gives their own explanation of the nature of love; these explanations build up to Diotima's, which is the culmination. However, one of the others is also important to our purpose here. The comic poet Aristophanes tells a ludicrous tale about how humans were originally spherical in shape with four legs, four arms, and four eyes (a typical symbol of wholeness, according to Jung). Because these primordial humans were too powerful, Zeus decided to split them in half. Some were split into a male and a female half, others into two male halves, and others into two female halves. Ever since then, we divided humans have been seeking our missing halves, either of the same sex or the opposite. Love is the desire to find our missing part and return to our well-rounded and potent wholeness.

Aristophanes's myth can be interpreted spiritually and psychologically: love is the desire to reclaim our lost part, our higher self, and so return to completeness. The higher self, the inner divinity, resides in the unconscious, and the most accessible archetype is the *anima* in a heterosexual man and the *animus* in a heterosexual woman. In straight people, this archetype has the opposite gender from the conscious ego. (Its gender in gays, lesbians, transsexuals, and transgendered people is less well understood.) The anima/animus often enters dreams and fantasies as an ideal erotic image, sometimes as the Seducer or Seductress. They may have magical power, as Svengali or Circe.

Hypatia again. "Diotima gets Socrates to realize that fundamentally love is a desire for the good, for possession of the good leads to happiness, which is its own end, for all beings by nature desire happiness. Furthermore, they desire to be happy so long as possible, to have everlasting happiness, and so they desire both the good and immortality.

> *Love is desire for eternal possession of the good.*[248]

"But, because bodies must die, the only immortality possible to embodied beings is through procreation, reproducing after their kind."

"Then the marriage bed," Gaius interrupts, "is the way to immortal happiness!"

Surprised by his outburst, Hypatia replies, "It is *one* way. Loving union transforms the lovers and creates new life, born of the union, but it could be a union of souls. Furthermore, Diotima argues, birth, whether physical or spiritual, depends on love's desire for beauty, for it is beauty that first awakens love.

> *Love is only birth in beauty,*
> *both in body and soul.*[249]

"That is, at the level of the body, Eros causes one person to seek union with another to create offspring, but at the level of the soul, Eros causes one soul to seek union with another to engender the good appropriate to the soul—that is, wisdom and the other virtues. This is explained in the following maxim, drawn from the *Symposium*:

> *Wisdom is a most beautiful thing,*
> *and love is of the beautiful;*
> *and therefore Love is also a philosopher,*
> *a lover of wisdom.*[250]

"Remember that the literal meaning of 'philosopher' is 'lover of wisdom.' Whether in body or soul, beauty inspires us to create, for beauty is the cause of creativity as well as its result.

"With this background," Hypatia continues, "you are ready to learn the Ascent by Love. There are four stages, corresponding to the planes of reality as symbolized in the

Tetractys (see figure): body, soul, nous, and One. The ascent proceeds upward from the body toward The One above, or alternatively, inward, from superficial physical beauty toward The One within, the 'Flower of the Soul.' But first, let's stretch our legs in the garden."

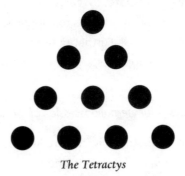

The Tetractys

Providential and Returning Love: Sit quietly with your eyes closed, breathe deeply a few times, and calm your mind. Depending on which of the Geocentric or Central Light Images (chapter 8) you find more natural, imagine pure, warm energy of love radiating toward you, either from the heavens or from the center of the earth. Breathe it into your heart. Feel it enlivening, harmonizing, and perfecting everything in the world, including you. Be grateful. When you feel full to overflowing with this love, direct it back toward it source, feeling yourself as a conduit through which the power of love circulates. When you feel the circulation is well established, allow the feeling to dissipate and return to normal consciousness.

AWAKENING—THE BODY

After a break, Hypatia resumes her explanation of the Path of Love. "You are embarking on the first path of ascent, but like anyone preparing for a journey into unfamiliar territory, you must be equipped with both knowledge and training. First, to make the ascent successfully and to get the maximum benefit from it, you should have your everyday life in order. This is why you have learned the first two degrees of wisdom and have been practicing them—I hope!—in your daily life. They will equip you with the godlike serenity and orientation toward divinity needed for the ascent.

"The first stage of ascent is symbolized by the row of four dots in the Tetractys. They represent the four *cardinal* or *social virtues* (moderation, fortitude, justice, practical wisdom), which govern relations among people, as well as the four traditional elements—earth, water, air, and fire—that constitute physical reality. This shows that the first stage of ascent, called *Awakening*, is at the level of the body and focuses on the physical beauty of your beloved. Thus it begins with your everyday perception of beauty, but heightens your awareness of the transcendent beauty behind it in order to prepare your soul for the ascent proper."

I mentioned briefly the four *cardinal virtues* or *excellences* at the end of chapter 7 in connection with the Stoic disciplines. Useful as they are as a framework for ethics and character, they have an added role in Neoplatonic ascents to The One, for they are reinterpreted on each level of ascent, as I'll explain later. In the first level, that of ordinary life, they are interpreted as *social virtues*, which govern our relations with each other.

Hypatia continues. "Let's begin with ordinary embodied love. First notice that the lover's response is out of proportion to the beloved's physical beauty, as disinterested observers can testify. That is, the lover perceives her beloved to be more beautiful than strangers would judge him. What is the source of numinous beauty? One answer is that the presence of the beloved is essentially an invocation of the god Eros. According to Platonism, the Idea of Love is implicit in any particular instance of love, but the physical presence of the beloved makes this Idea salient; it dominates consciousness." Psychologically, the Eros archetype has been activated, which transforms perception of the beloved.

"Therefore," Hypatia explains, "the first stage (at which most people experience love and beauty) makes use of sensation, the mental faculty that we share with other animals. That is, at this stage love is the desire of beauty through the senses. The focus is on the particular beauty of an individual body, that of the beloved. Even here the lover must keep in mind that the body is not the source of beauty, but only an imperfect reflection of the beauty of the soul, which ultimately comes from the Good, the source of all beauty. Therefore the lover must learn to look beyond superficial beauty.

"The lover feeds her soul with the sight and sound of her beloved, for only sight, hearing, and the mind are capable of appreciating grace of form, proportion, and harmonious measure.[251] According to some philosophers, because the lovers' intentions are spiritual, their physical loving may proceed so far as kissing, for the mouth expresses the soul, and by kissing the lovers may unite their souls as well as their bodies. When the soul advances to the lips it takes the first step toward separation from the body. Here is an exercise for the first stage."

Observed Beauty: Sit and talk with your beloved for a few minutes for your mutual pleasure in your usual way. Castiglione suggests gentle caressing and kissing, but sexual arousal is not the point; the goal of this exercise is to move beyond the body. Therefore, rest in a state of quiet contemplation of your beloved. Allow yourself to become aware of the beauty of your beloved, which is more than his or her physical beauty. Appreciate the grace in your beloved's movements and behavior. See your beloved as an expression of divine beauty and grace, and feel your love as a kind of adoration. You may be awestruck by the mysteriousness of love. Contemplate your beloved in this manner for as long as you like. I hope you will agree that this is an exercise worth practicing regularly! If you are not currently romantically involved with someone, you can still perform this exercise. In fact, the customs of courtly love required that the beloved be inaccessible to the lover (typically because the beloved was married to someone else). You can do the same today, loving someone who is beyond reach, either with their consent or without, if you behave with discretion. Just make sure it someone you actually love, and not just lust after. No doubt many of Hypatia's students adored her, not as a romantic interest, but as an embodiment of the beautiful soul. Nevertheless, if you cannot find a suitable beloved, there is no harm in proceeding directly to Purification, the first stage of the actual ascent.

Courtly love is a spiritual practice in which the heroic lover invokes and invites possession by Eros, and the beloved lady invokes and invites possession by divine Wisdom. The lover longs for, comes to know, and ultimately unites with the goddess; the beloved comes to identify with the goddess and to experience the flow of divine Wisdom through herself. The beloved bestows the Providential Love and care of a goddess, and the hero returns her love through service. Both are elevated, for a time, into the celestial realm, the sphere of Nous. Therefore the lover typically refers to his beloved by a *senhal*, or symbolic name (e.g., "Precious Stone Beyond all Others"). This has the practical effect of disguising her identity (for she is married to someone else), but the spiritual effect of reminding them both that she is representing the eternal Beloved, so they both should behave accordingly. Since the intended relation is archetypal, it is appropriate for each to set aside their egos. Nevertheless, neither party should forget that they are both mere mortals, not divinities.

For this spiritual practice to succeed, each party has to strive to embody the ideal they represent, to be a suitable vehicle for the divine energies. In medieval chivalry, the beloved lady would strive to be a living embodiment of divine Wisdom and Virtue, an inspiration and guide for her lover, the knight, so that he could accomplish his heroic destiny. The knight in turn would strive to love the Eternal Feminine through his lady. He would prove his worthiness by subjecting himself to tests and by adhering to the *chivalric virtues*, which are *moderation, service, prowess, patience, chastity, secrecy,* and *compassion.* In legend, the knight must go on quests, slay dragons, defeat sorcerers, protect the innocent, and rescue fair maidens. Psychologically, these chivalric tasks are the challenges that must be faced in achieving an integrated personality. Specifically, they represent the rejected parts of the psyche (the *Shadow,* in Jung's terms) and other psychological complexes that must be acknowledged and consciously integrated. These include the opposites of the chivalric virtues: excess, egotism, cowardice, impatience, promiscuity, gossip, and indifference.

> *Courtly Love:* You can adapt the spiritual practices of courtly love to our time. Both you and your beloved (who need not be your spouse, but should agree!) attempt to embody your respective archetypes, the lover and the divine Beloved (also Wisdom, the Good). If your partner is not your spouse, then you may want to follow the rules of courtly love and limit your interaction to the first four "lines of love." From ancient Rome to the Middle Ages poets enumerated the *five* lines of love: gazing, speaking, touching, kissing, and coitus. Obviously everyone must agree on limits.

> *Courtly Love (continued):* On the other hand, *separation* was common in courtly love, because a mortal lover cannot enjoy the ecstasy of permanent union with the immortal Beloved. Therefore, the lover might be separated from his beloved for long periods; indeed, they might never have met in person. Through separation you, as lover, prove your faithfulness. Moreover, desire feeds the flame. You can also celebrate your beloved, as symbol of divine Beauty and Goodness, in poetry or song.

We turn our attention back to Hypatia's imaginary lesson. "Union is achieved through sight and hearing, but also through the mind. In the second phase of Awakening, the lover internalizes the image of the beloved in her imagination, so she may have it with her always. In this way his beauty is separated from matter, which can reflect only imperfectly his true beauty. Thus the beloved's immaterial beauty is kept safe in the lover's heart; that is, the beloved is assimilated into the lover's soul. As you all know, you can hold in your heart love for someone who is absent, or even who has died. In this way you take a first step away from the realm of Becoming, from the flux of 'coming-to-be and passing-away,' toward immaterial and eternal Being.

"In this way you turn inward, shifting from exterior sensation to interior imagination. Your imagination of your beloved is also an invocation of archetypal Eros, who illuminates the image of your beloved in your soul. The goal of Awakening is to further inspire the lover to seek the source of this transcendent beauty. I will explain the technique."

> *Imagined Beauty:* This exercise may be practiced as a continuation of *Observed Beauty* by simply closing your eyes, or it can be practiced on its own in the absence of your beloved. The practice is simply to imagine your beloved and to feel your overwhelming love for them. See them in your mind's eye, imagine their voice, recall graceful or endearing habits, their touch, their smell—everything that will create a vivid representation of your beloved in your soul. Feel your adoration for them and the power of your love.

We get the word *narcissism* from the ancient myth of Narcissus, which Hypatia uses as an allegory.[252] "I'm sure you all remember the story of the beautiful youth, Narcissus, who was loved by both boys and girls, but rejected them all, most tragically the nymph called Echo. Therefore he was cursed by his heartless beauty. One day he bent down to take a drink from an especially clear pool and saw his own reflection in the water. He was completely enraptured by the beautiful boy that he saw, and he unsuccessfully attempted to kiss and embrace him. Despite his frustration he kept returning to the pool. At first, he didn't realize it was his own reflection, but when he did, the impossibility of the situation drove him to despair. In Ovid's *Metamorphoses*, Narcissus cries,

> *It is my self I love, my self I see;*
> *The gay delusion is a part of me.*
> *I kindle up the fires by which I burn,*
> *And my own beauties from the well return.*[253]

"Yet he cannot tear himself away from the beautiful image, and eventually, through neglect of himself for the sake of the reflection, he pines away and dies.

> *As wax dissolves, as ice begins to run,*
> *And trickle into drops before the sun;*
> *So melts the youth, and languishes away,*
> *His beauty withers, and his limbs decay;*
> *And none of those attractive charms remain,*
> *To which the slighted Echo su'd in vain.*[254]

"All that is left of him is 'a yellow stalk, with yellow blossoms crown'd,' the narcissus.

"We philosophers interpret this myth allegorically.[255] The pool of water represents the material world, for water is a traditional symbol of materiality, continually in flux, always coming to be and flowing away. Therefore Heraclitus said you cannot step in the same river twice, for it is ever changing, ever different. Narcissus represents the soul, and his reflection represents the imperfect image of the beauty of the soul in the physical body.

"The word *narcissus* is related to the word *narcê* (numbness), which refers to sleep and death, which is why we plant these flowers on graves. But it also suggests rebirth, which is why the narcissus is used in the initiations of the Eleusinian Mysteries. Its straight yellow stalk and blossoms, reaching toward the sun, show us the way upward, the path to the Flower of the Soul. The narcissus reminds us to wake up—from our numbness, from our sleep, from death.

"The Ascent by Love begins with the beauty of the body, for even this beauty is divine in origin. The danger is that the soul is so easily seduced by the beauty of the body, as Narcissus was seduced by his own reflection in the fluid depths. He loved the beautiful image and lost sight of its source. As Ovid says,

> *What kindled in thee this unpity'd love?*
> *Thy own warm blush within the water glows,*
> *With thee the colour'd shadow comes and goes,*
> *Its empty being on thyself relies;*
> *Step thou aside, and the frail charmer dies.*[256]

"It is the soul that animates the corporeal image, that brings it warmth and life. When the soul forgets itself out of love for the body, and when the soul neglects its own well-being out of fascination with the body, then it withers and loses its beauty, as Narcissus did. 'As wax dissolves, as ice begins to run,' the soul flows away into materiality.

"In summary, the Ascent by Love begins with Awakening, the conscious recognition that physical beauty is impermanent, that no mortal, embodied beauty can be perfect, for each person is beautiful in some respects but not in others, and that physical beauty has a source outside the body. Thus we seek a more perfect beauty than is possible in any body. Awakened, we can proceed to the ascent itself, which has three stages—Purification, Illumination, and Perfection—but let's take a break before discussing them."

Interlude—Gaius's Story

This is a good opportunity to tell a memorable story about Hypatia and how she awakened one student so he could see the beauty that transcends superficial beauty. He had requested a private meeting with his teacher, which was not unusual, for

Hypatia's disciples often met alone with her to discuss their personal problems and to seek private philosophical advice. Hypatia is sitting in a divan in a private room when a servant leads Gaius through the door.

"Good afternoon, Gaius," she says as the servant departs. "What did you want to discuss?"

The young man is obviously flustered, and after stammering a few words of greeting, falls to his knees, clutches the hem of her gown, and speaks in a rush. "Dear mirror of Athena, Athena's other self, dear Aphrodite next after Aphrodite, who in your excellence outshines all other mortal women, daughter of divine Zeus, god above all gods! Blessed your father, blessed she who bore such spotless charms! Blessed the womb that nurtured you and offered you to the sun's light! Hear my prayer and pity my desire! You, who teach the Mysteries of Love and Beauty, heed the law of Eros and Aphrodite, and their Mysteries—darkly sealed to maidenhood—will be revealed! Yield then to love and the marriage bed! Revere the sweet divine law of the heart-winning gods and accept me as your worshipper and, if you will, as your husband, for although Athena led me here, Love has slain me with his arrows for Aphrodite's sake. Lady, forgive my boldness!"

Hypatia is not surprised. She has noticed him staring at her during the lessons, and when she has looked at him and smiled, he has blushed and looked quickly away. Now she holds up a hand to stop his protestations of love, and silently hands him the shallow, covered basket from the table beside her. Perplexed, he takes it, and she says, "Open it."

Gaius looks inside, and his expression quickly changes from surprise to shock and revulsion, for the basket contains a menstrual napkin, brown with dried blood.

"Great gods, my lady! Why have you shown me this?"

"Because," Hypatia answers quietly, "this is what you actually desire, my young friend, but it's not so beautiful, is it?"

Gaius mutters, "It's disgusting," and buries his head in his hands in shame.

"No," says Hypatia, "it's the mystery of female fertility, and a sign that I have chosen not to be a wife and mother, for I am dedicated to the virgin goddess of wisdom, Athena. My path is to reproduce through the fecundity of my soul rather than that of my body."

"I am so ashamed, my lady."

"Don't be," she says, stroking his head, "for you have learned a valuable lesson. What is it?"

Gaius looks up, thinks a moment and replies, "That bodily beauty is much inferior to the beauty of the soul, but I have confused the two. And that I should seek the higher beauty and shun the foul and false beauty of this world."

"There is nothing false in the beauty of this world," says Hypatia, "but it is imperfect and impermanent, so you should be careful never to mistake it for the Beauty that is the ultimate desire of philosophers. The one can lead us to the other."

As a result of Hypatia's instruction, Gaius is awakened, and experiences a complete change of mind and heart.[257]

Purification—The Soul

Later in the afternoon, Hypatia resumes her lesson. "The ascent proper begins when you rise above the level of the body to that of the soul, or equivalently, when you turn inward toward the psyche, for the way *up* is also the way *in*. The stage is conventionally called *Purification*, since it begins the separation of the soul from the body: dying before you die. In Plato's *Phaedo*, Socrates explains:

> *"'Purification … consists in separating the soul as much as possible from the body, and accustoming it to withdraw from all contact with the body and concentrate itself by itself, and to have its dwelling, so far as it can, both now and in the future, alone by itself, freed from the shackles of the body.'*[258]

"Therefore Socrates reminds us,

> *True philosophers make dying their profession.*[259]

"Purification begins by concentrating your spiritual energy inward and upward, making your soul more like The One and lifting her toward it. You do this by turning your attention toward the spiritual and away from the body and everyday affairs, so that these will not distract your soul.

"Therefore, the first step is to calm the lower parts of your soul, which are in contact with the body. Let minor disturbances pass away by continuing your inward focus. Pleasures and pains are both distracting, so you should avoid them when possible, and when they occur, attach no more significance to them than as signals of the condition of your body, which you cannot ignore entirely. Therefore, to avoid these disturbances you should try to live healthily, with proper diet, sleep, and exercise.

"Many of the Epicurean and Stoic practices are useful here, for controlling appetites, emotions, sensations, etc. to achieve a state of tranquility. Suffering should not be allowed to affect your soul above its lowest levels; its higher part should remain inviolate, autonomous, and calm: an inner acropolis. This is facilitated by premeditation of possible future good and bad fortune, so that you are prepared to respond appropriately to whatever may happen. With these preparations, you can focus on Beauty at the level of Soul, ascending there by the ray of Love. This is how it works.

"As I've explained, the soul is the dynamic process that generates the body and gives it movement. Therefore the beloved's soul is the source of his beauty and grace. Thus love draws the philosopher upward in order to approach and embrace its source, her beloved's soul. My dear disciple Synesius finishes one of his hymns thus:

> Stretch forth Thy hand, draw me, and call
> My suppliant soul from nature's thrall.[260]

"Furthermore, the lover's principal love is for the soul of her beloved, not for his body, since her love continues and even grows in spite of his body's aging. In fact, as the beloved's body ages, his soul's beauty may shine through it more clearly, perhaps because physical appearance is less of a distraction. But how can we see the soul's beauty more directly?"

The students can't answer, so Hypatia continues. "Remember that the row of three in the Tetractys symbolizes the soul, which exists in time: past, present, and future. Therefore, the faculty of reason—the ability to form consecutive connected images or thoughts—resides in the soul. You apply this in the Purification stage by constructing, through the soul's powers, an image, the ideal of human beauty, perfect in all respects. In this way we abstract away from the inherent imperfections of matter and space, and by the soul's sequential operations create a moving pageant of images. Since the soul provides the elements of beauty from which this perfected human Form is created, the soul must be honored even more highly than this ideal human Form, for you should admire and love the creator more than its creation. Thus you turn inward to learn to love the soul, which is the fountainhead of this ideal beauty. I will now lead you through this exercise."

The Ideal Beloved: Sit in a comfortable position. You may do the preceding exercises *Observed Beauty* and *Imagined Beauty* to begin to turn your soul away from your body. With closed eyes, imagine an ideal beloved, perhaps a god or goddess, a saint, a hero or chivalrous knight, a wise and clever maiden—whatever your vision is of the perfect beloved. Do not try too hard to construct this ideal according to your preconceived ideas about what the perfect beloved *ought* to be. Rather, let your imagination follow its own course, for you want an image that will fire your love, not an intellectual abstraction. In this way you will activate the complex in your psyche that has formed around the anima / animus archetype. That is, you will become acquainted with the daimon engendered by the Ideal Beloved in the Cosmic Nous. Begin to shift your attention from the perfect beloved's physical attributes to the characteristics of his or her soul; that is, let your imagination reveal how your spiritual beloved thinks and acts. See him or her in action.

Hypatia concludes the exercise and explains, "Don't worry that this imaginative activity is disloyal to your worldly beloved. In fact, it's a disservice to project such perfection onto a mortal. On the contrary, this exercise will help you to avoid confusing your real beloved and your imaginary beloved.

"Just as you try to make yourself attractive for the sake of your real beloved, making yourself beautiful in appearance but also graceful in behavior, so in the Ascent by Love you strive to make your soul more beautiful for the sake of the image of the ideal Beloved in your soul. Remember that, as Diotima said, love seeks union in order to beget in beauty. In this part of the ascent, the union is of souls, and so your soul should beautify herself as she goes to meet her bridegroom. Therefore Ficino prays,

> *Grant, O God, that my soul may be beautiful*
> *and that those things that pertain to my body*
> *may not impair the beauty of my soul,*
> *and that I may think only the wise are rich."* [261]

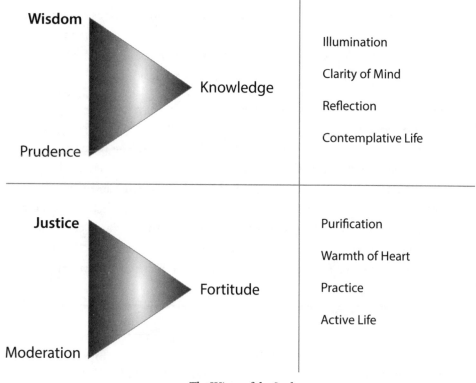

The Wings of the Soul

The lover purifies her soul by practice of two kinds of virtues, which Ficino likens to the two wings by which the soul ascends back to heaven. In the first stage the soul is purified through three *moral virtues: moderation*, which makes us tranquil; *fortitude*, which gives the strength and courage to live philosophically; and *justice*, by which we treat others fairly: we may put them all under the name *Justice*. These virtues, which govern our *active lives*, are acquired through practice and habit and lead to warmth of the heart. You should have acquired them in the first two degrees of wisdom—the philosophies of the Garden and the Porch—but there is always room for improvement.

The other wing of virtue, which builds upon the moral virtues as foundation, comprises the *intellectual* (or *noetic*) virtues, also called *reflective virtues*, because they are acquired through reflection in a contemplative life. These are *prudence* (*practical wisdom*), which illuminates human matters; *knowledge*, which illuminates natural (scientific) matters; and *wisdom*, which illuminates divine matters: we may class them as *Wisdom*. As Justice (the moral virtues) results in the warmth of the heart, so Wisdom (the reflective virtues) leads to clarity of the intellect (nous). In this way we progress from Purification to Illumination. Plotinus reminds us:

> *We're beautiful when we're truly ourselves;*
> *we're beautiful when we know ourselves.* [262]

> *Beauty in the Soul:* Developing the beauty in your soul is not a practice you do at special times, but an activity for all your waking hours. The primary part of this is to practice the first two degrees of wisdom in your everyday life, but you can take it to a higher level by imagining, in all your thoughts and actions, how your perfect beloved would react to them. None of us is perfect, but you can beautify your soul by striving to make yourself attractive to your ideal beloved. In all your actions, ask yourself, "What would my beloved think?" You may want to reflect on your progress in your journal, or discuss it with your teacher or others on the path.

ILLUMINATION—THE NOUS

Our imaginary lesson continues as Hypatia moves on to the World Nous. "The next stage in the ascent to The One is usually called Illumination, since it involves contact with Ideas in the Cosmic Mind, which illuminates the soul with its ideal Form. There are two steps in Illumination, which correspond to ideal Beauty and the Good, symbolized by the row of two in the Tetractys; they also correspond to the determinate Mind and the indeterminate Mind, which I've explained in my public lectures [chapter 8]. Ideal Beauty depends on determinate Forms, but the Good is an all-pervasive indefinite continuum of well-being.

"To understand the illumination by ideal Beauty, it is necessary to recall the characteristics of the noetic principle, which is both the divine Nous and the world of Forms as Ideas in the Cosmic Nous. The Forms are living, conscious Ideas in a state of mutual contemplation, which constitutes a living, conscious whole. The whole implies all its parts, and each part implies the whole; the Forms are transparent and interpenetrating. Among the Forms are all the immortal, divine nouses, including the gods (or angels) and the noetic souls of people. The noetic relation is more like intuitive contemplation than logical, reflective thought.

"As pure form devoid of matter, the Forms achieve perfection and hence constitute the perfect Beauty of the All moving in its intuitive necessity. The beauty of nature is, of course, a reflection of this ideal Beauty.

"In the preceding stages of the ascent your soul has retained its individual identity, but in this stage its noetic part experiences itself as an integral part of the All. Therefore your soul must set aside the non-being that makes it an individual (by imposing finiteness and separation on it). In this way your soul abandons the individual, particular, and contingent, and ascends to the universal and eternal."

Aedesia raises her hand and says, "I don't understand why non-being makes a soul individual."

"To be an individual," the teacher replies, "it must be connected in itself, which gives it unity, but it must also be separate from other things, which differentiates it from the others. So there must be a sort of gap or break in existence, non-existence to separate the existence of the one from the existence of the other. In other words, non-being is what separates one being one thing from being another. Do you understand?"

"I think so. We are supposed to ascend from the level of individual existence, which depends on non-being, to the level of universal being, where everything is unified."

Hypatia nods approvingly. "That's correct. To reach this level, your soul must not *think* about the Forms, or even contemplate them as other, but must *become* them and experience their organic, fluent mutual contemplation. In this intuitive flow, your soul is unselfconscious and loses its awareness (as in our everyday experiences of completely absorbed, competent activity). However, we cannot maintain this state for long, for the human soul is inherently conscious, so we soon fall back to a lower level. Let's give it a try with an exercise."

Contemplation of Ideal Beauty: The remaining stages of the Ascent by Love are more difficult than the preceding, since they are at the level of the nous, and you cannot strive to bring them about, for sequential mental activity—thinking—will drop you back to the level of the soul, where thinking takes place. Begin by making yourself comfortable and then ascending to the level of the Soul, as described in *The Ideal Beloved.* When you have established the image of your Ideal Beloved's body and soul in your mind, and you are feeling love for it (for this is the origin of the beauty of your real beloved), try to maintain this image and love in your mind. You are attempting to rise above the level of time, so this should not be a moving image, but a stable thought (an Idea). Your mind will wander from time to time, and when it does, reestablish your contemplation at the level of the soul, and then return to the noetic level. The goal is to remain as long as possible in a state of stable contemplation, devotion, and love for your Ideal Beloved.

After the students have been allowed some time for contemplation, Hypatia resumes her teaching. "The object of the second stage of illumination is to turn away from the nous's contemplation of itself and to direct its attention upward, toward the Good. To accomplish this it must eliminate form so that it may rise above the multiplicity of the world of Forms and approach The One. That is, it must transcend the duality inherent in the world of Forms. For aid, we may pray as Proclus prays to a goddess:

> *Breathe into my love*
> *a power great and capable*
> *to raise me up again*
> *from Matter's bosom to Olympus.*[263]

"In this stage Eros reaches out to your soul from beyond Nous and draws your nous toward the Good, which has awakened desire, as the lover is drawn to the beloved. Thus your nous orbits The One. This love is superior to the Beauty in the world of Forms, for it is luminous and alive, moving with grace; it is an (unwilled) act of grace by The One. Your soul must ignore everything but the luminous energy of this love.

"By transcending the duality of thought (even of intuition), the calm, sober Nous extends beyond itself and enters a state experienced as *inebriation*: drunk on divine nectar, or on the love of the Good."

This divine inebriation is a frequent theme in the poetry of mysticism, such as that of Rumi:

Look at my body's poor leaking shelter, regard
The proper element of my soul, Love has made
The one drunk and has dismantled the other.

                    ...

Suddenly, my heart is laid open, penetrated by Love
It sees Love's ocean; like a springing gazelle it leaps up
Dancing away to that waiting diamond sea, shouting:
"I can't stay, I must find the way. Come, come now
Follow me!" ...
(Raficq Abdulla, trans.[264]*)*

"Your soul," Hypatia explains, "through identification with the Nous, comes into immediate contact with the Good, although they are still two (as subject and object, or lover and Beloved). You experience this as the all-consuming happiness, bliss, and joy of love. This illumination appears suddenly and usually does not last for long, since it can be maintained only so long as you don't become conscious of it. Here are some practical suggestions."

Love of the Good: In the final stage of Illumination, you reside in a state of intense and intoxicating love for the Good, of which ideal Beauty is an emanation. You may find yourself in this state, sooner or later, while practicing *Contemplation of Ideal Beauty*. Experience it without trying to focus on it, for if you think about it you will drop back to the level of distinct Ideas (the determinate Mind), or even down to the Soul level. (As soon as you think, "Wow, I did it!" you're not doing it anymore.) With practice you will get better at remaining in this state, and at allowing incipient thoughts to dissolve before they interrupt your contemplation.

Hypatia remarks, "At this level, Providential Love and Returning Love nearly coincide; both depend on the duality of lover and Beloved, who have drawn into contact, embracing one another. But the Path of Love leads not to distant adoration of the Divine, but to intimate union with it. The final stage, Perfection, achieves complete unity in a state of Abiding Love."

PERFECTION—THE ONE

The last stage of the ascent is traditionally called Perfection, which sounds pretentious to say the least, and would seem to undermine the humility required for spiritual progress. Of course we can call these stages whatever we like, but it is worth explaining the meaning of "perfection" in the context of the Ascent to The One.

"Perfection" translates the Greek word *teleiôsis*, which is related to a verb (*teleô*) meaning to complete, fulfill, or accomplish. It is also related to the word *telos*, which means the *end* of something, both in the sense of its final state and in the sense of its goal or purpose (as in "means and ends"). Therefore, something is "perfect" (*teleios, teleos*) when it is fulfilling its natural function in the most complete way possible. In particular, the "perfect" human is someone who lives a *human* life to the fullest extent possible.

There is a significant parallel between the stages of the ascent and the degrees of initiation in the ancient mystery religions, such as the Eleusinian Mysteries: *Initiation, Illumination,* and *Vision.* The English word *initiation* comes from the Latin verb *initio,* "to initiate," which comes from *initium,* "a beginning or entry into," for the initiate has entered a new life. The Greek word for initiation and sacred mystery is *teletê,* which refers to the fact that the initiate has been completed, fulfilled, or perfected (*teleô*). In his *Phaedrus,* Plato describes the philosopher who has achieved union:

> initiated (*teloumenos*) into perfect (*teleios*) mysteries (*teletê*), he becomes truly perfect (*teleos*).[265]

Hypatia takes a drink of water and a deep breath before continuing. "How then can one live the human life completely and fully? Ancient sages teach us that this requires being in conscious communion with divine reality, for that is the way we may best express the human Form. This may be accomplished by returning to our source and seeking union with it. Therefore the state of Perfection is also called *Union* and *Deification.*"

Deification may sound even more pretentious than Perfection, even to the point of madness, but in the context of ancient philosophy it means to become godlike to the greatest extent possible to humans. Perfection is equivalent to psychological *individuation*, which means to become complete, whole, and undivided (Latin, *individuus*), a genuine individual, but Jung emphasizes that this is not so much a state or accomplishment as a process of continually trying to live the godlike life.

Petrus, one of Hypatia's Christian students, is visibly upset. "This talk of perfection and deification is sacrilegious. We are all sinners; only God is perfect! The serpent said, 'You shall be as gods,' and now he crawls on his belly in the …"

Hypatia holds up her hand to stop him. "Certainly, as you say, we all make mistakes and do things we regret. Nevertheless, our master Plotinus said,

Our goal is not to be flawless, but to be god.[266]

"What do you think he means?"

The students are perplexed, but Hermias says, "I can't make any sense of it, for the gods are flawless. Besides, you have just said that the goal of the ascent is Perfection."

Aedesia, who is sitting close by Hermias replies, "Could he mean that one part of us is flawed, but another is divine?"

"What parts might they be?"

Aedesia ponders a moment before answering. "Could they be the soul and the nous? For our souls are bound in time and space. They have limited information, their reason is imperfect, and they can make mistakes. They can be swayed—for good or ill—by daimons who dwell in the world and in our souls. But my nous is an image of the Cosmic Nous, the realm of the gods, and my true self, the inmost flower of my nous, is an image of The One. Is that what Plotinus means?"

"Very good, Aedesia! Indeed, so long as we are embodied, we have our souls, which are subject to many influences and limited in their ability to learn, know, and understand. Although we need our souls to live, we can choose to focus our attention into the spark of divinity in each of us, and to dwell as a god among the gods. That is the goal of the ascent."

Permit me to interrupt Hypatia to put this in more contemporary terms. None of us is flawless; we all have finite cognitive abilities, limited knowledge, biases and prejudices, a host of complexes, and especially our Shadows, which lead us to make many mistakes and to fall short of our ideals. *Ecce homo!* (Behold, the human!) To believe you are faultless is indeed madness. Nevertheless, through the practices you are learning in the third degree of wisdom, you can contact the transcendent archetypal forces governing human life and your individual destiny. This is individuation. By consciously centering your life in the archetypal realm, your true self can indeed dwell as a god among the gods.

Back to Hypatia. "In the fourth and last stage of the ascent, the soul advances from her particular understanding, which cannot completely comprehend heavenly Beauty, to universal understanding, which comes from union with divine Beauty. Some explain union with divine Beauty in this way. As the moth is attracted to the candle and is consumed by it, so the lover's soul sacrifices herself as a burnt offering to Love. As common fire refines gold, so the holy fire of divine Beauty refines the soul, burning away her grosser elements. As the mortal parts are consumed and the immortal parts purified, she becomes capable of uniting with divine Beauty so that, in the end, lover and Beloved become one. The soul is made divine and immortal, for she enjoys a feast of nectar and ambrosia with the gods. Heavenly Beauty is unveiled, and the soul experiences the supreme ecstasy. This is the endpoint of desire, the remedy for all pain, sickness, and misery, and the refuge from all troubles; here is bliss; here, peace, gentle love, certainty, well-being, ineffable delight. However, this union is imperfect and temporary, for true union cannot be achieved before death.

"Beyond Beauty is the Good, a place of tranquil blessedness beyond the intense desire for Beauty. This is where the soul reaches her Beloved, now become bridegroom, and achieves union with him. The marriage of the soul and God is an old theme, hinted at by Plato, and explained by Philo of Alexandria, the Jewish Platonist. We find it in King Solomon's 'Song of Songs' and in the Persians' impassioned mystical poetry. It is also behind the well-known story of Cupid and Psyche (that is, Love and Soul) from the *Metamorphoses* by Apuleius, the Platonic philosopher. This is all I can suggest:

> *Union with the Good:* There is really nothing that can be done to achieve this state of union, except to keep in mind that "like knows like," and so to achieve union with The One you should make yourself as like it as possible. That is, unified, whole, stable, impassive, tranquil, and—especially for this practice—filled with love. Then you must wait, for it is a grace that comes at the right time.

"Divine union is not a common event. Dear Synesius expressed this in a lovely hymn that he wrote when he was first studying with me ten years ago:

'Tis hard for man to rise with outspread wings,
Borne upwards by the love of heav'nly things.
Do thou but nerve thy heart with the desire
Of godly wisdom's joy; to heaven aspire;
And soon thou'lt see thy Father near thee stand,
And, bending o'er thee, stretch a helping hand.
For a soft ray from heaven will run to guide
And light thy way, and show that boundless land
Where the noetic lights forever dwell,
And whence true beauty and true joy expand
From the deep fountains of God's love which well.[267]

"Porphyry reports that his master Plotinus experienced union only four times in the six years they studied together; the disciple experienced it only once, in his sixty-eighth year."

Euoptius, Synesius's younger brother, asks, "How many times have you achieved union?"

"Modesty prevents me from reporting on myself," Hypatia replies. "You should be suspicious of anyone who boasts of their own spiritual accomplishments. That is enough for today; next time you'll learn the Ascent by Truth." The students quickly stand as Hypatia leaves.

Invocation of Love: You may find this exercise helpful in ascending through the degrees of Illumination toward Union. To practice it, you will need a name or short phrase that calls your ideal Beloved to mind. It could be the name of a god or goddess (e.g., Apollo, Artemis, Aphrodite, Eros, Sophia, Shekhinah, Kuan Yin, Brigid, Mother Mary, Jesus), but you don't need to use the Beloved's name. You can use a short phrase (an "arrow prayer"), such as these lines from al-Hallaj: "I am He / She whom I love, and He / She whom I love is I." Repeat the name or prayer as a devotional practice, first out loud, and then in your mind, while feeling genuine love for your Beloved. Repeat it incessantly, even as a background to your other activities. Eventually the lover and the Beloved, and the Love between them, will unite into One, a state of bliss and ecstasy. (See *Arrow Prayers and Invocation of the Name* in the next chapter for more on this exercise.)

The Ascent by Love is summarized in the following table:

Structure of the Ascent by Love						
Level of Reality		Love as Desire for …	Mental Faculty		Stage of Ascent	
World Body		Physical beauty	Sensa-tion	Vision	Awaken-ing	Observed beauty
				Imagin-ation		Imagined beauty
World Soul		Universal beauty	Reason		Purifica-tion	Calm lower soul
						Concept of perfect beauty of soul
						Beautifi-cation of soul: Moral virtues
						Intel-lectual virtues
World Nous	Being	Ideal Beauty	Nous		Illumina-tion	Contemplation of Ideal Beauty
	Good-ness	The Good				Love of the Good
The One		Divine Beauty	The god within		Perfection (Union)	

CHAPTER ELEVEN

THE PATH OF TRUTH

INTRODUCTION

In this chapter you will learn the second path of ascent to The One, the Ascent by Truth, also known as the Philosophical or Contemplative Ascent.[268] Like the Ascent by Love, it proceeds in four initiatory stages represented by the rows of the Tetractys (see figure): Awakening, Purification, Illumination, and Perfection. As you will learn, each stage has its own distinct *virtues* or *excellences*, which you should practice. You could devote about a week to each of the stages as a focus for your practice. Along the way you will also learn the fivefold basis of understanding and the Neoplatonic practice of prayer.

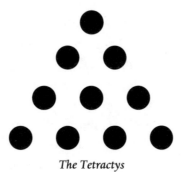

The Tetractys

Hypatia's students have gathered again, this time to learn the Ascent by Truth. The chatter ceases as she enters and begins. "The second path of ascent rises on the ray of Truth, which connects all things to the Wisdom of The One. Whereas the Ascent by Love emphasizes the faculty of desire, the Ascent by Truth emphasizes the faculty of reason. The guides on this path are Athena, patroness of wisdom, and Hermes, the guide of souls, messenger between gods and mortals, and patron of those who cross the boundaries between different realms."[269]

Aedesia raises her hand. "I am devoted to Athena, and in turn she cares for me and helps me in many ways. Does that mean the Path of Truth is best for me?"

"It very well could be, especially for someone who is a thinker and nature lover, as I know you are, Aedesia. But you are also passionate."

Hermias glances toward Aedesia, who blushes.

"So," Hypatia continues, "the Ascent by Love might be easy for you as well. Don't make the mistake of thinking there must be *one right way*. As a true philosopher you should learn and practice them all; know your way on all three paths. Different ascents will be easier at different times in your life or in different circumstances. Do you understand?"

Aedesia nods.

"Like the Ascent by Love," Hypatia continues, "the Ascent by Truth is also symbolized by the Pythagorean Tetractys, whose four rows correspond, from bottom up, to the four levels of reality in the macrocosm and the microcosm: Body, Soul, Nous, and One, and to the four stages in the ascent. As you will see, the dots in each row symbolize separate steps or rungs of each stage, with the last step of each stage bringing your psyche into contact with the next level and forming the bridge to it. If you hang these ideas on the Tetractys they will be easier to remember and practice."

Awakening

Hypatia proceeds to the first stage. "As the Ascent by Love is awakened by love of beauty (*philo-kalia*), the Ascent by Truth is awakened by love of wisdom (*philo-sophia*), which is why it's also called the Philosophical Ascent. The first stage is called the *active practice*, in contrast to the ascent proper, which is the *contemplative practice*. The active practice has four rungs, corresponding to the row of four in the Tetractys. These begin with a *change of mind*, which refers to your recognition that there is another, better way to live, namely philosophy, and to a commitment to follow it. This is the literal awakening of the soul. With opened eyes you can see a new path through life.

"Awakening leads to the second practice, *watchfulness* or *vigilance*—that is, to paying attention to each moment and to behaving philosophically in it. Since the change of mind is like waking up from a drunken stupor, and becoming aware of your drunkenness, this practice is also called *sobriety*, but this is a metaphor; it refers to the inebriation of thoughtlessness and the sobriety of self-awareness."

Hermias, who is sitting beside Aedesia, raises his hand. "Master, I am confused because when you explained Illumination in the Path of Love, you said we could become drunk on love for The One, which is good."

"You are correct," says Hypatia, "but why is it good?"

"Because it is the intoxication of a mind in contact with divinity?"

"Very good," Hypatia smiles. "The sobriety I am discussing here is opposed to the foggy thinking, blurred perception, and confused goals of someone who is not completely awake. Instead of wandering aimlessly, you have a purpose in each step. Thus, vigilance applies to the choices you make in each moment, as you learned in the second degree of wisdom, the vigilance of the Porch. Conversely, it refers to the practice of being aware of the quality of each moment, so that you can recognize the best time for any action. In summary, vigilance consists in being awake and paying attention.

"Awakening and watchfulness lead to the third practice, *discrimination* or *discernment*, which is remaining attuned to the rightness or wrongness of each situation and action. That is, having woken up and looked around carefully, now you must evaluate what you see. The practices of the Garden and Porch provide a foundation for discernment, for they help you to separate what you should judge as good or evil from those things on which you should suspend judgment. Remember:

> *Virtue is a quality of the soul*
> *that leads you by discernment*
> *to bliss."*[270]

Olympius, a student wearing a large, golden cross, remarks, "This continual vigilance and discernment seems like a burdensome way to live."

"It's not," says Hypatia, "for discernment becomes a habit, and you will develop a 'nose' for good and evil, which becomes a guide to right action. This is supplemented by other spiritual practices, such as meditation, prayer, and contemplation, which lead to your attuning to the archetypal forces of human nature, the eternal spiritual principles."

As I mentioned in chapter 9, Platonism includes the idea of a *guardian daimon*, which corresponds to the guardian angel of many religious traditions. This daimon is experienced as a separate personality, which speaks in our minds or in other ways inclines us toward or away from actions. Psychologically, the guardian daimon is a complex that grows, through habitual judgment, around a moral archetype. When activated, it manifests in consciousness as an agent of moral evaluation. Although the guardian daimon originates in the Cosmic Nous or Angelic Mind, it will not develop unless it is cultivated, both by parents and society, but also by the individual, who must tend to their own guardian daimon. In a hymn, Hypatia's disciple Synesius prays:

> A holy angel mighty send
> To be my guardian and guide—
> In heaven-taught prayer to keep my soul,
> And body in temptation's tide.[271]

"Discrimination," Hypatia continues, "leads to the fourth rung of active practice, called *guarding the heart* (that is, the nous); its purpose is to protect your inner spiritual core or higher self (the nous and the god within). You want to be guided by the spirit, as opposed to being driven by the appetites and feelings of the body. The latter should not be repressed, but transfigured and recruited toward spiritual progress (as in the Ascent by Love). One technique is the Stoic practice of suspending judgment. Your goal is joyful tranquility, as taught by the Porch, not absence of feeling. This state is called 'purity of the heart (nous).' Tranquility is achieved first on the level of the body, and later, through Purification, on the level of the soul. These are all practices you have learned in the first two degrees of wisdom, but now you have a name for them."

Philosophical Awakening: If you have read this far in this book, then that is good evidence that you have experienced a change of mind, the first step of Awakening. Nevertheless, you can practice the change of mind by reminding yourself from time to time that you have chosen a new, philosophical way of life, which then implies other changes in your attitudes and choices. The other steps of Awakening—vigilance, discernment, and guarding the heart—are implicit in the practices of the Garden and the Porch that focus on your moment-by-moment attitude and behavior in order to govern your lower soul. Explore your successes and difficulties in your journal and with others on the path.

Hypatia continues her lesson. "The Ascent by Truth involves the Platonic virtues. But the *virtue*—or *excellence*—of anything refers to the ways in which that thing is authentically what it is, its authentic being. For example, the virtue of a knife is to be sharp and strong. Therefore, we understand the virtues differently at each level of ascent. For example, Porphyry defines four degrees of virtue, corresponding, from bottom up, to the body, the animal soul, the human soul, and the nous, which is your divine mind; Proclus adds a fifth degree, which corresponds to The One.[272] The corresponding means of cognition are first, sensation; second, opinion and belief; third, discursive reason and contemplation; fourth, noetic (intuitive) intelligence; fifth, union and deification. In this way each of the four cardinal virtues or excellences—wisdom, fortitude, self-control, justice—is reinterpreted at each level of ascent. I will discuss each degree of virtue as we come to it, but let's begin with those associated with Awakening." (All the degrees are listed in a table at the end of this chapter.)

"Porphyry tells us that the goal of the first degree of virtue, *Practical Virtue*, is to moderate your feelings and to follow the guidance of reason in the responsibilities and actions of your life.[273] Therefore these virtues have both a personal aspect, regulating your behavior with respect to yourself, and a social aspect, regulating it with respect to other people. You learned this in the first two degrees of wisdom, which you must continue to practice. Naturally one cannot hope to become divine until one has become a good human being. Write down these maxims:

One must first be persons, then be gods.[274]

The Practical Virtues make persons,
and the sciences lead to Divine Virtue
and make them gods.[275]

"The Practical Virtues focus on the sensible world, the body, and sensation; they moderate the feelings and govern the irrational parts of the soul. In this way we conform our behavior to (rational) human nature, but many animals also exhibit these excellences, for they learn to regulate their behavior individually and in relation to other animals.

"Since the practical virtues are appropriate both to the individual and to the group, there are two sublevels, the Ethical Virtues and the Social Virtues. The first three Ethical Virtues govern the three parts of the lower soul: the irrational part, the will, and the appetites. The virtue of *prudence* or *practical wisdom* refers to the rational part's government of the irrational part. *Fortitude* governs the will, restraining it or acting on it according to reason. *Self-control* or *moderation* refers to the regulation of the appetites according to reason. *Justice* consists in the harmony of all the soul's faculties, so that each fulfills its proper function, either to command or to obey.[276]

"The Social Virtues make us kind in our dealings with each other, uniting us into a community.[277] At this level *practical wisdom* is sound judgment about what is good for society, *fortitude* is an appropriate attitude toward what should be feared or not, *moderation* refers to the relation between the government and citizens, and *justice* is defined as a harmonious relation among all the groups and individuals making up the community, so that each receives what it is due according to reason.

"In summary, the active practices of Awakening are represented by the four dots at the bottom of the Tetractys. They symbolize both the four practical virtues, namely practical wisdom, fortitude, moderation, and justice, and the four rungs of active practice—that is, a change of mind, vigilance, discernment, and guarding the heart. Now let's take a break."

Is your head is swimming with all these steps of awakening, "virtues," and other terminology? Don't despair! Certainly, you can succeed in the Ascent by Truth without memorizing all this esoterica. The bottom line is this: continue to practice what you have learned in the first two degrees of wisdom and stay awake with a changed mind, vigilance, discernment, and a pure heart, and you will be ready for the ascent.

PURIFICATION 1: THE PURIFYING VIRTUES

The contemplative practice, the ascent proper, begins with Purification, which was also the first initiation in the ancient mysteries. As Hypatia will explain, there are three rungs in the practice of purification, which progressively develop your contemplative abilities.

After her students have settled into their chairs, Hypatia begins. "Purification is represented by the second level of the Tetractys, which has three dots. They correspond to ethics, logic, and physics, and to the three parts of the soul: the animate soul (which we share with other animals), the rational soul (which includes the faculties of language and discursive reason), and the noetic soul (which is the image of the Cosmic Nous in each of us). Purification operates on each of these parts of the soul in order, and there are corresponding degrees of virtue, for Plotinus says,

Virtue demands preliminary purification.[278]

"The ascent commences with the *Purifying Virtues* by which you begin assimilation to The One. For it is said:

Just as the bleary, unclear eye cannot behold exceeding brightness,
so a feeble soul that's weak in virtue
cannot look and gaze upon the Beauty of Truth.[279]

"Preliminary purification is necessary; remember:

It's not lawful for impurity to touch the pure.[280]

"The Purifying Virtues begin the separation of your soul from your body and its concerns. They are the first stage of philosophical 'dying before you die,' because you intentionally separate your soul from your body by the power of the soul, whereas death separates your body from your soul because of the death of your body. Death to one's old life is the first stage of initiation in the mysteries, also called Purification. Therefore Plotinus says,

The object of virtue is to disentangle the soul from the body.[281]

"First your animal soul is purified by disengaging it from the concerns of the body, its feelings and concerns. Therefore the Purifying Virtues focus on your lower soul and your faculty of belief, which you share with many other animals. We reinterpret the four cardinal virtues in this first rung of Purification to represent a soul that has purified itself from the concerns of the body. In brief, *practical wisdom* consists in not forming opinions according to your body and its sensations, but in accordance with reason; *self-control* consists in not being disturbed by the state of your body or its feelings; *fortitude* consists in not fearing your soul's separation from the body (as though it were to die); and *justice* is the subjection of the soul to the power of reason. The first two degrees of wisdom support these virtues."

> *The Purifying Virtues:* The Purifying Virtues are supported by the practices and way of life you learned in the first two degrees of wisdom. In your journal or in discussion with your teacher and other practitioners, assess your progress in the four Purifying Virtues.

PURIFICATION 2: DIALECTICS

"The second rung of Purification," Hypatia continues, "is directed to the rational soul with its power of discursive reason. Its principal practice is *dialectics*, which is a philosophical method central to Platonism; it's illustrated by the Socratic method evident in the Plato's dialogues. Dialectics is a practice in which two or more people use logical analysis to reveal the truth. As we do in our lessons, a teacher usually leads the pupils in an exploration of the realm of Forms, but philosophers can also explore it collaboratively, criticizing and testing each other's discoveries.

"The practice of dialectics is a logical corrective to our tendency to fool ourselves or to be satisfied with inadequate proofs of what we are already inclined to believe. That is, it is a means of greater objectivity in philosophical matters. It is motivated by desire for the Truth and aims at a Logos that transcends our individual opinions. This is especially important in spiritual investigations.

"In accordance with the Triadic Principle—the threefold movement of Abiding, Proceeding, and Returning—dialectic explores the relation of Ideas three ways: in their own essence, in relation to their effects, and in relation to their causes. That is, it explores Ideas first as they abide in themselves, in their essence or Being. It also follows Ideas as logical causes, proceeding outward to their consequences. Finally, it investigates Ideas by looking backward toward their premises or causes, ascending ever higher in the Chain of Being toward the First Cause, The One. This may be difficult, but Plato reminds us:

> The way upward and downward,
> through all its stages,
> produces knowledge through effort and toil.[282]

"Mathematics is the most familiar example of the dialectical process, exploring the realm of Forms through this upward and downward process. For example, mathematics may begin with well-known Ideas, such as numbers, magnitudes, and geometrical figures, such as circles and triangles. It works downward, investigating the consequences of these ideas, deriving and proving theorems about arithmetic and geometry (such as formulas for area). It also works upward, striving to discover the definitions and postulates that give numbers and shapes their properties and that explain them. When this process is carried out methodically and when mathematicians collaborate, checking, criticizing, and improving each other's work, then the structure of mathematical ideas can be discovered and expressed precisely in words, symbols, and diagrams. (Traditional Euclidean geometry remains an outstanding example of a result of dialectics.) This is why over the entry to Plato's Academy was posted, 'Let no non-geometer enter.' But mathematics is just training for applying dialectics in the spiritual realm."

"I despair of ever learning mathematics," says Theotecnus, who has a snowy white mane and beard. "Am I unworthy to be a Platonist?"

"Most certainly not, father," Hypatia says kindly. "Mathematics is a useful stepstool for the ascent, but it's not necessary. Even for this purpose, it is sufficient to appreciate the eternal, immaterial nature of mathematical objects, in which they are like the Ideas. But I know from our personal conversations that you have already a deep understanding of the Ideas."

"That is a great relief, my lady."

"Another useful dialectical practice is textual commentary, such as I practice with you. We select some venerable text—it might be one of Plato's dialogues or one of Aristotle's essays, or an inspired text such as the poems of Homer and Hesiod, or the *Chaldean Oracles*—and either I comment on it myself, or assign it to one of you for commentary. Other teachers might choose the Torah or the Gospels. The task of the commentator is to expound, analyze, and criticize the text, revealing its inner meaning. But we also want this to be a collaborative activity, with the commentator responding to questions and challenges, either orally or in writing."

Through the preceding, Petrus has been growing more visibly upset.

"Do you have a question, Petrus?"

"Forgive my boldness, my lady, but how can you mention in the same breath the holy Gospels and the false Pagan fables of the gods? Moreover, the Gospels are beyond criticism, for they are the literal word of God."

"Which gospels do you have in mind?" snorts Athanasius—always ready to pick a fight—"For you Christians have them by the bushel, all mutually contradictory!"

"There are only four that are genuine," pronounces Olympius. "There must be four, like the four pillars that support the earth, but we must be patient until the holy synods finally decide which four. All the others are heresy!"

"Why don't they approve of the Gospel of Thomas?" asks Cyrus, a Christian suspected of Pagan leanings. "It is excellent."

"Aren't there also gospels of Eve, Mary, and Sophia?" asks Aedesia.

"Heresies!" cries Olympius.

The students begin to talk at the same time, until Hypatia raises her hand and they instantly fall silent.

"There is much of truth and value in our sacred and inspired texts—*if* you know how to read them. Do the *Iliad* and *Odyssey* record the true history of the Trojan War? While I have no doubt there was such a war, I *do* doubt that these poems record every detail correctly. That is not their purpose. Nor do I believe the literal truth of Hesiod's stories of the violence the gods commit against each other. Plato teaches us that such violence is against their nature.

"Nevertheless, these sacred, inspired texts, these scriptures, contain deep and profound truths. But you must set aside their literal meanings and read them—or hear them—*symbolically*. Then you will pass beyond the trivial particularities of time and place, the literal meaning, and penetrate to their universal and eternal meaning in their hearts. When we discussed the Ascent by Love, we did this in our analysis of the myth of Narcissus, a silly enough story if read literally! So remember:

Mythic truth is truer than literal truth.

"Moreover, as you will learn when we discuss the Ascent by Trust, long meditation on a symbolic interpretation allows the symbols to act in your soul, bringing about spiritual transformation. But enough of dusty books and brittle scrolls for now! The weather is very pleasant, so let's move our lesson to the garden."

Textual commentary is often viewed as a sort of low-grade, secondhand philosophy, but it is a spiritual exercise inculcating humility and love of truth. Nowadays we tend to value novelty for its own sake, but ancient philosophy was aimed at the truth as a guide for living. Whether an idea was new or old was not the point, and philosophers recognized that an old idea, which had been tested and refined for centuries, might be much more valuable than an untested innovation. Therefore, at its best, textual commentary acknowledges the time-tested value of a philosopher's work, while simultaneously trying to enhance human well-being by making incremental improvements to the philosophy's doctrines and practices and by adapting them to contemporary circumstances. (This is in fact my hope in presenting Hypatia's philosophy as a contemporary spiritual practice.)

Dialectics also includes reading and studying texts, both primary texts and secondary commentaries or analyses. An important part of this activity is allegorical interpretation and dialectical analysis of inspired texts or scriptures in order to reveal their inner meaning. Therefore, as part of your program of spiritual development you should continue to read critically books of philosophy, mythology, and spiritual wisdom, both ancient and modern. See the following exercises and the "Additional Reading" section at the end of this book for some suggestions.

Textual Commentary: You can practice textual commentary as a group exercise. First, pick some text of mutual interest with a spiritual orientation. Obvious choices would be any of Plato's dialogues. Traditionally Neoplatonists studied them in a prescribed order,[283] but that is not at all necessary; I recommend the *Phaedo*, *Symposium*, and *Phaedrus* as accessible dialogues with direct relevance to spiritual practice. Another good, challenging choice would be Plotinus's *Enneads*, since they are the foundation of Neoplatonism. If you are not ready to read them all, there are some good selections available, such as those by Dodds, O'Brien, Katz, and Uždavinys (see this book's bibliography).

Textual Commentary (continued): A more advanced exercise would be to work through Proclus's *Elements of Theology*, which attempts to establish the Neoplatonic system by systematically stating and proving 211 propositions. Of course, there is no reason to limit your exercises to Platonic texts. For each meeting, pick some text or part of a text for discussion, which the participants should read before the meeting. One person can be designated as the commentator when the text is picked, or the commentator can be chosen at the time of discussion (which helps ensure that everyone does their reading!). The commentator should present the text and attempt to reveal its inner meaning and significance. The other participants ask questions to clarify the text, to analyze or criticize it, and to explore its wider connections and implications. Keep in mind the dialectical exploration of ideas in themselves, in their implications, and in their presuppositions. If you reach any conclusions, it is worthwhile to have someone write them up; in any case you should record your own conclusions in your journal.

Allegorical Interpretation: Allegorical interpretation is an important Neoplatonic spiritual practice, for any inspired text has multiple levels of meaning. The most superficial level—the literal meaning—is the least important. Neoplatonists believe that penetrating into the deeper levels of meaning will grant you profound insights and even cause a spiritual transformation. Ancient mythology is especially valuable for this exercise. For example, you could use selections from Hesiod's *Theogony*, Homer's *Iliad* and *Odyssey* (a favorite of Neoplatonists), Ovid's *Metamorphoses* (with its Pythagorean allegories), or Apuleius's *Golden Ass* or *Metamorphoses*. Your goal is to use your intuition to find the hidden meaning(s). Record your interpretations and discuss them with your spiritual companions.

PURIFICATION 3: THE CONTEMPLATION OF NATURE

Hypatia settles on a stone bench in the garden, and her students take up positions around her. Aedesia and Hermias lean against a tree; Olympius has brought a folding chair of carved wood.

"In the Ascent by Truth," Hypatia begins, "your goal is the timelessness of the Forms. So after dialectical analysis is complete, discursive reason should retire and make way for contemplation. Thus the third stage of Purification addresses your noetic soul and turns it toward contemplation of the Forms. This discipline is called *Physics*, but you must remember that this word refers to Nature as a whole, spiritual as well as physical, so this practice is more accurately described as *Contemplation of Nature*. Although I am a scientist, this practice is not about equations and science, although these, properly approached, can contribute to the contemplation of Nature. The goal here is not a rational or scientific analysis of the physical world, but an intuitive contemplation of Nature, at all levels of reality, from an interior as well as an exterior perspective. As you know, the Pythagoreans and many of their Platonic successors were inspired by the mathematical structure of Nature, but for them numbers were not just quantities. They were also symbols of the noetic structure of the cosmos."

Contemplation of Nature is familiar to contemporary Pagans and followers of other earth-oriented religions, but the path to God through nature is a part of many spiritual traditions. The Neoplatonic practice takes your appreciation of nature to a new depth by developing your intuitive insight into the interconnectedness of all things and your place in the cosmos. This is valuable for your spiritual development, even if you are a city dweller!

"According to Platonic philosophy," Hypatia continues, "all things *proceed* from The One, or God, through the eternal Forms in the Cosmic Nous, and through their expression in space and time in the Cosmic Soul, to create the individual things that constitute the material world. Therefore in this practice you contemplate all the objects of the material world, human as well as non-human, non-living as well as living, human-made as well as natural, in order to see them as expressions of The One."

There is more to this than simply wonder, awe, and romantic appreciation of Nature and her beauty. The goal is to understand intuitively, not necessarily scientifically (that is, with the heart, not the head; with the nous, not discursive reason) each particular thing's place in the cosmic order. Each thing has its individual logos (formal structure, archetypal foundation), which is an emanation of the Universal Logos. Your contemplation should be directed toward the logos in each thing, which you grasp with your noetic understanding or intuition.

There are two ways to do this. The first focuses on how all things emanate from The One, which organizes and harmonizes everything in nature. The second focuses on how each individual thing in the universe looks back toward The One, and through its own unity becomes an individual symbol of The One. Let's listen as Hypatia explains the purpose and practice of both contemplations.

"A consequence of this contemplative practice is that you begin to see yourself as a part of this cosmic order. You see the divine order not only in the exterior macrocosm, but also in the interior microcosm. In particular, you will come to understand the unique position of humankind, for we are a microcosm combining a material body with an interior image of the entire macrocosm, from The One to the Ideas to individual souls. Therefore we are embodied divinities, combining material and divine realities, for humans are intermediate, combining aspects of the animal world and of the angelic world. Through our conscious engagement with the archetypal world, we can function as mediators between nature and divinity. This perspective helps us to understand our proper role in the totality of reality.

"Don't confuse Contemplation of Nature with the View from Above, which is intended to help you keep your individual concerns in perspective by seeing them in the greater context. The View from Above aims to reduce your attachment to matters that are out of your control and not really your concern. In contrast, contemplation of your place in the macrocosm helps you to see what *should* be your concern, so that each of us may come to know our greater purpose.

"Contemplation of your place in the macrocosm is also different from aimless daydreaming, for it requires you to pay attention to each thing and event in its particularity in time and space, to be completely present in the moment. Thus it depends on the excellence of Watchfulness, but also on the practice of living in the present, which you have learned in the first two degrees of wisdom. Let's try the Contemplation of Nature."

Seeing All Things in The One: Contemplation of Nature is best practiced, of course, in nature, but this is not necessary, for everything is nature. Therefore sit comfortably where you can see some thing or phenomenon that you want to contemplate (the *focus*). Quiet your body and lower soul by breathing gently, allowing any bodily feelings, moods, or thoughts to pass away without stress or anxiety. Place your attention on your focus, but do not stare at it; eventually you may want to close your eyes, since you will be contemplating it with your inner vision (your *insight*), not with your eyes. Without trying to be too scientific, turn your attention toward the ultimate Cause of the universe, however you conceive it: The One, God, the Great Spirit, the Absolute, the laws of physics, etc. Think how from it flow all the Forms and Patterns that give things their nature and organize their behavior, from the fundamental particles and forces of the universe, up to through the organization of all things, living and non-living. In particular, see your focus as the convergence of myriad forms and processes, all ultimately arising from The One. Try to allow your mind to grasp the immensity of this organized, integrated process, stretching across the diameter of the universe, evolving from the Big Bang into the unimaginable future. Realize that you too are a part of this Cosmic Soul, yourself a part of this totality. Allow your intuitive mind to abide quietly and motionlessly in this contemplation as long as you are able. Be completely present in the present. If your mind wanders or you drop down to the level of sequential thought, gently return to your contemplation. When you are done, record in your journal any insights you might have had.

Hypatia and her disciples have been contemplating here and there in the garden. She calls them together and resumes her teaching. "That is good for now; you should practice longer contemplations on your own and with a variety of focuses, but now I want to go deeper into the technique of contemplation. According to the Triadic Principle, all things revert back to their cause and ultimately to The One. Therefore, while the Contemplation of Nature focuses first on Nature as contained in The One, proceeding from it, it also turns back toward The One, by contemplating divinity in Nature.

"In this practice we see each existing thing as a *symbol* for some aspect of divinity. The Inexpressible One cannot be expressed in words, therefore symbols are required to point toward it. Symbols become increasingly important with more advanced spiritual practices, and so it is important that you cultivate the habit of seeing things symbolically. This requires a deeper than ordinary kind of sight, which we may call *symbolic seeing*. We have to see through the surface, the exterior reality of a thing, to see its inner reality—not the physical interior, but the divine logos within, which points to its cause."

Hypatia tells her students that symbolic seeing is aided by "purity of the heart" (the nous), which turns you away from superficial matters and attunes your nous, your intuitive mind, to the image of the Forms in the material world. Don't limit your contemplation to things that are obviously sacred, such as religious symbols, or to glorious sunsets, majestic mountains, ancient redwoods, and wild stallions. Practice contemplating all things—even those that are uninspiring or unappealing—and seeing how they embody ideals that point back to The One. Suspend your habitual reaction, as would a scientist or artist. George Herbert (1593–1633) described this penetrating vision in these verses from *The Elixir*:

> Teach me, my God and King,
> In all things thee to see,
> And what I do in any thing,
> To do it as for thee.
>
> A man that looks on glass,
> On it may stay his eye;
> Or if he pleaseth, through it pass,
> And then the heav'n espy.[284]

Seeing The One in All Things: In the same way as we can see a drawn or cutout triangle as an imperfect image of the Form Triangle (as in the Triangle Contemplation exercise), or a particular just act as a reflection of ideal Justice, so we can see all existing objects or processes as images pointing to their source of Being. However, because this exercise is intended to purify the noetic soul, rather than the rational soul, we do not want to limit ourselves to literal representations of an Idea. We want to practice symbolic seeing. Therefore, pick a focus as before, but select one that captures your attention.

Seeing The One in All Things (continued): Quiet your body and lower soul, and let your imagination lead you from the focus to significant Ideas. Don't let your mind wander, but keep drawing it back to the focus. You will begin to form a connected complex of Ideas associated with the focus. This is the beginning of your comprehension of the symbolic meaning of the focus. Some of this meaning will be personal, arising from your personal unconscious, but some of it will be universal, arising from the collective unconscious. In this way you begin to map the Ideas in the Cosmic Nous—read God's mind, if you will—and prepare yourself for illumination. You can never really capture a symbol in words—indeed the value of symbols lies in the fact that they transcend words—but you should record some of your strongest impressions in your journal. Draw pictures or write poetry, if you can express yourself better that way. Come back to the same focus from time to time, and you will deepen your understanding of its symbolic significance.

Hypatia resumes her exposition. "When you have concentrated your soul into its nous in order to contemplate the Cosmic Nous, you will be practicing the third degree of virtue, the *Contemplative Virtues*. In other words, the Contemplative Virtues refer to your spiritualized soul turning toward Spirit. This practice is still at the level of the soul, since this contemplation takes place in time, but it is directed toward the eternal Forms in the Cosmic Nous.

"The cardinal virtues have a new meaning at this higher level: *wisdom* consists in contemplating the Beings or Ideas in the Cosmic Nous; *justice* consists in the soul fulfilling its natural function, which is to act in accordance with the Forms in the Cosmic Nous (that is, the gods); *self-control* is orientation of the soul toward the Cosmic Nous; and *fortitude* is impassiveness or tranquility of the soul, for the Cosmic Nous is impassive, and in this way the soul makes itself like the Nous. But I see that our lunch is prepared, and we must attend to our bodies, so let's eat."

INTERLUDE—THE FIVE THINGS [285]

After lunch, Hypatia and her disciples settle themselves into their chairs; the students take up their tablets and styluses. Almost immediately Aedesia raises her hand.

"Teacher," she begins, "over lunch Hermias and I were discussing the Five Things that Plato mentions, but we have them all mixed up. Can you explain them to us?"

"Certainly, for they are quite relevant to the Ascent by Truth. In his *Seventh Letter*, the divine Plato describes Five Things that are necessary to the philosophical understanding of anything. The First Thing is the object's *name*—for example, 'circle.' The Second Thing is its verbal *definition*, *logos*, such as 'a circle is that which is everywhere equidistant from the extremities to the center.' [286] The Third Thing is the object's image, for example, any physical circle, whether drawn on paper, painted on a surface, stamped or molded out of metal, or made in any other way.

"These Three are necessary prerequisites to *conceptual knowledge* of the object, which is the Fourth Thing, and by systematic exploration of the Three, by persistent questioning and answering, the Fourth is finally discovered.

"Plato explains that the knowledge of any object forms an integrated whole, which cannot be adequately expressed in words. For words are ambiguous, definitions are incomplete or ambiguous (because made of words), and images are imperfect. Therefore, Plato says, he never wrote down his most important doctrines, but taught them orally. In his *Seventh Letter* he wrote:

> "'There does not exist, nor will there ever exist, any treatise of mine dealing with
> [the highest truth]. For it does not at all admit of verbal expression like other studies,
> but, as a result of continued application to the subject itself and communion therewith,
> it is brought to birth in the soul on a sudden, as light that is kindled by a leaping spark,
> and thereafter nourishes itself.' [287]

"Plato's dialogues only hint at the highest truths of philosophy, which cannot, in any case, be expressed in words. That is why I have invited you for this private instruction.

"In spite of their limitations, a thorough investigation of the Four, ascending and descending through them, is required before you can obtain the Fifth, which is an intuitive understanding of the eternal Form, its Being. After much diligent philosophical investigation, the Fifth may be revealed, as by a bolt of lightning, if the philosopher is awake and the eyes of her soul are open. As Plato says,

> "'At last, in a flash, understanding of each blazes up, and the nous,
> as it exerts all its powers to the limit of human capacity, is flooded with light. [288]

"Nevertheless, Plato teaches that investigation of the Four is not sufficient for winning the Fifth. You must be intellectually prepared and receptive, but this will be insufficient without a natural affinity to the Idea. For example, you will never be illuminated by the Idea of Justice, nor be able to identify with it, if you don't have a natural, inborn affinity to justice, or if you have been so corrupted to destroy your receptivity to the Form. Therefore a moral character, rooted in nature as well as nurture, is the foundation of illumination, which is why purification precedes illumination, in the Mysteries as well as in philosophy.

"In summary, the Five are Name, Definition, Image, Knowledge, and Idea. The First Two Things (name, definition) are the purview of dialectics, which makes use of discursive reasoning. The Third Thing, the image, corresponds to the contemplation of nature, which makes use of symbolic inner and outer vision, which transcends language. These Three lead to the Fourth, which is conceptual knowledge of the Forms, but this falls short of the Fifth, whereby you are illuminated by intuitive understanding of the Forms and identification with them. Thus purification opens the way toward illumination.

"Dialectics and physics can ascend the ladder of Being, but they cannot enter the non-being of the Indeterminate Mind or reach The One. Thus through dialectical and contemplative exercises the master who has achieved union can prepare you for the final leap, and sometimes you can prepare yourself, but the leap itself must be accomplished by other means. This brings us to the threshold of Illumination."

Illumination

Everyone takes a deep breath, and Hypatia drinks a little water before she continues. "This afternoon I will explain the last two stages in the Philosophical Ascent, Illumination and Perfection. If Purification is a kind of death—a separation of the soul from the body—then Illumination is a kind of resurrection or apotheosis, in which the soul ascends to the Cosmic Nous or Angelic Mind, taking its place among the other eternal Beings.

"Corresponding to Illumination is the fourth degree of the virtues, called the *Exemplary Virtues* in reference to the 'Exemplars'—that is, the Forms or Ideas. These virtues focus on your nous, which is an image of the Cosmic Nous, and on its faculty of intuition or direct, noetic knowing. Your mind turns toward the Forms of virtue—or authentic being—that reside in the Cosmic Nous, which are the formal causes of the virtues at the lower levels. Having directed your mind toward these higher virtues, you await their illumination.

"The Exemplary Virtues, which you should cultivate, may be summarized as follows: *wisdom* consists of intuition and noetic cognition; *self-control* is turning toward your inner self; *justice* is fulfilling your natural function—that is, living a human life; and *fortitude* is your soul's perseverance in remaining concentrated in your nous and separate from your body and the lower parts of your soul—that is, in maintaining its spiritual purity. These virtues support the spiritual practices of Illumination.[289]

"The row of two in the Tetractys symbolizes the two parts of the Cosmic Nous: Determinate Being and Indeterminate Being. Contemplation begins at the level of Determinate Being, where the Ideas are separate and distinct, and then proceeds to Indeterminate Being, which approximates the ineffable unity of The One. Now pay attention, for this is difficult.

"Contemplation at the level of the Determinate Being attaches definite thoughts, images, concepts, or assertions to specific Forms. This is called the *affirmative way* and follows from dialectical analysis and from knowing the Forms noetically. We Pagans contemplate the many gods who govern our lives. For Jewish and Christian Platonists, this practice includes contemplation of the names of God and his qualities. But we know that The Inexpressible One cannot be expressed in words, understood conceptually, or visualized.

"Therefore, in order to transcend Nous and Being and to approach The One, we must ascend to the level of Indeterminate Being, where all these specific assertions must be denied. This is the *negative way*. Beside each affirmation, such as 'The One is good,' we should put its negation, 'The One is not good.' Against 'The One is infinite,' we place 'The One is not infinite.'

"However, such negations are themselves affirmations, for to say, 'The One is not infinite' is the same as saying, 'The One is finite.' Therefore, we have not succeeded in transcending the realm of Being and Not-being, and so a more radical denial is required. We accomplish this by denying *both* the affirmations and the negations. Since we cannot assert anything, we must remain silent in the face of The Inexpressible. In this way we are open to hearing God.

"Being in this quiet, receptive state requires inner tranquility, a state of quiet expectation. However, as you have probably experienced, it is difficult to remain in this state for very long. Rather than attempting to enter directly into a state of meditative emptiness, it is often easier to repeat a simple inner chant, called an *arrow prayer.*"

ARROW PRAYERS AND INVOCATION OF THE NAME

Some example arrow prayers follow, but of course you can pick your own, or your teacher might give you one. If you are Neopagan or Wiccan, you could choose a short chant or an extract from a longer one that is especially meaningful for you.

Alone with The Alone. [Numenius and Plotinus[290]]

I'm beautiful when I'm truly myself;
I'm beautiful when I know myself. [after Plotinus[291]]

I contain part of the Supreme. [after Plotinus[292]]

My soul is a child of The One. [after Plotinus[293]]

God is the author of liberty. [Plotinus[294]]

My goal is not to be flawless, but to be god. [Plotinus[295]]

Remove everything. [Plotinus]

Bear and forebear. [Epictetus]

Hen to Pan (The All is One). [Greek, alchemical[296]]

As above, so below; as within, so without. [Hermetic]

My god, my nous, my thought, my soul, my body. [Monoïmos the Arab[297]]

Ribbono shel Olam (Master of the Universe). [Jewish[298]]

Shalom (Peace). [Jewish]

Elohim (on inhale); Ha-Shem (on exhale). [Jewish names of God]

Kyrie, eleison (Lord, have mercy). [Greek, Orthodox Christian[299]]

O God, make haste to help me.
O Lord, make speed to save me. [Christian[300]]

Allah. [Muslim]

Allāhu akbar (Allah is great). [Muslim]

La ilaha ilallah (There is no god but Allah). [Muslim]

Lā wa lā lā (Not and not not) [Abu Yaqub al-Sijistani, Muslim Neoplatonist]

Love is the law, love under will. [Thelemite]

IAÔ. [Gnostic]

AUM (Om). [Hindu, Buddhist, Jain]

Om mani padme hum. [Buddhist]

Namo Amitābhāya (Homage to Infinite Light). [Sanskrit, Pure Land Buddhism]

Namu Amida Butsu (I take refuge in Amitābha, Buddha of Infinite Light).
[Japanese, Pure Land Buddhism]

Hare Krishna Hare Krishna
Krishna Krishna Hare Hare
Hare Rama Hare Rama,
Rama Rama Hare Hare. [Sanskrit, Hindu]

Tat tvam asi (Thou art that). [Sanskrit, Hindu]

San Ching Jiao Tzu Wu Liang Tien Tzun (Three pure ones, founders of Daoism, limitless honored in heaven). [Chinese, Daoist [301]]

As you can see, most spiritual traditions have the practice of arrow prayers—for example, the Hindu repetition of mantras (*japa*) and the Sufi chanting of the divine name (*dhikr*).

An arrow prayer gets its name from the idea that it flies straight to God, that it carries the soul directly into the heart of The Inexpressible One. I think it's interesting that shamans often use a magic arrow as a means of ascending through the levels of reality to the gods, beating it on their drums to enter a trance state. According to legend, the healer-sage Abaris (seventh to sixth centuries BCE) traveled on such a magic arrow, which he later gave to Pythagoras, who was supposed to be the semi-divine son of Apollo, a solar god of healing and prophecy, often seen with his bow and arrows. In any case, an arrow shot into the sun is a symbol of ascent to The One.

Similarly, the well-known Sanskrit mantra *AUM* is interpreted as the bow that shoots the arrow, representing the true self (*atman*), into Brahman (Absolute Reality). Its letters represent the triadic principle: Creation, Preservation, and Destruction. The Gnostic *IAÔ* can be interpreted similarly as the Neoplatonic triadic principle: Abiding, Proceeding, and Returning, respectively.

Notice that an arrow prayer may be as simple as a divine name or attribute; its purpose is to keep your mind focused on the deity, until the repeater and the repeated merge together. Also, most of these prayers do not ask for something or attempt to change God's mind, and so they may seem a little different from the prayers familiar to you. According to Neoplatonic philosophy, prayers are not intended to persuade the gods, flatter them, rouse their pity, or otherwise suppose the gods are like super-humans subject to human emotions. Rather, the gods or angels in the Cosmic Nous are Beings outside of time, impassive and steadfast in their governance of change here below. And this applies even more to The One. The purpose of Neoplatonic prayer is not to bring divinity down to our level, but rather to raise our souls up toward the divine. The purpose of a prayer is not to change God, but to change us. Therefore, a Neoplatonic prayer is more like an affirmation, which is intended to keep us focused on our goal, which is The One. This is the target of the arrow.

Petrus, one of Hypatia's Christian students, raises his hand and asks, "What is the proper posture and technique for this contemplation? Some Pagans mock our holy men who dwell in the desert, and call them 'navel gazers.'"

Hypatia laughs. "It's true that the Pagan practice is a little different, and Christian method seems odd to us. However, I see that Synesius, who has recently arrived in Alexandria, has slipped into the back of the room. As you know, he was my pupil many years ago and has since converted to Christianity, so he can explain the practice of your desert hermits."

Synesius is caught off-guard, but proceeds to the front and addresses the disciples. "Thank you, my lady, for this honor. Our ascetics are called 'navel gazers' because they bend forward until they can stare at their navels, the center of their vitality. Sitting on a stool in this posture causes tension in their shoulders and necks, but especially constriction around their hearts. This keeps them alert, but also aids concentration of the vital spirit into the heart. They compress this spirit with each breath, which they hold while they mentally invoke God, and which they release briefly between invocations. By focusing on their navels, they shift their attention from external things into themselves and master the inner beast." Synesius takes an empty seat.

"Thank you, my friend," Hypatia says, "for this clear explanation. I'm sure it is an effective technique, but we do it differently, sitting with an erect spine and our eyes closed or focused a short distance away. For us, an erect posture symbolizes the natural state of humans as intermediate beings, able to choose to look downward to material reality or upward to divine reality. The three parts of our souls are arranged along our spines, which symbolize the Cosmic Axis, Olympus, or the 'World Tree' connecting earth and heaven together. Neither is complete without the other, and we must look both up and down to understand all of reality."

"Forgive me, master," Petrus interrupts, "but is navel gazing wrong?"

"There are many ways," she replies, "all effective, but some work better for some students than for others. Partly it is just a matter of habit, or of your teacher's preference. Since you have Christian teachers, Petrus, you should probably practice after their fashion."

Arrow Prayer: Select an arrow prayer from those in this chapter or find one elsewhere. Generally you should use a meaningful arrow prayer so that you can focus on its meaning, which will keep you alert. The practice is to sit in a comfortable position, quiet your soul, and raise and concentrate it into your nous. Repeat the arrow prayer silently, without any accompanying image. Do so in a relaxed way, without excessive stress or loudness in your inner voice. Try synchronizing it with your breath.

FOUR DEGREES OF PRAYER

Hypatia explains that there are four degrees of prayer of decreasing materiality and increasing subtlety, ascending toward The One. The first is "prayer of the lips"—that is, prayer spoken out loud, which is the way people usually prayed in the ancient world. (If someone whispered a prayer, others suspected them of praying for something bad.) "Prayer of the lips," she says, "corresponds to the level of the body. The second degree of prayer is more inward, at the level of the soul. In this case you repeat the prayer in your mind, but since it goes word by word in time, it is at the level of the soul. This practice is especially valuable if your mind is filled with pointless chatter. Do you know what I mean?"

Athanasius raises his hand but cannot restrain himself. "My brain is always talking to itself: repeating the arguments I have won, or agonizing over those I lost, repeating what I should have said, if only I had thought more quickly. Or it's planning what I will say in an upcoming conversation, or what I should say, if ever I chance to discourse on some topic. Is this wrong?"

"It's not wrong," Hypatia replies, "but governing your inner dialogue is an essential part of the virtue of self-control. If you are going to speak or write about something, then it is certainly wise to plan your words. But then you should let it go, without causing yourself mental anguish by imagining all the ways it may turn out. Likewise, it's pointless to gloat over past triumphs or to rehearse the mistakes you've made in the past, suffering again the humiliation, pain, guilt, or regret.

The present is all that is real."[302]

Petrus raises his hand and says, "Master, I think often on the sins I've committed, and on those I'm tempted to commit. I believe this makes me a better person."

"Certainly," Hypatia replies, "it is worthwhile to recall our mistakes and to think how we could have avoided them, so we are less likely to make them in the future. As Epicurus said,

The beginning of salvation is the recognition of faults.[303]

"In fact—that is the point of one of our spiritual practices, Examination of Conscience, but it is always for a purpose, our moral and spiritual progress. Wallowing in guilt over our failures—or for that matter in pride at our successes—is a waste of the soul's energy. When you hear your soul chattering in this way, turn it toward an arrow prayer, which will replace the useless inner noise. Indeed, no matter what you are doing, unless your inner talk is serving some purpose, it's best to mentally recite an arrow. You will find it remarkably calming.

> *Do not continually stir the water;*
> *let it be,*
> *and the sediment will settle out.*

"The third degree of prayer, which is at the level of nous, is called 'prayer of the nous,' 'prayer of the heart,' or 'the prayer of simple gaze.' Here you must rest in a state of timeless contemplation, one Being turned toward the cause of all Being. At this level prayer is a *state*, not an *action*. The fourth and highest degree, at the level of The One, is the 'self-acting prayer,' in which the state of contemplation is replaced by a feeling of divine presence and love. This is not anything that you *do*, but rather something that happens *to* you, an effect of the First Cause. You may experience a kind of ecstasy, which results from contact with The One just prior to Union."

Continuous Prayer: Experiment with the continuous prayer of the soul, especially if you find yourself constantly repeating past or future dialogues in your head, whether these scripts are positive or negative. Unless there is some specific purpose to thinking these thoughts, switch to an arrow prayer, so that it becomes the background to whatever you are doing. As this practice becomes habitual, you may find that active mental praying sometimes vanishes into a calm state of contemplation.

Twelve Thousand Arrows: If you want a more intense practice of continuous prayer and a quicker experience of its benefits, you can try this practice. It prepares the ground in which self-acting prayer can germinate. Make a commitment to repeat your arrow prayer one thousand times each day. Use prayer beads (Buddhist malas, Pagan prayer beads, or a rosary) to help you count.

Twelve Thousand Arrows (continued): One thousand prayers is not as many as it seems; if you repeat the arrow at a comfortable rate, as you should, it will take less than an hour (depending on the length of your arrow). Continue this practice for a week (at least during the time you are learning the Ascent by Truth). If you have more time to devote to your practice (e.g., on vacation or during a retreat), then every week you can increase the number of daily repetitions in steps to 3,000, 6,000, and 12,000 (the practical limit: about ten hours). You do not need to do them all at one sitting, and you can engage in limited activities while you say them.

Perfection—Union

Hypatia pauses to make sure everyone is paying attention. "Now we come to the goal and culmination of the Philosophical Ascent. Union with The One is symbolized, of course, by the dot at the top of the Tetractys. This is not so much an achievement as a gift. As you have seen through all three degrees of wisdom, living philosophically involves an acceptance of Destiny, Universal Nature, Providence, or God's Will, whatever its name. This does not imply an apathetic passivity, of course, but it does imply a realistic and wise understanding of your place in the cosmos, which we can get from philosophy and spiritual practice. This is especially the case with the final stage of ascent—called Perfection, Deification, or Union—for each person has a spiritual destiny, and practice only prepares the ground for it; the seed must come from above.

"Union may be experienced as plenitude—that is, as fullness or a merging with everything in the universe at every level of reality. This is often accompanied by an experience akin to light, which can be called the Divine Light. Therefore The One is often symbolized by the sun. Since the sun is a source of warmth and comfort and sustains life, Union is also an experience of feeling illuminated by the goodness of The One, and of experiencing everything else as so illuminated. On the other hand, the Divine Light of The Inexpressible One is so brilliant and incomprehensible, that Union is also experienced as a kind of darkness, the impenetrable depths of existence."

"Since The One is devoid of activity, form, and thought," she continues, "the philosopher must abandon activity, form, and thought to identify with The One. These maxims are from Plotinus; they can be used as arrow prayers:

We develop toward ecstasy by simplifying the soul.[304]

We ascend by flight of the alone to The Alone, face to Face.[305]

"Then center will be joined with Center, the flower of the soul to The Inexpressible One. However, as I said, neither this experience nor the preceding ones can be brought about by will; it is a kind of grace, a gift. You can only prepare and wait patiently. The goal of the philosophical life is perpetual attention to the divine, a metamorphosis or deification. However, while still attached to a human body, you cannot maintain the concentration and tension of union, so you must eventually return to the world. Nevertheless, as a result of union you will return with improved mildness, gentleness, and receptivity, and with an improved knowledge of your true self. You will be better able to see the light of The One reflected in the everyday world and, by bringing that light back, to illuminate others.

"When you have experienced divine union, you will of course be anxious to return to it, and you can prepare for union by exercising the virtues and the other spiritual practices you have learned. Don't be impatient, but remember:

According to the Rules of Order,
little things must precede the greater,
if we would make the ascent.[306]

"The philosophical life is 'amphibious': a double life, cycling, turning now toward the light, now toward the earth. The philosopher is like the moon in her orbit, turning her face first to the earth (when she is full), then to the sun (when she is new). When the moon approaches closest to the sun, when they are in *conjunction*, there is an eclipse; that is like the philosopher's union with the source of divine light, when the earthly realms are left in utter darkness. But when the philosopher returns, and turns her face again to the earth, then she illuminates it with light reflected from the source. The stages of the ascent are not one-time accomplishments, but practices of continual ascent and descent, since continuing practice at the lower levels allows you to stay at the upper levels longer. They are comparable to the iterative processes of reversion, abiding, and procession in dialectic. When sufficiently practiced, however, the adept may remain 'beyond' indefinitely. This is all I have to say now about the Path of Truth."

The Ascent by Truth is summarized in the following table.

Structure of the Ascent by Truth

Macrocosm	Microcosm	Faculty	Stage of Ascent		Virtues	
World Body	body	sensation	Awakening	Change of Mind	Practical	Ethical
World Body	body	sensation	Awakening	Watchfulness	Practical	Ethical
World Body	body	sensation	Awakening	Discernment	Practical	Social
World Body	body	sensation	Awakening	Guarding the Heart	Practical	Social
World Soul	soul — animal	belief	Purification	Purific. Virtues	Purifying	
World Soul	soul — human (rational)	reason	Purification	Dialectics	Contemplative	
World Soul	soul — human (noetic)	contemplation	Purification	Physics	Contemplative	
World Nous — Det.	nous — archetypes	noetic intelligence	Illumination	Affirmative Way	Exemplary	
World Nous — Indet.	nous — Self	noetic intelligence	Illumination	Negative Way	Exemplary	
The One	the god within	union	Perfection		Hieratic	

CHAPTER TWELVE

THE PATH OF TRUST

INTRODUCTION

In this chapter you will learn the third of the three paths of ascent to The One, the Path of Trust, which uses the rituals of *theurgy*, the "high magic" of Neoplatonism.[307] I will begin by comparing it to the other paths, and give some further suggestions on which path you might prefer. Next you will learn the use of material and immaterial symbols, which are the principal tools used in theurgy to contact and communicate with gods (or archetypes or angels) and their use in the *invocation* of gods and other spirits. Next I will teach you how to perform four important theurgical practices: *animation* ("ensouling") of a divine image as a means of communication; *incubation*, as a method of evoking healing and prophetic dreams; the formation of *alliances* with gods and other spirits; and finally *deification*, in which you ascend to union with the gods and are reborn, spiritually enlightened.

DIFFERENT WAYS TO THE ONE

As Hypatia's private students arrive and are admitted to her house, they take their accustomed places on the chairs that surround the master's empty chair. One of these chairs has a ribbon reserving it for Synesius, who is visiting in Alexandria after his successful diplomatic mission in Constantinople. The disciples talk quietly with their neighbors, but there is an uncommonly palpable excitement, for the topic of the day is theurgy, a subject of controversy both within the Platonic community and among the wider Alexandrian intelligentsia. Her Christian students are especially eager to hear what she

267

says, for some of their religious leaders have been very critical of Hypatia and her philosophy on account of theurgy.

The master and Synesius, in conversation with each other, enter from an adjoining room and take their chairs; without ado she begins. "As I explained previously [chapter 10], there are three paths of ascent, which look back toward three attributes of The One—its Beauty, Wisdom, and Goodness—and ascend on the corresponding 'rays' emanating from The One, called Love, Truth, and Trust. Love fills you with the warmth of The One and Truth illuminates you with its Light, but Trust brings you into direct contact with the divine fire. Today I will describe this last ascent, the Ascent by Trust, more commonly known as the art of *theurgy* or the *hieratic*, or priestly, *art*.

"The Ascents by Love and Truth are contemplative; for the most part they are practiced by sitting quietly and either observing attentively or turning inward. In contrast to this inward orientation toward ideas, the Ascent by Trust is oriented outward through ritual action and the use of material symbols. In many ways theurgy is more concrete and active than the other paths.

"The deities associated with this path are Hecate, a moon goddess, and Helios, Sol, a sun god. According to tradition, Hecate is a goddess of magic and a patron of witches, but she is also the patron of theurgy, for she is the goddess who oversees the Cosmic Soul, where the daimons reside, who are the primary concern of theurgists. The Sun, as we have seen, is a symbol of The One and the divine, life-giving illumination proceeding from it. Therefore the Sun represents the *procession* of the Good, whereas the Moon, which turns back toward the Sun and reflects its light, represents the *return* to the Good. Thus theurgists look to Hecate to lead them and guide them on the Path of Trust, which is motivated by love of the Good (*phil-agathia*)."

There is scholarly disagreement about whether Hypatia practiced theurgy. Some say that on the whole, Alexandrian Neoplatonism tended to follow Porphyry, who criticized theurgy. But there are reports that suggest Hypatia practiced it. For example, John of Nikiu, writing three hundred years after her death, accused her of devotion to "magic, astrolabes, and instruments of music," [308] but he can hardly be considered a unbiased witness, for he approved of her murder. More sympathetic is her disciple Synesius of Cyrene, Bishop of Ptolemais, who reminisced about Hypatia in a letter to a fellow student: "We have seen with our eyes, we have heard with our ears the lady who legitimately presides over the mysteries of philosophy." [309] He uses the terminology of the mystery religions, which suggests that they were both witnesses of mystical rites. Also, when Synesius was inspired by God, as he said, to write an essay on how dreams reflect the interaction of the divine and mortal worlds, he sent it immediately to Hypatia for her comments. These and other remarks in his letters hint that Hypatia and her advanced students had a private ritual practice.

In ancient times astrology was often confused with astronomy, and they both were classified under the mathematical arts, which were frequently supposed to be among the magical arts. This is not only because mathematics uses arcane symbols and diagrams, but also because it could function as a legitimate spiritual practice leading first to the Forms and then to the gods. Music, too, had spiritual and magical connotations, and central to the mystical Orphic religion was the legend that Orpheus, who (nearly) brought his wife back from the dead, had charmed the animals, trees, and even stones with his music. The ancient Pythagoreans practiced music therapy, and a story has been passed down that Hypatia used music to redirect the attentions of her infatuated disciple (although the menstrual napkin was the more likely instrument of his awakening).

We have even better evidence that the interests of Hypatia's father, Theon, extended beyond mathematics and astronomy. In addition to Pagan religion and ritual, he studied astrology and other forms of divination, and he wrote on the spiritual practices of the Orphics and on the works of Hermes Trismegistus, the legendary founder of Hermetic philosophy. He also wrote a poem praising Ptolemy, in Orphic terms, as one blessed by the gods, who through long practice and devotion had ascended to divine illumination. It is worth remembering that Ptolemy, on whose works Theon and Hypatia spent much time, was not just an astronomer, but also the author of one of the oldest surviving astrology texts. Such a range of interests would not be unusual for ancient Alexandrian philosophers.

Therefore, it is not unlikely that Theon's spiritual practice included theurgy and that Hypatia learned it from him. She might have continued to teach it and to practice it in private with her most advanced students. Since it was more closely tied to her Pagan religion than were other Neoplatonic practices, she would have deemphasized it in her public lectures, which were addressed to non-Pagans as well as Pagans. Also, theurgy might be misunderstood or misrepresented as sorcery, as John of Nikiu demonstrated.

Some people suppose that theurgy would have been incompatible with Theon's and Hypatia's scientific interests, but this is a modern prejudice. As the Ascent by Truth shows, spiritual and empirical approaches to the understanding of reality are complementary, not inconsistent. This was taken for granted in ancient philosophy.

Regardless of whether Hypatia practiced theurgy, she certainly understood it. I have included it in this book because its techniques are spiritually valuable and have important similarities to modern techniques for pursuing psychological integration.

Let's turn our ears again to Hypatia's lesson. "There are three keys or passwords that open the way on the paths of ascent:

The Love of Beauty, Wisdom, Truth
—philokalía, philosophía, philagathía—
these are the desires that draw us upward.

"You will see that the Theurgic Path has much in common with the Paths of Love and Truth, the major difference being the use of rituals involving symbolically meaningful material objects, such as statues, stones, herbs, and incense. Because it makes use of these material aids, some claim that theurgy is easier or more accessible than the more interior paths through Love and Truth."

"Does that make theurgy inferior," Petrus asks, "because its orientation is more material than spiritual?"

"On the contrary, the divine Iamblichus ranks theurgy higher than the other ascents, since it is able to transcend the limits of your nous. This is because the nous can ascend only so far as Being, but as I mentioned earlier, the Good, which is the goal of the Theurgic Ascent, is prior to Being, as is The Inexpressible One. This takes place beyond the reach of words, in the realm of silence. Don't forget:

A holy silence hides what lies beyond,
Where mind and thought unite in ceaseless bond,
One Fountain and one Root, whence all flow on.[310]

"These words are from a hymn written by Synesius, who is attending our lesson again today." She smiles at him and he nods in acknowledgment.

"Knowledge of The One," Hypatia continues, "is not obtained by thinking or even by intuition, but by *contact* and *union*—that is, by direct experience. This must be a kind of non-rational belief, for rational belief is based on knowledge of causes, but The One has no cause, for it is the First Cause. However this knowledge is not unfounded, for it is based on direct experience, like the knowledge we get from our senses (which is the basis for all scientific knowledge). We can trust our experience to be as we experience it, and so it doesn't require some sort of proof. Therefore, theurgy is the Path of Trust, which is capable of transcending the limit of Being to reach The Inexpressible One."

Cyrus raises his hand and asks, "I am more confused than ever! Which of the three ascents is best?"

"In my experience," Hypatia replies, "different ascents work better for different persons, and so they are all valuable. I encourage you to explore them all and to follow the paths that call you. Remember:

We're descended from different gods,
with different ways to The One.

"If you are in the lineage of Aphrodite, then the Path of Love might suit you best, or the Path of Truth if you have descended from Athena. If your ancestor is Hermes, then a more Hermetic practice might work better for you; if you are descended from Ares (Mars), then a martial practice might be best. Theurgy is especially suited for those with Hecate or the Moon in their blood."

In more modern terms, our unconscious behavioral patterns and predispositions are a function of both nature and nurture, which regulate the development of our individual versions of the universal human archetypes (a function of our individual genotypes) and of the complexes that form around them in the courses of our individual lives. These are the gods from whom we are descended and the daimons who accompany us. As a consequence of differences in these unconscious personality factors, some practices work better for some people, others for others. Give them all a try and see which works best for you.

A few remarks on the etymology of *theurgy* will help you see its purpose. The root meaning of *theology* is "divine words" (*theioi logoi*)—that is, discussions, explanations, or accounts of divine matters. In contrast, *theurgy* means "divine works" (*theia erga*), which refers both to the ritual actions (as opposed to talk) and to the consequent intervention of divinity in human lives. Thus you might say that theurgy brings theology into practice.

Ritual was common in the ancient Pagan religions, and if you are Pagan or Wiccan, you are probably comfortable with it and appreciate its spiritual value. Although ritual lingers in other religions, and in government, the military, and other institutions where tradition is valued, it is alien to many people nowadays. Therefore you might find theurgy a bit bizarre, but psychology supports ritual as a means of spiritual development. We are embodied beings, and the spiritual is not independent from the physical. Therefore physical actions can contribute to spiritual practice.

Theurgy is a practice that was developed in the cultural context of ancient polytheistic Paganism, and so I will present it from that perspective—that is, as a means of contacting gods and daimons, negotiating with them, and seeking their aid. If you are Pagan or Wiccan, you will find this viewpoint very familiar. However, as I explained in chapter 9, Christian Neoplatonists, such as St. Dionysius, adapted the polytheistic perspective to monotheism by interpreting the gods and daimons as angels. So in the monotheistic theurgy taught by St. Dionysius and others, the object is communication with angels as mediators between humans and God. Therefore, in the discussion of theurgy you can think of gods and daimons in this way if that makes more sense to you. But perhaps you think of angels as a superstitious idea left over from the Middle Ages. In that case you may find the perspective of depth psychology more reasonable.[311] The gods correspond to the archetypes of the collective unconscious, and daimons correspond to the complexes in the personal unconscious that have grown out of the archetypes. Both have a solid grounding in biology and have an enormous impact on our psychological well-being, but we cannot access them directly (because they are unconscious). Therefore, we have to use techniques and practices that activate them, so that they intervene in conscious experience and interact with us. Theurgy is simply a collection of techniques developed over the ages for doing this. Now let's listen in as Hypatia explains how to do it.

SYMBOLS

Hypatia resumes her exposition. "When things that are informed by the divine Ideas, whether they are found externally in physical reality or internally in psychical reality, are used in theurgy, they are called *symbols*, *tokens*, or *signs*, but we can understand better their role in theurgy if we begin by looking at the root meanings of the Greek words. They refer to things put together or devised, agreed-upon signals, passwords, passports, or indeed any tokens or signs. More generally, they may refer to pledges, pacts, covenants, or agreements, or to tokens of these relations. Further, they may refer to a communion or connection between two parties. Thus, in the context of theurgy, a *symbol* is a password or sign, given to us by the gods, in token of and to facilitate our communion with them."

Hypatia explains that a *symbol* brings together (*symballein*) two things. She begins with the most concrete meaning: "In ancient times the parties to an agreement might break a small bone, pottery shard, or coin into two pieces; the two parts, each retained by one of the parties, fit together like lock and key. So also a seal impression in wax or clay, such as made by a signet ring, is a *symbol*, a good metaphor for the impression of the Forms on matter. The material Form or embodied Idea is the signature or imprimatur reflecting the sanction of the god. The symbol is a sign of goodwill, and thus in theurgy of a god's goodwill. The signet ring and like tokens are proofs of identity, the passwords and secret signs that allow one to proceed and, in a theurgic context, to approach and contact the gods. Such a password can take the form of *sign and response*, and so also in theurgy there can be an interchange of signs. The god gives the signs; if you respond appropriately, you will be admitted. So also, the symbol becomes a token of the agreement, treaty, contract, pact, or covenant between the parties; here, between the god and the theurgist. In particular, the symbol as secret sign leads to its meaning as allegory, omen, portent, or occult sign." (And through these senses we arrive at the ordinary meanings of the English word *symbol*.)

Hypatia continues. "The signs and symbols are in the 'lineages' or 'chains' of the gods, which I've already explained [chapter 8]. By these chains we are elevated to the gods; through them the symbols are connected to the divine Forms or Ideas. They are in the gods as the gods are in them. They are found everywhere, as the *Chaldean Oracles* attest:

Paternal Nous sows symbols all throughout the World;

He thinks the Thoughts, called Beauties Inexpressible.[312]

"Literally, the *Nous* intuitively-thinks [*noeî*] the Ideas [*Noêta*].

"Once you understand the general principles of signs and symbols, you can see that they take many different forms: anything in the god's lineage, anything partaking of the divine Idea.

"For example, a symbol may be *material*. To cite an ancient example, gold and golden-colored objects, such as the stone citrine, are in the lineage of the sun, itself in the lineage of the god Helios. So also are animals, such as the cock, which welcomes the sun, and plants, such as the heliotrope, which turns toward the sun. Hot spices, such as cinnamon, are symbols of the sun, and may be used in ritual food, offerings, or incense. Obviously images of the sun or of the god Helios participate in the Form of the sun and may be used as symbols. More abstractly, various 'characters'—gestures, figures, and geometric shapes that participate in the divine Form—may be used. Such figures may be written, drawn, or engraved, or they may be uttered or otherwise enacted in time.

"Symbols need not be so material. For example, a poem celebrating the sunrise or a hymn to Helios may serve as a symbol. Indeed, the symbols need not be external at all, but may be constructed or imagined in your mind, and contemplated and offered to the gods upon that most sacred altar: your soul.

"Traditionally the celestial gods—those associated with the planets and stars— are important mediators by which the Ideas *proceed* into the material world and by which we *return* to the gods, and so astrological correspondences are important symbols, and astrological considerations enter into the timing of theurgic rites."

"Excuse me, master," interrupts Athanasius, a student with an argumentative streak, "but doesn't the divine Plotinus ridicule astrologers and prove that the stars and planets cannot determine human characteristics or their fates, and that heredity is the stronger cause?"

Heculianus, Cyrus's older brother, a Christian student devoted to philosophy and literature, raises his hand and Hypatia nods in his direction. "On the contrary, in Book 1 of the *Third Ennead* he wrote that those who look at the stars and read their writing, and interpret it by the method of analogy, can predict the future."

"You are both correct," says Hypatia, "but the divine master's teachings are more complicated. The stars and the entire sphere of the sky above us affect conditions on Earth, the seasons, the climate, the tides, the flooding of the Nile, the growth of plants, and the life cycles of animals. All farmers, herders, and sailors know this. People born in different lands and tropics, under different parts of the sky, have different appearances and characteristics. The philosophers of the Porch, too, teach that this world is a single Cosmic Body, coordinated and harmonious, an organism with sympathetic connections among all its parts. Therefore you can see that in the material world there are many influences on the fate of an individual: heredity, as Plotinus said, but also the circumstances of one's time and place of birth. These may be a consequence of our prior lives—the rewards or punishments of Providence—as the young philosopher Hierocles says. Perhaps we may read some of this fate in the planets and the stars by means of analogy. But Plotinus also teaches that the stars and planets can affect only those things below them—that is, in the material world and in our bodies and lower souls. It is the body and lower soul that is subject to fate. The upper soul, which harbors a spark of the divine, has the power of choice, and may choose to ascend to the divine realms and elevate itself above fate. This is the freedom we achieve by the ascent to the divine, and in this freedom we become godlike. Furthermore, don't forget:

> All the heavens are inside us;
> both the light of life resides there
> and the origin of heaven.[313]

"Master," Herculianus asks, "are you referring to the microcosm?"

"Exactly," Hypatia replies. "For all the planets move inside our souls, conjoining, opposing, and aspecting each other, as they do in the heavens. These celestial gods grant seven divine gifts. Jupiter gives peace, generosity, law, and good government; Mercury grants reason and eloquence; while Venus gives us joy and love. Mars brings generosity and Saturn contemplation; the haste of the former ought to be tempered by the deliberateness of the latter. The Moon keeps the body and soul continuously moving, and her gift is procreation. But there will be order in the microcosm only if the Moon periodically looks toward the Sun, for he is the god within, who grants us intelligence and prophecy.

"So let us return to the Ascent by Trust. You do not need to believe in astrological prediction or astrological influences to use astrological correspondences in theurgy; what is important is their symbolism. For the zodiac and the planets—with their risings, settings, aspects, and so forth—are symbolic systems, and we can use these symbols just like other signs and tokens, to connect to the divine energies that they symbolize. They are by no means essential, but many theurgists have found them useful."

If astrology seems like a silly belief for mathematicians, scientists, and philosophers, it is worth remembering that ancient people were much more aware of the rhythms of nature—of the earth, stars, and planets—than most of us are today. Most of the civilizations around the Mediterranean used a lunar calendar, so religious and civic activities varied with the phases of the moon. Agriculture was dictated by the rising and setting of certain stars and by the solstices and equinoxes; the rising of Sirius signaled the flooding of the Nile, which brought the fertile silt, and so on. Furthermore, the stars and planets—which are still awe-inspiring, if we let them be so—were understood as *visible gods*, and so it seemed natural that they would influence the earthly realm. Astrology also became a symbolic system for talking about human personality types, which some contemporary psychologists still find useful.

How can we, who have not grown up in these ancient traditions, learn these divine signs and symbols? Sometimes they have been handed down by tradition and can be learned from ancient mythology. The more recent work of depth psychologists, such as Jung, can also be helpful, as can dictionaries of symbolism. But none of these sources should be accepted uncritically. At the very least, they should be tested by your own intuition, for your individual nous participates in these same Ideas. (Hypatia would say that the gods place the symbols in our souls as well as in the material world; that is, they are in the collective unconscious.) Practices such as the Contemplation of Nature (chapter 11) can reveal divine symbols. True symbols are not arbitrary; they are numinous. There are also cultural symbols, especially from the various religious and spiritual traditions, of course, and these can be very potent, even though they are not universal.

"In the final analysis," Hypatia concludes, "we must learn the tokens and symbols from the gods themselves: they teach us the appropriate signs and responses. One of the principal ways to learn them is by theurgy, which is therefore the means as well as the end. By theurgy we learn the rites and symbols for more advanced theurgy. For example, the goddess Hecate revealed the theurgical techniques in the *Chaldean Oracles* to Julian the Theurgist. In a hymn, our Synesius prays for the illumination of his intellect (nous) by the symbols.

> *O Father, wisdom's Fount, dispel with light,*
> *From Thy breast make my nous, my mind full bright;*
> *Comfort my heart by wisdom's beam from Thee,*
> *And give Thy sign and token, for the way*
> *That leads to Thee; and from my life and prayers*
> *The darker daimons ever drive away."* [314]

INVOCATION

An important function of theurgy is to allow communication with divine beings or, in psychological terms, with archetypes and their derivative complexes. Signs and symbols are used to activate these spiritual principles—to invoke them into consciousness—so that our ordinary selves can communicate and even negotiate with them, for they function as autonomous personalities.

As Hypatia begins to explain the process to her students, Cyrus asks, "Is it true that theurgists can command gods and daimons to do their will?"

> She shakes her head and replies, "When you invoke the gods you do not in any sense command them to come to you. Nevertheless, your actions, including the invocations, are instrumental in the god's arrival. I can explain this by analogy. You cannot order the sun to shine, but by uncovering and cleaning your windows you can allow the sunlight in. So also, you cannot order a god to come, but by proper theurgic cleansing of your soul, you may make it a suitable receptacle for the divine presence."

To update Hypatia's analogy somewhat, light follows its own law and sunlight contains all the colors. You cannot command a certain color to descend from the sun, but you can put a colored filter over a window to admit only one color, bathing everything in that hue. Or you can paint an object or make it of a material that reflects only one color; for example, a golden object manifests the yellow light in the sun's rays. That is, by appropriately skilled means, you can create a receiver that is "tuned" to a particular color as a radio receiver is tuned to a radio frequency. So also in theurgy. Although all the gods are everywhere, like the colors in the sunlight, the theurgist arranges suitable receivers or receptacles that are tuned to a particular god or divine force. This tuning is accomplished by means of divine symbols. Like one half of a broken token, the symbols match and engage the divine energy, causing it to resonate and reflect, illuminating the world and the theurgist's soul with this energy. Psychologically, the symbols activate an archetype or complex. Like all analogies, these are imperfect and should not be taken too literally. Nevertheless, it is astonishing how much theurgy can be learned from them, and you will be rewarded for contemplating them carefully.

ANIMATION

> Hypatia's students have heard rumors about theurgy, and some of them have mixed feelings about its legitimacy. No matter what their preconceived ideas, they are anxious to hear about it from Alexandria's best-known philosopher. Unconsciously they lean forward as she begins by explaining that there are a number of theurgic "operations," but today she is explaining only the most useful four.

The first operation is called in ancient Greek *telestikê*, a vague term that means "mystical" or "initiatory." (I discussed related words in connection with "perfection" in chapter 10.) In this case it refers to a particular mystical art or science. In English the procedure is often called "animating a statue," which might suggest statues dancing around the room, unless you remember that *anima* is a Latin word for soul, and thus *animation* is literally giving a soul to something. In Greek the technical term for this process is *empsychosis*, since it puts a soul (*psyche*) into something.

"Normally," Hypatia explains, "animation is used to cause a divine or daimonic soul to occupy an *icon*, or sacred image; thus this soul is given a material vehicle through which it may operate. Therefore in this, as in all theurgic operations, you become god-like by participating in the creative activity of the Nous, specifically, in the animation of the material world. Such an operation can be used to consecrate an icon (for example, to be the principal divine image in a shrine), or to provide a medium of communication with divinity, or to purify your soul by helping to mold it in the divine image.

"To repeat, you cannot compel a god to occupy the image, but you can prepare the image as a suitable receptacle for the divine power, so that it may actualize its energy in the material world. It is like preparing an object to reflect a certain color of light, but the light must be present already for the reflection to take place. This preparation is accomplished by using the divine signs and symbols in the preparation of the image. The more symbols you use, the better the image will reflect the divine energy.

"For example, the divine image could be a statue or a picture of the god in a characteristic pose, or an image of an attribute associated with the god, such as an animal sacred to the god (for example, an owl for Athena), or the god's instrument (such as a lyre for Apollo). Christian examples include an image of Jesus, a cross, and a lamb.

"The statue can have a receptacle in its back or base into which you can put the god's tokens. These might include gemstones, metal objects, herbs, plants, and animal parts, such as a claw, feather, or bit of fur. If the image is a picture, you can mount it on a box in which you put the tokens, or hang it above the box. You can fumigate the image with incense appropriate to the god and anoint it with appropriate oils or perfumes. You can address invocations, prayers, chants, poetry, or other texts to the god, sing hymns, or play music appropriate to the god. Finally, the icon will be a better receiver if you construct or consecrate it at a time that is astrologically auspicious for attracting the god's power. The general principle should be clear: the more signs, symbols, and tokens you can combine in the icon, the better the receiver it will be. They all serve to connect you to a particular divine energy. Many theurgists report that phenomena of light may appear around the icon, and that the god may grant prophetic dreams, manifest omens, or deliver revelations."

The image will become numinous when it is animated by the divine energy; psychologically, the archetype or complex is projected onto the image, a projection that is invited by appropriate symbols. When this projection occurs, the divine energy will be actualized in your psyche, and the image may induce deep insights; psychologically, the archetype or complex has been activated by the symbolic image and is interacting with your conscious experience.

This attention to a physical image could be misinterpreted as superstition or even idolatry, but it is not, for there is no supposition that the image *is* a god. To think that the deity is literally in the image would be as foolish as supposing that the President is inside your TV when he or she gives the State of the Union address. In both cases you have an artificial contrivance designed to translate the omnipresent energy into a form that humans can perceive. As a consequence, the speech is present in viewers' minds.

In the Christian world, St. John Damascene (c.675–749 CE), among others, advocated the use and veneration of icons. He said they might serve as "books for the unlettered," but more importantly that they have inherent power, for the archetypal Form is really present in the icon. The veneration of icons was approved at the Second Council of Nicaea (787 CE).[315]

Animating an Icon: If you want to try animating a divine image, here is a way to do it. Pick a divine figure that holds meaning for you. If it is a figure from a traditional religion, then do a little research to find other symbols associated with the deity (angel, saint, hero, etc.). Create a small shrine to house the image and put other associated divine symbols in or on it. When you are ready to consecrate it, place some offerings, such as flowers, on it. If you know how to do so, you can pick an astrologically appropriate time, or a time that is symbolically significant in another way.

Animating an Icon (continued): Light a candle in the shrine, and some incense if you like. Sit or stand comfortably before the image, and calm your body and soul. Contemplate the icon for a few moments, and try to feel it as a link to the divinity. It may seem to glow in the divine light. Recite a prayer requesting the divinity to reveal itself through the icon. (Psychologically you are arranging for a projection of subconscious content onto the image.) You may follow the prayer with a quiet chant calling the deity (e.g., an arrow prayer). Request that the deity allow its energy to remain in the icon so that you can use it as a means for connecting with the divine energy. Pray before and venerate the icon as long as you like, and then thank the deity for its presence. Any time you pray before the icon in this way will increase its capacity to hold the divine energy.

INCUBATION

In all cultures and all times, people have noticed their dreams, and occasional "big dreams" seem potent with meaning and significance. Therefore dreams have been an important means of engaging spiritual forces from ancient shamanism to modern analytical psychology.[316] In particular, from Pythagoras to Hypatia and beyond, philosophers interpreted dreams. In modern terms, since dreams arise from the unconscious mind they can give insight into unconscious processes and developments. Many are insignificant, but others, especially the "big" or archetypal dreams, may be critical to your psycho-spiritual development.

Since ancient people attached so much importance to dreams, they could not always wait for an archetypal dream to occur on its own, so they practiced *dream incubation* to encourage a big dream in answer to a question or problem. The basic idea is simple: after psychological preparation, you go to rest or sleep in a sacred place, and hope to have an archetypal dream. Afterward, a spiritual therapist helps you to interpret it and apply it to your situation.

The most widespread use of incubation in the ancient world was at some four hundred *Asclepeia*, temples of the healing god Asclepius. For more than a thousand years, beginning in the sixth century BCE, many thousands of sufferers came to these temples to have their physical and mental afflictions cured.[317] Apparently many of them went away satisfied, for they left inscriptions recounting their cures or plaques representing the cured part, and we have many thousands of these, which you can see in museums.

Hypatia explains:"The procedure in the Asclepeia will help you understand how to practice incubation. After traveling, perhaps a long distance, to the temple, you pray, make offerings, and are purified. Among other things, this puts you into an appropriate mental and spiritual state to have an archetypal dream. An attending priest-therapist performs divinations to determine if the time has arrived for an archetypal dream, and sometimes you may have to wait for months. When the time comes, you retire at night to the sanctuary, where you lie down on a couch by the animated statue of the god. The god might come to you in a dream, or you might have a vision of the god in a semi-waking state. The god might cure you with a touch or prescribe a cure. In some cases you converse with the god, either in a waking vision or in a *lucid dream*—that is, a dream in which you are aware you are dreaming. Sometimes you have to wait many nights for a healing dream. The next morning the therapist-priests help you to interpret the dream. It is important to interpret the dreams symbolically, not literally, for symbols are the language of the gods and the unconscious. For example, the god might prescribe surgical procedures, which are to be interpreted symbolically. When the interpretation is complete, you have the dream inscribed on a tablet—for it is a revelation from the god—and post at the temple. In addition you make thanks offerings and, of course, follow the god's prescription, either literally or symbolically, as appropriate."

"I myself have been cured at Epidaurus by a dream sent from the god," says Euoptius, Synesius's brother, "but it was an ordeal."

"It is certainly an elaborate procedure," Hypatia remarks, "arduous, lengthy, and expensive, and so most people do it rarely and only as a last resort. However, dream incubation does not have to be so complicated, and you can do it in your own bed. Since Synesius has recently completed an essay *On Dreams*, I have asked him to say a few words explaining the operation. Please, Synesius." She nods toward him and gestures to a place by her dais.[318]

Synesius stands a little awkwardly and faces the other students. "Thank you, my lady, for this opportunity to explain dream divination, which I have learned entirely from you. Please forgive me my errors."

Looking at his tablet, he begins. "Dreams are the gods' great gift to us, for they allow us to divine many things without lengthy journeys to the oracles or temples, without expensive instruments and sacrifices, and without consulting soothsayers and priests. Remember:

> *Through divination by our dreams*
> *we always enter relationships*
> *with gods who give us council*
> *and answer us in oracles*
> *and care for us in other ways."*[319]

"And do you claim," Athanasius interrupts, "that it is possible to know the future from dreams?"

"In one sense, yes," answers Synesius, "for the source of dreams is the Cosmic Nous, the realm of Being, which is outside of time. At this level of reality, past, present, and future are meaningless; they apply no more than they do to the ideal Triangle, or to the timeless cycles and epicycles in which the planets move. It is the Cosmic Soul that expands timeless Being into temporal Becoming, while still comprehending all time in itself. Therefore there is no contradiction in the Soul projecting images from the future into current dreams, which arise in the imagination, which resides in the subtle fluid or vital spirit that binds the soul to the body."

In terms of contemporary psychology, the collective unconscious, which corresponds to the World Nous, contains the archetypal ideas, which are (effectively) eternal patterns of human behavior and development. The World Soul represents their embodiment, as regulatory mechanisms, in the individual brain, as well as their personalization by means of the complexes. Since the archetypes and complexes regulate and guide your behavior, including your conscious experience, in a sense they do "know" your future (so far as it can be known), because they are among the determinants of your development, motivations, and predispositions to act. As Jung noted, archetypes and complexes can affect the content of dreams to prepare your consciousness for the psychological future that they are orchestrating.

Let's return to Synesius's presentation. "The language of dreams is obscure, like that of other oracles. For the gods know each other's minds simultaneously, in a constant present, and without the need of language. For speaking and learning are things that happen in time, but gods are outside time. For humans it is different. We learn things bit by bit, with effort over time, and express our knowledge in sequential speech and cogitation. So the authentic language of the gods is symbols, which express these ineffable connections, and to understand our dreams we need to learn that language. We can look inside, by contemplative practices to discover the divine speech. Fix in your mind:

> *Before all else we ought to seek*
> *to know the sacred speech of dreams,*
> *for it comes from us,*
> *is within us,*
> *and is the special possession of the soul*
> *of every one of us."*[320]

Olympius, who wears a richly embroidered robe, raises his hand and asks, "I have acquired a rare book, *The Interpretation of Dreams* by Artemidorus; is it the best book for understanding dreams?"

Synesius sighs and shakes his head. "I'm afraid I laugh when I read these books; they are nearly worthless."

Olympius looks disappointed.

"This is the problem," Synesius explains. "Here below, in the material world, everything is hard and definite, and so what one person perceives with their sense organs is much like what another perceives. And so we can say how one thing goes with another independently of the observer. But dreams come from above and are projected into the imagination, which resides in the vital spirit. Now this spirit is not the same for all, and it differs from one person to the next for many reasons. And just as an image reflected in water looks different if it is calm, or if it is flowing, or if it is stirred up in some way, so the dreams come differently to each of us. So you cannot rely on the dream book of Artemidorus; perhaps it was correct for him, but it will not be for you."

"How can we interpret our dreams without such books?" asks Cyrus.

"Just as we keep a *day book*, or diary, which records the events of the day, so also we can keep a *night book*, which records the events of the night. If you keep careful records of your dreams in this book, and study it, you will discover your own meanings. Look for connections, within dreams, between dreams, and between dreams and waking life. Then you will discover the pattern of your whole life, both its day and night halves."

"My brother," says Euoptius, "you have explained dream divination well, but you haven't told us the operation by which we can obtain a dream oracle. Do we need a lamp? Are there secret words to be written or spoken? Incense or offerings to be burnt?"

"First, you must practice philosophy and perform its purifications so that your imaginative spirit is calm, pure, and unclouded. If you keep this spirit purified by a life in accordance with nature, you will have an instrument ready to hand, which comprehends your spiritual disposition and has, therefore, sympathy with it. Beyond that, the procedure is simple; remember these words:

> *Pray to the god for a dream;*
> *if you are worthy, the god will arrive.*[321]

> *It's enough to wash your hands,*
> *to keep a holy silence,*
> *and to sleep."*[322]

Synesius returns to his seat. "Thank you, Synesius, that was excellent," says Hypatia and calls for a break.

Dream Journal: A dream journal is a valuable tool for getting and keeping in touch with the spiritual side of life. Make sure you have a notepad or notebook, a pen, and a night-light by your bed. When you wake up from a dream, write down as quickly as possible everything you can remember, for the memory fades quickly. Try not to move too much from your sleeping position, since this will also dissipate the dream. In the morning you can write out the dream more carefully in your journal, and additional details may return to you as you do so. Interpreting the dream is discussed in the next exercise.

Dream Interpretation: In dreams your unconscious mind speaks to you through the language of symbols. Sometimes what it has to say is important, but often not. Some of these symbols—the archetypal ones—are universal to humans, others are cultural, and many are personal. It is helpful to study the universal symbols of humankind and of your culture, but ultimately what matters is what the symbols mean *to you*. The One is talking to you through your nous. So try to let each figure, object, event, situation, color, etc., in your dream speak to you. Contemplate it in the context of your dream, and see what moods, ideas, and images arise. You can make a diagram to show the connections, with lines from each dream image to the things that it elicits. Don't assume that the first meaning that comes to mind is the relevant one; it may be only the most obvious or superficial meaning. Symbol meanings exist in levels, and when you dig down to a deeper one, you may find that it has the light of significance for *your* dream. Sometimes you can amplify the meanings of dream symbols by studying archetypal images, but popular dream dictionaries have limited value. You may have to return to a big dream many times, and you may never discover *all* of its meaning. You can learn a lot about dream interpretation by studying the analytical psychology literature. Even better would be to work with a depth psychologist who uses dream interpretation.

Dream Incubation: This is a simple modern procedure for dream incubation. Pick a bed, couch, or chair on which you can recline comfortably. Have a pen, journal, and night-light available so you can make notes. It is better if you have by you a consecrated image of the deity you want to contact, but this is not necessary. You can make offerings and light a candle and incense. Contemplate and pray before the icon until you have a distinct impression of the deity's presence, and ask about whatever you want to know. Then if you have lit a candle, extinguish it (for safety's sake), lie back in the dark, and close your eyes. Keep your mind on the question, but don't obsessively repeat it to yourself.

> *Dream Incubation (continued):* Let your mind be gentle and drift, but try not to daydream about mundane matters. You may find it helpful to recite mentally an arrow prayer. If you drift in and out of sleep—that is good. If you discover that you have been having a dream that seems important, or if you have seen visions or heard sounds in a semiconscious state, then write them down as quickly as possible. Interpret the dream as you have learned. Keep in mind that your dream might not be an answer to your request; the deity might be telling you something more important.

ALLIANCE

Having explained incubation with Synesius's help, Hypatia continues to the next procedure. "The purpose of this operation is to meet and form an alliance with a god, angel, or daimon for the sake of cooperation. By means of such an alliance you can place yourself under a divinity's guidance and protection—tutelage, in the ancient sense—or you may secure the assistance of a deity for furthering divine purposes."

Translating Hypatia's words into psychological terms, you are engaging in conscious interaction with the universal archetypes and your personal complexes. These unconscious dynamical forces intervene continually in our lives, and if you are unaware of them, deny their existence, or attempt to repress them, they will nevertheless have their effect on you, but without your conscious participation. Through theurgy you can interact consciously with these unconscious powers, not fighting them, but cooperating with them to live an authentic life of meaning.

The teacher continues. "The archetypal gods exist outside of space and time; they are virtually identical among people and, in this sense, 'know' us only as representatives of humankind. Therefore it is usually easier, more beneficial, and more common to have an alliance with a god's attendant daimons, for these exist in time and space and are concerned with you as an individual. Since these spirits are intermediate between humans and gods, they are ideal mediators and are especially suited as messengers [*angeloi*, angels] between the human world and the Noetic Realm of the gods. We may bring our individual problems to these attendant spirits and request their guidance and aid in our individual lives."

This talk of daimons may seem less strange from a psychological perspective. The daimons correspond to unconscious complexes, which adapt the activity of the universal archetypes to our individual lives. The complexes nucleate around the archetypes as they are activated in the circumstances of each of our lives. As structures in the psyche they incorporate personal material from our external and internal lives into their being, and can be said to be "concerned" with us as individuals.

"You cannot assume," Hypatia warns, "that the deity you invoked is the deity who arrived. You prepare the receptacle, but the Nous fills it as it wills. Sometimes another divinity has a more important message for you than the one you invoked. Therefore, when you feel the presence of the deity, it is a good idea to ask their name."

"Must they answer truthfully?" asks Cyrus.

"No, you cannot simply accept that a spirit is who they say they are."

"How, then, can you trust anything they say?"

"You can't! Even if you are confident that you are communicating with one of the high gods, you should not believe uncritically what they say—or what you think they say—or blindly accept their advice or commands. Certainly, the goal of theurgy, and of many Platonic practices, for that matter, is to know divine Providence, so that you can submit your conscious ego to The One and live in harmony with it. Nevertheless, your conscious, rational mind serves a purpose, and you should use it. Do not abandon your critical reason or your moral autonomy. They are essential to our role as humans in the divine order."

Modern analytical psychologists as well as ancient theurgists emphasize that you should subject all spiritual experiences and revelations to conscious critical evaluation, including consultation with other experienced spiritual practitioners.

Hypatia reminds her students that they all have personal spirits who accompany them throughout their lives and perhaps beyond; psychologically, these are complexes closely connected to our individual identities. "For example," she says, "each of you has a guardian spirit, who mediates between you and the god who originates

your lineage—that is, who is the specific Form of your soul. In particular, your guardian watches over you and strives to guide you according to your destiny; some say
that this guardian is your advocate between lives. In any case, your cooperation with
your guardian will be facilitated if you make their acquaintance and form an alliance
with them. Thus a liaison with your guardian is especially worthwhile; life will go much
smoother."

"Master," says Cyrus, raising his hand, "I have heard that there are evil daimons, who
lead us astray."

"Daimons are not evil per se, but they have their own desires and agendas, which
are not always in our best interests or even lawful."

"Surely we should not invoke such beings," Cyrus presses.

"Always remember," Hypatia replies:

Invoked or not, daimons are here.

"If you ignore them, you risk possession. It is far better to acknowledge their presence, become acquainted, and communicate with them."

"How can we protect ourselves in these dealings?" asks Cyrus.

"Your practice of the first two degrees of wisdom is your protection. Indeed, all
daimons have valuable gifts, if you negotiate from this position of strength. Moreover,
never forget that you each have your own 'bad daimon,' which you have created un-
wittingly. You should meet it some day!"

As I discussed in chapter 9, another personal spirit is the Shadow complex, which is born
from the rejected potentials and energies of a person's soul. That is, everything that you,
consciously or unconsciously, whether by conscious decision or by cultural and environ-
mental osmosis, take to be *bad*, all those qualities will be the characteristics of your Shadow. Psychologically, it is the complex that has formed around the Idea of Evil.

Such might seem to be the last sort of spirit one might hope to meet (since it's demonic
in the colloquial sense), but that attitude is misguided. Because if you ignore the existence of
the Shadow, he or she (its gender is the same as yours) will act outside your awareness, "possessing" you or, by projection, possessing those with whom you interact. For the Shadow
behaves as an autonomous personality that wants to live and act, and will find a way to do
so. And, as Jung explained, a repressed archetype or complex will appear in its most primitive
and uncivilized form, so repression is not a wise choice.

Therefore it is much better to establish an alliance with your Shadow. Become acquainted so that you will recognize him or her: whether seizing you or another person, or simply hovering as a disconnected mood. (Recall the exercise *Seeing Your Shadow* in chapter 9.) Find out this spirit's needs, desires, and issues with you, so that you may form an agreement that satisfies the Shadow without sacrificing your personal needs and moral autonomy. By this alliance your Shadow, who was created from rejected parts of your own soul, may be recruited to work for your higher (divine) purpose. The Shadow holds great power, rejected from your psyche, and by a proper alliance you may reclaim this power for divine ends. By reclaiming the lost parts of your soul, you become more whole.

For many centuries Western culture has rejected and denied the Shadow, both individual and collective (for the collective consciousness of a culture, nation, or religion also creates its Shadow); this is the reason these destructive powers are rampaging ungoverned around our world. They cannot be banished; the only solution is a cooperative alliance in conformity with modern society and ethics.

The students scratch on their wax tablets as Hypatia gets to the technique. "To return to the operation of forming alliances with spirits, the invocation begins with cleansing and purification. Usually you take a ritual bath and dress in ceremonial attire, which puts you in the right frame of mind. You can wear symbols of the god to be invoked, and also garlands and other divine symbols as appropriate. You may purify the ritual area, typically with incense appropriate to the divinity. During the invocation itself you can stand on characters and figures that are symbols of the divinity. In general, as when you animate an icon, the more signs and symbols you can use, the better your soul will be prepared for the arrival of the divinity. To help achieve a trance state, you can use a point of *focus*, such as an oil lamp, a candle, an animated icon, or a character or other divine symbol."

"How do you tell if the invocation is successful?" asks Cyrus.

"There are various signs that experienced theurgists can use to tell if the divinity is present. For example, you might observe the lamp focus to transform from the ordinary 'mortal light' to a numinous 'strong immortal light.' Also, experienced theurgists can tell from the luminous apparitions what sort of spirit is present. According to Iamblichus, formless luminous apparitions are more reliable indicators of divine presence, since they are truer to a god's form than are recognizable shapes. In confirmation, the *Chaldean Oracles* state:

But when you see the very holy shapeless fire,
which shines by leaps and bounds throughout the whole world's depths,
attend the fire's voice ...[323]

"In any case, spirits are incorporeal and adopt a corporeal form only for our benefit, as explained in the *Oracles*,

... for you these bodies have been bound
upon the witnessed apparitions ...[324]

"Once the spirit is present, you should engage in a dialogue directed toward establishing an alliance. This might include vows on your part in thanks for the divine aid, and other agreements on symbols, signs, and tokens by which you and the spirit can communicate."

Hypatia takes a deep breath and concludes. "At the end of the ritual, bid the divinity to depart (if necessary) and thank them for their presence. Again, in theurgy we understand that a god cannot be 'banished.' Rather, this dismissal begins the 'detuning' of your soul from the divine power and back to the material realm, thereby allowing the divine projection to dissipate. Once you begin to return to normal consciousness, you can accelerate the process by turning away from the focal lamp and turning your attention to everyday matters. Focusing on your body is a good strategy. You may step off of the god's characters, if they were used, and extinguish the incense and focal lamp. These and other characters and symbols of the god may be covered. Finally, you should remove your ceremonial robes and any symbols of the god you might be wearing. This ends the rite. Note that the goal is not to sever all contact with divinity, but simply to conclude the rite."

The following exercises give some practical suggestions for establishing alliances with spirits (complexes and archetypes). The practices are related to the technique of *active imagination* developed by Jung and used in analytical psychology.

Spiritual Alliance: The theoretical basis for invoking a spirit and forming an alliance with it has been explained in this chapter. Once you understand how it works, you can adapt the procedure to fit your own spiritual practice and taste; these are general suggestions. It is easiest to communicate with a spirit if you have an "animated" image of it, but that's not required. A focus may be sufficient, but when you are practiced, you can invoke a familiar spirit at any place and any time. The simple procedure is to recall the spirit into the divine image in the usual way. When you feel its presence, you can begin communicating for any purpose. It is helpful to have a notebook (sometimes called a *spirit journal*) to record both sides of the conversation. You may be worried that you are making up the dialogue, but unless you are consciously scripting it, there is no need for concern; soon enough it will take surprising directions. All practitioners, from ancient theurgists to modern analytical psychologists, assert that you should be polite and respectful in dealing with spirits (personified complexes and archetypes). You should be questioning, assertive, and firm, and maintain a critical attitude. It is especially important that you stand your moral ground. Keep in mind that archetypal deities have their own agendas, which serve humankind and nature as wholes, but we are moral agents living in a twenty-first-century society. Humility is important, since they may have more important things to tell you than you have come to ask. If the spirit is aggrieved in some way, then you should negotiate, without of course abandoning your core values. If the spirit has some power (creativity, courage, compassion, and so on) that you desire, then you can negotiate the spirit's aid. You can also arrange mutual signs, words, or actions by which you can invoke the spirit or the spirit can get your notice. (I have expressed these practices in theurgical terms, but from a psychological perspective you are using symbols to activate and interact with complexes and archetypes. Some of this sounds like hocus-pocus, but the ritual of invocation may be as simple as sitting in a favorite chair and stating your wish to speak to a particular subpersonality.)

Alliances with Unknown Spirits: Generally, when you think of forming a spiritual alliance it is with a definite figure, such as a named god, angel, saint, or other spirit. But sometimes we need to contact a spirit known only through its effects. An example would include a dream figure that recurs, or that has had an important role in a big dream. It could also be a spirit that possesses you in an undesirable way, such as a feeling of fear, depression, or anger; or it could be an addictive or obsessive tendency. These are all complexes, which can cause trouble if neglected or denied. It could also be a positive possession—an inspiration—such as by a creative muse who visits too rarely. These are also complexes, whose growth we would like to encourage. In all these cases we would like to negotiate a better relation with the spirit, even if we do not know its name. The procedure is straightforward. When the feeling or idea is occupying your mind (that is, when the complex is active), give it a name. You could call it "Fear," "Shadow," "Muse," or anything else, including a personal name. Associate with that name any other ideas that arise with it, for example, how it appeared in a dream, an image, a color, a smell, a sound, surroundings; these can serve as symbols to help invoke it. Once you have this handle on the spirit, you can invoke it, negotiate with it, and form an alliance with it as with any spirit. As you become better acquainted, you may agree on signs, words, or actions by which to invoke the spirit. (Note: Sometimes a spirit will appear with the face of someone you know. This should be avoided because this can lead to confusion between the person and the spirit. Simply ask the spirit politely to change its shape.)

DEIFICATION

After taking a sip of water and contemplating for a moment, Hypatia resumes her teaching. "We now come to the last, and most advanced, theurgic operation, the Theurgic Ascent (also known as the Hieratic Ascent).[325] Although the procedures are similar to the operations I've already discussed, there is a crucial difference between this ascent and all the other operations, for in those operations the divinity is always experienced as 'other,' but by means of this exercise you ascend so that your soul, so

far as is possible for a mortal, unites with divinity. In this way you experience deification."

"My lady," says Cyrus, raising his hand, "if I remember correctly, the last lines of the
Pythagorean Golden Verses are:

> *Then stripped of flesh up to free Aether soar,*
> *A deathless god, divine, mortal no more.*[326]

"But your words imply that we can become a god only 'so far as is possible for a
mortal.'"

"But surely you recall," injects Athanasius, "that in Book 9 of the *Second Ennead*, the
divine Plotinus criticizes the Gnostics for their arrogance and foolishness in thinking
that they alone can become gods, and without any need of virtue, so long as they are
initiated into certain secrets. By scorning others they reveal their own failings for, as
Plotinus says, wise people have a mild disposition:

> *In proportion to a person's excellence,*
> *they're well disposed to everything,*
> *including people.*[327]

"The master also says we must know our limitations:

> *The person of real dignity*
> *must ascend in proper measure,*
> *without boorish arrogance,*
> *and only go so far as human nature can.*[328]

"For indeed:

> *Arrogance defeats becoming god,*
> *even so far as possible to human souls."*[329]

Several other students begin to speak at once, and Hypatia holds up her hand
until everyone is quiet. She replies, "Deification is not a matter of simple ritual, as some
Gnostics think. The divine Plato himself wrote,

> *To become like God is*
> *to become holy, just, and wise.*[330]

"We must strive to become good, holy, and wise. Therefore in philosophy we seek the Good through cultivation of the virtues, we seek the Truth through contemplation, and finally we seek Purity through the theurgic arts. This is achieved by separating yourself—for a time—from everything that differs from divinity. In this way we become divine, so far as humanly possible."

"Why should we strive for deification?" asks Cyrus.

"The goal of theurgic ascent—as well as the other ascents—is union with a god, and this may be any god, including even The Inexpressible One—an especially difficult accomplishment! By means of this union you may experience your own inherent divinity and your connection with The One, and thus, by means of the union, come to be in better harmony with Providence. Consciously experiencing your participation in Providence gives meaning to life. You become a willing agent of Providence.

"By the principle of like knows like, it is the image of The One in your own soul—which we Platonists call the *flower of the soul*—that is able to unite with The Inexpressible One. By means of this 'knowledge through identification,' your individual One comes to participate more perfectly in The One Itself. This is the turn back toward The One—the ultimate source—known as the *Return*, by which your soul becomes the *energy* actualizing the *power* of The One. This is our destiny."

In terms of Jungian psychology, the Self, which is the unconscious foundation of each person's psyche, the God-image within, is a part of the psychophysical unity that is the universe. By conscious contact and identification with your inner Self, you can come to comprehend (to some degree) and to participate consciously in your individual destiny as part of this totality.

Hypatia continues. "To accomplish the ascent, the parts of your soul that are more like The One must be separated from those that are less like it. This separation is accomplished by a symbolic death: 'dying before you die.' Therefore the operation includes a symbolic funeral. Before describing the procedure I must add that the ascent is a cooperative activity between the initiate, who makes the ascent, and an initiator or theurgist, who usually has assistants. It is possible, but difficult, for you to make this ascent on your own.

"Preparatory to the ascent is *Purification* of the soul, of its 'vehicle'—the vital spirit that connects it to the body—and of the body itself. The principal goal is to facilitate the ascent by making the initiate as similar to the gods as possible. Purification of the soul is directed toward quieting the lower parts of your soul, which do not ascend. To this end, the techniques of the Contemplative Ascent [chapter 11] are useful.

"Purification eliminates those influences that may impede your ascent, but we facilitate it by using the signs and symbols appropriate to the deity. You may wear the symbols, ingest them—if they're edible!—or place them in the ritual area. Nonphysical symbols, such as hymns, prayers, and chants, will be recited out loud or in the initiate's mind as the ascent proceeds."

In more contemporary terms, by connecting, internally as well as externally, with these symbols of the archetype or complex, by making them part of yourself, you activate the archetype or complex so that it manifests in your conscious experience. You awaken the god within you (which also transcends you). This begins the identification of you and the god.

"The next steps are a symbolic death, funeral, and burial. When complete, the theurgic director begins to call forth your soul, invoking the inner 'soul spark' born of the Cosmic Nous, to draw your soul forth from your body. The director declares you to be clothed in shining raiment, girded by the substance of the celestial spheres, bids you to concentrate your nous upon the signs and symbols, and calls your soul to come forth to scale the fiery rays. The theurgist continues with various sacred formulas to evoke your soul, and the assistants begin singing chants and hymns to aid the separation. While the theurgist calls forth your soul, you focus on your breath and begin to breathe more deeply and quickly, in time with the chanting or music. One of Synesius's hymns expresses the initiate's intention:

> Giver of noetic life and fire!
> Behold me, and regard my soul that cries,
> Which from the earth does upward flights desire,
> Light up, O King, my heaven-seeking eyes.
> Cut off all ties; and nimble make my wing;
> Up to Thy halls and breast, may I swift spring!"[331]

We now know that breathing exercises and rhythmic chanting and music are common shamanic techniques for modifying neurophysiology to achieve a trance state. Shamans also decorate themselves with signs and symbols intended to facilitate their spiritual journeys and to ensure their success. As the theurgist ascends the fiery rays to The One, so shamans often ascend the World Tree, World Axis, or Sacred Mountain, through seven heavens, to enter the divine realms. But let's return to Hypatia's imaginary lesson.

"Through the following stages the assistants, under direction of the theurgist, adjust their chanting, singing, or other music to aid the elevation of the initiate's soul. Henceforth, the initiate may breathe through the mouth and intone chants selected to aid their ascent. But once the initiate has ascended above the celestial sphere, they should focus on chanting the signs and symbols in their mind rather than out loud, for they are ascending through the immaterial empyrean spheres. As Synesius wrote in a hymn when he was studying with me:

> Rash harp be silent, nor profanely dare
> The secret worship, which no rites declare,
> To men to tell; go, sing of things beneath;
> Let Heaven be unpolluted by thy breath,
> The soul alone may roam through worlds of thought.[332]

"Here—in the Cosmic Nous—you may encounter the gods, who may assist your ascent, drawing you upward with helpful hands.

"Ultimately you may ascend all the way to The Inexpressible One. At this transcendent pinnacle you will be beyond duality, beyond language and conceptual thought, indeed beyond all differentiation and change. In this eternal realm, beyond time itself, you experience immortality and deification.

"A mortal cannot remain in the state of unification for very long, and when you sense its dissipation you must begin to re-descend and to don again the layers of your outer soul. The experienced theurgist will perceive that you are falling from the unitive state and will assist your re-descent with appropriate formulas, chants, songs, prayers, and hymns. When your descent is complete, the company welcomes you—the reborn initiate—with joyous hymns of welcome and praise.

"As a result of the ascent, you are transformed, reborn with a new soul. Although you have returned to the material world, henceforth your soul retains roots planted in The One. With this permanent connection to the transcendent source of divinity, you henceforth consciously embody divinity on Earth.

"The theurgic ascent is a difficult and hence infrequent rite, for which years of preparation may be required. But when it is successful, the initiate is transformed into a god-person, one of the so-called 'perfected or immaculate beings,' who by their very presence on Earth bring grace to humanity and to all of Nature. They are the divine people who have founded our religious traditions. Synesius concludes his hymn with these words:

> *Upward, my soul! drink from th' Eternal Fount*
> *Of heavenly good; with earnest prayer entreat*
> *Thy Father! Halt not—leave this earthly mount,*
> *For Godlike thou shalt be—in God complete."* [333]

With that, Hypatia rises and leaves the room.

Theurgic Ascent: If you want to practice Theurgic Ascent, you will have to find your own way forward, but I will give a few hints. First it is essential that the theurgist and his or her other assistants be experienced in all the other theurgic practices, the other two ascents, and of course the first two degrees of wisdom. In particular, they must be experienced in animating images and have established alliances with deities that can aid the ascent (that is, that they are in conscious relation to the relevant archetypes). The initiate should also have a solid foundation in these skills. This means that all the participants are experienced in using symbols as means to connect through the Cosmic Nous to The One. Then you will have to design a ritual or symbolic drama centered on the idea of rebirth. You will have to pick the cultural, religious, and spiritual details to speak symbolically to the participants. For example, the ritual or drama could be based on Greek mythology, some other Pagan myths, the Christian resurrection, a modern near-death experience, a science-fiction scenario, or anything else, provided it is authentic (and not hokey). You will have to experiment, and your procedure will be proved by your success. Don't expect it to work every time. It is not a recipe; it is a preparation to receive divine grace.

INDIVIDUATION

You may be wondering what could be the value of these practices today. The answer is that they help you to live in harmony with your true nature and the nature of the universe.

From a polytheistic perspective, theurgy provides the means for contacting the gods and daimons who govern the universe. In this way you can learn the individual role you are supposed to play and can undertake it consciously. Interacting with these spirits allows you to placate those divinities who stand in the way and to recruit them and others as assistants in the conscious fulfillment of your individual destiny.

The monotheistic perspective is not much different, since theurgy provides means for communicating with the various ranks of angels who are the mediators between you and God. This allows you to get more specific information from angelic beings and to recruit their aid in fulfilling your individual purpose on Earth.

Even from a purely psychological perspective, theurgy is a valuable practice (called *active imagination*). The archetypes represent the major innate governing forces of our collective unconscious; they provide the psychological and biological foundation of our individual life cycles and thus of the evolution of our species. They are the ultimate sources of meaning in our lives. Therefore, to live consciously meaningful lives, as individuals who understand their roles in the whole drama, it is helpful to consciously engage the archetypes and their dependent complexes. By consciously integrating the archetypes into our lives, we progress along the path of spiritual development that Jung called individuation. Remember:

Our goal is not to be flawless, but to be god.[334]

> *Final and First Exercise:* Chances are, you have rushed through this book to get to the end. That's fine. Now go back through it again and make the practices a part of your life. As Epicurus said, you can't get healthy by reading about exercises and cures; you have to *do* them!

CLOSING REMARKS

You've come a long way, and if you have been practicing the exercises as you've advanced through the three degrees of wisdom, you have acquired some important life skills. In the Garden you learned how to live with greater joy and tranquility by governing your desires and by living simply. From the philosophers of the Porch you learned three valuable disciplines. The Discipline of Assent accepts the true, rejects the false, and suspends judgment on the uncertain. The Discipline of Impulse governs your choices, with an emphasis on altruism. The Discipline of Desire guides your decisions about what is good, what is bad, and especially about those things to which you should be indifferent. These disciplines are helping you to lift your concerns from the level of material contentedness to a higher and wider perspective, and aiding you to live your destiny. Finally, from the philosophy of Hypatia you have learned three ways of ascent to The One, the Paths of Love, Truth, and Trust, which will lead to greater psychological integration and harmony with the cosmos. You have learned as well a Neoplatonic system of psycho-spiritual practices to develop and support a way of life that draws from the deepest wellsprings of meaning and is guided by the eternal forces that govern our lives. Through the exercise of these arts you will fulfill your destiny.

However, your mastery of the sublime philosophy of Hypatia does not imply that you should forget the life skills that you learned in the Garden and the Porch. For they will allow you to live your everyday life wisely and will provide a foundation of serenity and happiness for your more ambitious spiritual practices.

I hope you will agree that the Neoplatonic way of life has much to offer to our world. Although its roots are thousands of years old, its central ideas and practices are grounded in human nature, which is the same now as it was in Hypatia's time and in earlier ages. Therefore the sources of meaning in human life are unchanged, and although much has changed in science and civilization, the practices that Hypatia taught are still effective. Furthermore, they are largely independent of specific religious or spiritual doctrine, and so they are compatible with many systems of belief: Pagan and non-Pagan, polytheist, monotheist, and even atheist. Although ancient, it is a spiritual path for our time. May we all find the wisdom we need!

ENDNOTES

ABBREVIATIONS

CO	*Chaldean Oracles* (see Majercik)
DL	Diogenes Laertius, *Lives*
ED	Epictetus, *Discourses*
EH	Epictetus, *Handbook* (also called *Manual* and *Encheridion*)
HC	Hierocles, *Comm. on Pythag. Gold. Verses* (see Dacier, Hierocles, and Schibli)
LM	Epicurus, *Letter to Menoeceus* (see Bailey, Oates, or DL X.122–135)
LS	Long and Sedley, *Hellenistic Philosophers*
LSJ	Liddell, Scott, and Jones, *Greek Lexicon*
MA	Marcus Aurelius, *Meditations*
OF	Epicurus's fragment in Oates
P7	Plato, *Seventh Letter* (in *Collected Dialogues*)
PD	Epicurus, *Principal Doctrines* (see Bailey, Oates, or DL X.139–154)
PE	Plotinus, *Enneads* (see *Plotinus*, Armstrong trans.)
PG	Plotinus, *Compl. Works* (Guthrie translation)
PLP	Porphyry, *Launching Points*
PS	Plato, *Symposium* (in *Collected Dialogues*)
RH	Reale, *Systems of Hellenistic Age*
SD	Synesius, *On Dreams*
SL	Seneca, *Letters to Lucilius* (*Ad Lucilium Epistolae*)
VS	Epicurus, *Vatican Sentences* (see Bailey or Oates)

1. Hierocles's *Commentary on the Pythagorean Golden Verses*, Proem 4, trans. Schibli.

2. The information about Hypatia's life and death is drawn from the books by Dzielska (1995) and Deakin (2007), the best current sources.

3. *The Chronicle of John of Nikiu* (ch. 84, §§87–103), quoted in Deakin (p. 148).

4. Damascius's *Life of Isidorus*, which tells Hypatia's story (Deakin, p. 142).

5. Plato, *Phaedo*, 69C, my trans. The literal translation is "narthex-bearers," for the Bacchic wand was made from a narthex stalk.

6. Quoted from Emerson's essay "Circles" (First Series, 10), but the analogy appears in a Hermetic text called *The Book of 24 Philosophers*, dated to about 1200; see Wind (p. 227, n. 30). See the similar idea in Plotinus's *Enneads* 5.2.2. Emerson incorrectly attributed the statement to St. Augustine.

7. Plato's *Phaedo* (80e–81a, Jowett trans.).

8. Epicurus's *Letter to Menoeceus* DL X.126). "DL" refers to books and chapters in Diogenes Laertius, *Lives of Eminent Philosophers*.

9. The Delphic Maxims were widely discussed in antiquity. In his *Protagoras* (343b), Plato mentions the two most famous, "Know thyself" and "Nothing too much." Eliza Wilkins's dissertation is an old but comprehensive review of interpretations of "Know thyself."

10. Verses 40–44 of *The Pythagorean Golden Verses*, adapted from Thomas Stanley's translation (Part IX, ch. v, p. 477). See Thom's *Pyth. Golden Verses* (pp. 38–43, 163–7) on these verses and their background.

11. Porphyry's *Life of Pythagoras* (sec. 40), adapted from K. S. Guthrie's translation (*Pyth. Sourcebook*, p. 131). It also appears in some texts of the *Golden Verses* immediately before "Don't suffer sleep …" See Thom's *Pyth. Golden Verses* (pp. 40–41).

12. Theorems and proofs are familiar from mathematics, but ancient Greek *theôrêma* means (among other things) a deduced principle contemplated or investigated by the mind (Liddell, Scott, and Jones—LSJ—s.v.).

13. Magic as "the art of changing consciousness at will" is widely attributed to Dion Fortune (Violet Firth), but I have been unable to find it in her writings. See, for example, Berger (p. 22) and Harvey (p. 88).

14. For more on the New Thought movement, see Braden's *Spirits in Rebellion*.

15. For a discussion of the ideal sage, see Hadot's *What Is Ancient Philosophy?* (pp. 220–23), where the sage is described as a "transcendent norm," and Hadot's *The Present Alone* (p. 117).

16. Hadot attributes this phrase to Victor Goldschmidt (Hadot, *The Present Alone*, pp. 55, 91).

17. The map is adapted from a public domain map available on Wikipedia at http://en.wikipedia.org/wiki/File:RomanEmpire_117.svg (accessed February 16, 2012).

18. For more on Pythagoras, Abaris, and shamanic connections with Mongolia and Tibet, see Kingsley's *A Story Waiting to Pierce You*.

19. There is scholarly doubt about the meaning of his nickname, *Sakkas*. It might refer to the fact that he dressed in a sack or in sackcloth, or that he was a sack-carrier at the docks. It apparently comes from *sakkos*, which means a cloth woven of coarse hair or a coarse beard. All the possible meanings point to a person of humble origins. See the *Oxford Classical Dictionary* (Ammonius Saccas) and LSJ, *Greek-English Lexicon* (under *sakkas* and *sakkos*).

20. Porphyry's *Life of Plotinus* (3.6–21, Guthrie trans.), which can be found as the first section of any edition of Plotinus's *Enneads*.

21. Porphyry, *Life of Plotinus* 2.26–27, trans. Armstrong (*Plotinus*).

22. Socrates Scholasticus's account of the events surrounding Hypatia's murder; see Deakin (App. D, Sec. B).

23. Damascius's *Life of Isidorus*, quoted in I. Hadot's *Studies on the Neoplatonist Hierocles* (p. 2). Hierocles was quoting the *Odyssey* (Bk. 9, line 347).

24. Pico is quoting the *Asclepius* 6, "magnum miraculum est homo." See Copenhaver for a recent translation.

25. From a letter by Epicurus, OF 37, trans. Erik Anderson, http://www.epicurus.info (accessed March 21, 2012). "OF" refers to the number of a fragment in Oates, *The Stoic and Epicurean Philosophers*.

26. From Pierre Gassendi (1592–1655), quoted in Thomas Stanley's old *History of Philosophy* (1655/1743), which collects a wealth of detailed information.

27. DL X.9.

28. Stanley, Pt. 5, "Epicurus," ch. 15 (p. 124).

29. From Thomas Jefferson's letter to William Short, October 31, 1819 (Forman, pp. 207–8).

30. Epicurus, *Letter to Menoeceus* (henceforth, "LM") is preserved in DL X.122–135. This quotation is adapted from the Hicks trans. of DL X.134.

31. For more on compatibilism, see Michael McKenna's "Compatibilism" (2009) in the online *Stanford Encyclopedia of Philosophy*, http://plato.stanford.edu/entries/compatibilism (accessed March 21, 2012).

32. The dialogue, of course, is fictional, except for the maxims, whose sources are documented herein. The *dramatis personae* are historically documented students of Epicurus. The same applies to the other dialogues in this book, which are printed in a distinctive typeface.

33. VS 59, adapted from Peter Saint-Andre's trans. http://www.monadnock.net/epicurus (accessed August 4, 2012). "VS" refers to the *Vatican Sentences* (VS), a collection of Epicurus's maxims.

34. VS 68, Saint-Andre trans.

35. This Delphic Maxim, which was discussed frequently in antiquity, is mentioned by Plato in his *Protagoras* (343b).

36. From Epicurus's *Principal Doctrines* (PD) 29, adapted from Saint-Andre trans. The *Principal Doctrines* are also known as the *Key Doctrines*.

37. VS 71, trans. from http://www.epicurus.info/etexts/VS.html (accessed July 3, 2012).

38. Lucretius, "On the Nature of Things (De Rerum Natura)," Bk. 2, lines 1–2.

39. OF 67, trans. from Hadot (1995, p. 87).

40. VS 63, trans. from http://www.epicurus.info/etexts/VS.html (accessed July 3, 2012).

41. OF 39, Saint-Andre trans.

42. Reale, *Sys. Hellen. Age*, p. 170.

43. This quotation is from DL X.130, trans. from http://www.epicurus.info/etexts/Lives.html (accessed July 3, 2012).

44. OF 70, adapted from Saint-Andre trans.

45. VS 77, trans. from http://www.epicurus.info/etexts/VS.html (accessed July 3, 2012).

46. PD 4 (Oates, p. 35).

47. PD 1, adapted from Saint-Andre trans.

48. Xenophanes, DK 21B11. This "Diels-Krantz number" is the standard way of citing the fragments the Presocratic philosophers. I've used the translation from Cornford (*Grk. Rel. Tht.*, 1950), p. 85.

49. PD 2, Saint-Andre trans.

50. Lucretius, "On the Nature of Things," Bk. 3, lines 978–79, William Ellery Leonard trans.

51. Lucretius, "On the Nature of Things," Bk. 3, line 1023, my trans.

52. LM (DL X.126), my trans.

53. LM (DL X.126), trans. from Long and Sedley (LS), *Hellenistic Philosophers*, 24A6.

54. PD 19, Hicks trans. (DL X.145).

55. The analogy between the perfection of a moment and of a circle was used by Seneca (*Letters to Lucilius* 74.27), who wrote, "Whether you draw a larger or a smaller circle, its size affects its area, not its shape."

56. From Philodemus, *Against the Sophists*, 4.9–14, my trans.

57. PD 21, adapted from Saint-Andre trans.

58. VS 14, trans from http://www.epicurus.net/en/vatican.html (accessed July 14, 2012).

59. Adapted from VS 58, Saint-Andre trans.

60. Plutarch (quoted in Reale, *Sys. Hellen. Age*, p. 177).

61. OF 86, trans. from Reale, *Sys. Hellen. Age*, p. 177.

62. Stevenson (trans.), *Ten Hymns of Synesius* (1865).

63. On Epicurean "evolutionary anthropology" see Lucretius, "On the Nature of Things," Bk. 5, and Porphyry's *On Abstinence from Meat*, Bk. 1, in *Select Works*.

64. PD 31, Saint-Andre trans.

65. PD 33, trans. adapted from http://www.epicurus.info/etexts/PD.html (accessed July 3, 2012).

66. PD 17, trans. from http://www.epicurus.info/etexts/PD.html (accessed July 3, 2012); cf. VS 12.

67. OF 81, Saint-Andre trans.

68. Peters, p. 40.

69. Trans. from LS 22S.

70. Trans. from LS 22P.

71. OF 80, trans. Bailey.

72. Porphyry, *On Abstinence* (trans. from LS 22M1).

73. Plutarch, "That a Philosopher Ought Chiefly to Converse with Great Men" §3 (Vol. 2, p. 374).

74. DL X.120.

75. VS 52.

76. PD 27.

77. VS 78.

78. VS 66, adapted from Saint-Andre trans.

79. OF 50, Saint-Andre trans.

80. DL X.22, Hicks trans. (*Stoic & Epic.*, p. 159).

81. Adapted from DL X.16, my trans.

82. VS 41, Saint-Andre trans.

83. VS 54, adapted from Saint-Andre trans.

84. VS 65, Saint-Andre trans.

85. VS 79, trans. adapted from http://www.epicurus.info/etexts/VS.html (accessed July 3, 2012).

86. OF 46, Saint-Andre trans.

87. OF 54, Saint-Andre trans.

88. OF 66, adapted from Saint-Andre trans.

89. OF 74, Saint-Andre trans.

90. LM (DL X.135), adapted from Saint-Andre and Hicks translations.

91. Diogenes Laertius (DL) VII.2–4; he probably wrote in the third century CE and was perhaps an Epicurean.

92. Crates's 6th Letter, translated in Sayre, *The Greek Cynics* (p. 7). These letters were not actually written by Crates, but reflect Cynic doctrine.

93. Crates's 21st Letter, trans. adapted from Sayre, *Greek Cynics* (p. 7).

94. Seneca, *Letters to Lucilius* (*Ad Luculium Epistulae Morales*) 74.27, trans. Gummere.

95. DL VII 40.

96. Aurelius, *Meditations* (MA), II 4.

97. MA XII 26.

98. MA VIII 7.

99. Epictetus's *Handbook* (EH) §5, trans. adapted from Hadot (*Inn. Cit.*), p. 109.

100. MA VIII 40.

101. MA VIII 49.

102. MA III 11.

103. The "naked" description of eating a steak is based on MA VI 13; the anachronistic references to germs and chemical stimulation of the tongue are mine.

104. MA VI 13. It astonishes me that this passage is censored, without comment, from some modern translations of Marcus's *Meditations*.

105. MA VII 68.

106. MA VIII 48.

107. MA IX 15.

108. MA XI 11.

109. MA VI 8.

110. MA V 25.

111. MA V 10.

112. MA II 1.

113. MA IV 49.

114. "The philosophical origins of cognitive therapy can be traced back to Stoic phi-losophers, particularly Zeno of Citium (fourth century B.C.), Chysippus, Cicero, Seneca, Epictetus, and Marcus Aurelius" (Beck 1979, p. 8). See especially Robertson (2010).

115. Marcus Aurelius describes it in *Med.* XII 3, and Hadot discusses it in *The Inner Citadel*, pp. 112–25; the quote is on p. 120.

116. MA XII 3.

117. Horace's *Satires*, Bk. II, 7, lines 83–88, translated by John Conington.

118. Epictetus's *Discourses* (ED) III 24.88, trans. Long.

119. Seneca, *Letters to Lucilius* (SL) 98.6.

120. MA VIII 36.

121. Of course some diseases and injuries, those affecting the brain, *do* impair your abil-ity to make moral choices. From a Stoic perspective, there are situations in which suicide or euthanasia might be justified.

122. ED IV 1.111.

123. ED IV 1.112, trans. P. E. Matheson.

124. ED IV 1.110, trans. P. E. Matheson.

125. MA II 13.

126. MA II 17.

127. DL VII 88.

128. ED I 14.12, modified from Matheson trans.

129. MA V 27.

130. MA IV 5.

131. MA IX 28.

132. See Schneider (2005) on the role of the second law of thermodynamics on creating order.

133. MA III 16.

134. This analogy is based on MA V 8.

135. SL 107.2.

136. MA V 8. This is also the source of the simile about the stones in a pyramid.

137. MA X 5.

138. MA III 11.

139. MA IV 40.

140. MA VII 9.

141. MA X 21.

142. MA VI 38.

143. This maxim occurs in several different forms, for example MA III 16, X 11, XII 27.

144. MA XII 14.

145. Seneca, *Nat. Quest*. I, preface, 3, quoted in Hadot, *Inn. Cit*. p. 157.

146. EH 8.

147. MA XII 29.

148. MA VII 69.

149. MA VIII 2.

150. MA VII 11.

151. MA X 2.

152. MA VII 55.

153. MA XII 30.

154. MA VII 13.

155. ED II 5.

156. MA VIII 34, ED. II 5.

157. MA IX 42.

158. MA XI 4.

159. MA V 6.

160. MA IX 42.

161. MA II 1, trans. Long.

162. MA VII 63.

163. Peters, s.v. sôphrosynê, p. 180.

164. MA XI 18.

165. MA IV 7, my trans.

166. MA X 4.

167. MA XI 13.

168. MA XI 18. Meditations XI 18 and II 16 are too long to quote in full, but they each provide organized series of rules for behaving ethically.
169. MA VI 27.
170. MA IX 11.
171. MA VIII 59.
172. MA VII 22.
173. MA XI 18.
174. MA VI 39.
175. Hierocles, *Commentary on the Pythagorean Golden Verses* (henceforth, "HC") VII 9, Rowe trans.
176. *The Pythagorean Golden Verses*, edited by Thom, verses 5–8, adapted from Thomas Stanley trans.
177. HC VII 11, Rowe trans.; a common Greek idea (e.g., Plato, *Lysis* 214d5–6).
178. MA VIII 29.
179. MA IX 27.
180. Adapted from Cassius Dio, 72.34.4, Foster trans.
181. MA XI 1.
182. Seneca, *On Benef.*, IV.33.2, adapted from Stewart trans.
183. MA X 12.
184. MA VIII 32.
185. MA VI 7.
186. MA VIII 32.
187. MA V 20.
188. MA IV 2.
189. MA VIII 35.
190. MA VIII 16.
191. ED II 5.
192. Epictetus, fragment 10, quoted by Aulus Gellius XVII.19, trans. Matheson. If you want to learn it in ancient Greek, it is *anékhou kai apékhou,* or in Latin *sustine et abstine.*
193. MA IX 1.
194. MA IX 9.
195. Adapted from Haines trans. of MA IX 9.
196. MA IX 9.
197. MA XI 37, paraphrasing ED III 24.

198. The relation between the three Stoic disciplines and the cardinal virtues is discussed at some length in Hadot, *Inn. Cit.* (ch. 9).

199. MA XII 15.

200. As it turns out, this persistent notion arises from a mistranslation of an idiom in Plato's *Phaedo*; see Appendix II in Archer-Hind's edition of the *Phaedo*. Nevertheless, it is an attractive metaphor.

201. As I explained in chapter 3, so far as we know, Hypatia did not write any philosophical works. Therefore, in this imaginary lecture I am putting words in her mouth, but the ideas are those of Alexandrian Neoplatonism during her lifetime.

202. The *levels or planes of reality* are technically termed *hypostases*, so The One is the first hypostasis, the World Mind is the second hypostasis, etc. As much as possible I have tried to avoid the technical terminology of Neoplatonism. From Plato's time on to Hypatia's and beyond, there have been differing analyses of the nonmaterial realm, generally subdividing the levels into sublevels in one way or another. For the most part we do not need to worry about these differences, and you will be learning techniques that will allow you to do your own exploration of the nonmaterial realms.

203. Many mathematicians have defended a Platonic philosophy of mathematics. Balaguer (1998) argues convincingly that there are two equally defensible philosophies of mathematics, one of which is "full-blooded Platonism," in which any logically consistent mathematical object exists.

204. The meaning of *idea* is in Liddell, Scott and Jones's *Greek Lexicon*, and its philosophical usage is discussed in Peters, *Greek Philosophical Terms*, under *eidos*.

205. We do not know the names of Hypatia's female students, and so I have made up Aedesia. In fifth-century Alexandria, there were married Neoplatonic philosophers named Aedesia and Hermias, but they would have been a little young to attend Hypatia's lectures.

206. Plato's *Sophist*, 246a–b, translation adapted from those by Jowett (*Dialogues of Plato*) and Cornford (in *Collected Dialogues*, ed. Hamilton & Huntington-Cairns).

207. Plato's *Sophist*, 246b–c, translation adapted from those by Jowett (*Dialogues of Plato*) and Cornford (in *Collected Dialogues*, ed. Hamilton & Huntington-Cairns).

208. Plotinus, *Enneads* (hence forth "PE") 4.8.3.

209. PE 4.8.5.

210. PE 4.4.13.

211. Plato, *Timaeus*, 37d.

212. My paraphrase of an Epicurean fragment quoted by Porphyry (*Letter to Marcella*, 31).

213. From Synesius's *Third Hymn*, translated by Alan Stevenson, which Synesius probably wrote in 402, shortly after returning from Constantinople (Bregman, *Synesius*, pp. 78–79).

214. From Synesius's *Fourth Hymn*, trans. Alan Stevenson. Synesius wrote this hymn in the period 404–406 CE while residing in Alexandria and before he was appointed bishop (Bregman, *Synesius*, p. 61).

215. PE 6.7.22.

216. Plato describes this ascent in his *Symposium*; you will learn it in chapter 10.

217. From Synesius's *Fourth Hymn*, trans. Alan Stevenson.

218. Maximus Tyrius, *Dissertation I,* trans. Thomas Taylor, pp. 5–6.

219. Verses 45–48 of the *Pythagorean Golden Verses*, adapted from the translation by Thomas Stanley.

220. Hierocles, *Comm. Pyth. Gold. Vers.* XXI.7, adapted from Rowe trans.

221. Homer, *Iliad*, bk. 8, lines 17–27, translated by Alexander Pope.

222. PE 3.4.3, line 22, my trans.

223. For more on the Trinity and subordinationism, see Bregman's *Synesius* (pp. 79–80) and the citations therein.

224. From Synesius's *Third Hymn*, trans. Alan Stevenson.

225. The Epicurean Paradox is attributed to Epicurus by Lactantius, *De ira dei* 13, 20–21.

226. There are many biographies of Jung, some of which are prejudiced and subjective. One that is unbiased and objective is Dierdre Bair's *Jung: A Biography*. Jung's autobiography, *Memories, Dreams, Reflections*, is valuable for giving his own perspective on his development.

227. In my papers listed in the bibliography I explore in more detail the connections, on the one hand, between Jungian psychology and Neoplatonism, and on the other, between Jungian psychology and evolutionary psychology. Much of my work on evolutionary Jungian psychology is based on that of Meredith Sabini and especially Anthony Stevens.

228. The human genome has about 3.2 billion bases.

229. Since there are ten digits but only four DNA bases (A, C, G, T), it takes only about 3.85 billion digits to number the possible 6.4 billion-long strings of the bases from the two parents.

230. I am referring to the *Baldwin effect*, which is one kind of *niche construction* by species.

231. Trans. Edwin Hamilton Gifford. http://classics.mit.edu/Porphyry/images.html (accessed September 25, 2012).

232. General information on the three paths of ascent can be found in Rosán's *Phil. of Proclus*, pp. 205–13, and Siorvanes's *Proclus*, pp. 189–99. See also PE 1.3.

233. Proclus, *Plat. Theol.*, trans. in Rosán, *Phil. Procl.*, p. 213.

234. Information on the troubadours and Cathars can be found in Anderson's *Dante the Maker* and in de Rougemont's *Love in the Western World*.

235. Rumi, *Mathnavi* I.109, trans. Raficq Abdulla, *Words of Paradise: Selected Poems of Rumi* (London: Frances Lincoln Ltd., 2000), pp. 46–47, used with permission.

236. al-Hallaj, "Kitab al-Tawasin" (see Nicholson's *Mystics of Islam*, p. 151).

237. I use the terms Provence, Languedoc, and Poitou more or less synonymously for the part of southern France that gave birth to Occitan poetry (poetry from the region where *oc* meant "yes"). Technically, Provence is the region east of the Rhône and Languedoc is west of it. Languedoc is part of Poitou, a region in west-central France. Poitiers was the capital of Poitou, which was part of (lower) Aquitainia. See the map in chapter 3.

238. Anderson, *Dante the Maker*, p. 83.

239. For example, Luigi Valli (*Il linguaggio segreto di Dante e dei "Fedeli d'Amore,"* Rome, 1928).

240. Cavalcanti, IV; in D. G. Rossetti, trans., *Early Ital. Poets*.

241. Judah Leon Abrabanel's *Dialogues of Love* is available in English as Leone Ebreo, *The Philosophy of Love*.

242. Among many sources for the Ascent by Love, I have found Friedländer's *Plato*, chapter 3, and Hadot's *Plotinus* to be especially informative. Castiglione's version of Bembo's ascent is in his *Courtier* (Book IV, chapters 50–70). I have followed Castiglione's fictional account because it is more genuinely Platonic than Bembo's original (*Gli Asolani*, Bk. III, pp. 173–95).

243. Plato, *Symposium* (henceforth, "PS"), 178a–c.

244. Hesiod, *Theogony*, lines 116–22, my trans.

245. PS 202e, after translation by Tom Griffith.

246. The original meaning can be found in the *Oxford English Dictionary*.

247. Quoted in Hadot, *Plotinus*, p. 58.

248. After PS 206a.

249. PS 206b.

250. PS 204b.

251. Ficino, letter 1.47 (Ficino, *Med. on Soul*, #80).

252. The myth of Narcissus can be found in Ovid's *Metamorphoses*, Book 3, beginning at line 341. I have quoted the classic translation by Dryden, Garth, Pope, Addison, Congreve, et al. The story of Echo immediately precedes that of Narcissus.

253. Ovid, *Met.*, Bk. III, Dryden et al., trans., lines 534–37.

254. Ovid, *Met.*, Bk. III, Dryden et al., trans., lines 567–72.

255. The allegorical interpretation is from Ficino, *On Love*, Sixth Speech, chapter 17 (Sears trans., p. 212).

256. Ovid, *Met.*, Bk. III, Dryden et al., trans., lines 496–500.

257. Gaius's story comes from Damascius (fr. 102), the last head of the Platonic Academy in Athens, who was writing about a century after Hypatia's death. Since the would-be lover is not named, I have called him "Gaius," which was the name of one of her students, about whom nothing else is known. The obvious assumption is that the menstrual napkin was recently used and set aside for this purpose, but another possibility is that it was from her menarche, preserved as a kind of talisman, as was sometimes done (see Deakin, pp. 62–63, 180). The basket is my invention, but it seems plausible that the napkin was contained in something. I have imagined a small *cista mystica* (mystic basket), such as used in the Mysteries. Dzielska (p. 50) observes that the story might preserve the only authentic quotation from Hypatia: "In truth, this is the focus of your yearning, young man, but it is nothing beautiful" (Deakin, pp. 141). Gaius's profession of love is adapted from Musaeus's lyric poem *Hero and Leander*, lines 135–52, using the translations by Sikes (p. 18) and Greene (pp. 9–10). Musaeus was probably a Christian Neoplatonist who wrote around a century after Hypatia's death and seems to have spent time in Alexandria (Loeb ed., pp. 297–302).

258. Plato, *Phaedo* (66c–d), Jowett trans.

259. Plato, *Phaedo* (67e), Jowett trans.

260. From Synesius's *Fifth Hymn*, trans. Alan Stevenson.

261. Adapted from Ficino, *Commentary on Plato's Symposium*, Sears trans., p. 214.

262. Adapted from Plotinus, *Enneads*, 5.8.13.

263. Adapted from Proclus's Hymn VII, To Polymetis (Athena); trans. van den Berg, pp. 304–5.

264. Rumi, *Divan* 310, trans. Raficq Abdulla, *Words of Paradise: Selected Poems of Rumi* (London: Frances Lincoln Ltd., 2000), p. 42, used with permission.

265. Plato, *Phaedrus*, 249c. I give the Greek words in their nominative singular form so that they are easier to compare.

266. Adapted from Plotinus, *Enneads*, 1.2.6, MacKenna trans.

267. From Synesius's *First Hymn*, trans. Alan Stevenson. I have replaced "intellectual" with "the noetic," which is less misleading. It is likely that he wrote this hymn between 395 and 397 CE while he was studying with Hypatia, or shortly thereafter, and before he converted to Christianity (Bregman, *Synesius*, pp. 25, 29). Bregman (p. 36) says, "We have here, then, in a hymn of only 134 lines, a complete outline of the entire Neoplatonic system."

268. Hesychast practices in the contemporary Orthodox Church retain many Neoplatonic practices, in a Christianized form. I have used Ware's *Orthodox Way* and Le-Loup's *Being Still* as sources on them.

269. The guides on the three paths are based on Proclus (Rosán, p. 188; cf. pp. 172–73).

270. Ficino, letter 1.106 (see Ficino, *Med. on Soul*, #3, p. 5).

271. From Synesius's *Fifth Hymn*, trans. Alan Stevenson.

272. This reference to Proclus is anachronistic, since he was born the same year Hypatia died. The Four Degrees of Virtue are discussed in Porphyry's *Launching Points*, also known as *Sentences Leading to the Intelligible World* (henceforth, "PLP"), pp. 27–33, and in Reale's *Schools of the Imperial Age*, pp. 408–9.

273. PLP 27.

274. Hierocles's *Commentary on the Pythagorean Golden Verses* (henceforth, "HC"), Proem 4, trans. after Rowe. Hierocles of Alexandria was a Neoplatonist and younger contemporary of Hypatia (see chapter 3). Translations of Hierocles's *Commentary* can be found in the bibliography under the entries for Dacier, *Golden Verses*, Hierocles, and Schibli (the best translation).

275. HC, Proem 4, after Rowe trans.

276. Plotinus, *Enneads* (PE) 1.2.1.

277. PLP 27.

278. PE 1.2.7, Guthrie trans.

279. HC, Proem 3, adapted from Hall trans.

280. HC, Proem 3, trans. after Rowe, but comes from Plato's *Phaedo* 67b2 and was often quoted by philosophers.

281. Plotinus, *Complete Works*, adapted from Guthrie trans. (henceforth, "PG"), p. 1332 #14.

282. Adapted from Plato's *Seventh Letter* (henceforth, "P7"), 343e, trans. Fowler et al.

283. The standard Neoplatonic curriculum began studying Plato's dialogues with these ten: *Alcibiades* I, *Gorgias*, *Phaedo*, *Cratylus*, *Theaetetus*, *Sophist*, *Statesman*, *Phaedrus*, *Symposium*, and *Philebus* (see Iamblichus, *Pyth. Way Life*, Dillon & Hershbell ed., 22).

284. Herbert, *The Temple*, p. 195.

285. P7 342a–344d.

286. P7 342b.

287. P7 341c–d, trans. Fowler et al.

288. P7 344b, trans. L.A. Post.

289. The summary of exemplary virtues is from PE 1.2.7.1–7.

290. In Greek, *monô monon*. Plotinus (PE 1.6.7.9, 6.7.34.8, 6.9.11.51) seems to have got it from Numenius (fr. 2, line 11; see Petty).

291. After PE 5.8.13, Guthrie trans.

292. PG, p. 1331 #3.

293. After PG, p. 1332 #22.

294. PG, p. 1332 #11.

295. After PE 1.2.6, MacKenna trans.

296. This is from one of the earliest alchemical manuscripts, *The Chrysopoeia of Cleopatra*, written by Cleopatra of Alexandria, who lived a century or so before Hypatia.

297. Monoïmos was Gnostic, quoted in Hippolytus, *Refutatio*, VIII 15, 2, my trans.

298. Kaplan, 57–58.

299. Ware, 122.

300. Psalms 70:1.

301. Cohen, 12.

302. This is, of course, common in both Western and Eastern spiritual traditions.

303. In Epistle 28.9, Seneca attributes this to Epicurus.

304. PG, p. 1331 #1.

305. After PG, p. 1331 #2 (cf. PE 6.9.11.50).

306. HC, Proem 4, trans. Schibli.

307. Iamblichus, *On the Mysteries* (*De mysteriis*), provides much of the Neoplatonic theoretical background for the theurgic art. For information on ancient theurgy, see Rosán (1949, pp. 204–17), Dodds (1951, pp. 291–99), Lewy (1978, chapters III, IV),

Majercik (1989, pp. 21–46), Shaw (1995, pt. III), Siorvanes (1996, pp. 189–99), and Clarke (2001). Van den Berg (2001) is a comprehensive discussion of Proclus's use of hymns in a theurgical context. Addey (2003, ch. 6) presents theurgy in a modern context.

308. John of Nikiu, in Deakin (p. 148).

309. Synesius, letter to Herculian (Deakin, p. 157).

310. From Synesius's *Second Hymn*, trans. Alan Stevenson.

311. Robert Johnson's *Inner Work* is a good, practical introduction to the techniques of *active imagination*, which is the contemporary analytic equivalent of theurgy. Many of Jung's writings on the topic are collected in Chodorow's *Jung on Active Imagination* (look under "Jung" in this book's bibliography); Hannah's *Active Imagination* is also informative. Two of my own papers (MacLennan, "Ev. Jung. Theurgy" and "Indiv. Soul") discuss theurgic practices from the perspective of depth psychology.

312. Majercik, *Chaldean Oracles* (henceforth, "CO"), fragment 108, my trans.

313. Adapted from Ficino's letter 4.46 (Ficino, *Med. on Soul*, #78), who adapts the last two lines from Virgil's *Aeneid* 6.730. The description of the planets and their gifts is from this letter, letter 3.8 (*Med. on Soul*, #89), and Ficino's *Commentary on Plato's Symposium* (Sixth Speech, ch. 4).

314. From Synesius's *Third Hymn*, adapted from the Stevenson trans.

315. The place of icons—venerated images—in Christianity, and its relation to Neoplatonism, is surveyed in Armstrong, *Camb. Hist. Later Gk. & Early Med. Phil.*, ch. 33.

316. Meier (1967) explains incubation from the perspective of depth psychology. Additional background is in Dodds (1951, ch. 4), Kingsley (1995, pp. 284–88; 1999, pp. 77–86), and Eliade (1964, ch. II, pp. 101–9).

317. For more on the dating of the Asclepeia, see Meier's *Healing Dream and Ritual* (ch. II); the entire book is an excellent discussion of ancient incubation in the context of contemporary depth psychology.

318. Synesius's imaginary presentation on dream divination is drawn largely from Synesius's *On Dreams* (henceforth, "SD"), trans. A. Fitzgerald, at http://www.livius.org/su-sz/synesius/synesius_dreams_01.html (accessed November 3, 2012).

319. SD (Migne p. 1288).

320. Adapted from SD (Migne p. 1288).

321. Adapted from SD (Migne p. 1301).

322. SD (Migne p. 1301).

323. CO, fr. 148, my trans.

324. CO, fr. 142, my trans.

325. The Theurgic Ascent is discussed by Lewy (1978, ch. 3) and Majercik (1989, pp. 36–45).

326. *Pythagorean Golden Verses*, lines 70–1, trans. adapted from Thomas Stanley.

327. Adapted from Plotinus, *Enneads* (PE) 2.9.9, lines 45–46, Armstrong trans.

328. PE 2.9.9, lines 46–48, Armstrong trans.

329. PE 2.9.9, adapted from lines 48–51, Armstrong trans.

330. Adapted from Plato, *Theaetetus*, 176b2, Jowett trans.

331. From Synesius's *Third Hymn*, adapted from Alan Stevenson trans. Technically it should read "noeric" rather than "noetic," but the distinction is not important for this book.

332. From Synesius's *First Hymn*, trans. Alan Stevenson.

333. The conclusion of Synesius's *First Hymn*, trans. Alan Stevenson.

334. Adapted from PE 1.2.6, MacKenna trans.

ADDITIONAL READING

We are now fortunate to have two excellent up-to-date books on Hypatia: *Hypatia of Alexandria* by Maria Dzielska (1995) and *Hypatia of Alexandria: Mathematician and Martyr* by Michael A. B. Deakin (2007). Both explain the political, cultural, and religious context of Hypatia's murder. I think that Dzielska captures Hypatia's philosophical orientation better, but Deakin (a mathematician) does better on her mathematical and astronomical work. Also, Deakin provides English translations of all the primary texts relating to Hypatia, which is very convenient. Both, but especially Deakin, seem reluctant to admit her spiritual practices (a common prejudice many academics have about Neoplatonism). To some extent we all project our ideals and expectations onto her.

Pierre Hadot's *Plotinus or the Simplicity of Vision* is perhaps the best explanation of the Neoplatonism of Plotinus and will do much to illuminate Hypatia's thought. It is a little gem. Hadot's *Philosophy as a Way of Life* and *What Is Ancient Philosophy?* are good explanations of ancient philosophy (including Neoplatonism) as a spiritual path and a practice of care for the soul.

The best current translation of Plotinus's *Enneads* is by Armstrong (in seven volumes with facing Greek). More accessible is the early-twentieth-century translation by Stephen MacKenna, which is less literal, but perhaps more inspired. It is available in many inexpensive editions, both complete and abridged. Uždavinys's *Heart of Plotinus* is a good, recent selection from the MacKenna translation, and a good place to start your study of the *Enneads*.

Books that treat Neoplatonism as a spiritual path for modern people include Tim Addey's *Unfolding Wings: The Way of Perfection in the Platonic Tradition* and Brian Hines's *Return to the One: Plotinus's Guide to God-Realization.* Stoicism as a practical philosophy is present-ed in several recent books, including *A Guide to the Good Life: The Ancient Art of Stoic Joy* by William B. Irvine and *The Stoic Art of Living: Inner Resilience and Outer Results* by Tom Morris. *Epicurean Simplicity* by Stephanie Mills celebrates modern Epicurean living with an ecological orientation. *The Swerve: How the World Became Modern*, by Stephen Greenblatt, is a good, recent appreciation of Lucretius.

There are a number of good introductions to Neoplatonism from an academic perspec-tive (i.e., history and analysis rather than practice). Most recent is *Neoplatonism* by Pauliina Remes (2008). R. T. Wallis's *Neoplatonism* (1995) is a new edition of a classic history of Neo-platonic philosophy. Chlup's *Proclus: An Introduction* (2012) is a readable presentation of the philosophy of Proclus, including theurgy.

There are several collections of readings to give a taste of Neoplatonism, including *Neoplatonic Philosophy: Introductory Readings*, edited by John Dillon and Lloyd P. Gerson, which they intend as a companion to Wallis, but some of the selections are quite technical. Another collection is *The Neoplatonists: A Reader*, edited by J. Gregory, and an older one is *Select Passages Illustrating Neoplatonism*, translated by E. R. Dodds.

To learn more about Stoicism, I highly recommend *The Inner Citadel* by Pierre Hadot, which focuses on Marcus Aurelius. Most of Marcus's *Meditations* are excellent reading; I usu-ally recommend skipping Book I on a first reading. However, it is worth reading eventually, since it expresses Marcus's gratitude toward his teachers, friends, and family, and shows us the personality traits he considered most praiseworthy. The *Meditations* can be a lifetime companion, but don't forget it is just Marcus's commonplace book; you should be compiling your own, which can be just as worthwhile.

At the present time there are at least two websites with good selections of Epicurean texts: *Epicurus.info—Epicurean Philosophy Online* (http://www.epicurus.info) and *Epicurus and Epicurean Philosophy* (http://www.epicurus.net). I am very grateful to Erik Anderson for his permission to use many of his translations from Epicurus.info. Epicurus's four-page-long *Letter to Menoeceus* is an excellent summary of his ethics (Oates, pp. 30–33).

There are many useful symbol dictionaries. Anthony Stevens's *Ariadne's Clue* is especial-ly good, since it is written from the perspective of evolutionary Jungian psychology.

There have been a number of fictional treatments of Hypatia. As the most famous female intellectual of the ancient world, who came to a tragic end and about whom we know rela-tively little, her history is an attractive frame around which authors can weave their stories. Best known is Charles Kingsley's 1853 novel, *Hypatia: Or New Foes with an Old Face*. It is widely available in reprint editions and online. Kingsley was a historian, and when he began his book he intended it as nonfiction, so in broad terms it is quite accurate. Nevertheless, it is a novel, and so he did not shy away from embellishing Hypatia's story whenever it suited his literary and ideological needs (as reflected in his subtitle). His fabrications are discussed by Dzielska, who reviews the whole Hypatian literary tradition, and by Deakin. In any case, Kingsley's *Hypatia* is entertaining and informative, for a Victorian novel, provided you don't forget you are reading fiction.

GLOSSARY

The following are short definitions of terms that appear frequently. For a fuller explanation, look them up in the index. If a glossary item refers to another glossary entry, the cross-reference is shown like this.

Analytical psychology: Jungian psychology.

Archetype: In Jungian psychology, dynamic structures in the unconscious mind, common to all humans, which are the psychical aspects of instincts, and govern human perception, motivation, and action. Correspond to Platonic Ideas or Forms and to polytheistic gods.

Ascent: A series of spiritual practices aimed at achieving Divine Union or Deification. The preparatory practice is Awakening, followed by the Ascent proper in three stages: Purification, Illumination, and Perfection.

Awakening: The prelude to the Ascent proper, which involves recognition of the desire to ascend.

Becoming: The familiar material world, in which everything is in flux (coming to be and passing away); contrasted with the realm of Being, where truths are timeless.

Being: The timeless realm of Platonic Ideas or Forms, in which things either are or are not; contrasted with the realm of Becoming (the material world), which things are constantly coming to be and passing away.

Cardinal virtue: See Virtue.

Chaldean Oracles: A collection of sacred verses allegedly revealed to Julian the Chaldean and his son Julian the Theurgist in the second century CE as a result of their <u>theurgical</u> operations. They were treated as scripture by the <u>Neoplatonists</u>, but survive only in fragments.

Collective Unconscious: In <u>Jungian psychology</u>, the unconscious <u>psychical</u> structures common to all humans, comprising all the <u>archetypes</u>.

Complex: In <u>Jungian psychology</u>, an unconscious network of ideas, images, feelings, and behavioral dispositions that form, during an individual's life, around an archetypal core, and adapt that <u>archetype</u> to the individual. Complexes, which are normal components of the unconscious mind, can act as autonomous inner personalities (<u>daimons</u>).

Cosmic Body: The physical body of the universe, the fourth emanation from The One and the lowest level of the Neoplatonic cosmos, corresponding in the <u>Macrocosm</u> to the human body in the <u>Microcosm</u>. The Cosmic Body is the realm of Becoming. Also called the <u>World Body</u>. See chapter 9.

Cosmic Mind: See <u>Cosmic Nous</u>.

Cosmic Nous: The first emanation from The One in the Neoplatonic cosmos, corresponding in the <u>Macrocosm</u> to the human <u>nous</u> in the <u>Microcosm</u>. The Cosmic Nous is the realm of Being, which contains the Platonic Forms or Ideas. Also called the <u>World Nous</u>. See chapter 8.

Cosmic Soul: The second emanation from The One in the Neoplatonic cosmos, corresponding in the <u>Macrocosm</u> to the human soul in the <u>Microcosm</u>. The Cosmic Soul is intermediate between the <u>Cosmic Mind</u> and the <u>Cosmic Body</u>, bringing the Platonic Forms or Ideas into manifestation in space and time. Also called the <u>World Soul</u>. See chapter 8.

Daimon: A spirit intermediate between a god and a human, mediating between gods and humans. Correspond to psychological <u>complexes</u>. See chapter 9.

Deification: The process of becoming godlike, so far as possible for mortals, which, in some sense, is the goal of all ancient philosophies. Specifically, deification is the final stage of the spiritual <u>Ascent</u>, also known as <u>Perfection</u> or <u>Union</u>.

Demiurge: The creator god (who is not, incidentally, the highest god) is called the Demiurge (Craftsman) in Plato's *Timaeus*.

Depth psychology: Primarily Jungian psychology, with its focus on the unconscious mind, especially the collective unconscious.

Embodied psychology: Contemporary approach to psychology which stresses the essential role that the body plays in psychological processes.

Enneads: The writings of Plotinus are organized into six *Enneads* (groups of nine).

Epicureanism: Teaches how tranquility and happiness may be obtained by governing desires. The first degree of wisdom.

Fate: In the context of Neoplatonism, Fate refers to the operation of purposeless, random, accidental, or meaningless processes in the universe. Contrasted with Providence.

Form: See Idea.

Garden, The: Nickname for Epicureanism.

Gnosticism: A religious movement, generally considered an early Christian heresy, which focuses on intuitive or mystical knowledge (Greek, *gnôsis*) as a means of spiritual Ascent and salvation.

Grove, The: Nickname for Platonism.

Guiding Principle: The power of conscious judgment and free choice, the higher soul of Stoicism.

Hedonism: The theory that pleasure is the ultimate good and standard of morality.

Hermetic: Refers to the spiritual practices traditionally attributed to the divine sage Hermes Trismegistus.

Idea: In Platonic philosophy, an Idea or ideal Form is the eternal and perfect principle of some class of objects (e.g., *Triangle* of triangles, *Gold* of pieces of gold, *Beauty* of beautiful things, *Horse* of horses).

Illumination: The second stage in the Ascent proper, involving contact with the archetypal Ideas.

Impassive: Not suffering emotions or feelings; tranquil.

Impulse: The impetus, cause, or inclination to an action in Stoic ethics.

Indefinite Duality: The first emanation from The One, which is no longer simple, but is still undifferentiated and indefinite. Also, the power by which unity expands into diversity and multiplicity. See chapter 8.

Indeterminate Mind: The unformed substance of mind that has the potential for containing <u>Ideas</u>, but from which Ideas have not emerged. See chapter 8.

Individuation: In <u>Jungian psychology</u>, the lifelong process of developing toward psychological completeness, integration, and authenticity.

Jungian psychology: The psychological theories originated by C. G. Jung, also known as <u>depth psychology</u> and <u>analytical psychology</u>.

Kabbalah: Jewish mystical tradition.

Logos: A Greek word with a complicated meaning, about which books have been written. Often translated "word," its meaning encompasses various kinds of articulated thought (speaking, reasoning, explanations, calculations, principles, causes) and, more generally, the rational or orderly principle of anything, whether an explanation in speech or thought, or an active organizational principle.

Love (Abiding, Providential, Returning, Mutual): As a universal force, Love obeys the <u>Triadic Principle</u>. It is *Abiding Love* when it remains in itself. It is *Providential Love* when it proceeds into lower levels, organizing them. It is *Returning Love* when the lower levels look back to their origin as a source of harmony. It abides within the multiplicity of the lower levels as *Mutual Love*, the manifestation of this harmony.

Macrocosm: The whole cosmos or universe as a model for the individual human viewed as a <u>Microcosm</u>. See chapter 8.

Mandala: A symmetrical, often circular, diagram representing the structure of cosmos and/or psyche.

Manichaeism: The religion established by the Babylonian prophet and religious reformer Mani (c.216–276 CE). It is especially characterized by a duality of good and evil powers.

Microcosm: A human being, taken as a whole, as a miniature universe or cosmos (the <u>Macrocosm</u>). See chapters 8–9.

Moral purpose: In Stoicism, the commitment to act in accordance with Stoic moral principles, which is the only inherent good (and its opposite, the only inherent evil).

Mysteries, The: Refers to the mystery religions and initiations of the ancient world, in which esoteric spiritual practices and truths were revealed to initiates, resulting in their spiritual transformation.

Neoplatonism: Platonism after about 245 CE, when Plotinus made many important contributions to its development. This is an academic term; ancient Neoplatonists called themselves simply "Platonists."

Neopythagoreanism: The revival of Pythagoreanism in first two centuries CE, which was an important influence on Neoplatonism.

Nous: The intuiting mind, which grasps the Ideas in their timeless relationships. Often, somewhat misleadingly, translated "mind" or "intellect."

One, The: The ultimate principle in Neoplatonism. It is the universal principle of unity, unifying the opposites, transcending even existence and non-existence, being and non-being. It is indefinable in ordinary terms, and hence described as ineffable, inexpressible, unspeakable, etc. See chapter 8.

Perfection: The third and final stage of the Ascent proper, its goal, in which Divine Union or Deification is achieved. Perfection refers to psychological integration, not being flawless or faultless.

Physics: In ancient philosophy, the study of nature (*physis*) in the widest sense.

Platonism: In the broad sense, Platonism is the philosophy originated by Plato (427–347 BCE) and its later developments.

Porch, The: Nickname for Stoicism.

Providence: The principle of intelligible order and purpose, both in the cosmos as a whole and in individuals. Contrasted with Fate.

Psychical: As opposed to physical or material; refers to mind, soul, spirit, etc., both conscious and unconscious.

Purification: The first stage in the Ascent proper, which is directed toward quieting the soul by turning it inward and away from the concerns of the body.

Pythagorean Golden Verses: A 71-line verse summary of Pythagorean ethical principles attributed to Pythagoras, but probably dating to the fourth century BCE. Hierocles wrote an extensive *Commentary* on it.

Pythagoreanism: The philosophy of Pythagoras (c.570 – c.495 BCE) and his followers. Pythagoreanism significantly influenced Plato and later Platonists and Neoplatonists.

Self: In Jungian psychology, the Self (with a capital "S") refers to the totality of the archetypes, the central core of the unconscious mind; the God-image in an individual's psyche. See chapter 9.

Shadow: In <u>Jungian psychology</u>, the unconscious complex formed of all the rejected, disowned, and unwanted aspects and potentials of the psyche. See chapter 9.

Shaman: In the broadest sense, practitioners who interact with the spirit world to heal individuals and ensure a harmonious relation between their community and nature.

Soul: In ancient philosophy, "soul" translates Greek *psychê*, which refers to the animating power in any animate thing. More colloquially, "soul" refers to the <u>psychical</u> aspect of human nature (both conscious and unconscious).

Stoicism: Teaches how we may live with serenity, freedom, and autonomy while actively contributing to the world. This is accomplished by understanding where our true freedom lies and by using it with wisdom. The second degree of wisdom.

Sufism: A mystical or esoteric sect of Islam focused on purification of the soul and its unification with God. Some scholars argue that Sufi practices predate Islam.

Symbol: In <u>Neoplatonism</u>, anything in the lineage of a god, which therefore participates in the <u>Idea</u> or <u>Form</u> of the god and can be used to connect with the deity or its <u>daimons</u>. In <u>Jungian psychology</u>, a symbol is an expression of something that is not otherwise expressible, in particular, that cannot be completely defined or expressed in words. Symbols may activate the <u>archetypes</u> and <u>complexes</u> with which they are associated, and thus are important means of relating to them.

Tetractys: A sacred symbol in <u>Pythagoreanism</u> and <u>Neoplatonism</u>, which is a triangular arrangement of ten dots (rows of 1, 2, 3, and 4 dots, from top to bottom) with many symbolic interpretations (see chapters 8, 10–12).

Theurgy: Spiritual practices and rites intended to facilitate communication and ultimately union with divinity. See chapters 10–12.

Triadic Principle: Three aspects of each plane of reality in the Neoplatonic cosmos, namely Abiding, Proceeding, and Returning. See chapter 8.

Tripartite Soul: Platonic three-part division of the soul into (1) the appetite or desiring part (the "belly"), (2) the will or spirited part (the "heart"), and (3) the mind or reasoning part (the "head").

Union: Spiritual unification with a divinity or with <u>The One</u>, the last stage of the <u>Ascent</u>, equivalent to <u>Deification</u>.

Virtue: The ancient Greek word commonly translated "virtue" (*aretê*) refers to the *excellence* of anything, the ways in which that thing is authentically what it is, its authentic being. <u>Neoplatonism</u> reinterprets the four "cardinal virtues" (wisdom, self-control, fortitude, justice) on each level of spiritual ascent (chapter 11).

World Body: See <u>Cosmic Body</u>.

World Mind: See <u>Cosmic Nous</u>.

World Nous: See <u>Cosmic Nous</u>.

World Soul: See <u>Cosmic Soul</u>.

BIBLIOGRAPHY

Abdulla, Raficq. *Words of Paradise: Selected Poems of Rumi*. London: Frances Lincoln Ltd., 2000.

Addey, Tim. *The Unfolding Wings: The Way of Perfection in the Platonic Tradition*. Somerset, UK: Prometheus Trust, 2003.

Anderson, William. *Dante the Maker*. London: Routledge & Kegan Paul, 1980.

Armstrong, A. H., ed. *The Cambridge History of Later Greek and Early Medieval Philosophy*. Cambridge, UK: Cambridge University Press, 1967.

Aurelius, Marcus. *Marcus Aurelius*, ed. and trans. C. R. Haines. Cambridge, MA: Harvard University Press, 1916. (Greek and English text of meditations, speeches, and sayings.)

———. *The Thoughts of the Emperor Marcus Aurelius Antoninus*. Translated by George Long. New York: Thomas Nelson & Sons, 1862.

Bailey, Cyril, trans. *Epicurus: The Extant Remains*. Oxford, UK: Oxford University Press, 1926.

Bair, Dierdre. *Jung: A Biography*. Boston: Little Brown, 2003.

Balaguer, M. *Platonism and Anti-Platonism in Mathematics*. Oxford, UK: Oxford University Press, 1998.

Beck, Aaron T., A. John Rush, Brian F. Shaw, and Gary Emery. *Cognitive Therapy of Depression*. New York: The Guilford Press, 1979.

Bembo, Pietro. *Gli Asolani*. Translated by Rudolf B. Gottfried. Bloomington: Indiana University Press, 1954.

Berg, R. M. van den. *Proclus' Hymns: Essays, Translations, Commentary*. Leiden, the Netherlands: Brill, 2001.

Berger, Helen A., ed. *Witchcraft and Magic: Contemporary North America*. Philadelphia: University of Pennsylvania Press, 2006.

Braden, Charles S. *Spirits in Rebellion: The Rise and Development of New Thought*. Dallas, TX: Southern Methodist University Press, 1963.

Bregman, Jay. *Synesius of Cyrene: Philosopher-Bishop*. Berkeley: University of California Press, 1982.

Cassius Dio. *Dio's Rome: An Historical Narrative Originally Composed in Greek During The Reigns of Septimius Severus, Geta and Caracalla, Macrinus, Elagabalus and Alexander Severus, Volume 5, Books 61–76 (A.D. 54–211)*. Translated by Herbert Baldwin Foster. Troy, NY: Pafraets, 1906.

Castiglione, Baldassarre. *The Book of the Courtier*. Translated by Leonard Eckstein Opdycke. New York : Charles Scribner's Sons, 1901.

Chlup, Radek. *Proclus: An Introduction*. Cambridge, UK: Cambridge University Press, 2012.

Clarke, Emma C. *Iamblichus' De Mysteriis: A Manifesto of the Miraculous*. Aldershot, UK: Ashgate, 2001.

Cohen, Ken. *Taoism: Essential Teachings of the Way and Its Power*. Boulder, CO: Sounds True, 1998.

Copenhaver, Brian P., ed. *Hermetica: The Greek Corpus Hermeticum and the Latin Asclepius in a New English Translation, with Notes and Introduction*. Cambridge, UK: Cambridge University Press, 1995.

Cornford, F. M. *Greek Religious Thought from Homer to the Age of Alexander*. Boston: Beacon Press, 1950.

Dacier, M. *The Life of Pythagoras with His Symbols and Golden Verses. Together with the Life of Hierocles and his Commentaries on the Verses*. Translated by N. Rowe. London: Jacob Tonson, 1707.

Deakin, Michael A. B. *Hypatia of Alexandria: Mathematician and Martyr*. Amherst, NY: Prometheus Books, 2007.

de Rougemont, Denis. *Love in the Western World*, revised and augmented edition. Translated by Montgomery Belgion. New York: Pantheon, 1956.

Dillon, John, and Lloyd P. Gerson, eds. *Neoplatonic Philosophy: Introductory Readings*. Indianapolis, IN: Hackett, 2004.

Diogenes Laertius. *Lives of Eminent Philosophers*, 2 vols. Translated by R. D. Hicks. Cambridge, MA: Harvard University Press, 1925.

Dodds, E. R. *The Greeks and the Irrational*. Berkeley: University of California Press, 1951.

———. *Select Passages Illustrating Neoplatonism*. Chicago: Ares reprint of London, 1923 ed.

Dzielska, Maria. *Hypatia of Alexandria*. Translated by F. Lyra. Cambridge, MA: Harvard University Press, 1995.

Ebreo, Leone. *The Philosophy of Love (Dialoghi d'Amore)*. Translated by F. Friedeberg-Seeley and Jean H. Barnes. London: Soncino Press, 1937.

Eliade, Micea. *Shamanism: Archaic Techniques of Ecstasy*. Translated by W. R. Trask. Princeton, NJ: Princeton University Press, 1964.

Emerson, Ralph Waldo. *Essays: First and Second Series*. New York: Random House, 1993.

Epictetus. *The Discourses of Epictetus, with the Encheridion and Fragments*. Translated by George Long. London: George Bell, 1877.

———. *Epictetus: The Discourses and Manual Together with Fragments of His Writings*. Translated by Percy Ewing Matheson. Oxford, UK: Oxford University Press, 1916.

Ficino, Marsilio. *Commentary on Plato's Symposium*. Text, translation, and introduction by Sears Reynolds Jayne. Columbia, MO: University of Missouri Studies, vol. XIX, no. 1, 1944.

———. *Meditations on the Soul: Selected Letters of Marsilio Ficino*. Rochester, VT: Inner Traditions, 1996.

Forman, Samuel Eagle. *The Life and Writings of Thomas Jefferson: Including All of His Important Utterances on Public Questions, Compiled from State Papers and from His Private Correspondence*. Indianapolis, IN: Bobbs-Merrill Company, 1900.

Friedländer, Paul. *Plato*. Translated by Hans Meyerhoff. New York: Pantheon, 1958.

Golden Verses of Pythagoras, with Commentary of Hierocles. Adapted from translation by N. Rowe. Santa Barbara, CA: Concord Grove, 1983.

Greenblatt, Stephen. *The Swerve: How the World Became Modern*. New York: W. W. Norton & Co., 2012.

Gregory, J., ed. *The Neoplatonists: A Reader*. London: Routledge, 1999.

Guthrie, Kenneth Sylvan. *The Pythagorean Sourcebook and Library: An Anthology of Ancient Writings Which Relate to Pythagoras and Pythagorean Philosophy*. Intro. and ed., David R. Fideler. Grand Rapids, MI: Phanes, 1987.

Hadot, Ilsetraut. *Studies on the Neoplatonist Hierocles*. Translated by Michael Chase. Philadelphia: American Philosophical Society, 2004.

Hadot, Pierre. *The Inner Citadel: The Meditations of Marcus Aurelius*. Translated by Michael Chase. Cambridge, MA: Harvard University Press, 1998.

———. *Philosophy as a Way of Life*. Edited by A. I. Davidson. Translated by M. Chase. Oxford, UK: Blackwell, 1995.

———. *Plotinus or the Simplicity of Vision*. Translated by Michael Chase. Chicago: University of Chicago Press, 1998.

———. *The Present Alone Is Our Happiness: Conversations with Jeannie Carlier and Arnold I. Davidson*. Translated by Marc Djaballah. Stanford, CA: Stanford University Press, 2009.

———. *What Is Ancient Philosophy?* Translated by M. Chase. Cambridge, MA: Harvard University Press, 2002.

Hannah, Barbra. *Encounters with the Soul: Active Imagination as Developed by C. G. Jung*. Santa Monica, CA: Sigo Press, 1981.

Harvey, Graham. *Contemporary Paganism: Listening People, Speaking Earth*, 1st ed. New York: New York University Press, 1997.

Herbert, George. *The Temple: Sacred Poems and Private Ejaculations*. London: Pickering, 1838.

Hesiod. Hesiod: *Volume I, Theogony. Works and Days. Testimonia* (Loeb Classical Library No. 57N). Edited and translated by Glenn W. Most. Cambridge, MA: Harvard University Press, 2007.

Hicks, R. D. *Stoic and Epicurean*. New York: Charles Scribners Son's, 1910.

Hierocles. *Hierocles upon the Golden Verses of Pythagoras*. Translated by J. Hall. London: Francis Eaglesfield, 1656.

Hines, Brian. *Return to the One: Plotinus's Guide to God-Realization*. Salem, OR: Adrasteia, 2009.

Hippolytus. *Werke, vol. 3, Refutatio Omnium Haeresium*. Edited by Paul Wendland. Leipzig, Germany: J. C. Hinrichs'sche Buchhandlung, 1916.

Homer. *The Iliad of Homer*. Translated by Alexander Pope, 1715–20.

Horace. *The Satires, Epistles, and Art of Poetry of Horace*. Translated by John Conington. London: Bell & Daldy, 1870.

Hornblower, S., and A. Spawforth, eds. *The Oxford Classical Dictionary*, 3rd ed. Oxford, UK: Oxford University Press, 1996.

Iamblichus. *Iamblichus on the Mysteries*. Translated by and introduced by Emma C. Clarke, John M. Dillon, and Jackson P. Hershbell. Atlanta, GA: Society of Biblical Literature, 2003.

———. *On the Pythagorean Way of Life: Text, Translation, and Notes*. Translated and edited by John Dillon and Jackson Hersbell. Atlanta: Society of Biblical Literature, 1991.

Irvine, William B. *A Guide to the Good Life: The Ancient Art of Stoic Joy*. Oxford, UK: Oxford University Press, 2008.

Johnson, Robert A. *Inner Work: Using Dreams and Active Imagination for Personal Growth*. New York: Harper & Row, 1986.

Jung, Carl Gustav. *Jung on Active Imagination*. Edited and introduced by J. Chodorow. Princeton, NJ: Princeton University Press, 1997.

———. *Memories, Dreams, Reflections*, revised edition. Edited by A. Jaffé and translated by R. & C. Winston. New York: Random House, 1963.

Kaplan, Aryeh. *Jewish Meditation: A Practical Guide*. New York: Schocken, 1985.

Katz, Joseph. *The Philosophy of Plotinus: Representative Books from the Enneads*. New York: Appleton-Century Crofts, 1950.

Kingsley, Charles. *Hypatia: Or New Foes with an Old Face*. London: Parker, 1853.

Kingsley, Peter. *Ancient Philosophy, Mystery, and Magic: Empedocles and Pythagorean Tradition*. Oxford, UK: Oxford University Press, 1995.

———. *In the Dark Places of Wisdom*. Inverness, CA: Golden Sufi, 1999.

———. *A Story Waiting to Pierce You: Mongolia, Tibet, and the Destiny of the Western World*. Point Reyes, CA: Golden Sufi, 2010.

LeLoup, Jean-Yves. *Being Still: Reflections on an Ancient Mystical Tradition*. Translated by M. S. Laird. New York: Paulist Press, 2003.

Lewy, Hans. *Chaldean Oracles and Theurgy: Mysticism, Magic and Platonism in the Later Roman Empire*. Paris: Études Augustiniennes, 1978.

Liddell, H. G., R. Scott, and H. S. Jones. *A Greek-English Lexicon*. 9th ed. Oxford, UK: Oxford University Press, 1968.

Long, A. A., and D. N. Sedley. *The Hellenistic Philosophers*. 2 vols. Cambridge, UK: Cambridge University Press, 1987.

Lucretius. *Of the Nature of Things*. Translated by William Ellery Leonard. London: Dent, 1916.

———. *On the Nature of Things*, revised ed. Cambridge, MA: Harvard University Press, 1924.

MacLennan, Bruce J. "Evolution, Jung, and Theurgy: Their Role in Modern Neoplatonism." In J. Finamore and R. Berchman (eds.), *History of Platonism: Plato Redivivus* (pp. 305–22). New Orleans, LA: University Press of the South, 2005.

———. "Evolutionary Jungian Psychology." *Psychological Perspectives* 49(1) (2006), 9–28.

———. "Evolutionary Neurotheology and the Varieties of Religious Experience." In Rhawn Joseph, ed., *NeuroTheology: Brain, Science, Spirituality, Religious Experience* (2nd ed., pp. 317–34). San Jose, CA: University Press, 2003.

———. "Individual Soul and World Soul: The Process of Individuation in Neoplatonism and Jung." In T. Arzt and A. Holm (Eds.), *Wegmarken der Individuation* (pp. 83–116). Würzburg, Germany: Königshausen & Neumann, 2006.

Majercik, Ruth. *The Chaldean Oracles: Text, Translation, and Commentary*. Leiden, the Netherlands: Brill, 1989.

Maximus Tyrius. *The Dissertations of Maximus Tyrius*, vol. I. Translated by Thomas Taylor. London: Evans, 1804.

Meier, C. A. *Ancient Incubation and Modern Psychotherapy*. Translated by M. Curtis. Evanston, IL: Northwestern University Press, 1967.

———. *Healing Dream and Ritual: Ancient Incubation and Modern Psychotherapy*. Einsiedeln, Switzerland: Daimon Verlag, 2009.

Mills, Stephanie. *Epicurean Simplicity*. Washington, DC: Island Press, 2003.

Morris, Tom. *The Stoic Art of Living: Inner Resilience and Outer Results*. Chicago: Open Court, 2004.

Musaeus. "Hero and Leander." In *Callimachus, and Musaeus. Callimachus: Aetia, Iambi, Hecale and Other Fragments; Musaeus: Hero and Leander*. (Loeb Classical Library No. 421). Translated by C. A. Trypanis, T. Gelzer, and Cedric H. Whitman. Cambridge, MA: Harvard University Press, 1973.

———. *Hero and Leander*. Translated by E. E. Sikes. London: Methuen & Co., 1920.

———. *Hero and Leander: A Poem*. Translated by E. B. Greene. London: J. Ridley, 1773.

Nicholson, R. A. *Mystics of Islam*. London: Bell, 1914.

Oates, Whitney J. *The Stoic and Epicurean Philosophers*. New York: Random House, 1940.

O'Brien, Elmer. *The Essential Plotinus: Representative Treatises from the Enneads*. Indianapolis, IN: Hackett, 1964.

Ovid. *Ovid's Metamorphoses in Fifteen Books*. Translated by Sir Samuel Garth, John Dryden, Alexander Pope, Joseph Addison, William Congreve, "and other eminent hands." 1717.

Oxford English Dictionary, 2nd ed. Oxford, UK: Oxford University Press, 1989.

Peters, F. E. *Greek Philosophical Terms: A Historical Lexicon*. New York: New York University Press, 1967.

Petty, Robert. *Fragments of Numenius of Apamea*. Westbury, UK: Prometheus Trust, 2012.

Plato. *The Collected Dialogues: Including the Letters*. Edited by Edith Hamilton and Huntington Cairns. Princeton, NJ: Princeton University Press, 1938, 1941, 1961.

———. *The Dialogues of Plato: A Selection*. Translated by Benjamin Jowett. Oxford, UK: Oxford University Press, 1893.

———. *The Phaedo of Plato*, 2nd ed. Edited by R. D. Archer-Hind. New York: Arno, 1973. Reprint of Macmillan, 1894 ed.

———. *Phaedrus*. Translated by R. Hackforth. Cambridge, UK: Cambridge University Press, 1952.

———. *Plato in Twelve Volumes: With an English Translation*. Translated by Harold N. Fowler, W. R. M. Lamb, Robert G. Bury, and Paul Shorey. London: W. Heinemann, 1914–30.

———. *Protagoras*. Translated by Benjamin Jowett. New York: D. Appleton and Company, 1898.

———. *Timaeus*. New York: Liberal Arts Press, 1949.

———. *Symposium of Plato*. Translated by Tom Griffith. Berkeley: University of California Press, 1993.

Plotinus. *Complete Works*. Translated by Kenneth Sylvan Guthrie. London: Bell, 1918.

———. *The Enneads* (5 vols.). Translated by Stephen MacKenna and B. S. Page. London: Philip Lee Warner, Publisher to the Medici Society, 1917–30.

———. *Plotinus* (Biography and *Enneads*, 7 vols.). Translated by A. H. Armstrong. Cambridge, MA: Harvard University Press, 1989.

Plutarch. *Plutarch's Morals. Translated from the Greek by Several Hands. Corrected and Revised by William W. Goodwin, with an Introduction by Ralph Waldo Emerson* (5 vols). Boston: Little, Brown, and Co., 1878.

Porphyry. *Life of Plotinus*. Translated by A. H. Armstrong. Cambridge, MA: Harvard University Press, 1966.

———. *Porphyry's Launching Points to the Realm of Mind: An Introduction to the Neoplatonic Philosophy of Plotinus*. Translated by Kenneth Guthrie. Grand Rapids, MI: Phanes Press, 1989.

———. *Porphyry's Letter to His Wife Marcella*. Translated by Alice Zimmern. Introduction by David Fideler. Grand Rapids, MI: Phanes, 1986.

———. *Select Works of Porphyry*. Translated by Thomas Taylor. Somerset, UK: Prometheus Trust, 1994.

Reale, Giovanni. *The Schools of the Imperial Age*, 5th ed. Edited and translated by John R. Catan. *A History of Ancient Philosophy*, vol. IV. Albany: State University of New York Press, 1990.

———. *The Systems of the Hellenistic Age*, 3rd ed. Edited and translated by John R. Catan. *A History of Ancient Philosophy*, vol. III. Albany: State University of New York Press, 1985.

Remes, Pauliina. *Neoplatonism*. Berkeley: University of California Press, 2008.

Robertson, Donald. *The Philosophy of Cognitive Behavioural Therapy (CBT): Stoic Philosophy as Rational and Cognitive Psychotherapy*. London: Karnac, 2010.

Rosán, L. J. *The Philosophy of Proclus: The Final Stage of Ancient Thought*. New York: Cosmos, 1949.

Rossetti, D. G. *The Early Italian Poets from Ciullo D'Alcamo to Dante Alighieri (1100-1200-1300)*. London: Smith, Elder & Co.,1861.

Sabini, Meredith. "The Bones in the Cave: Phylogenetic Foundations of Analytical Psychology." *Journal of Jungian Theory and Practice*, Fall 2000, Issue 2, 17–41.

Sayre, Farrand. *The Greek Cynics*. Baltimore, MD: J. H. Furst, 1948.

Schibli, Hermann S. *Hierocles of Alexandria*. Oxford, UK: Oxford University Press, 2002.

Schneider, Eric D. (2005). *Into the Cool: Energy Flow, Thermodynamics, and Life*. Chicago: University of Chicago Press.

Seneca. *Ad Lucilium Epistolae Morales* [Letters to Lucilius] (3 vols.). Translated by Richard M. Gummere. Cambridge, MA: Harvard University Press, 1962.

———. *L. Annaeus Seneca On Benefits*. Translated by Aubrey Stewart. London: Bell, 1887

Shaw, Gregory. *Theurgy and the Soul: The Neoplatonism of Iamblichus*. University Park: Pennsylvania State University Press, 1995.

Siorvanes, Lucas. *Proclus: Neo-Platonic Philosophy and Science*. Edinburgh, UK: Edinburgh University Press, 1996.

Stanley, Thomas. *The History of Philosophy Containing the Lives, Opinions, Actions and Discourses of the Philosophers of Every Sect*, 4th ed. London: A. Millar, 1743.

Stevens, Anthony. *Archetype Revisited: An Updated Natural History of the Self*. Toronto: Inner City Books, 2003.

———. *Ariadne's Clue: A Guide to the Symbols of Humankind*. Princeton, NJ: Princeton University Press, 1998.

———. *The Two Million-Year-Old Self*. College Station: Texas A&M University Press, 1993.

Stevenson, Alan. *The Ten Hymns of Synesius, Bishop of Cyrene A.D. 410 in English Verse and Some Occasional Pieces*. Edinburgh, UK: T. Constable, 1865.

Synesius. *The Essays and Hymns of Synesius of Cyrene, Including the Address to the Emperor Arcadius and the Political Speeches* (2 vols.), trans. Augustine Fitzgerald. Oxford, UK: Oxford University Press, 1926 and 1930. (See also http://www.livius.org/su-sz/synesius/synesius_dreams_01.html.)

Thom, Johan C. *The Pythagorean Golden Verses: With Introduction and Commentary*. Leiden, the Netherlands: Brill, 1995.

Uždavinys, Algis. *The Heart of Plotinus: The Essential Enneads, Including Porphyry's On the Cave of the Nymphs.* Bloomington, IN: World Wisdom, 2009.

Wallis, R. T. *Neoplatonism*, 2nd ed. Indianapolis, IN: Hackett, 1995.

Ware, Kallistos. *The Orthodox Way,* revised ed. Crestwood, NY: St Vladimir's Seminary Press, 1999.

Wilkins, Eliza Gregory. *"Know Thyself" in Greek and Latin Literature.* Chicago: University of Chicago Libraries, 1917; New York: Garland Publishing, 1979.

Wind, Edgar. *Pagan Mysteries in the Renaissance*, revised and enlarged ed. Middlesex, UK: Penguin, 1967.

INDEX

TO WRITE TO THE AUTHOR

If you wish to contact the author or would like more information about this book, please write to the author in care of Llewellyn Worldwide Ltd. and we will forward your request. Both the author and the publisher appreciate hearing from you and learning of your enjoyment of this book and how it has helped you. Llewellyn Worldwide Ltd. cannot guarantee that every letter written to the author can be answered, but all will be forwarded. Please write to:

Bruce J. MacLennan, PhD
℅ Llewellyn Worldwide
2143 Wooddale Drive
Woodbury, MN 55125-2989

Please enclose a self-addressed stamped envelope for reply,
or $1.00 to cover costs. If outside the USA, enclose
an international postal reply coupon.

Many of Llewellyn's authors have websites with additional information and resources. For more information, please visit our website at http://www.llewellyn.com.

GET MORE AT LLEWELLYN.COM

Visit us online to browse hundreds of our books and decks, plus sign up to receive our e-newsletters and exclusive online offers.

- **Free tarot readings • Spell-a-Day • Moon phases**
- **Recipes, spells, and tips • Blogs • Encyclopedia**
- **Author interviews, articles, and upcoming events**

GET SOCIAL WITH LLEWELLYN

Find us on Facebook
www.Facebook.com/LlewellynBooks

Follow us on twitter™
www.Twitter.com/Llewellynbooks

GET BOOKS AT LLEWELLYN

LLEWELLYN ORDERING INFORMATION

Order online: Visit our website at www.llewellyn.com to select your books and place an order on our secure server.

Order by phone:
- Call toll free within the U.S. at 1-877-NEW-WRLD (1-877-639-9753)
- Call toll free within Canada at 1-866-NEW-WRLD (1-866-639-9753)
- We accept VISA, MasterCard, and American Express

Order by mail:
Send the full price of your order (MN residents add 6.875% sales tax) in U.S. funds, plus postage and handling to: Llewellyn Worldwide, 2143 Wooddale Drive Woodbury, MN 55125-2989

POSTAGE AND HANDLING

STANDARD (U.S. & Canada):
(Please allow 12 business days)
$25.00 and under, add $4.00.
$25.01 and over, FREE SHIPPING.

INTERNATIONAL ORDERS (airmail only):
$16.00 for one book, plus $3.00 for each additional book.

Visit us online for more shipping options. Prices subject to change.

FREE CATALOG!

To order, call 1-877-NEW-WRLD ext. 8236 or visit our website

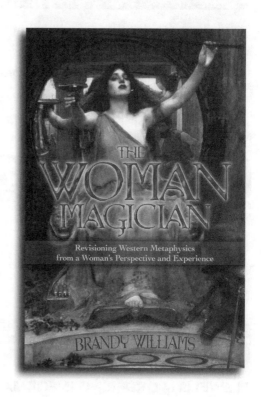

The Woman Magician

Revisioning Western Metaphysics from a Woman's Perspective and Experience

BRANDY WILLIAMS

The Woman Magician is a thought-provoking and bold exploration of the Western magical tradition from a female perspective, celebrating the power of women's spirituality and their vital role in the magical community.

Drawing on thirty years of study and personal experience, Brandy Williams reframes magic around women, examining and challenging traditional Western notions of women's bodies, energies, and spiritual needs. She discusses women's roles throughout magic's history, gender issues, and honoring the voice within to live authentically as women and magicians.

Part Two features personal and group initiatory rituals based on Egyptian cosmology, created by the Sisters of Seshat, the first all-female magical order since the French Revolution.

978-0-7387-2724-0, 384 pp., 6 x 9 $19.95

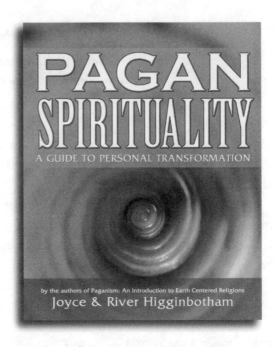

PAGAN
SPIRITUALITY
A GUIDE TO PERSONAL TRANSFORMATION

by the authors of Paganism: An Introduction to Earth Centered Religions
Joyce & River Higginbotham

Pagan Spirituality

A Guide to Personal Transformation

JOYCE HIGGINBOTHAM AND RIVER HIGGINBOTHAM

In a world filled with beginner books, deeper explanations of the Pagan faith are rarely found. Picking up where their critically acclaimed first book *Paganism* left off, best-selling authors Joyce and River Higginbotham offer intermediate-level instruction with *Pagan Spirituality*.

Respected members of their communities, the Higginbothams describe how to continue spiritual evolution though magick, communing, energy work, divination, and conscious creation. Learn how to use journaling, thought development, visualization, and goal-setting to develop magickal techniques and to further cultivate spiritual growth. This book serves to expand the reader's spiritual knowledge base by providing a balanced approach of well-established therapies, extensive personal experience, and question-and-answer sessions that directly involve the reader in the spiritual journey.

978-0-7387-0574-3, 288 pp., 7½ x 9⅛   **$16.95**

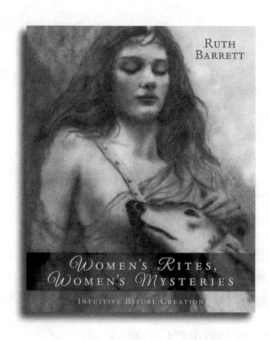

Women's Rites, Women's Mysteries

Intuitive Ritual Creation

RUTH BARRETT

How can women turn birthday parties, baby showers, and other rites of passage into empowering celebrations brimming with meaning and fiery feminine spirit?

Emphasizing the Dianic Wiccan tradition, Barrett shows women how they can create empowering, transformative rituals that strengthen their profound connection to the Goddess. Instead of providing shortcuts, scripts, or rote rituals, she teaches women how to think like a ritualist. Step by step, readers learn the ritual-making process: developing a purpose and theme, building an altar, preparing emotionally and mentally (energetics), spellcasting, and more. For beginners or experienced ritualists, solitaries or groups, this thorough, engaging guide to the art of ritual-making can help women commemorate every sacred milestone—from menstruation to marriage to menopause—that touches their lives.

978-0-7387-0924-6, 360 pp., 7½ x 9⅛   **$16.95**

To order, call 1-877-NEW-WRLD
Prices subject to change without notice
Order at Llewellyn.com 24 hours a day, 7 days a week!